BRONTERRE

BRONTERRE

A Political Biography of
Bronterre O'Brien 1804–1864

Alfred Plummer

London · George Allen & Unwin Ltd
RUSKIN HOUSE   MUSEUM STREET

First published in 1971

ISBN 0 04 923054 9

9 2
Q 13 p

Printed in Great Britain
in 10 point Plantin type
by The Aldine Press, Letchworth

Inveniat viam aut faciat.   Seneca

'In having manifestations before our eyes, that exertions for liberty are not barren toils, there is a source of animation sufficient to make old men feel young, and to repay with the richest returns, labours the most arduous.'

John Cartwright

'My life was not useless; I gave important truths to the world. . . . I have been ahead of my times.'

Robert Owen

Preface

This biography was suggested by that learned historian, Mr E. Lipson, formerly Reader in Economic History at Oxford, whose opinion was that too little was known of James Bronterre O'Brien's life and writings. The research was helped forward in the early stages by the late Professor G. D. H. Cole, who always showed interest in the work and kindly gave me access to his excellent library which contained a collection of relevant scarce books, tracts and pamphlets.

Since that time I have called upon the services of many librarians and keepers of records in different parts of Great Britain and Eire, e.g. London, Dublin, Edinburgh, Oxford, Manchester, Newcastle-upon-Tyne, Birmingham and Brighton, and I wish to express my sincere thanks for their unfailing patience and efficient help.

I wish also to acknowledge my indebtedness to Professor Theodore Moody, to Mr Edward P. Thompson and to his wife, Mrs Dorothy Thompson, for their candid but kindly criticisms and valuable constructive suggestions. I am grateful to Professor Asa Briggs and Mr H. L. Beales for their interest and encouragement during the later stages of the work; and to Mr Chimen Abramsky I offer thanks for so willingly placing at my disposal several rare pamphlets, not available elsewhere so far as I know. Mr W. H. Marwick and Miss Elizabeth Mein of Edinburgh very kindly helped with information about one of Bronterre O'Brien's Scottish friends, and the Reverend G. C. Taylor, Rector of St Giles-in-the-Fields, London, supplied some clues to the history of the old Dudley Court Chapel, Denmark Place. Above all, I cannot sufficiently thank my good friend, Alfred Peacock, for so generously helping me to revise a draft which, over the years, had grown too bulky. I hope he will be pleased with the book as it now appears.

Woodford Green   A. P.
Essex

Contents

Preface   *page* 9

   I. Bronterre's Beginnings   15

   II. A Recruit for the Radicals   26

   III. Unstamped Defiance   44

   IV. Revolution in Retrospect   59

   V. Prelude to 1839   73

   VI. Sharp Arguments   94

   VII. Benbow's Bantling   123

   VIII. Counter-attack   139

   IX. Beckoning Mirage   164

   X. A Centre in Soho   193

   XI. The Wane of Life   236

   XII. Appraisal   247

APPENDICES

  A   Thomas A. Devyr on the Newport Rising and the Projected Rising in the Newcastle District.   261

  B   Bronterre O'Brien's Address to the Electors and Non-electors of Newcastle-upon-Tyne, written in H.M. Prison, Lancaster Castle, in June 1841.   264

  C   Some Notes on Twelve of Bronterre O'Brien's Friends and Disciples.   267

  D   The National Reform League, the Eclectic Institute and the *Working Man*.   274

Bibliography   277

Index   283

Illustrations

		facing page
1.	Bronterre O'Brien aged 46	16
2.	Bronterre O'Brien and Feargus O'Connor in 1839	17
3.	Henry Hetherington	32
4.	The Tree of Taxation	33
5.	The Chartists march through London	208
6.	A physical force Chartist arming for the fight	209
7.	The last Pantomime of the Season	224
8.	The Eclectic Institute in Soho	225

Chapter I

BRONTERRE'S BEGINNINGS

CHARTISM was the first working-class political movement on a national scale in British history. Bred by economic hardship out of social injustice, it aimed at 'whole-hog' parliamentary reform as a means to the achievement of economic and social justice for the working masses. Its programme – the People's Charter – contained six 'points' gleaned from earlier Radical reformers: universal manhood suffrage, vote by (secret) ballot, no property qualifications for membership of Parliament, payment of M.P.s, equal electoral districts, and annual parliaments. Chartism filled the early years of Queen Victoria's reign with widespread political agitation and the clamour of crowds. It was a mass movement, drawing into its ranks men and women workers in the textile, mining, and metal-working districts, supported by some – but not all – of the artisans of London, Birmingham, Manchester, Leeds and other large cities; yet many of its leaders sprang from the professional and middle classes. These men brought the country to the very brink of revolution and were prosecuted and imprisoned for their activities. Afterwards most of them renounced their early extremism and became more restrained; some, indeed, disappeared from the Chartist scene completely; others continued in, or on the fringes of, the Movement, often at odds with the recognized leadership. Such a man was James Bronterre O'Brien,[1] once regarded by the authorities as one of the most dangerous agitators in the land.

James O'Brien was born at the beginning of February 1804 in Granard, County Longford, a small town in the centre of Ireland, 53 miles north-west of Dublin. Normally it was 'a comparatively quiet and easy-going sort of place', but during the last stages of the Great Rebellion which drenched Ireland in blood throughout the hot summer of 1798 (less than six years before James O'Brien's birth), Granard was the scene of a battle between its garrison of regular troops, with reinforcements from Cavan, who defended the town against the United armies of Longford and Westmeath. The latter, made up largely of

---

[1] His baptismal name was James; he later adopted the name 'Bronterre', which he often used as a *nom de plume*.

peasants armed with pikes and pitchforks, were attempting to link up with General Humbert's small force of some 850 French veterans, which had fought its way from Killala in County Mayo, where it had landed – much too late to save the rebellion from failure – on 23rd August. By 5th September, with about 1,000 Irish allies, the French were making a desperate drive towards Dublin. At Granard, on that day, the men of Longford and Westmeath attacked the town and for four hours 'the garrison, reinforced by Major Porter's 250 yeomanry, shot, sabred and bayonetted their attackers. Only two men were wounded on their side. The official estimate of the rebels' losses was 400, but others put it nearer a thousand'. Three days later the French general, surrounded and hopelessly outnumbered, surrendered near Ballinamuck, 'just out of sight of the great moat of Granard'. During that dreadful summer thousands of Irishmen were killed in battle or sentenced to death or transportation. Brave – often reckless – but poorly co-ordinated and short of arms, ammunition, and military training, the United Irishmen, despite some local successes, were defeated and suppressed, save for a few die-hards who, operating alone or in small groups, continued their 'vagrant hostilities'.[1] The desperate deeds, heroism, and grievous losses of this bitter conflict were long remembered in Ireland, and James O'Brien, as a boy, must have listened, spellbound, to many a tale of the 'troubles' of '98.[2]

In and around Granard, with its 2,000 inhabitants, the manufacture of coarse linen was extensively carried on, and one or two handlooms were to be seen in every poor man's cottage. Set in the midst of some of the richest soil in Ireland, the town was the main trading centre for the produce of the surrounding countryside. Every Friday brought a busy market in provisions, corn and linen, and among the chief events of the year in Granard were two fairs, one in May for store cattle, and the other in October for fat cattle. The latter was seen by John Christian Curwen, M.P., an interested and observant Cumberland squire who toured Ireland in 1813. He found the long, straight main street crammed

---

[1] The story of this conflict inspired the poet W. B. Yeats to write his visionary one-act prose play, *Cathleen ni Houlihan*, which produced a galvanic effect upon Irish nationalism early in the twentieth century. See also James Sexton's *Autobiography* (1936), p. 18.

[2] Baptism Register of Granard R. C. Church; entry 12th February 1804. The same register records the baptism of a second child, a girl, named Catherine, on 5th January 1806. T. Pakenham, *The Year of Liberty: the Story of the Great Irish Rebellion of 1798* (1969) pp. 294–326; *Annual Register*, 1798, pp. 162–5; R. Postgate, *Story of a Year: 1798* (1969); J. P. Farrell, *Historical Notes and Stories of the County of Longford* (1st edn, Dublin, 1886), Ch. 3; J. C. Beckett, *Making of Modern Ireland* (1966), pp. 261–7.

1. Bronterre O'Brien aged 46. From a daguerreotype photograph taken in 1850.

2. Bronterre O'Brien (seated) and Feargus O'Connor in 1839. From a contemporary engraving.

to capacity – 'possibly four thousand people were crowded into it' – a dense jostling concourse of country folk, decently dressed for the most part, lively and good-humoured, their shouts and laughter ringing out above a deep bass 'ground' provided by protesting cattle.[1]

James O'Brien's parents were respectable 'middling sort of people' such as farmers, graziers, shopkeepers, dealers and the like, so well known and observed by Maria Edgeworth (1767–1849), that talented popular writer and practical woman of affairs who lived many busy years in their midst. The eldest child of Daniel O'Brien and his wife Mary (née Kearney), a Catholic couple, James was baptized in Granard Catholic Church on 12th February 1804. His father, who carried on a wine and spirit business supplemented, probably, by the sale of tobacco and snuff, was evidently not a bigot, for he sent his son, in due course, to the Granard Parochial School, a 'free and pay' school which had Protestant connections and received support from the Board of Governors of Erasmus Smith [2] and from the Society for the Education of the Poor in Ireland, commonly known as the Kildare Place Society.[3] The school premises comprised 'a good slated house, with apartments for the master', which had been built by private subscriptions supplemented by a grant of £50 from the Association for Discountenancing Vice. This establishment, which was open to boys and girls 'of all religious persuasions', could take about 80 pupils, of whom some were free scholars, but 'the greater part' paid tuition fees which ranged from 2s 6d to 5s 5d a quarter. The ratio of boys to girls was normally around four to three; and the ratio of Protestant to Catholic pupils was approximately five to three.[4] The school master and mistress at Granard, usually a married couple, were Protestants, and their joint income

[1] J. C. Curwen, *Observations on the State of Ireland* . . . (1818), II, pp. 208, 217. J. C. Curwen of Workington Hall was a zealous patron of various coal-miners' friendly societies, and his wife was a patroness of the Sisterly Society, a 'female friendly society' with a membership (*c.* 1795) of 225. F. M. Eden, *The State of the Poor* (1797), new edition, ed. A. G. L. Rogers (1928), pp. 158, 164–6; Arthur Young, *Tour in Ireland*, 1776–1779, ed. A. W. Hutton (1892), II, pp. 11, 14; Edward Wakefield, *An Account of Ireland* (1812), I, pp. 80–1.

[2] The Board of Governors of Erasmus Smith was incorporated by Royal Charter in 1669.

[3] Founded in 1811; it has now become a Church of Ireland Training College for men and women teachers. See H. K. Moore, *An Unwritten Chapter in the History of Education* (1904).

[4] *Second Report of the Commissioners of Irish Education Enquiry* (1826), Appendix No. 22. The Protestant to Catholic ratio of 5 : 3 may seem surprising in a parish where only 790 out of 7,600 were returned as 'Protestants' in 1805; but many Irish Catholics, although anxious to have their children educated, refused to use the Protestant-sponsored parochial schools. *14th Report of the Board of Education in Ireland* (1812), p. 331.

17

amounted to £37 per annum (the odd £7 being raised by a charge on a neighbouring parish) and free living accommodation. Between them they provided a 'course of instruction' comprising 'spelling and reading, writing and arithmetic'.[1]

Although Granard was a thriving town in the early years of the nineteenth century, and although Irish drinking habits at that time were nothing short of excessive, Daniel O'Brien's wine and spirit business failed while his son was still at the parochial school. In the hope of mending his fortunes, Daniel O'Brien migrated to the West Indies, leaving his wife and family behind; but it seems that he died shortly after his arrival. This double family disaster might have put an end to James's school career, had not an extraordinary combination of circumstances provided a golden educational opportunity – a great chance which might so easily have slipped away for ever. It was more than fortunate for young O'Brien that, situated as he was in a small community in the very centre of rural Ireland, he found himself at about the right age, within a stone's throw of a new, experimental school in which he received a secondary education well nigh unique at that period, followed by no less than seven years of uninterrupted studies at university level. James's high intelligence and studious habits had so impressed his schoolmaster at Granard that he made a special effort to secure a place for the boy in the new school at Edgeworthstown, a large village only seven miles away. This brought him under the immediate notice of the Edgeworths.

Edgeworthstown School was planned by that remarkably versatile reformer and educationist, Richard Lovell Edgeworth (1744–1817), father of Maria Edgeworth and her half-brother, Lovell. The Edgeworths, originally an English family, acquired land in Ireland during the reign of Elizabeth I. In 1732, Richard Edgeworth married Jane Lovell, daughter of a Welsh judge and granddaughter of Sir Salathiel Lovell, a Recorder of the City of London in James II's time, and of this union Richard Lovell Edgeworth was born. He was brought up a Protestant and, in his youth, became an undergraduate, first of Trinity College, Dublin, and afterwards of Corpus Christi College, Oxford. Subsequently, over the years, he contracted four marriages from which no fewer than twenty-two children were born to him, of whom only four died in infancy. Within his populous domestic circle he was a kindly, well-intentioned – if somewhat interfering – autocrat, 'and a more benevolent embodiment of the principle of autocracy has perhaps never flourished'.[2] His superabundant energy, like the variety of his

---

[1] *Eleventh Report of the Board of Education in Ireland* : Parish Schools (1810).
[2] E. Lawless, *Maria Edgeworth* (1904), p. 38.

18

interests and activities, is astonishing. He travelled much abroad and appeared almost as completely at home in France with people of quality and *les philosophes*, as in England or Ireland where he was accepted in the highest social and literary circles and was *persona grata* with such well-known scientists as Sir Joseph Banks (during whose Presidency of the Royal Society Edgeworth was elected F.R.S.), Sir William Hamilton, Joseph Priestley and his fellow members of the Lunar Society, and Dr Erasmus Darwin, scientist and physician, grandfather of the great Charles Darwin. By such contacts, he tells us, his mind 'was kept up to the current of speculation and discovery in the world of science and continued hints for reflection and invention were suggested to me'.[1] He wrote and published *An Essay on the Construction of Roads and Carriages*, and among his inventions was a semaphore telegraph, an 'odometer' or perambulating land-measuring machine (which gained a silver medal from the Society of Arts), a turnip-cutter, and a 'wheel-boat' or 'sailing-carriage' which 'ran with amazing velocity'.[2] Ireland, however, was 'the worst abode for an inventor; had he lived in an industrial district of England he might have reaped a rich reward . . .'.[3]

Edgeworth inherited the family estate in 1769 at the age of twenty-five but he did not settle permanently at Edgeworthstown House until 1782. Thereafter he became – *rara avis!* – a model Irish landlord. Ingeniously, he tried to improve the soil – even reclaiming some bog land – and strove to meliorate the lot of his tenants and labourers. This latter objective, combined with his enlightened ideas on the education of children, led him to subscribe to seven or eight different schools and, eventually, to formulate his own plan to found a boys' school at Edgeworthstown for the children of the poorer classes on what were, for those days, very advanced lines. 'Experimental education,' he wrote in 1801, 'is . . . in its infancy and . . . boundless space for improvement remains . . .';[4] and, eight years later, 'New schools should give a fair trial to experiments in education. If nothing can be altered in the old schools, leave them as they are . . . but let the publick try whether they cannot have something better.'[5] In his own 'Sketch of a Plan of an Elementary School for the Lower Classes' he explained his ideas more fully,

[1] R. L. Edgeworth, *Memoirs* (1820), I, p. 351.
[2] *Ibid.*, I, p. 152.
[3] H. J. and H. E. Butler (eds.), *The Black Book of Edgeworthstown and other Edgeworth Memories, 1587–1817* (1927), p. 231.
[4] M. and R. L. Edgeworth, *Practical Education* (1801), II, p. 358; J. P. Farrell, *op. cit.*, p. 123. Oliver Goldsmith spent two years in a Latin School at Edgeworthstown before going up to Trinity College, Dublin, in 1745.
[5] R. L. Edgeworth, *Essays on Professional Education* (1809), pp. 39, 48.

19

stressing the importance of obedience, truthfulness, cleanliness, and sobriety, together with 'a sense of religion without superstition'. There should be a good playground and proper alternation of active and sedentary lessons or occupations. 'This elementary school,' he promised, 'should be established whenever a master and what is of more consequence, a mistress of the house, can be provided, for whose manners, morals, tenderness, knowledge and successful experience in teaching, I can dare to pledge myself.' [1]

There this attractive project rested until 1815, the year in which Edgeworth's son, Lovell (1775–1842), slowly recovering from the effects of eleven years of captivity in France as a civilian detainee during the Napoleonic war, spent the summer travelling in England to see the Bell, Lancaster, and certain other free schools, as a prelude to opening one of his own. Maria noted with pleasure that her brother's 'enthusiasm about these schools' seemed to have 'quite cured all his complaints and to have inspired him both with new body and new soul'. He was, of course, actively encouraged by his father, who, true to form to the last, despite grave illness, wrote a manual specially for the new school, which was opened on a modest scale in 1816.[2]

When his father died in June 1817, Lovell Edgeworth inherited the estate and with it the means to develop the school more rapidly. Free from the influence of the benevolent autocrat, he began to introduce ideas of his own. Whereas his father had intended the school only for the benefit of children of the poorer classes, Lovell extended its scope to admit day boys and boarders *of all classes*; a proposal which had been urged upon him by many gentlemen and farmers who promised to pay a fee of £40 per annum for each boy. Thus encouraged, Lovell Edgeworth spent considerable sums building new schoolrooms and a boarding house, and became, as Maria tells us,

'. . . a gentleman schoolmaster . . . of no common school, and . . . in general his benevolence, his exertions, and his skill as a preceptor were the admiration of numbers who came from different parts of Ireland, either to put their children to the new school or to visit it from curiosity . . . all ranks, gentlemen's sons, middlemen and the poorest day scholars were . . . taught together in the same schoolroom and the same classes'.

---

[1] *Memoirs*, II, pp. 451–3.
[2] E. Inglis-Jones, *The Great Maria* (1959), pp. 59, 127, 132–3, 212–13, 239–41; Constantia Hill, *Maria Edgeworth and her Circle* (1910), Preface and pp. 78–80, 86, 138–142; F. F. Roget, *Un Anglais Prisonnier à Verdun, 1803–1814* (Geneva, 1916), pp. 10–30.

By way of school uniform all boys wore a linen smock over their clothes, but to guard against

'. . . the alarming appearance of a democratic tendency in the mixture of the poor and rich scholars, gentlemen's sons and those of the lowest class, it was enjoined and made known that the pupils were never to mix in this manner or meet together upon this equality except in the school-room and during school hours'.[1]

Lovell Edgeworth devoted himself to the school: planning and organizing, superintending and teaching, trying to carry forward the torch kindled by his father. According to its founders, the school's aim was not to cram the pupils with facts learned by rote, but to instil 'habits of industry and application, and the ability to reason accurately'. Lessons were short, learning gradual, and the teaching method largely conversational, the children being constantly exercised in 'their powers of observation, reasoning and invention'. The 'three Rs', including mathematics, were taught, of course, and the classical languages and French. To these subjects 'everyday science' was added, taught by 'practical demonstration and experiment in connection with the phenomena that daily meet the eye'. Children 'intended for business, or for any active life' were taught book-ekeping, the principles of domestic economy and trade, and the 'first principles of natural philosophy, which are universally useful'. Religious education was given on Saturdays; the Protestants, with the Rector, the Rev. George Keating, were taken in one room, and the Catholics, about equal in number, with their priest, Father Donoghue, in another. These two men were 'quite free from bigotry, and . . . on the best terms with each other, without the slightest mutual jealousy'.[2]

Edgeworthstown school was by no means a closed community; on the contrary, it educated its pupils by encouraging them to contribute in various ways to social life in the village. For example, plays were produced and acted by the boys in the village theatre, and there was a school band able to give acceptable public performances. In 1819, when Lovell Edgeworth's aunts, Charlotte and Mary, returned to their old home at Edgeworthstown House after an absence of many years, they were greeted by crowds of people from the village, the school, and the surrounding countryside, and saw something of the way the presence of the school had improved local amenities. 'There was a line of children

[1] *The Black Book of Edgeworthstown*, pp. 219–20, quoting from a *MS.* written by Maria Edgeworth.
[2] *Memoirs*, II, pp. 451–3; J. G. Lockhart, *Narrative of the Life of Sir Walter Scott* (1848), II, pp. 163–7.

on each side of the road,' Maria Edgeworth records, 'from Lovell's school . . . such huzzaing! . . . such shouting! such bonfires!' In the evening a large schoolroom was 'lighted up for the people that they might have a dance'.[1]

James O'Brien was almost certainly among the boys assembled to welcome 'the Good Ladies', for he entered the school in 1818 at the age of fourteen, two years after its opening, when it was 'a flourishing seminary' of some 170 boys. Little more is known about the future Chartist's school career, but that he was a clever boy is obvious from his subsequent record at the university. It may well be, as is suggested by Robert G. Gamage, one of the early historians of Chartism and himself an O'Brienite-Chartist, that O'Brien was chosen to be a monitor,[2] which means that he would have been entrusted with teaching and supervising younger boys. As a possible pointer to young O'Brien's qualities it is interesting to recall the opinion of Richard Lovell Edgeworth, who was in favour of the monitorial system but sounded a sensible warning note against 'the indiscriminate appointment of monitors; great care must be taken in the selection; only the best informed, and the best tempered boys should be employed; good temper should be preferred to ability, because in teaching, good temper is of more consequence than the most shining abilities'.[3]

In 1822, when he was nearly nineteen, O'Brien went up to Trinity College, Dublin, entering not as a sizar (i.e. a poor student allowed a free education in return for performing certain, at one time menial, duties), but as a pensioner, a grade almost invariably made up of students from middle-class families of modest means, but able to afford the £7 10s entrance fee and £7 10s tuition fees for every half-year, plus additional charges for rooms and 'commons' (food and drink).[4] Probably O'Brien was financed mainly by the Edgeworths (Lovell and Maria) who decided not 'to spare the ship for a ha'porth of tar', deeming the money well spent, for O'Brien was an extremely promising student and did, in fact, graduate with honours after a dis-

---

[1] E. Inglis-Jones, *op. cit.*, pp. 160–1, 209, 211; and Maria Edgeworth's *MS.* memorandum on the school. In stark contrast to O'Brien's school life we have Richard Cobden's 'cruel and disgusting mockery of an education' from 1814 to 1819, when he was 'ill fed, ill taught, ill used', which raises an awful vision of Squeers and the horrors of Dotheboys Hall. Morley, *Life of Richard Cobden* (1881), I, pp. 4–5: cf. also C. F. A. Best, *Shaftesbury* (1964), pp. 15–16.

[2] R. G. Gammage, *History of the Chartist Movement* (Rev. edn 1894), p. 72.

[3] *14th Report of the Board of Education in Ireland* (1812), p. 340.

[4] *Alumni Dublinenses*, p. 627; *Dublin University Calendar, 1833*, pp. 64 *et seq.* The four undergraduate grades or categories were: Noblemen, Fellow Commoners, Pensioners, Sizars.

tinguished college career. The university entrance subjects in O'Brien's time were Greek (New Testament, Homer, Xenophon and Lucian) and Latin (Virgil, Horace, Terence, Sallust and Livy), and the Arts degree course consisted of the study of Greek, Latin, Logic, Astronomy and Physics. Leave to sit the degree examination was gained by 'keeping' at least eleven terms and passing that number of terminal examinations. Although all examinations at that date were conducted orally and were much less searching than university examinations today, young O'Brien evidently did all that was required of him by his examiners, gaining prizes in classics and science on several occasions, and crowning his undergraduate career in Michaelmas Term, 1825, by winning the gold medal for science, the highest honour a Dublin undergraduate could achieve. Finally the 'candidate bachelor' in Arts had to prepare and read a Latin thesis *in laudem philosophiae*; two 'declarations', in Greek and Latin respectively; and to oppose or defend certain set questions in 'Logics, Natural Philosophy or Morality'.[1]

Long before O'Brien's B.A. degree was conferred upon him early in 1829, he had begun to prepare for a legal career by gaining admittance as a student to the King's Inns, Dublin, in Michaelmas Term, 1826, when he was in his senior sophister (i.e. fourth academic) year, but before he attained the status of candidate bachelor. The Honourable Society of King's Inns, the principal law school of Ireland, correspond-ing to the English Inns of Court in London, is an ancient body founded in the Middle Ages. Its present fine Georgian building on Constitution Hill, Dublin, was designed and built by the famous architect, James Gandon, at the turn of the eighteenth and nineteenth centuries. In 1826 its spacious dining hall had been in use little more than twenty years, and doubtless O'Brien greatly enjoyed reading in the beautiful library of King's Inns, newly built in adjacent Henrietta Street, to Frederick Darley's designs, and opened in 1827. But although the Irish law students were handsomely housed at that period, their legal education was very much a go-as-you-please process, and a student could usually 'get by' with a little Latin and 'a minimum of inventiveness and presence of mind'. No tests by written examinations were imposed; the 'ancient tests' of liberal education and personal knowledge of character – in which the eating of dinners played an important part – were deemed to be quite sufficient. Nor were the requirements any more stringent in Gray's Inn, London, to which O'Brien transferred in 1830 in order to

---

[1] *Dublin University Calendar, 1833*, p. 204; *Catalogue of Graduates, University of Dublin, 1591–1868*, p. 433. Every Dublin graduate must sign the Register of Degrees; James O'Brien's signature appears in the register used from 1794 to 1855.

'keep' the six terms at an English Inn of Court which 'an anachronistic survival of Tudor educational policy' made compulsory upon all Irish graduate candidates. In London, as in Dublin, legal education was so unsystematic that the law student was left very much to his own devices. Law lectureships at Gray's Inn and the Inner and Middle Temple were not set up until 1847 – long after O'Brien's student days – and the Inns of Court did not introduce compulsory examinations until 1872.[1]

At the age of twenty-six, after more than seven years of higher education, O'Brien came to a fork in the road; a decisive point at which he cast aside the study and administration of existing laws and chose instead the alluring but hazardous prospect of making new ones. The Edgeworths must have been deeply disappointed when the news reached them, but there was little they could do. Among the family papers there is a brief memorandum, dated 13th January 1835, which closes the chapter: 'James O'Brien, Married & settled in London – he is an Editor of one or more papers, but I don't like his politicks, but he is very clever.' 'My friends,' confessed O'Brien himself, 'sent me to study law; I took to Radical Reform on my own account. . . . Having a natural love of truth . . . I soon got sick of law, and gave my soul to Radical reform.' Among the influences which brought him to this crucial decision were Ireland's wrongs – the quasi-military occupation (Granard had barracks for a garrison of 300 soldiers), England's determined discrimination against Irish trade and industries, the evils of absentee landlordism, and above all, the manifold miseries of the Irish poor. 'I have seen [he told the readers of Bronterre's National Reformer] thousands of Irish who have never had animal food or fish or wheaten bread twice a year since they were born. I have seen them whole days together without even potatoes or salt . . . I have seen them living, or striving to live, on nettles and other weeds, till their blood actually lost the colour of blood and turned yellowish. I have seen them living, or striving to live, in sooty mud cabins, or rather sties, and in deep holes burrowed under bushes on the roadside, or under turf banks, where there was not

---

[1] *Reynolds's Political Instructor*, 30th March 1850; *Admission Book of King's Inns, Dublin*, Michaelmas Term, 1826; *Admission Book of Gray's Inn*, 24th March 1830; B. T. Duhigg, *History of King's Inns* (1806); W. F. Littledale, *The Society of King's Inns, Dublin: its origin and progress* (1859); *The Law Journal* (Irish F.S. Section), 5th March 1932, pp. 55–6; C. P. Curran, *Address to the Old Dublin Society* . . . (1943); typescript in the Library of King's Inns, Dublin; R. B. Dowell and D. A. Webb, *Hermathena* (1935); *Northern Ireland Legal Quarterly*, June 1965; W. J. Reader, *Professional Men* (1966), pp. 55–8; D. Guinness, *Portrait of Dublin* (1967), p. 42. Non-graduates were required to keep eight terms in England.

24

even the iron pot which Cobbett speaks of. . . . All this . . . have I seen in Ireland – not in solitary instances, but over whole districts . . . and often did my blood boil with rage to think that I could not strike the assassins dead who caused such misery. I have always loved the poor. I have always felt how unnecessary as well as unmerited was their treatment.' [1] So it was that, of his own free choice, he was called, not to the Bar, but to thirty years of political agitation, becoming not an advocate for the rich, but a champion of the poor. Always a zealous, persistent agitator with a firm faith in 'one man one vote', he spent a lifetime on the frontier of politics and did much to pioneer the way to the welfare state.

[1] *Bronterre's National Reformer*, 7th, 28th January, 4thFebruary 1837. There are many contemporary witnesses as to the state of Ireland; e.g. Richard Cobden, who made his first journey in Ireland in September 1825; see Morley, *Life of Richard Cobden* (1881), I, p. 11, and John O'Driscoll, quoted by B. Inglis, *The Story of Ireland* (1956) p. 132. J. G. Lockhart, *Narrative of the Life of Sir Walter Scott* . . . (1848), II, pp. 163–7. In 1834 William Cobbett, at the age of seventy-one, travelled 180 miles in Ireland on the last of his famous rural rides, and even he, familiar though he was with the privations of English farm labourers, was shocked by the widespread starvation, nakedness and filth in Ireland; G. D. H. Cole, *Life of William Cobbett* (1927), pp. 352, 424–7. Edgeworth Papers, Document M2320, Irish Record Office, Dublin.

Chapter II

A RECRUIT FOR THE RADICALS

JAMES O'BRIEN's decision to enter politics rather than the law was taken on the eve of one of the most tense periods in modern British history. During 1828–9, his last years in Ireland, he had seen Daniel O'Connell and his popular, powerful Catholic Association pressing forward, in a dangerously explosive political atmosphere, towards Catholic emancipation or civil war, and achieving an astonishing victory at Westminster when the Duke of Wellington's Tory ministry forced through Parliament the Catholic Relief Act, 1829, which opened the way to Roman Catholics (on taking a new oath instead of the Oath of Supremacy) to both Houses of Parliament, to all corporate bodies, lay judicial offices, and political offices except those of Regent, Lord Chancellor in England and Ireland, and Lord-Lieutenant of Ireland. Doubtless this new Act delighted O'Brien because, although nominally a Roman Catholic, he approached the Catholic emancipation question less as a religionist than as a Radical standing for the abolition of all indefensible limitations upon civil liberty.[1]

Not only in unhappy Ireland, but in England also, the political atmosphere was highly charged. Discussion of 'Reform' filled the air on every side and at all social levels. Lord Campbell, later to be Lord Chancellor, wrote: 'The Catholic Relief Bill having passed in 1829, it hung in the balance whether the Duke of Wellington's Government was to be progressively *Liberal* or . . . was to return to the old principle of *Toryism*.' Whigs and Tories alike were torn asunder and reduced to confusion by the 'ever-varying combinations of the political groups' into which they had split.[2] The moderate reformer, Sir Francis Burdett, declared his opinion that 'the only struggle really worth making was for Reform in Parliament', adding that 'the people of England were at last beginning to bestir themselves'. The great and growing industrial towns, such as Manchester, Birmingham and Leeds, with populations

---

[1] On the influence of William Cobbett's opportune best-seller, *A History of the Protestant Reformation*, see G. D. H. Cole, *The Life of William Cobbett* (1927), Ch. XIX.

[2] J. R. M. Butler, *The Passing of the Great Reform Bill* (1914), pp. 51–2.

recently risen to between 120,000 and 180,000, were ripe for representation. At the same time and in the same regions people like the handloom weavers and stocking knitters, and the child-workers in the factories, who were the principal victims of the new industrial power-production system and the emergent age of steam and steel, were in desperate straits, as indeed were the farm labourers in almost every county.

Radical politicians looked for the remedy in Radical reform of Parliament. Year after year, said the Reverend Sydney Smith in a speech at Taunton, 'the question of Reform has been pressing upon us, till it has swelled up at last into this great and awful combination, so that almost every City and every Borough in England are at this moment assembled for the same purpose and are doing the same thing we are doing'.[1] The London Radical Reform Association, founded in July 1829, urged the formation of local societies to agitate and press for annual parliaments, universal suffrage and the secret ballot. A few months later an enthusiastic assembly of Birmingham reformers meeing in Beardsworths Repository, with Thomas Attwood in the chair, resolved 'to obtain by every just and legal means such a reform of the Commons House of Parliament as may ensure a real and effectual representation (in that House) of the lower and middle classes of the people', and to that end formed the Birmingham Political Union. These proceedings were widely reported throughout the country. *The Times*, though hostile, gave $4\frac{1}{2}$ columns to a report on the meeting, while the somewhat more favourable *Morning Chronicle* gave it $5\frac{1}{2}$ columns.[2] Young James O'Brien arrived in London from Ireland in time to witness the formation, in March 1830, of the Metropolitan Union of Radical Reform at a mass meeting at which Henry Hunt, Daniel O'Connell, Richard Carlile and Henry Hetherington were the chief speakers. But in the House of Commons a stonewalling policy still persisted, and on 28th May 1830 O'Connell's universal suffrage bill was contemptuously thrown out by a majority of 306. Four weeks later, George IV, the 'indolent, voluptuous prince' of Thackeray's lectures on the four Georges, died (26th June 1830). Under a statute then in force, this means the dissolution of Parliament and an imminent general election. An intriguing situation, indeed, for a budding politician!

Nor was this all. Abroad the Belgians in the Southern Netherlands

[1] E. Hobsbawn and G. Rudé, *Captain Swing* (1969), *passim*; J. H. Clapham, *Economic History of Modern Britain* (1926), I, pp. 139–40; J. L. and B. Hammond, *The Village Labourer* (1920), Chs. XI and XII; Sydney Smith, *Works* (1850), p. 558; Barbara Kerr, *Bound to the Soil: A Social History of Dorset, 1750–1918* (1968), pp. 100–15 and Appendix E.

[2] J. R. M. Butler, *op. cit.*, pp. 57, 61–2, 68; On the revival of the Birmingham Political Union see Brit. Mus. *Add.MSS.* 27,819(73), (172).

were in revolt against the Dutch; the Poles had risen against their Russian masters; while nearer home another bitter struggle was taking place in France where monarch and ministers were even more unpopular than their opposite numbers in England, and where the climax was the revolution of 27th–29th July 1830, when the people of Paris forced abdication upon the Bourbon reactionary, Charles X. Eleven days later the French Chamber of Deputies raised to the throne the more liberal Duke of Orleans, who began his reign as Louis-Philippe I. 'France,' says the French historian, Victor Duruy, 'welcomed this separation from the men of 1815 with practically unanimous acclamation. In taking again the flag of 1789, she seemed to have taken possession of herself and of her liberties.' Across the Channel, too, the tricolour, emblem of revolution, liberation and a new order, had a special significance at that time. There is abundant testimony to the intense political excitement sparked off by the July Revolution in France. Towards the end of July, communications between Paris and London were interrupted for several days, and hope and apprehension held all classes in London at fever heat. When, at last, news came of the defeat of the government in Paris, scores of jubilant meetings were held to congratulate the revolutionaries. Francis Place recorded that the 'temper and determination' of the metropolitan working classes were 'admirable', and that the news 'has already done something towards our political regeneration and will, if need be, do more'.[1] 'It roused my utmost enthusiasm,' wrote John Stuart Mill, 'and gave me, as it were, a new existence'; [2] and Richard Carlile, the Fleet Street bookseller and veteran Radical, believed that the action of the Parisians was approved of by 'nine-tenths of the people of this island'. William Cobbett, the greatest popular agitator of the day, announced that 'the tri-coloured flag is enough for me; if that flag keep up, *reform in England is inevitable* . . . and the wise way would be to make it *now* when it can be done without a struggle'. 'Does not every man of you,' he asked his readers, 'feel differently from what you did twenty days back? . . . You, without any reasoning, feel that there must be, and will be, *a total change in the system.*' [3] Between the end of August and early October 1830, Cobbett gave eleven lectures to huge audiences in the Rotunda, Blackfriars, on the revolution in France and 'borough-mongering' in England. Equating the enemies of the English working class with those over-

---

[1] B.M. *Add.MSS.* 27,789(162–3), (166); cf. *Annual Register* (1830), Vol. 72, p. 144.

[2] J. S. Mill, *Autobiography* (1873), p. 172; Duff Cooper, *Tallyrand* (1932), pp. 314–25.

[3] *Political Register* 7th and 14th August 1830, pp. 181, 197.

thrown by the French revolutionaries, he urged his hearers to follow the example of the French who had shown what labouring men could do when they liked to bestir themselves, and had made 'the working classes see their real importance, and those who despised them see it too'. Though far removed from Cobbett in politics, the Whig reformer, Henry Brougham, saw the upheaval in France as 'the greatest event for liberty in modern times' and likely to be 'most advantageous' to reform in England because it threatened 'wrath and destruction on those who would by force withstand the popular opinion'. Lord Grey, later to become the Prime Minister responsible for the 'Great Reform Bill', echoed these sentiments, and so did many of the more radical members of his party.

Even the dignified deliberations of the Corporation of the City of London did not proceed undisturbed. Charles Welch tells us, in his annals of the City, that although addresses to the new king, William IV, in the traditional loyal terms were agreed to by the Court of Mayor and Aldermen and by the Common Council, a Common Hall, held on 28th July 1830, voted for an address to the King protesting against high taxation – 'at least 60 millions of taxes are annually wrung from the industry of the people' – and deploring the increase of poverty and crime. But the king refused to receive this address 'upon the throne'.

All this political excitement was like mountain air to young O'Brien. Exhilarated beyond measure, he was more than delighted to find himself in the storm-centre of the amazing reform agitation which led up to the passing of the Act of 1832 – and beyond. Shortly after his arrival in London – the London so vividly sketched by 'Boz'[1] – he made the acquaintance of some of the leading Radicals of the day. He often heard, and was on good terms with, 'Orator' Henry Hunt, who won Preston for the Radicals in 1830. With his remarkable stentorian voice Hunt was, according to Francis Place, 'in almost all respects the best mob orator of the day'; but he had become vain and overbearing, and Hunt's namesakes, the brothers John and Leigh Hunt, thought him 'vulgar'. O'Brien got to know Cobbett (who had a great liking for young people) and attended his lectures; he also went regularly to the meetings of the London Radical Reform Association where he heard lively discussions on universal suffrage, the secret ballot, annual parliaments, and other essentials of the Chartist programme which was to appear later. At this time, too, he met Henry Hetherington, a prominent and intrepid Radical publisher and member of the L.R.R.A. – a contact which, some two years later, ripened into a fruitful militant partnership, as we shall shortly see. Moreover, O'Brien's knowledge of French brought

[1] Charles Dickens first published his London *Sketches* in 1835–6.

him into touch with political refugees – *les proscrits* from the Continent.

A highly-charged political atmosphere persisted throughout the whole of 1830. During the second half of the year O'Brien heard of serious disturbances, now known as the 'Swing' riots, among the poorly-paid farm labourers. From Kent and Surrey in June, July, and August came news of labourers' strikes and protest marches by day, often marked by threshing-machine breaking; and of arson (mainly rick-burning) by night. Threatening letters signed 'Swing' or 'Capt. Swing' were mysteriously delivered to farmers, parsons, landlords; inflammatory speeches were made and, here and there, tricolours appeared; higher wages, or food, or money were often demanded with menaces. A steady stream of reports flowing into London in the autumn and early winter revealed not only the spread of the disturbances to the Home Counties, Hampshire and the West Country, the Midlands, East Anglia, and Yorkshire, but the reaction of the authorities – arrests, trials, fines, prison sentences, transportations, and executions. 'In all 1,976 prisoners were tried by 90 courts sitting in 34 counties.' Of these prisoners, 481 were transported to Australia, and 19 were executed; while at the other extreme 800 were acquitted or bound over.[1] In London and Westminster the introduction of Peel's new Metropolitan Police force, formed in 1829 and welcomed by the well-to-do, was fiercely resented by the working class. A number of 'incidents' erupted in the streets early in November 1830. The King's carriage was followed from Covent Garden by a milling mob bawling 'No New Police' and 'Down with the New Police'. Stones were thrown at the Duke of Wellington, and policemen were set upon by rioters shouting 'Here's the Revolution of Long Acre'. One policeman was killed and twenty rioters were arrested. When the traditional procession and other festivities of Lord Mayor's Day (9th November) were hastily cancelled for fear of rioting, 'great alarm spread over the Metropolis, the Funds fell three per cent, the Tower moat was flooded by way of precaution, the guards at the Bank were doubled'. On 8th November a marching mob, having passed through the City, clashed with the new police at Westminster, and the disturbances continued on the next day, when 'some of the rioters diverted themselves' by standing within the City boundary at Temple Bar and pelting the Metropolitan Police who were stationed just outside the boundary![2] However, on the Wednesday

[1] See Hobsbawn and Rudé, *Captain Swing* (1969), p. 262 and Appendix III, in which nearly 1,000 incidents and disturbances are listed and classified.

[2] When three policemen were killed in a riot in 1833, a London jury brought in a verdict of 'justifiable homicide'. G. M. Young (ed.), *Early Victorian England* (1934), I, p. 196.

(10th November) tranquillity gradually returned. Crowds gathered in the City's streets it is true, but they were harmless people who had merely come to see 'the magnificent but abortive decorations'.[1]

Amid this swirl of events, O'Brien soon began to emerge as a public orator. According to George Howell, the young Irishman was 'not at first a fluent speaker', but he seems quickly to have overcome his early hesitancy, for in the annual report of the L.R.R.A. for 1829–30 tribute is paid to the 'spirited speeches of Mr Hunt, Mr O'Brien and Mr Grady'. *The Prompter*, also, mentions him as having appeared at Radical meetings with speakers as experienced and popular as 'Mr Cobbett, Mr Hunt, Mr Lovett, Mr O'Connell, [and] Mr Hetherington'. Among O'Brien's earliest public speeches was one made at a meeting at the London Tavern, Bishopsgate Street, in January 1831, with Thomas Wakley in the chair, to celebrate Henry Hunt's election as M.P. for Preston. O'Brien's task was to propose a vote of thanks to the people of Preston for having returned Mr Hunt to the House of Commons. After attacking the Whigs on their Irish policy and their opposition to the secret ballot, O'Brien warned his audience against 'moderate Reform' which, he said, was 'but another name for fraudulent Reform' and was being offered as a thief gives up a sovereign or two so that 'he may retain a firmer grip on the fistfull . . . still in his possession'.[2]

This speech, and an article published a few weeks later, show that, young and politically inexperienced as he was, O'Brien saw clearly the danger that the working people might be cheated of their most cherished objectives, especially universal suffrage.

'Of the utter insincerity of the Whigs [he wrote] what further proof do we want than that they have always had the power of compelling a reform of the Commons House to any extent they wished, yet they never till now made the slightest effort to do so; and now (if I am not completely deceived) their policy is to effect a sham reform, which will have little else than the name; a miserable something that will have the semblance without the reality – a something to stop the people's mouths for a season. . . .

'I implore my readers to have no confidence whatever in the Whig ministry . . . and the rogues in England who wish to swindle the people out of real, substantial, Radical reform . . . but to work for themselves

---

[1] Quoted J. R. M. Butler, *op. cit.*, p. 86; *The Times*, 1st–11th November 1830; Brougham, *Life and Times* (1871), III, pp. 59–65; C. Welch, *Modern History of the City of London* (1896), p. 166.

[2] *A Penny Paper for the People by the Poor Man's Guardian*, 21st January 1831.

as earnestly, and with as little reliance on the "highest quarters" as if the Devil himself were Premier, and all his ministers in office.' [1]

Events proved that O'Brien's fears had been justified, for when, by dint of a widespread, determined, and sustained agitation the Reform Bill eventually became law, the Act not only fell far short of the radical measure demanded, for instance, by bodies like the L.R.R.A., but it made matters worse in some respects by extinguishing the old popular franchises in scot and lot boroughs, where all ratepayers could vote, and in the 'potwalloper' boroughs, in which the voters were the occupiers of premises with a fireplace where a pot could be boiled. These numbered 59 boroughs returning 118 members. Bitterly, working folk soon realized that they had been betrayed by the middle classes, who had banged the doors of Parliament in their faces and were now about to enjoy the fruits of their successful chicanery. This outcome, so clearly foreseen by O'Brien, greatly inflamed his hatred of the Whigs and their middle-class supporters; an attitude which he shared with many thousands of Radicals throughout the nation, whose frustration and disillusionment were the more intense because of the high hopes they had previously cherished. The great majority of the new electors, O'Brien told his readers on another occasion,

'. . . are middlemen, who thrive by your degradation. They get their living by buying your labour at one price and selling it . . . at another. . . . Your thorough-going middleman is never a Reformer from benevolence; hatred of tyranny or love of justice has nothing to do with his politics. . . . While the philanthropist glows with benevolence and the patriot burns with indignation, the frosty, flinty middleman is coolly inspecting the balance sheet. When times are good, that is to say when he is making a fortune out of other people's labour, he cries, "Church and King" and "Down with the Jacobins". When times are bad . . . he becomes a demi-Jacobin himself, and joins the "lower orders" against the higher. Into this alliance, however, he carries the prudence of the counting-house; he will be a "reformer" but not a "revolutionist"; that is to say he will reform *down* to himself, but not one jot will he reform *up*. Every change in the constitution of Parliament which gives him co-ordinate authority with the aristocracy, he calls reform, but every change that would give the honest artisan a co-ordinate authority with *him*, he calls "revolution".' [2]

---

[1] *Carpenter's Political Letters*, 18th February 1831.
[2] G. Slater, *Poverty and the State* (1930), pp. 89, 89n. *Poor Man's Guardian*, 15th December 1832.

3. Henry Hetherington (1792–1849), radical and freethinker, proprietor and publisher of the *Poor Man's Guardian*.

THE TREE OF TAXATION.

4. The Tree of Taxation – a cartoon from the *Northern Liberator* of 13th October 1838. Designed to be cut out and displayed in the workmen's homes.

It was clear to O'Brien that henceforward the working class must 'go it alone' and that the primary need in the struggle that lay ahead would be a cheap, unfettered periodical press carrying pungent political comment specially written to give 'political instruction' in true, thorough-going Radical principles to the untutored masses. Besides taxes on paper and advertisements there was the stamp duty on newspapers which at that time stood at a prohibitive level. Successive increases had raised the tax from one penny in 1795 to fourpence in 1815, so tending to put newspapers beyond the reach of the ordinary working man. He could, of course, read them – or hear them read aloud – at a tavern or coffee shop or workmen's club. He might be given his master's paper – probably a week old; or he might, if he could afford it, hire a paper, or club together with others to buy or share a copy. Francis Place said that the hire of a journal 'for a time scarcely sufficient to read one-half of it' cost twopence; and the duties of booksellers' and stationers' apprentices, like the young Michael Faraday, often included the delivery and collection of newspapers out on hire.[1] Such expedients were obviously unsatisfactory and their positive effects upon the spread of political knowledge among the working masses probably very small, if not negligible. The crying need was to bring cheap newspapers and periodicals within the reach of Everyman, who ought to have his own copies to hand whenever he had time for reading.

O'Brien's first contribution to the Radical press was an article in William Carpenter's unstamped *Political Letter*. It was entitled 'A Political Mirror' and was signed 'Bronterre', a *nom-de-plume* by which O'Brien was known to friend and foe for the rest of his life. This article, which appeared on 7th January 1831, and the two that followed are worth noting at some length, indicating as they do the author's current ideas, reflecting the impact of his experiences to date (he was nearly twenty-seven), and showing the conclusions he had so far drawn from his life and studies in Ireland and his small part in the early stages of the Reform struggle.

To begin with, Bronterre discussed the political union between Great Britain and Ireland. He defended Daniel O'Connell (later to be regarded by the Chartists as one of the greatest enemies of the working class) against 'the base imputation of sinister motives' contained in a *Times* article of 1st January 1831, which he denounced as 'from beginning to end, one tissue of fraudulent assumption [and] fallacious reasoning'. Linking the Irish question with that of political reform in England, O'Brien wrote in terms revealing his class attitude to the struggles then

[1] B.M. *Add.MSS.* 35,154(137); D. Gunston, *Michael Faraday* (1962), p. 27.

taking place. Given the repeal of the Union between the two countries (which, as an Irish patriot, he ardently hoped to see), and the sweeping away of the rotten boroughs – 'the elements of corruption and infamous trafficking in the "rights of man"' – nothing could prevent the Irish people from securing fair representation in the new Irish parliament. And it is

'. . . the dread of this influx of democratic influence into the legislature (not the mere existence of a local parliament for Ireland) which has thrown the whole body of the Aristocracy and the usurious capitalists into such paroxysms of fury and premature hostility to this great and just measure. It is the fear of losing the exclusive hold they heretofore have had on the property and power of the community, through the instrumentality of the hell-born borough and banking systems, which makes these heartless sons of monopoly so ludicrously fretful on this subject. . . . Thus we see the grand secret . . . the hostility of all the monied interest and higher orders (as they call themselves) to the repeal proceeds not from a desire to "preserve the connection between the two countries", which is in no danger from the measure, but from a desire to preserve *another connection*, which is much nearer their hearts; namely, the connection which ever subsists between exclusive representation and the exclusive enjoyment of wealth and power . . . a connection, in short, between the fingers of the boroughmongers and the pockets of the people. This is the connection they wish to keep up, – the rest is fudge.'

As for the alleged economic advantages to Ireland, stressed by *The Times*, is it, O'Brien asks, an advantage to the Irish people

'. . . to have the food taken away from the mouths of those who produce it, and brought to England to be sold at twice the price which Englishmen would have to pay for better food from the Continent, if not prohibited by Corn Laws? What impudence to talk of exclusive advantage to the Irish, who, living in a land which would maintain three or four times the present population, if properly cultivated, are, notwithstanding absolutely dying in thousands every year, of starvation and disease induced by poverty. . . . [Only] the landowners – the absentee Aristocracy – not the cultivators of the soil . . . benefit by the system. The main body of the people of both England and Ireland are deeply injured, almost ruined. . . .'

The *Political Letter* of 21st January 1831, carried 'Bronterre's First Letter to the People of England', in which he avowed his determination to diffuse 'wholesome political knowledge amongst the great body of the wealth-producing classes'.

'It is now sufficiently evident,' he wrote, 'that a great change is about to take place in the institutions of the civilized world. The crisis is arrived! the moral world is in a state of rapid transition; the reign of chicanery is about to close for ever, and the black empire of church and state mystery will cease henceforward to terrify and enslave mankind . . . god-like humanity proclaims aloud that a mighty moral revolution is necessary, and about to take place.'

As his speech at Henry Hunt's meeting shows, O'Brien expected nothing from Whig reform, but he did not, at this time, advocate violent measures. How, he asked, 'is change to be effected without bloodshed, violence or spoliation? . . . only by cheap publications, emanating from an enlightened, honest, and independent press, unshackled by taxes and unawed by threatened penalties'. He challenged the easy false philosophy which described as 'the will of God' the sufferings of those who, like the Irish poor, were condemned to try to live upon 'rape, nettles, and even sea-weed', and to die of starvation in the midst of abundance. Such words of ignorance, he said, obscure the fact that these miseries were caused by 'the will of inhuman tyrant man' operating through a cruel and unjust social system. He compared the lot of the iron-founders or the coal-miners with the horses in the field; 'strike an account between, and I ask you on which side is the balance of felicity?' Or compare these men of toil with the aristocrats who may be seen every day living in a state of luxury made possible because 'they contrive by superior cunning, and by always acting in concert together (just as thieves and banditti do) to monopolize the sole power of making laws, which laws they contrive to make so many cloaks, under which they disguise the hand of systematic rapine and legalized murder'.

'Bronterre's Second Letter to the People of England' which appeared on 12th February 1821 begins by defining 'aristocracy' as

'. . . that system of injustice and oppression which enables one man or body of men, to live in idleness and luxury at the expense of another man or body of men; that system which . . . would maintain an un-natural division of society into classes, *viz.*, those who labour and produce as well as consume, and those who consume only . . . as we are not at present likely to see realized Mr Owen's state of human perfect-ability, we must content ourselves with looking for that species of reform, which will make the present state of society most tolerable to the productive classes. . . . It is evident that such a plan of reform must invest the productive classes with real legislative power . . . with the power of gradually making whatever modifications they choose in existing institutions, and even in the constitution of society itself.'

In the remainder of this letter, printed in the *Political Letter* of 18th February 1831, he attempts to compute the amount of 'spoliation' by the aristocracy of England upon the masses, and arrives at the 'enormous sum' of £150,000,000, of which the working people, who had no power as tax-makers, were 'robbed' annually 'for the benefit of the aristocracy and their dependents'. Here, too, he introduces what became known later as his 'home-colonization' project.

'Look then at the monstrous injustice done to the wealth-producing, or labouring people. It may be thus stated in a simplified way; they are compelled by laws, in the framing of which they have no voice directly or indirectly, to raise property to the amount of £150,000,000 annually to be distributed, under innumerable names and pretences, among men who give them nothing valuable in exchange. . . . As regards the result to themselves it is precisely the same thing as if they were compelled to support twenty millions of people at £30 a year for each family; that is to say, in a style of living far superior to their own, generally speaking. . . . But let no one for a moment imagine that this is the whole amount of injustice done to the industrious classes . . . [for] after being compelled to toil and raise countless luxuries for the knaves and fools and strumpets and villains, who first rob them, then degrade them, then despise them, and sometimes hang them – after all this, the working people are absolutely disabled by the system from raising even the necessaries of life for themselves, though possessing all the skill and strength and leisure and will to do so. How many hundreds of thousands of men and women, and grown boys and girls are there in England and Ireland, who with all the eagerness in the world to get employment and give their labour and time for the tenth part of what they are fairly worth, yet cannot succeed in procuring a sordid subsistence even on those terms. . . .

'It would be competent for . . . a capable parliament, fairly representing *all the people*, to make whatever changes they might think necessary in the "settled institutions" of the country . . . for the enlightened and humane purpose of establishing free schools . . . for purchasing the 150 million acres of waste land now in the United Kingdom, whereon to locate our famishing fellow-countrymen; and above all for putting machinery and scientific power into the hands of

36

the wealth-producing classes, so as to make it auxiliary to manual labour, instead of permitting it to come into competition with, and supersede it.'

These articles are important for an understanding of O'Brien at an early stage in his career, revealing as they do the naïve optimism of a young man fresh to Radical politics, who believed that simply to expose the evils in Society would suffice to sweep the masses into the movement. Once the reformers had ranged behind them the power of the mighty multitudes, political reform would surely follow and then a parliament of the representatives of labour would 'abolish nine-tenths of the present taxes, together with such other numerous evils and abuses as are separable from even the present state of society; and thus gradually prepare the way for the adoption of the social or co-operative system, by diminishing the numbers of all interested opponents and giving us a perfectly free and unshackled press'. Any political reform, he insisted, must manifestly be such as will diminish as much as possible the number of non-producers and at the same time give the producers the power of retaining for their own enjoyment as much as possible of the wealth they produce. Without such legislative power the real producers will continue to be mere beasts of burden; with it, the Corn Laws would never have been passed; neither would English treasure have been poured out 'in order to frustrate the will of the French people in 1793'. Such an honest, genuine reform of Parliament would, O'Brien hoped, usher in an era of socialistic legislation and progress – a 'mighty moral revolution'.

This series of articles, which established Bronterre O'Brien as a Radical to be reckoned with, brought him, in the spring of 1831, the offer of the editorship of the *Midland Representative and Birmingham Herald*, a new, stamped, Radical weekly. He accepted at once and moved to Birmingham where the first issue of the new paper appeared on 23rd April 1831.[1] The struggle for the Reform Act was at its height and Birmingham was the centre of a tremendous agitation led by the Birmingham Political Union. Into these wild waters Bronterre eagerly plunged, writing and speaking chiefly, but not exclusively, on reform and 'anti-reform'. Poor Law maladministration and the paupers' miseries, including the 'Dreadful conditions of the Irish poor in Southwark', also received a good deal of attention. O'Brien prided himself upon giving fair play in his columns to writers of 'all sects, parties, and shades of opinion – Jew, Gentile, or Change-alley Jobber', provided

---

[1] *A Penny Paper for the People by the Poor Man's Guardian*, 15th April 1831, pp. 6 and 8.

they had something to say 'likely to interest or benefit the public'.[1]

O'Brien's speaking engagements at this time included one at a meeting held on 23rd January 1832 to press for repeal of the 'taxes on knowledge', at which he was the principal speaker. His carefully prepared, cogent speech was adequately buttressed with recent statistics, and, despite its length, was extremely well received. Another outstanding occasion was his address to the Second Co-operative Congress held in Birmingham from 4th to 6th October 1831. The *Proceedings* show that Robert Owen was there, surrounded by his most ardent admirers and disciples, and that O'Brien addressed the assembly on the second day. What they heard from him was not so much a flattering commendation of Co-operation, as an exposure of the essential evils of Capitalism.

'I have been,' he said, 'early in life a Co-operator. The more I have reflected on human nature, and the means of human happiness, the more firmly are my feelings and judgement rivetted in favour of the system. . . . A Reform of Parliament can effect little good except in so far as it may conduce to a reform in the construction of society. . . . By Co-operation every man able and willing to work will be always sure of abundance, for then there will be no limit to the production of wealth, besides [other than] the wants and capabilities of the community. How different from this is the present system of competition. Colquhoun . . . calculated in 1812, that every working family in England produced then, at an average, wealth to the value of about £260 a year, and that of this they were permitted by existing institutions to retain *less than a fifth part* for their own enjoyment. Since that time the productive powers of the community have been prodigiously increased. By recent improvements in chemical and mechanical science, we could now produce (if free to do so) seven or eight times more wealth of every description than as rational beings we would need to consume. Observe, then, the injustice done to the working classes. They are . . . robbed by competition of at least four-fifths of their earnings; and . . . disabled from producing necessaries for themselves after creating all manner of luxuries for others. Their labour is held in servile subjection by a tyrant called Capital, who *suspends* as well as *expands* production at pleasure [and] virtually tells the millions they may eat or drink, live or die, be prosperous or miserable, just as he likes. There is no escaping from this tyrant Capital: he is an essential element in every work of enterprise. No matter what may be a man's abilities, or industry, whether intellec-

---

[1] *Midland Representative and Birmingham Herald*, 23rd April–2nd June 1832, *passim*.

tual or mechanical, he can do nothing without the capitalist! The consequence is, the bulk of mankind are slaves – disguise it as we may. . . . When the capitalist finds the market glutted, his warehouse full . . . the question with him is never, whether any proportion of Society does or does not want the articles he manufactures, but whether or not they will yield him a remunerating profit. What a frightful prospect is this for the unfortunate workman! With every ability and disposition to work, he must withal rest his hopes of existence on sordid speculations of individuals called capitalists. When the capitalist wants him, he keeps him hard at work, 12 or 14 hours a day, for just as much as keeps him alive and able to resume his work next day, and when the speculator's convenience no longer requests it, he sends the wretch away, telling him to go and starve for a fortnight or so. Can this be called a rational form of Society? Ought human life to be thus one continued gambling speculation? On the contrary, ought not every human being to enjoy an abundance of all that is good for man's enjoyment, provided he be able and willing to produce it? Common sense – common justice – common humanity – say, *yes*.

'If it be true that working Englishmen are now deprived by existing institutions of four-fifths of their earnings, and if it be equally true that they have no share or consent in the formation of such institutions, it follows that they are as effectually robbed in this way, as they could be by a highway robber. . . .

'What, then, is the remedy for these evils? My opinion is, Co-operation. By Co-operation they can do *collectively* what it is impossible for them to do *individually*. They can become capitalists, and thus intercept the profits of trade in addition to the wages of labour. . . . Without capital they must continue slaves. . . . The law will but protect them as individuals from one another . . . but there is no protection for them *as a class*, to save them from being the prey of all other classes. The legislature excludes them from all share in the government on the ground that they are too ignorant to vote wisely, and too poor to vote independently, whilst at the same time it takes especial care to keep them both poor and ignorant. . . . Between Church and State they contrive to make useful machines of us, letting us use our feet freely [and] our hands, but *not our minds*, because these we could not exercise freely without reaping the benefit ourselves.'

This forthright speech 'was interrupted with frequent applause' and ended amidst a loud outburst of cheering.[1]

---

[1] *Proceedings of the 1st, 2nd and 3rd Co-operative Congresses, 1830–2* (Goldsmith's Library, University of London).

Although attracted and strongly influenced by Owenism, O'Brien never became a completely convinced Owenite Socialist. 'While I admire both Babeuf and Robert Owen,' he wrote, 'and agree, generally, with both as to the end sought, I am obliged to dissent from both as regards means.'[1] O'Brien based his hopes upon universal suffrage followed by the election of a House of Commons truly representative of the *whole* nation. Like Thomas Carlyle he cherished a firm belief in 'a willing Legislature' and the wonders it might work for the health and happiness of the working class – men, women and children – once the law-making power had passed into the hands of the true representatives of the people. Next should come the gradual acquisition of the land *by* the nation, *for* the nation; and such a thorough reform of the banking and currency system as would make the working man's wilderness blossom as the rose. O'Brien believed in state intervention in the processes of production and distribution, so as to ensure a just share of wealth for the working class. This points towards the nationalization of industries. Robert Owen, on the contrary, had not the slightest faith in political action. It has been well said that he 'had a vacant place in his mind where most men have political responses', and nobody ever convinced him that economic maladies could be cured by political medicines. Education and Owenite co-operation were, he thought, the only firm foundations upon which to build a better society. He saw as clearly as anybody the crying need for complete reform of the social order, and he believed that it would be achieved more quickly and peacefully through the communities of co-operation of which he dreamed than in any other way. This faith of Owen's was unshakable, and throughout his long life he ever remained utterly opposed to political action, to the class struggle idea, and to violence in any form.

On 27th May 1832, while O'Brien was still editor of the *Midland Representative*, he wrote to Owen urging him to make a bid for a larger measure of popular support:

'To you who know human nature so well, and whose writings afford abundant evidence that you are as well conversant with the nature of existing governments, I need not say that these governments have ultimately no other basis of support than public opinion. Be they ever so complicated or simple, be they monarchical or republican, they stand or fall, move retrograde or forward, solely in obedience to Public Opinion. It is therefore of vital importance to gather up this Public Opinion, to concentrate it on the social system and make it bear irresistibly on the government, by the weight, unity of direction, and

---

[1] O'Brien's translation of *Babeuf's Conspiracy* (1836), p. 214n.

simultaneous action of all its parts. With this view I respectfully suggest that the Association in Gray's Inn Road [1] should be made of a more popular character. I would in fact recommend you to take the Birmingham Union as your model so far as organization is concerned. . . . I would admit all persons as members who paid 1s per quarter or upwards, in order to secure the attendance of great numbers of the working classes at the lectures, council meetings, etc. I conceive that by proper arrangements you might get from five to ten thousand members. . . . If these and like duties [i.e. of the Council of the Association] were performed judiciously and your own peculiar opinions on Religion, Responsibility, etc., kept in the background, at least for a short time, I believe we could very soon, to use the language of Mr Attwood, roll up such a massive power, such a giant strength, as would be perfectly irresistible.

'I have said, my dear Sir, that I think the present time most auspicious. I think so because the suffering and deluded people are fast recovering their senses, sick and weary as they are of Public meetings, Reform discussion, Speechmaking and all that sort of thing; there are already hundreds, perhaps thousands in this very town, who have wit enough to perceive that this boasted Reform Bill will not bring them the good they once expected from it. As respects my allusion to religion, responsibility, etc., I beg you to understand me not as pleading indulgence for my own prejudices, but for those of others. If I mistake not, your ideas and my own are the same, or nearly so, on these subjects – but the people, the unhappy, the ignorant, the debasingly superstitious people are *frightfully sensitive* and, if you like, *insane* on these points.' [2]

Neither this letter nor a subsequent debate on 'Co-operation *versus* Political Rights' as a means of conferring immediate benefits upon the working class, had the slightest effect upon Owen. O'Brien, for his part, was quite convinced that Owen was on the wrong track, because the remedy offered by Owenite Socialism was, at best, only partial and likely to be painfully slow, if, indeed, it did not end in utter failure. For O'Brien the first objective stood out clearly – universal manhood suffrage: [3] 'Mr Owen and his followers may preach about co-operation

---

[1] i.e. The Institution of the Industrious Classes for Removing Ignorance and Poverty by Education and Beneficial Employment, founded by Robert Owen in December 1831.

[2] Manchester Collection of Robert Owen's Correspondence; cf. *The Power of the Pence*, Vol. I, No. 16, p. 242.

[3] *Poor Man's Guardian*, 22nd and 29th September 1832; 20th April 1833. O'Brien later dropped the word 'manhood' and referred always to 'universal suffrage'.

till they are hoarse as frogs, but no co-operation will there ever be till the rich are stripped of the exclusive privilege of law making – this is a change which must precede every other.' O'Brien's attitude towards Owenism was confirmed and strengthened by time, thought and experience. In January 1847 he wrote in his *National Reformer and Manx Weekly Review*:

'. . . with the Charter, [and] national ownership of land, currency and credit, people would soon discover what wonders of production, distribution, and exchange might be achieved by associated labour, in comparison with the exertions of isolated individual labour. Thence would gradually arise the true social state, or the realities of socialism, in contradiction to the present dreams of it. And doubtless the ultimate consequences would be the universal prevalence of a state of society not essentially different from that contrived by Owen. But the idea of jumping at once from our present iniquitous and corrupt state of society into Owen's social paradise, without any previous recognition of human rights and without establishing a single law or institution to rescue the people from their present brutalised condition of ignorance and vassalage, is a chimera.'

So throughout their lives, although they remained on terms of mutual respect, these two pioneers, Bronterre O'Brien and Robert Owen, continued to differ on this highly important question; [1] and, as Professor Harrison says, 'the advocates of independent political action went their own ways, taking with them such parts of Owenism as suited their purposes'. Owen's total opposition to political action seems the more remarkable since it was maintained in the midst of the great Reform Bill agitation which, month after month, shook the country from end to end. In the middle of May 1832, when the battle for the Bill was well-nigh won, O'Brien repeated a loud and clear warning to his working-class readers:

'Whatever Whigs or knaves may pretend to the contrary . . . the Bill was never intended to do you, the working people, one particle of good. We are well aware what vengeance and secret malignity this declaration will excite . . . but as the *Midland Representative* was established chiefly by and for you, the working classes, and as this is probably the last time

---

[1] *Ibid.*, 21st June 1834. An exchange of letters published in the *Poor Man's Guardian* in March 1835 shows that their views were as wide apart as ever; cf. J. F. C. Harrison, *Robert Owen and the Owenites in Britain and America* (1969), pp. 214–16. For Francis Place's views of Owenism see B.M. *Add.MSS.* 27,791(268) and 27,819(7), and cf. Asa Briggs, 'Robert Owen in Retrospect', a centenary lecture printed in *Co-operative College Papers No. 6*, April 1959.

we shall have an opportunity of addressing you through its columns, we are determined to tell you what we believe to be the truth, cost what it may.'[1]

The Reform Bill was passed on 4th June 1832, just two days after O'Brien's first editorship came to an end with the taking over of the *Midland Representative* by the *Birmingham Journal*. This meant that, after a strenuous, satisfying year, O'Brien found himself out of work.

During the autumn of 1832 he had a number of speaking engagements, including a meeting held to whip up support for the *True Sun* newspaper, at which O'Brien's platform colleagues were 'Orator' Henry Hunt and William Lovett (both already known to him), and the corpulent Owenite-Chartist Vicar of Warwick, the Reverend A. S. Wade, D.D., – a curiously assorted quartet united only by their common devotion to Radicalism and the democratic ideal.[2] Meantime, in London, Thomas Mayhew, the eldest of a 'literary band of brothers' (which included Henry Mayhew, who later became famous as chief assistant to Mark Lemon, the first editor of *Punch*, and as a pioneer investigator of the lower levels of London life), was on the point of giving up the editorship of the *Poor Man's Guardian*.[3] Henry Hetherington, proprietor of the *Guardian*, looking around for a successor to Thomas Mayhew, remembered O'Brien and invited him to fill the vacant chair. Bronterre was more than willing, for he saw this timely opening as a challenge and a golden opportunity to strike a blow for Radicalism and a free press. Without a moment's hesitation he returned to London.

[1] *Midland Representative and Birmingham Herald*, 12th May 1832.
[2] Report of the proceedings at the Public Meeting to support the *True Sun;* H.O. Papers 64(18).
[3] Athol Mayhew, *A Jorum of 'Punch'* . . . *the Early History of the London Charivari* (1895), p. xiv; G. M. Young (ed.), *Early Victorian England* (1934), II, pp. 86–7.

Chapter III

UNSTAMPED DEFIANCE

O'BRIEN became editor of the *Poor Man's Guardian* in November 1832, by which time the Radicals had gone over from the defensive to the attack in the battle for a free press. William Carpenter had been prosecuted to conviction by the Stamp Office for publishing his *Political Letters* (each one directed to a different addressee), despite his ingenious plea that since each issue was a separate paper and not one paper appearing in parts, it was not liable to the tax. This argument was of no avail; Carpenter's defence was rejected and he was imprisoned.[1]

Carpenter's conviction had an electric effect on Henry Hetherington who 'at once accepted not the prohibition to publish, but the decision that . . . evasion would be futile . . . we will not trespass, but deny the authority of our "lords" to enclose the common against us'. 'Defiance,' he declared, 'is our only remedy.' Within a few weeks after Carpenter's trial, Hetherington deliberately published the *Poor Man's Guardian: A Weekly Paper for the People* (eight quarto pages for a penny), unstamped, 'in defiance of "Law", to try the power of "Right" against "Might"'. He threw down the gauntlet with the words – 'Knowledge is Power', and 'Taxation without Representation is Tyranny, and ought to be resisted';[2] and when he said 'resisted' he meant *resisted openly* so that all men might see who stood for 'Right' and who wielded the weapons of 'Might'. Volunteers were urgently needed to undertake the hazardous

---

[1] *Political Letters*, 4th February 1831, p. 16; cf. the argument in the *Letter to the People of England*, 1st October 1830, signed 'M' (probably Thomas Mayhew), published by Hetherington; *Poor Man's Guardian*, 21st May 1831. This weekly had grown out of a series of penny papers dating from 1st October 1830; *Report of the Trial of Mr William Carpenter* (pub. Carpenter, 1831). The Radical journalists, publishers and booksellers had long been at grips, no holds barred, with successive governments.

[2] Hetherington had worked as a printer's apprentice under Hansard; see G. J. Holyoake, *Life and Character of Henry Hetherington* (1849), and *Sixty Years of an Agitator's Life* (1902), Chs. 51 and 106; W. Lovett, *Life and Struggles* (1876), p. 59; E. P. Thompson, *The Making of the English Working Class* (1965), pp. 720, 728.

business of selling the paper. 'Wanted ads' appeared prominently in the *Guardian*:

'WANTED: Some hundreds of poor men out of employment, who have nothing to risk, some of those unfortunate beings to whom distress occasioned by a tyrannical government has made a prison a desirable home. An honest and moral way of finding gaol bread and shelter, and, moreover, of earning the thanks of their fellow-countrymen, now presents itself to such patriotic Englishmen as will, in defiance of the most odious "Laws" of a most odious tyranny, imposed upon an enslaved and oppressed people, sell to the poor and ignorant

THE POOR MAN'S GUARDIAN
A Weekly "Newspaper" for the People.

Published contrary to "law" to try the power of "Might" against "Right".

N.B. A Subscription is open for the relief, support and reward of all such persons as may become victims of the Whig Tyrants.'

Many volunteers responded, ignoring or discounting the risk. Some were keen to get into the fight for a free press; others were attracted by the prospect of the gift of a stock of papers and £1 for every month, or part of a month, during which they might be imprisoned for selling them. By 20th August 1831, six persons had been imprisoned for selling the *Guardian* openly in the streets: but this was only a preliminary skirmish. At the end of March 1833 the *Guardian* printed an official return of the number of persons committed for selling unstamped journals during the seven months between 26th July 1832 and 27th February 1833. The total was 254. From July 1831 to the end of 1834 over 800 vendors of 'the Unstamped' were arrested, of whom over 500 were fined or gaoled, or both.

Among those who took part in this great struggle was that Radical revolutionist and seasoned campaigner, William Benbow, whom we shall meet again in connection with his plan for a 'grand national holiday' or general strike. So passionate was his hatred of despotism in all its forms that he fought for a lifetime to destroy it. An essential weapon against the entrenched enemy was, he well knew, a free and cheap press; so in 1832, declaring that 'the people shall no longer be duped', he brought out an unstamped twopenny monthly entitled *The Tribune of the People* which was printed for him by R. E. Lee, who afterwards attacked Benbow in a pamphlet entitled *Victimization, or Benbowism Unmasked* for failing to pay his printing bills. Benbow also

45

helped O'Brien and Hetherington by collecting Victims' Fund contributions at his coffee-house.

Young Julian Harney, too, fought in this battle, for he was employed at the time by Hetherington as a printer's shop-boy in the *Poor Man's Guardian* office, where he met O'Brien and was deeply impressed by his ideas and ability. Considering that Harney was twelve years younger than O'Brien and greatly his inferior in education, it is not surprising that O'Brien's influence upon Harney, and through him, eventually, upon the lively, left-wing London Democratic Association, was strong and lasting. These two spirited young men, filled with revolutionary fervour, were united in their conviction that given universal suffrage and the dispersal of mass ignorance – objectives which were, they believed, within the people's grasp – 'the march of regeneration would be swift and sure; all that was oppressive would be overthrown, and triumphant Justice would take the place of extirpated Wrong'. And in this decisive battle they were determined that the *Guardian*'s banner should be kept to the fore. Harney boldly hawked unstamped papers in the streets and, while still in his teens, was thrice imprisoned and compensated from the Victims' Fund.[1]

Editor Bronterre O'Brien published, from time to time,

'. . . a few facts to show that neither age nor sex is spared in this onslaught. On Monday, a child of eight years old was taken into custody for selling this paper; on the same day Sir Peter Laurie committed another child, only 10 years old, for a month to Bridewell, for the same offence, observing . . . "I shall commit every one, old or young, for this offence". On the same day, an old man . . . aged 62 was committed (at Bow Street) to the House of Correction for selling the *Weekly Times*. In all these cases, the parties were robbed as well as incarcerated, for their parcels, which were their whole property, were taken from them. One of the children . . . had 57 papers taken from him. The old man, who declared that he had no other means of living, was robbed of . . . 128 papers, after which he was sent to Coldbath-fields [prison] . . . for 25 days . . . [with] rogues and vagabonds of every sort'.

'A middle-aged respectable-looking female' charged with selling the *Poor Man's Guardian* in Oxford Street told the Marlborough Street magistrate that she could see nothing dishonest about it, and certainly 'it was better than starving'. She was sent to prison for fourteen

---

[1] B.M. *Add.MSS.* 27,821(5); H.O. Papers 64(18); A. R. Schoyen, *The Chartist Challenge: A Portrait of George Julian Harney* (1958), Chs. I and II, and p. 281.

days.[1] The two principal sellers of unstamped papers in Leeds, a man and a woman, were sentenced to six months' imprisonment. The choice offered by the magistrate was to pay an enormous fine of £80 and 'give up shop as a vendor of the Unstamped, or to go to York Castle for six months'. They both went to prison.

There were, also, many secret sellers of the unstamped papers; people who coveted the profit but feared the punishment. A letter on this subject was addressed to O'Brien in August 1833.

'Brother, It is not, I think, so well known as it ought to be that there are many booksellers who sell the unstamped secretly, and who by this means enjoy a share of that profit which in my opinion belongs to those who have boldly stood forward to fight the good fight. I do not blame the booksellers, many of whom may be good men and true, and afraid openly to sell the works for fear of injuring their present interests . . . I earnestly entreat all who dare to read these works . . . to buy only of those who dare to sell. . . .

A Socialist.' [2]

Thus, openly or secretly, in the teeth of every sort of interference, hindrance and discrimination, including free carriage of their stamped rivals by the Post Office, the unstamped journals were distributed throughout London and the provinces. At a time of strictest vigilance on the part of the authorities, large numbers of John Cleave's *Police Gazette* were packed into coffins and solemnly carried out of an undertaker's shop near the printing office.[3] This ruse succeeded well until people began to talk. (Why so many coffins but so few funerals? Very strange!) James Burn, who lived through this period, says that in the large towns

'. . . there were certain places where the people dropped their pence into narrow apertures, and papers to the amount made their appearance immediately, as if by magic. I knew an instance in which a young man was sent down from London to push this business in Glasgow, and it is a fact that his machinery was so perfect that he kept the officers of the

---

[1] *Working Man's Friend*, 22nd December 1832. Many children in those days had to earn an independent livelihood; see e.g. H. Mayhew, *London Labour and the London Poor* (1851), *passim*.

[2] *Poor Man's Guardian*, 24th August 1833. This is one of the earliest appearances of the word 'Socialist'.

[3] C. D. Collett, *History of the Taxes on Knowledge* (1899), p. 46; J. Grant, *The Newspaper Press* (1871), II, p. 307; R. D. Altick, *The English Common Reader* (1957), pp. 340-2; quoting House of Commons Newspaper Stamp Committee, *Evidence*, 1851.

47

law dancing about his premises for months, if not for years. He continued to elude all the snares which were laid for him, and he is now a man of independent means, with a place of business considerably less than a thousand miles from Greenside, in Auld Reekie. Many men in the business, however, were both fined and incarcerated, and not a few reduced to ruin.' [1]

Another seller of unstamped papers who prospered eventually was Abel Hayward, whose name became as famous in the provinces as Hetherington's in London, and who twice became Mayor of Manchester.

The Duke of Wellington was disturbed, not in London but in the rural solitude of the south where, hitherto, newspapers were seldom seen in the villages and farmhouses. 'I hear a great deal of the circulation of "Cobbett" and the *Poor Man's Guardian* in this district,' he wrote from Hampshire to Lord Melbourne in November 1832.[2] There is, moreover, good reason to think that the unstamped papers were getting into the hands of the troops. Bronterre O'Brien, speaking as the voice of the working class, addressed 'the soldiers of the United Kingdom' in the following terms:

'Though you are apparently our enemies, we call you brothers and friends. Though enlisted . . . to enslave us, and fed upon taxes wrung from our toil, we nevertheless see in you but fellow-citizens reduced to the same state of degradation as ourselves, and by the same means. . . . The government and its supporters are responsible to God and man for your bloody deeds. . . . The rulers of this country know that all crime springs from ignorance and poverty; they know equally well that it is no man's choice to be poor and ignorant. . . . We hear that a spirit of enquiry has got into the army . . . and that the *Poor Man's Guardian* has already found its way into a great number of regiments. . . . Be assured that millions of honest Englishmen will shout with ecstasy when they hear you are become good republicans.'

The harsher the prosecution of the unstamped papers and the stouter their resistance, the greater their popularity. Such audacious flouting of 'authority' *alias* 'tyranny' delighted the Radical working men, who characteristically sided with 'the little 'un' in his desperate fight against 'the big 'un', and looked upon a Radical publisher's imprisonment as an honour, not a disgrace. Every issue of an unstamped paper was a defiant snook cocked at a tyrannical government. Anthony Fonblanque of *The Examiner*, a powerful journalist and man of principle,

---

[1] James Burn, *Autobiography* (1882), p. 378n.
[2] Lord Melbourne's Papers, p. 150; P. Guedalla, *The Duke* (1931), p. 409.

saw the struggle as a 'contraband trade' called into existence to hawk 'cheap illicit spirit, ten times over proof . . . among the working classes'.

The Victims' Fund, too, buttressed the movement and contributed greatly to its success. In his autobiography (*Life and Struggles*, Ch. III), William Lovett tells us that the Fund was administered by a committee of nine – himself, Cleave, Watson, and six others – who 'met weekly in an upstair room at the Hope Coffee House, King Street, Smithfield, then kept by Mr John Cleave, and subsequently at his house in Shoe Lane'. In his capacity as bookseller and publisher John Cleave was a most dedicated fighter for a free press, and suffered grievously in the struggle through fines, imprisonment and loss of business. Not only did the Victims' Fund committee meet on his premises, but the victims, many of them poor, ragged and dirty, came there to be paid. This was too much for some of Cleave's customers!

At the height of the campaign against 'the taxes on knowledge' in 1834–5, it appears that something like 150,000 copies of the unstamped papers were defiantly distributed each week; every copy likely to be passed from hand to hand, studied in coffee-houses and taverns, and read aloud to groups of non-readers eager to hear what the Radical journals had to say and how the fight was going. Even the journeymen handloom silk weavers of Spitalfields and Bethnal Green, desperately poor though they were, for their trade was disintegrating, tried hard to save a copper to buy a copy. According to O'Brien, the sales of the *Poor Man's Guardian* increased every time Hetherington was arrested, and within three years of its first appearance the weekly circulation reached some 16,000. Also in the battle were Richard Carlile's *Gauntlet* (a symbol of challenge), John Cleave's *Weekly Police Gazette*, and four or five other vigorous unstamped weeklies edited by such men as James Watson, J. H. B. Lorymer, R. E. Lee and James Morrison. Outstanding among the unstamped journals produced in the provincial towns like Manchester, Leeds, Bradford, and taking their tone from the *Poor Man's Guardian*, was Joshua Hobson's weekly *Voice of the West Riding*. Hobson, who employed John Francis Bray for a short time as printer in charge of the office, began publication in June 1833, when he was only twenty-two. He had been a handloom cotton weaver in Oldham, but had turned from this doomed occupation to joinery and, later, to printing. His publication of an unstamped journal soon brought about his conviction in 1833 and he had to choose between paying a fine or going to prison. He chose prison and was accompanied to Wakefield Gaol by a cheering concourse of supporters and sympathizers.[1] He

[1] *Poor Man's Guardian*, 9th March 1833; *Economica*, November 1940, p. 399, article by H. J. Carr on John Francis Bray.

continued his activities and suffered a second gaol sentence in 1836.

Hetherington, a giant among giants, led the van of these determined forces. Nothing could shake his will to win. Often, he had to disguise himself as a waggoner, a costermonger, or a Quaker. Dummy parcels of the *Guardian* were carried in one direction by persons instructed to make all possible resistance to constables who seized them, while real parcels were sent by another route. Hetherington's shopmen were imprisoned, his premises forcibly entered and his property confiscated. The constables paid men to smash his press with blacksmiths' hammers. The reactionary papers made him the target for their virulent attacks and gross misrepresentations. *The Standard*, for example, erroneously described him as an Irish papist (confusing him, perhaps, with his editor, O'Brien), and his principles as 'Jacobinical of the deepest and bloodiest dye'.[1] Lovett says that Hetherington's radicalism was so obnoxious to many of his customers that they withdrew their printing from him.

'One of his most useful apprentices, too, refused to work on such a radical publication, and was sanctioned in his disobedience by the magistrates, who very readily cancelled his indentures. I remember being present on one occasion when one of Mr Hetherington's customers, in a large way of business, offered to give him as much printing as he could do on his premises, provided he would give up his radical publications; but this splendid offer (in a pecuniary sense) he very nobly refused; although to my knowledge his shelves were then filled with thousands of his unsold and returned publications, and all his relations and connections were loudly condemning him for his folly. Mr Hetherington, however, was not the kind of character to yield under such circumstances.'

At every turn the editors, printers, publishers and vendors of the unstamped papers were dogged by spies. Constables ransacked the coach offices and coffee shops for copies of the unstamped journals, while 'all parcels which a peace-officer may choose to suspect as containing unstamped newspapers' could be seized in the street and retained indefinitely for investigation. Many copies of Carpenter's *Political Letters*, the *Poor Man's Guardian* and other unstamped papers were seized and sent to the Home Office where they were labelled 'Seditious'. Copies of the *Republican* and the *Poor Man's Guardian* of

---

[1] *Dict. Nat. Biog.*, article 'Henry Hetherington'; B.M. *Add.MSS.* 27,822(23); Maccoby, *English Radicalism, 1832–1852*, p. 414. The true-blue Tory view of the 'destructive' or 'pauper' papers was given in *The Standard*, 10th September 1833.

23rd July 1831, were despatched to the Home Office with the following 'Morning Report':

'I made enquiry last evening respecting the meeting that is to take place on Monday, 1st August. Nothing is settled at present who is to take the chair. . . . I was informed at Mr Hetherington's that it is the intention of the principals to employ a number of persons to vend the annexed publications and if sent to prison to allow them 1s per day during the time they are in confinement and a reward of 10s on the day of their liberation and let them confine ever such a number they will furnish a fresh supply. They informed me that since the first prosecution the sale of them is increased to 3 times the number. 27th July 1831.' [1]

The *Poor Man's Guardian* of 10th December 1831, which carried a speech by William Benbow declaring that his 'Holiday' or general strike would effect the most glorious revolution ever heard of, was heavily marked in places by a government secret agent who attached a note pointing out that '*The Guardian* is more than usually violent today – at the bottom of the 4th page you will find more about the "Holiday" and also in the middle of the 6th page, that it has formed one of the resolutions at the Huddersfield meeting'.

Early in 1833 the Radicals had cause for rejoicing when Colley and Currey, an unsavoury pair of Stamp Office spies and *agents provocateurs*, were brought to book for 'a most abominable conspiracy' to entice boys to sell unstamped papers and afterwards to inform against them for the sake of the 20s 'bloodmoney' obtained for each conviction.[2]

An interesting and amusing sidelight upon the sort of obstacles overcome by men like Hetherington, O'Brien, and their allies during this struggle is furnished by a manuscript note gummed inside a copy of the *Bonnet Rouge*, No. 1, of 2nd February 1833:

'This number was never issued to the Public, two hundred were struck off but all immediately destroyed with the exception of some two or three. Application was made to several printers to print this number but they refused owing to its very strong destructive principles: it was ultimately printed by a man living in a garret in Holywell Street [Strand] who was drunk at the time, which may account for the misplacing of the pages. Mr J. — [James Lorymer] wrote the leading articles. . . . The *real* first number came out on the 10th and is the *acknowledged* first number of the *Bonnet Rouge*.   1833. S.P.'

The mis-placed pages run – 1, 6, 5, 2, 3, 8, 7, 4.

[1] *H.O. Papers*, 64 (17 and 18).
[2] *Poor Man's Guardian*, 12th January 1833.

Notwithstanding every kind of obstacle and the most ruthless opposition, the *Poor Man's Guardian*, under Bronterre O'Brien's editorship, rapidly became the foremost penny paper and 'undoubtedly the finest working-class weekly which had (until that time) been published in Britain'.[1] He made it an exceedingly lively paper, allowing free expression in its columns to all sections of the working-class movement and every shade of opinion. True to its motto 'Knowledge is Power', the *Guardian* sought to provide information and to encourage discussion on a wide variety of current economic and political topics as a means of banishing 'that greatest of all national evils, political ignorance', and educating working people for the eventual exercise of political rights and responsibilities. To this end the importance of sustained effort to create a widespread, well-organized, working-class movement, independent of middle-class meddling, was stressed again and again. The more unmercifully O'Brien hammered the 'Whig tyrants' the more he heartened his readers. Much space was given to Robert Owen and the Grand National Consolidated Trades Union, and to the case of the persecuted Tolpuddle labourers. (It was O'Brien who pointed out, in July 1835, that only eighty-four M.P.s out of 658 had voted for the recall of these transported victims.) The *rights* of property were shown to be the *wrongs* of labour. The worst horrors of the new and expanding factory system – especially child labour – were exposed by extracts quoted from the evidence given before the commissions of enquiry then in session. The 'Poor Men of England' were told in a passage which, like the address to the soldiers, had a distinct republican flavour, that

'. . . there is no law for you in this country – no law, we mean, for your protection. There are plenty of laws to plunder you, to pauperize you, to overwork you, to starve you, to whip you, to transport you, to hang you; but – we repeat it emphatically – there is no law for your protection. The rulers of this country are a band of villains whose actions prove them to be leagued together for your and our destruction . . . then lose not a moment to prove to our oppressors that you are with us . . . to root out of England the disguised cannibalism of Monarchy – in a word, to exchange the wrongs of enslaved subjects for the rights of enfranchised citizens. God save the Guardian.'

In a leading article O'Brien explained why the working classes should reject the ballot '*unless accompanied by a great extension of the suffrage*: . . . with an enlarged constituency (i.e. electorate) – say universal, or

[1] E. P. Thompson, *The Making of the English Working Class* (1965), pp. 811–12.

even household suffrage – the ballot is an invaluable palladium of liberty; but with a narrow, sordid, jealous constituency of shopocrats and middlemen slave-drivers . . . the Ballot would be a poignard in the hand, and a mask on the face, for all that is usurious, hard-hearted, and liberticidal in society'.[1]

From February 1833 onwards, O'Brien also edited *The Destructive and Poor Man's Conservative*, for publishing which Hetherington was fined £180 in 1834. This was a twopenny journal, larger than the *Guardian*, including an analysis of the debates in 'the New Parliament'. Its politics were identical with the *Guardian*'s, and as to its title, 'suffice it to say that while we desire to be destructive of evil, we are still more zealous to be conservative of good'. Nevertheless the word 'destructive' had a sinister sound, very difficult to explain away. Therefore, towards the end of 1833 the paper's title was changed to *The People's Conservative and Trade Union Gazette* in deference to the wishes of many friendly critics and 'those who desire to see us identified, in name as well as in fact, with those powerful associations called Trades Unions'.

By their sustained efforts Bronterre O'Brien's two papers and the various other unstamped journals succeeded in keeping up a feverish excitement among working people, many of whom believed that a resounding revolution was close at hand. 'In the great event approaching' wrote a London working man to Robert Owen, 'all little individual views and feelings are contemptible compared to the great objects before us.' *The Republican* encouraged its readers to prepare for armed conflict, and gave an estimate of the numbers of soldiers and police in the Metropolis. And as to stores, it said, let them read William Benbow's *Grand National Holiday* and they would 'learn something worth knowing'. J. H. B. Lorymer's *Bonnet Rouge* was said to be circulating in certain regiments and causing disaffection among the rank and file. James Morrison's *Pioneer* confidently announced, in October 1833, that 'The crisis of our condition is at hand – close upon us. The contest affects all alike; and woe unto the man who deserts his post. The question to be decided is, Shall Labour or Capital be uppermost?' R. E. Lee in *The Man* forecast the 'approaching storm' and actually offered for sale the 'Outlines of a New Constitution'. In March 1834 a government spy named Ball '. . . called at Lovett's Coffee House, Hatton Garden [and] met Preston who said Lovett would make a prime Chancellor of the Exchequer . . . and [spoke of] the great probability of a successful Triumph of the cause of the people, as he is certain it is on the eve'.[2] O'Brien, for his part, had already given

---

[1] See *Poor Man's Guardian*, 1833–5 *passim*.
[2] *The Man*, 24th November 1833; H.O. Papers, 64(19).

warning that 'the people must prepare themselves for a desperate struggle. We suspect they [the Whigs] will begin with the unstamped. Indeed they have already dispatched emissaries to all parts of the country to ascertain the channels through which they circulate. No matter, *we defy the rascals*. . . .'

This warning coincided with the release of 'Citizen' Hetherington from the Clerkenwell 'Bastille' where he had been imprisoned for six months. But the government had not yet finished with him. Before the close of the year (1833) O'Brien was writing in the *Guardian* about 'a bill of indictment found against Mr Hetherington some six months ago by the Grand Jury of Middlesex, and which . . . we had every reason to believe was abandoned'; and in the middle of January 1834 a leading article heralded the approaching trial, the outcome of which, as we now know, astonished everybody.

The case, *The Attorney-General v. Hetherington*, was tried in the Court of Exchequer on 17th June 1834 before Lord Lyndhurst and a special jury.[1] Hetherington, accused of the illegal publication of two papers, the *People's Conservative* and the *Poor Man's Guardian* (both edited by Bronterre O'Brien), put up an outspoken and vigorous defence, stressing the well-worn Radical complaint that the law was, in practice, enforced in an extremely partial and unjust way, because many of the cheap Radical papers produced for working-class readers were relentlessly persecuted, while a paper like Knight's *Penny Magazine*, selling some 150,000 copies weekly which certainly contained news items, was never prosecuted, perhaps because it had influential patrons. The Solicitor-General ignored this point and argued that both papers were clearly newspapers, as the jury would, on inspecting them, see. Lord Lyndhurst said that

'. . . the *Poor Man's Guardian* was a much more meagre publication than the *Conservative*; but the jury could inspect them, and they knew as much about a newspaper as he did.'

'Verdict for the Crown upon the *Conservative*, with two penalties – £160 for not delivering the affidavit, and £20 for selling them unstamped; and verdict for the defendant upon the *Poor Man's Guardian*.

The Defendant: I am glad of that for it legalizes the publication.

Lord Lyndhurst: Mr Hetherington is anxious that it should be understood that the jury do not think that the *Poor Man's Guardian* comes within the Act.'

[1] An Act of 1825 required a member of a special jury to be of the rank of 'esquire', or a merchant or banker. Special juries were abolished in 1949.

'This paper,' wrote O'Brien exultantly after the trial, 'after sustaining a Government persecution of three years and a half duration, in which upwards of 500 persons were unjustly imprisoned and cruelly treated for vending it, was . . . in the Court of Exchequer before Lord Lyndhurst and a special jury, declared to be a strictly legal publication.' [1] The almost incredible new status of the *Guardian* brought an unexpected result; for after the publication of a further seventy-nine issues, its troubled, triumphant career came to an end. Working men, it seems, would buy an illegal paper, for that was to aim a blow at the Government; but when the paper – even the famous and gallant *Guardian* – became 'respectable', their support declined. Hetherington himself, when before the Court of Queen's Bench in December 1840, accused of publishing a blasphemous libel, said, 'I have been prosecuted, as I think with great injustice, for the publication of a paper called *The Poor Man's Guardian* . . . I was twice imprisoned, for six months on each occasion, and the circulation of the paper, thus prosecuted, more than paid my losses; but at last . . . a jury found a verdict in my favour . . . and as soon as it was known that the *Guardian* was a legal paper, it went down at once, I could not sell copies enough to pay the expenses!' [2] Just before it ceased publication the *Guardian*'s weekly circulation was only 4,000 copies. In the very last issue Hetherington, looking back more in sorrow than anger, addressed his readers, recounting some of his experiences and recommending to them the *Twopenny Dispatch* and O'Brien's projected writings: 'I have myself been four times convicted for publishing it [the *Guardian*] – twice imprisoned for six months – indicted for libel, but never brought to trial, for denouncing the brutal conduct of the police at the Calpthorpe-street meeting . . . the indentures of my apprentice were cancelled by the Magistrates . . . on the ground that he was employed on an illegal publication. . . . The *Twopenny Dispatch* will henceforth embody the principles of the *Guardian* . . . a series of letters on highly important subjects will also appear in it from the Editor [O'Brien] . . . I trust the importance and utility of the forthcoming historical works, announced by the Editor, and designed as an antidote to the frauds of history . . . will be found worthy of extensive popular encouragement. The first work will be Babeuf's *Conspiracy*, one of the most deeply interesting narratives ever issued from the press.' [3]

[1] *The Times*, 18th June 1834; Grant, *op. cit.*, II, pp. 305–6; Collet, *op. cit.*, Ch. II.
[2] *Reports of State Trials* (New Series), IV (1840), pp. 563, 574–5: The Queen *v.* Hetherington.
[3] *Poor Man's Guardian*, 19th and 26th December 1835.

Beginning in January 1836, O'Brien set to work to infuse the force and spirit of the *Guardian* into Hetherington's *Twopenny Dispatch*, in which he wrote weekly 'letters' to his readers over the now well-known signature 'Bronterre', because, he said, it seemed 'more convenient and familiar to write in the first person, as a man would write who desired to make his readers his friends, the cold editorial 'we' being a sort of damper to that feeling . . .'. 'My object,' he wrote, 'is to supply the best instruction and the best substitute I can' for the . . . *Guardian*, 'the loss of which, as every week's correspondence informs me, is much regretted by the working classes.' [1] In this spirit 'Bronterre' continued to write upon the familiar themes which were to fill his mind and heart throughout his life: false and true religion; universal suffrage; the great gulf between rich and poor; falling wages, sweated labour, unemployment, poverty and starvation; the evils of the new Poor Law; every point driven home by 'modern instances' of tyranny, injustice, and suffering.

Universal suffrage was the key which would release the sufferers, and O'Brien was optimistic about the chances of carrying a substantial measure of reform at the next general election. In July 1836 he made an interesting reference to 'the first National Convention – the germ of that self-government' which, it was hoped, would shortly prove to be the true means of improving the condition of all working people. Five weeks later he urged the people to

'. . . unite, petition, demonstrate, organize . . . to obtain universal suffrage. Without the franchise they can do nothing except by armed force, and at present *that* is out of the question. It is now while they are in full employ that they ought to form Unions, raise funds, and organize the labouring masses all over the country. . . . It is not when whole districts are out of employ and absolutely starving that operative unions can be formed. It is while the people are in full employ and wages comparatively good. That is the time to unite and raise funds'.

In another issue of the *Dispatch* 'Bronterre' attacked the capitalist system and the king's speech at the prorogation of Parliament.

'I do not pretend,' he wrote, 'to describe a system which is perfectly indescribable. . . . If the reader desires more he has only to look abroad in society. He has only to observe the monstrous inequalities – the inhuman circumstances that everywhere abound – the insolent luxury of one class – the hopeless slavery of others – the universal hypocrisy and cunning – the frightful demoralization – in short the chaos of woe and wickedness in which the whole population is involved.'

[1] Hetherington's *Twopenny Dispatch*, 2nd January 1836.

As for the king's speech, O'Brien dismissed it contemptuously as a 'meaningless farrago of commonplaces', and substituted his own version of what the king ought to have said, couched in terms bitterly scornful of the public functions and private lives of 'my lords and gentlemen'.[1]

Doubtless O'Brien's anger was envenomed at this time by the Government's unremitting attacks on the unstamped papers, even when legislation to reduce the newspaper stamp duties was actually before Parliament in 1836. During 1835 and the first quarter of 1836 there were 219 prosecutions for selling unstamped papers. John Cleave was fined £500 in February 1836 for publishing the *Weekly Police Gazette*, and as late as August, according to O'Brien, seven parcels of the *Dispatch* had been seized in one week and 3,000 copies in the following week in a desperate eleventh-hour attempt to destroy the paper.

When at last the new Act came into force, on 15th September 1836, the stamp duty was substantially reduced from 4d to 1d; but newspaper proprietors still had to bear the expense of getting their journals stamped, and they lost the duty on all copies stamped but not sold. The retention of duty at one penny still left the working-class journals at a disadvantage, for few workmen could afford more than twopence, while, on the other hand, production costs plus the duty made it difficult to publish, without loss, a well-printed paper at less than 4d or 5d a copy.

Immediately after the new Act was passed, O'Brien and Hetherington came to terms with the situation by bringing out the *London Dispatch and People's Political and Social Reformer*. It was, in fact, the *Twopenny Dispatch* increased in price to $3\frac{1}{2}$d, – one penny extra for the stamp and a halfpenny to cover additional expenses due to the stamp. To attempt to continue the struggle in the old way by remaining unstamped was now impossible because of the Government's increased powers of confiscation under the new Act. Against such powers, said O'Brien, personal courage alone could not hope to prevail; therefore they must reluctantly resort to the rather less hazardous alternative of charging $3\frac{1}{2}$.

The effect of such a decision upon the poorer readers is exemplified by the reaction of the Spitalfields silk weavers. These men, we are told by William Bresson, an observant velvet weaver and loom broker, in his evidence to the Hand-loom Weavers Commissioner in 1838, used to read the unstamped papers, but when 'the new law, which accompanied the reduction of the stamp-duty on newspapers, put down the un-

[1] *Ibid.*, 27th August 1836.

57

stamped papers . . . without substituting stamped papers sufficiently cheap in their place . . . there is now less reading than formerly'.[1]

*   *   *

The agitation for *complete* repeal of the taxes on newspapers, advertisements and paper went on until, in 1852, it seemed that one more heave might remove the last obstacles. On 1st December a large crowd assembled at Exeter Hall for the annual meeting of the Association for Promoting the Repeal of the Taxes on Knowledge. In the chair was Douglas Jerrold, journalist and playwright, a friend of Dickens, noted for his highly successful comedy, 'Black-eyed Susan', and his contributions to *Punch*, especially 'Mrs Caudle's Curtain Lectures', who had recently become editor of *Lloyd's Weekly News*. Richard Cobden was the principal speaker. O'Brien and two of his close friends and disciples, John Rogers and Charles Murray, were in the audience. The business before the meeting was a resolution and a proposed petition to Parliament for total abolition of the three taxes. After a sparkling, witty opening by Jerrold, it was proposed and seconded: 'That the duties on paper and advertisements, and the penny stamp on newspapers, tend to injure literature, to obstruct education, and to hinder the progress of the people in intelligence and morality.' Cobden made a long speech, and then the O'Brienites went into action pointing out that the resolution made no reference whatever to the palpably unjust 'security system' created under Section 8 of the Act, 60 Geo. III, C. 9 (which required guarantees to be given to answer for libels which might be committed in the future, before a newspaper was allowed to be published), and proposing, 'amid some interruption', an addendum calling for the repeal of Section 8. This important proposal received support from the platform and was made part of the original resolution, which was then carried unanimously. Finally, arrangements were made for the preparation and presentation of the petition to Parliament.[2]

The advertisement duty was repealed in August 1853; but, owing to fluctuations of fortune in the political arena, the 1d newspaper stamp remained in force until 15th June 1855. The duty on paper was the last to go – in October 1861.

[1] W. E. Hickson's *Report on the Condition of the Hand-loom Weavers* (1840), Appendix, p. 78; G. Wallas, *Life of Francis Place* (Rev. edn 1918), p. 348.

[2] *The Times*, 2nd December 1852. For C. D. Collet's version of this incident see his *History of the Taxes on Knowledge*, p. 94, and on the security system see Ch. XXI; see also G. J. Holyoake, *Sixty Years of an Agitator's Life* (1902), I, p. 292, in which he names Milner Gibson, Charles Knight, Rev. Thomas Spencer, George Henry Lewes, and Samuel Wilderspin among the prominent people present at this meeting. Douglas Jerrold's biography was written by his son, William Blanchard Jerrold, and published in 1859. See also *D.N.B.*

Chapter IV

REVOLUTION IN RETROSPECT

In HIS late twenties, Bronterre O'Brien was living little more than a generation after the French Revolution of 1789, which many middle-aged and elderly people could still remember, and he was fascinated by its history and ideology. William Lovett and his Radical friends sought to create links with continental revolutionaries by exchanging fraternal greetings and addresses. O'Brien decided that he could do more by making known to British working men the story of the revolutionary struggle in France, as he understood it, explaining the more significant ideas and profitable lessons to be learned. How this was to be done he announced to the readers of the *Poor Man's Guardian* at the end of 1832 – the year of the 'Great Reform Act' in Britain:

'We have already referred to Buonarroti's history of Babeuf's Conspiracy for a true picture of those times. . . . To these volumes we again refer; and take this opportunity to announce, that . . . we will shortly publish a translation of the whole work . . . to which we will affix annotations and arguments of our own, so as to present that famous Revolution in a point of view as *novel* to the British public, as it will be *true* to reality.' [1]

Four years were to elapse before O'Brien fulfilled his promise; but in 1836 his translation of Buonarroti's *Gracchus Babeuf et la Conspiration pour l'égalité dite de Babeuf*, appeared under the title

'*Buonarroti's History of Babeuf's Conspiracy for Equality*; with the author's reflections on the Causes and Character of the French Revolution, and his estimate of the leading men and events of that epoch, also his views of Democratic Government, Community of Property and Political and Social Equality.'

This book, intended for the edification of working men, was originally printed and published by Henry Hetherington in twenty parts at two-pence each. It is a daunting document of 454 closely printed pages

---

[1] *Poor Man's Guardian*, 24th November and 22nd December 1832. O'Brien's translation of Buonarroti's book, bound in cloth, sold at 4s.

copiously annotated by Buonarroti, and with more than sixty additional notes by the translator. It opens with a biographical sketch of Philippe Buonarroti and an illuminating note giving O'Brien's reasons for translating the work, and revealing the trend of his thinking about politics and the intriguing problem of historical truth.

'1st. Because Buonarroti's book contains one of the best expositions I have seen of those great political and social principles which I have so long advocated in the *Poor Man's Guardian* and other publications, and which I am still endeavouring to inculcate through the columns of *Hetherington's Twopenny Dispatch*. The application of these principles I deem to be of paramount importance to the human race. Society has been hitherto constituted upon no fixed principles. The state in which we find it is the blind result of chance . . . the right of the strongest – the only right acknowledged by savage men – appears to be still the fundamental charter of all "civilized" states. . . . What the savage or uncivilized man does individually and directly, by the exercise of mere personal prowess, the civilized man (so called) does collectively and circuitously, by cunningly-designed institutions. The effects of these institutions are well depicted by Buonarroti. He shows, with admirable ability, how, in trying to escape the evils of savage life, man has unconsciously plunged into another state, which he terms that of "false civilization". He shows that to correct the evils of this latter state, without at the same time retrograding to the former, was the grand problem sought to be resolved by the first French Revolution; and in discussing the principles and institutions deemed necessary to that end by the leaders of the Revolution, I was so forcibly struck by the coincidence of Buonarroti's ideas with my own, that I immediately resolved to translate the book, and thereby present to the English reader the doctrines of the *Poor Man's Guardian* under a new form and dress. . . .

'2nd. Because it contains what to me appears the most luminous and correct estimate to be found in any language, of the leading men and events of the great French Revolution. In this respect I deem republication of Buonarroti's work an imperative duty. In no other book have I seen the frauds of history so effectually exposed. . . . History has been defined to be "Philosophy teaching by examples". A just definition, no doubt, if applied to *true* history; but how melancholy to think that the youth of a nation should have its opinions formed by . . . a "philosophy" that has falsehood for its means and slavery for its end . . . with aristocratic historians . . . [the] middleman's gains being of more consequence in their eyes than the poor man's life, whatever interferes with the one is "violent", while the other is very lightly dealt with. . . .

60

'3rd. Because "Babeuf's Conspiracy for Equality" appears to me the only event of the kind recorded in history that was sincerely and comprehensively designed for the benefit of human kind ... a plot for the emancipation of France – for the regeneration and happiness of mankind. It was a conspiracy to restore the democratic Constitution of 1793, and ... the reign of political and social equality.' [1]

Philippe Buonarroti, born in 1760, was an Italian of noble parentage who studied philosophy, politics, history and music at the University of Pisa. Despite his aristocratic origin he developed democratic views and towards the end of 1792, fired with enthusiasm for the revolution, he made his way to Paris where, in the Convention itself, he made an eloquent and successful plea for French citizenship.

'Free men,' he said to the assembled revolutionists, 'I was born in Tuscany. In my adolescence my tutor, who had been the friend of Rousseau and Helvetius, inspired me with the love of liberty and my fellow man. I acted, I spoke, I wrote, according to his precepts. I have received my reward. The great denounced me as a scoundrel, the imbeciles as a fool. ... Your Constitution requires five years' domicile and a French wife or property, for naturalisation. I have been here only four years, and my wife is the daughter of an Italian and an Englishwoman. My property is in Tuscany. I demand naturalisation.' [2]

The Convention had not the heart to refuse him, and he soon found himself among Robespierre's inner circle of friends.

Francis Noel Babeuf, the leading figure in Buonarroti's *Conspiration*, was born at St Quentin in the same year as Buonarroti. He was the son of a former French cavalry officer who had once been tutor to the Emperor Joseph II, [3] but who was working as a tax-collector at the time of his son's birth. At the age of sixteen the boy was apprenticed to a *commissaire à terrier*, a nobleman's agent, whose duties included land surveying, keeping complicated accounts, and exacting from the tenantry those onerous feudal dues and services which were so much the warp and weft of French life before the revolution. At the age of twenty-five young Babeuf had become a *commissaire à terrier* in his own right – a very creditable achievement. By this time, however, his

---

[1] 'Restore' is not the *mot juste* here, for this new, markedly democratic Constitution—'a prime document of democracy' providing for universal suffrage, yearly parliaments, the referendum, etc.—was never given practical effect.

[2] Quoted by W. S. Ward, *Maximillian Robespierre: A Study in Deterioration* (1934), p. 143.

[3] Joseph II was Emperor of the Holy Roman Empire from 1765 to 1790.

61

'distasteful, oppressive duties' had bred in him a fanatical hatred of the *ancien régime*, and in a correspondence he conducted with Dubois de Fosseux, secretary of the Academie royale des Belles-Lettres d'Arras, between 1785 and 1788, ideas of utopian egalitarianism clearly emerge. The outbreak of revolution gave Babeuf his chance to cut adrift from a hated profession and turn to political journalism. In 1789 his ideas were being discussed in the National Assembly, while he himself was moving over more and more to the aggressive left-wing of popular agitation, making many enemies in the process, especially among the Jacobins. After Robespierre's downfall and death in July 1794, Babeuf stood out against the flood tide of bourgeois liberalism and reaction, and strove to have the Constitution of 1793 made operative as a means of bringing in, ultimately, a true, unadulterated communistic state of society. He did not want, he declared, the replacement of 'a band of ancient scoundrels by a band of new ones'. The open expression of such views led to his arrest and imprisonment in February 1795. While in prison he set about the final formulation and elaboration of his principles of Communism, and when, after seven months, he was released 'on the turbulent world of the Directory . . . the journalist had become an experienced conspirator . . . a professional revolutionary'.[1]

After his release Babeuf began to take part in the clandestine activities of the Society of the Pantheon, and thus he met Buonarroti, who

[1] The sources and authorities on both Babeuf and Buonarroti are numerous, mainly in French, and are discussed in a note to David Thomson's *The Babeuf Plot: The Making of a Republican Legend* (1947), pp. 107–10. The chief printed documentary sources are Philippe Buonarroti, *Conspiration pour l'égalité dite de Babeuf* . . . (2 vols 1828); Victor Advielle, *Histoire de Gracchus Babeuf et du babouvisme d'aprés de nombreux documents inédits* (2 vols 1884); the official *Débats des Procés* (4 vols 1797) which contain a full report of the trial of Babeuf, Drouet, and their fellows, and the *Judgements of the High Court*, 1795–7. Other important works are Maurice Dommanget, *Babeuf et la conjuration des Égaux* (1922), and the same author's *Pages Choisies de Babeuf* (1935). Also in French there is Josette Lépine, *Gracchus Babeuf* (1949) (which includes a list of manuscript sources in the bibliography), and J. Kuypers, *Les Égalitaires en Belgique: Buonarroti et ses Sociétés Secréts* (Brussels, 1960). In English we have E. B. Bax, *The Last Episode of the French Revolution* (1911); H. W. Laidler, *A History of Socialist Thought* (1927); K. Martin, *French Liberal Thought in the 18th Century* (1929); R. Soltau, *French Political Thought in the 19th Century* (1931); H. J. Laski, *Studies in Law and Politics* (1932), pp. 68–75; A Gray, *The Socialist Tradition: Moses to Lenin* (1946); G. D. H. Cole, *Socialist Thought: The Forerunners, 1789–1850* (1953), pp. 12–17; and R. Postgate, *Revolution from 1789 to 1906* (1920), which contains translations of documents embodying Babouvist doctrines. In Italian there is Alessandro Galante Garrone, *Buonarroti e Babeuf* (1948); A. Saitta, *Filippo Buonarroti, Contributi alla Storia della sua Vita e del suo Pensiero* (2 vols, Rome 1950–1).

described secret midnight meetings in the crypt of the Convent of Sainte Géneviève, where the flicker of torches made sinister shapes and shadows, and the hollow echoes of the conspirators' voices might have been the mutterings of uneasy ghosts. The Society, unfortunately, was disunited; the former Jacobins disagreed with Babeuf's egalitarianism, and there were traitors in their midst who kept Barras and the Directory fully informed of what was going on. The chief spy, Grisel, was ferreted out many years later by Babeuf's eldest son, who killed him in a duel.

Both Babeuf and Buonarroti were members of the secret inner *Comité insurrecteur* of the Society, whose favourite rendezvous was the *Café des Bains-Chinois*. The other members were Darthé, Debon, Le Pelletier, and Silvain Maréchal, who wrote popular songs for the movement and drafted the *Manifeste des Égaux*, a bold, uncompromising, intensely idealistic document which declared:

'We desire real equality or death. . . . We aim at something more sublime and more just [than mere division of the land, namely] the Community of Goods. . . . Vanish at last revolting distinctions of rich and poor, great and little, masters and servants, governors and governed. . . . The French Revolution is but the precursor of another revolution, far greater, far more solemn, which will be the last. . . . The time has come to found the Republic of Equals, that great guesthouse of all mankind. The days of restitution have arrived. Weeping families take your seats at the common table nature spreads for all her children.' [1]

Babeuf and his fellows planned a *coup d'état*, aiming to win over the soldiers and police by intensive propaganda (some of their publications being distributed by the prostitutes of Grenelle), and to form numerous cells of insurrectionists. The Government, however, forestalled them. We are told that their meeting place was closed by General Napoleon Bonaparte himself, a man who, in Buonarroti's eyes, had betrayed every revolutionary and republican ideal. Finally, the leaders were arrested on 10th May 1796, and in the following days between 200 and 300 other members or suspected members were seized.

In a great public trial lasting from 20th February to 27th May 1797, forty-seven prisoners, accused of conspiring to 'usurp sovereignty', appeared before a special high court of eight judges and a jury of sixteen. 'Before long the prosecution found itself outmanœuvred by the skill of Babeuf and his colleagues' who turned 'every question into a

---

[1] *Manifeste des Égaux* (1796), copied from papers seized in the place where Babeuf was arrested; printed in English in Postgate, *op. cit.*, pp. 54–5.

defence of the Constitution of 1793 and an indictment of the Directory'.[1] At the end Babeuf and Darthé were condemned to death, Buonarroti and six others were sentenced to imprisonment or deportation, and the rest were let off. Many of these survivors became the depositories of a tradition which they were convinced the new generation would be eager to cherish. Bronterre O'Brien belonged to this new generation.

Buonarroti, his sentence completed, lived first in Switzerland and, later, in Belgium, where he created a number of secret societies, directed by him simultaneously but separately, through which he attempted to keep Babeuf's ideas alive and to prepare the way for a large-scale communist revolution. In 1828, after an interval of more than thirty years, he kept a promise made to Babeuf and Darthé 'in the presence of the aristocratic axe, which was ready to fall upon them . . . to avenge their memory by an exact recital of our common intentions, which party spirit had so strangely misrepresented and disfigured'.[2] This was the work which O'Brien translated for the benefit of the British working man.

Buonarroti's book was based mainly on his own recollections, the writings of fellow conspirators, and the records of the judicial proceedings in which they all figured. At that time it was deemed prudent to substitute anagrams for the real names of the conspirators, and these would have been repeated in O'Brien's translation but for a fortunate chance. One of O'Brien's advertisements of his forthcoming work happened to come to the notice of Buonarroti, who was then seventy-five years of age and living again in Paris. He wrote to O'Brien in May 1836, giving him the names of the conspirators and enclosing an essay he had written (probably between 1833 and 1836) in defence of Robespierre, 'dont la publication me parait utile; peut être jugerez vous apropos d'en faire usage'.[3]

Buonarroti's book in its original form (O'Brien's translation was an abridged version) was reviewed by the *Quarterly Review* as a well-timed work written by a disinterested person (*sic*) who

. . . has rendered an important service to society by the publication of these memoirs. There never was a book more trustworthy in all its state-

---

[1] D. Thomson, *The Babeuf Plot* (1947), p. 57.

[2] O'Brien's translation of Buonarroti's Preface.

[3] In 1837 Buonarroti's essay on Robespierre was printed anonymously in *Le Radical*, and reprinted, again anonymously, in *La Fraternité*, a Paris monthly, in September 1842. Another reprint appeared nine years later. In 1912 a new edition under the title 'Observations sur Maximilien Robespierre par Philippe Buonarroti', with an introduction by Charles Vellay, was brought out as one of the publications of the Société Robespierre, which was founded as the 'Section Robespierre' in 1832.

ments; Buonarroti is chargeable with disingenuousness only for having been silent respecting the previous history of his confederates. On the subject of the conspiracy his authority is *omni exceptione major*: he is perfectly explicit, both as to the object at which he aimed, and the means by which it was to be brought about.'[1]

Babeuf's movement, Buonarroti argued, was the logical outcome of the French Revolution, which had had equality as its original goal. But the Jacobin way had not led to it. Babeuf's ideas are fairly well known and need not be re-stated here. Suffice it to say that, in the main, O'Brien went enthusiastically along with him (and Buonarroti), occasionally adding ideas of his own in a form calculated to appeal to his British readers. For example, according to Buonarroti, the break-up of huge cities would be one of the many boons and benefits of Communism. The existence of great urban communities was, in his view, symptomatic of a public malady, the forerunner of civil convulsions, and a source of innumerable vices. Around a nucleus of 'over-grown proprietors, large capitalists, and opulent merchants', gathers a parasitic multitude of undesirables and vagabonds of every sort, attracted by the chance of easy riches and the prospect of dissipation. O'Brien agreed, and commented:

'How dear old Cobbett would have enjoyed this phillipic of Buonarroti against the vices of city life! Who does not recollect some of that able writer's descriptions of the "Wen", as he used to call this metropolis? Buonarroti, however, possesses this advantage over Cobbett – that he tells the whole truth, while Cobbett tells only a part. The taxes and the tax-eaters were all that seemed to trouble Cobbett. Buonarroti takes a wider and juster view of things. Without assigning a pre-eminence of mischief to any one class in particular, Buonarroti shows what must inevitably be the vices of all city populations – vice which can be no otherwise remedied than by the application of some such principles as those inculcated in his book.'[2]

The Babouvists' conspiracy and programme were remarkable in many ways; for example, their organization before the attempt to seize power; their plan of action carefully prepared for the next stage; the doctrine of the inevitable antagonism of classes, except under Communism, and the necessity of a post-revolutionary dictatorship to guard and preserve the new communist civilization. The close resemblance between Babeuf's programme and that of the twentieth-century

[1] *Quarterly Review*, April, 1831, pp. 167 *et seq.*
[2] O'Brien's translation, pp. 161–3.

Russian Communists was pointed out by Harold Laski in his *Studies in Law and Politics*, and – even more striking, in his opinion – the 'similarity of ultimate temper which runs through the two movements': the exhilaration of spirit, the bitterly drawn sharp distinction between friend and foe, the burning desire to make all things new, the relentless dissection of the weaknesses of contemporary society, the genius for propaganda and invective and the self-confident optimism.[1] 'The French Revolution,' the Babouvists proclaimed with fanatical assurance, 'is but the precursor of another revolution, far greater, far more solemn, which will be the last.'

★   ★   ★

From Babeuf, O'Brien turned his attention to Robespierre, in whom, it may be, he discerned a twin soul, as George Julian Harney did in Marat. He may even have imagined himself in the rôle of Robespierre in a British revolution. Both O'Brien and Robespierre were lawyers by training, and both were politicians by inclination. Both were moved by high ideals and sincere political convictions; both had fought for the freedom of the press; both believed that laws should be based upon just principles and that by this route the ultimate goal of universal social justice could be reached. Each had his vision of an ideal democracy in which civic virtue, blossoming freely, would produce an abundant harvest of private contentment and public prosperity. Each aimed to become a popular leader of the working class, and, up to a point, succeeded. Each, in his own style, was a lucid, effective speaker whose oratory won for him, for a brief space, great popularity.

In the summer of 1835 Bronterre O'Brien set out for Paris to collect material on Robespierre. Travelling by coach from Calais through Abbeville and Beauvais, he reached Paris on 5th August, to find a great public funeral in progress and all normal traffic at a standstill. For two hours he was held up in the Rue Faubourg Montmartre. Naturally, he was not only impatient, but curious to know the cause of the delay.

Nine days earlier, on the morning of 28th July, during a military review and procession to mark the fifth anniversary of the July Revolution of 1830, one Fieschi, a convicted criminal, attempted to assassinate the King by means of a home-made 'infernal machine' consisting of twenty-five gun barrels loaded with bullets and fired simultaneously by a train of gunpowder. This crude contraption was discharged from a second floor window as the royal party rode by. The King's horse was hit, but Louis-Philippe and his sons had miraculous escapes from the hail of bullets which spread sudden death around the monarch and

---

[1] Laski, *Studies in Law and Politics* (1932), pp. 98–9.

among the onlookers. The veteran Marshal Eduard Mortier (Duc de Treviso), one of Napoleon's marshals, who had been Military Governor of Moscow in 1812, commanding the French rearguard during the disastrous winter retreat across Russia and who had fought gallantly in the desperate defence of Paris against the advancing Allies in the spring of 1814, was killed instantly, as were several other high-ranking officers in the King's entourage. Many of the National Guard and a number of civilians – over thirty all told – were either killed or wounded. The assassin himself was wounded when one of the gun barrels burst, and he was soon arrested.[1] It was the spectacular funeral procession of fourteen of the victims, on its solemn five-hour progress through the city, which delayed O'Brien [2] and evoked the following caustic comment:

'There were [he wrote] 100,000 men in arms including the National and Municipal Guards, the Troops of the Line, and the gendarmes.... *There was the government of France!* . . . 100,000 men who would put Nero himself on the throne, if they could find no other base enough to bend himself to the oppression of the working classes. The major part of this force consisted of Parisian shopocrats and usurers. The rest were unfortunate devils, hired at the rate of two sous and their keep, to fight *for* any body and *against* any body that the shopocrats bid them. We speak, of course, of the soldiers of the line, who looked the most hungry and deplorable set of pigmy wretches that we ever beheld. To contrast these creatures (the average height of whom appeared about 4 ft 6 ins) with the sleek pot-bellied fellows that composed the National and Municipal Guards, you might see at once where the government resided.'

O'Brien spent eight days in Paris, visiting the slums as well as the districts inhabited by those 'guzzling accumulators, the rich'. The more he saw, the more he was amazed that the poor of Paris could put up with such 'a horrible and inhuman state of things'. Powerful vested interests acting on 'the conservative principle' maintained a great restrictive system of high protective tariffs and import prohibitions which, despite widespread smuggling, kept the cost of living terribly high, and contributed largely to the appalling conditions observed by O'Brien: dreadful slums, long hours of labour, large-scale employment

[1] *Cobbett's Political Register*, III, p. 867; Alan Palmer, *Napoleon in Russia* (1967), pp. 163, 181, 198, 204. Fieschi was tried and executed with two others, Morey and Pepin, early in 1836.
[2] *The Times*, 30th and 31st July; 1st–8th August 1835; Victor Duruy, *A Short History of France*, II, p. 474.

of the puny scrofulous children of the poor, low wages, the pawn-brokers' pitiless grip, and restrictions 'upon any means by which the workers might have achieved less intolerable conditions'. O'Brien left for home filled with loathing for the prevailing system in France, and more firmly convinced than ever that 'the people's oppression arises not from this monarch or that, but from the fact that the rich and would-be rich have the exclusive making of the government'.[1]

O'Brien made two more visits to Paris. In the summer of 1836 he went to seek out Buonarroti, who, as we have noticed, had written to him early in May,[2] and in the following year he paid his third visit, taking Mrs O'Brien with him, and receiving a cordial welcome from a number of leading French democrats.[3]

Buonarroti's book, his pamphlet on Robespierre, and his conversations with O'Brien greatly changed and consolidated the latter's views on his subject. In 1831 O'Brien had written about 'the Robespierres, the Marats, the Dantons, and other such demons of the day as were thrown up to the surface in the seething of the revolutionary cauldron';[4] but two years later he was singing a very different song. The mountains of calumny heaped upon Robespierre 'by ten thousand venal men' had, he declared, been scattered to the winds by men like Buonarroti, who had shown that Robespierre had been the last luminous hope of the republican movement in France, and that

'. . . the assassination of Robespierre, and a few other real friends of the people, terminated the revolution. On the ninth Thermidor . . . 1794, the men of the Fauxbourgs were seduced to desert their faithful leaders. Had the brave workmen . . . only done their duty to Robespierre on that day, the shopocrats of the Sections would never have triumphed – France would have continued a republic. . . .'

Thenceforth O'Brien's aim was to reveal to the world what he called the true character of Robespierre, whom he depicted as a martyr on the altar of the people's cause.[5] Robespierre's deterioration, his falling away from his ideals, 'the Incorruptible' finally corrupted by power; all was ignored, denied, or ingeniously excused. The key-note of the work is sounded by such press advertisements as the following, which

[1] J. H. Clapham, *Economic History of France and Germany, 1815–1914* (1936), Ch. III; cf. A. Horne, *The Fall of Paris* (1965), pp. 294–5; McDouall's *Chartist and Republican Journal* (1841), Vol. I, pp. 47, 54, 62, 70.
[2] Hetherington's *Twopenny Dispatch*, 30th July 1836.
[3] *Reynold's Political Instructor*, 30th March 1850.
[4] Carpenter's *Political Letter*, 21st February 1831.
[5] *Poor Man's Guardian*, 27th April 1833.

appeared early in 1838, usually under the headline, 'French Revolution of 1789'.

'Now publishing, in Weekly Numbers, at Threepence each: and in Monthly Parts at One Shilling:

BRONTERRE'S LIFE and Character of Maximilian Robespierre, Proving by irrefragable Facts and Arguments, that that 'blood-thirsty Monster', and wholesale barbarian Murderer of the French People, was one of the most humane, virtuous, noble-minded, and enlightened Reformers that ever existed in the World.

(Published by James Watson, 15 City Road, London).'

The first volume of O'Brien's *Robespierre* was also offered, bound 'in neat cloth boards', for six shillings.[1] How well it sold we do not know. Certainly it was not well suited to the public O'Brien was trying to reach, for it was too long and tightly packed: too solid. The work-people in 1838 had little leisure, except the enforced leisure of unemployment, and they were not readers by training and habit, only by dogged determination and sacrifice.

In a lengthy introduction of twenty-three pages addressed to his 'Friends and Fellow Labourers' the radical and social reformers of Great Britain and Ireland, O'Brien declared that his main aim was to discredit the so-called history concocted by 'the aristocracy in support of their liberticidal systems', and to redeem 'the glorious cause of democracy' from the obloquy cast upon it by all such false histories. Chapters 1 to 4 deal with Robespierre's early life, the growth of his reputation as a barrister, and his social and literary activities at Arras; and in Chapter 5 O'Brien gives an analysis of what he considered were the 'proximate causes' of the French Revolution – the return from America of French troops imbued with new political ideas, and a financial crisis deliberately engineered by the ambitious monied middle classes who aimed at securing control of the public finances but never intended 'a revolution that would emancipate the labouring millions'. O'Brien went on to deal with Robespierre's exposure of the wholesale jobbery and plunder carried on under pretence of constructing roads, bridges and other public works; his election to the States-General in 1789; his growing influence, and (at considerable length) his membership of the Constituent Assembly, wherein, according to O'Brien, he counted for little because 'his opinions were too honest to have any weight with the aristocrats and hypocrites who surrounded him'.[2]

---

[1] *Northern Liberator*, 17th February 1838; *London Dispatch*, 12th August 1838.
[2] O'Brien, *Robespierre*, pp. 179, 202.

Subsequent chapters dealt with Robespierre's views on taxation, the royal veto, his fight for 'simple and unconditional' freedom of the press in 1789, his attitude to violence, insurrection, slavery and the death penalty.[1] O'Brien's handling of Robespierre's views upon this last problem is typical of his treatment of his subject.

Robespierre was, according to O'Brien, a humane man to whom bloodshed was repugnant. In 1791 he made a celebrated speech against the death penalty, but, O'Brien contended (using the sort of argument so often used in more recent times), the sentiments Robespierre was uttering then were those intended for a later stage in the revolution. When the revolution was firmly established, 'the authority of the law, emanating like the law itself from the whole community, would be so omnipotent over individuals, as to preclude all necessity for sacrificing human life'; but until then a very different state of things existed. Until then – and here again O'Brien's words have a remarkably modern ring – bloodshed was justified 'on those fatal occasions when counter-revolutionary plots or the rage of parties rendered the shedding of blood indispensable, to prevent the greater effusion of innocent blood'. In the matter of the King's execution in 1793, Robespierre acted in defence of the revolution when it was threatened and 'jeopardized by the monarch, the monarch's partisans, and the factions which succeeded them . . . *the law of natural defence* was Robespierre's justification for co-operating with the Convention in decreeing their deaths'.

Robespierre's part in 'The Terror' of 1793–4 was not discussed by O'Brien, for this critical and catastrophic period of French history was to have been dealt with in his second volume, which was promised but never published. In 1848, the year of European revolutions, he published a short essay on Robespierre in his little journal *The Power of the Pence*, but not until 1859 was the *Life* rounded off, in some slight measure, by O'Brien's *Dissertation and Elegy on Maximilian Robespierre*; a work in which Robespierre, Marat, St Just, and Couthon were held up as alone admirable and worthy among all the leaders of the French Revolution. In fairness to O'Brien it must be said that several modern scholars, using, over a century later, far more ample sources and facilities than were available to him, have confirmed at least some of his opinions and judgments upon Robespierre's career and character.[2]

In 1836 O'Brien had announced that closely following his works on Babeuf and Robespierre he proposed to bring out 'several new works' including 'A Real History of the French Revolution', a history of the

[1] *Ibid.*, p. 241. Later, at the peak of his power, Robespierre was opposed to complete freedom of the press.

[2] See e.g. M. J. Sydenham, *The French Revolution* (1965), pp. 86–8, 100.

English Commonwealth, and an essay on the 'Existing State and Future Prospects of Society'. But these works never saw the light of day. Evidently he had been overspending, especially on his journeys to Paris, and shortly after the publication of the first volume of his life of Robespierre, his belongings, including his precious books and papers, many of which he had collected in Paris, were seized and sold for debt. 'I discontinued the work [he wrote] only after I had been literally turned into the streets with a young and helpless family, without a roof to shelter them, a chair to sit on, or a bed to lie on. . . .'[1]

Apart from a few brief scattered references to his wife and 'young family', little is known of Bronterre O'Brien's private life. We know that he married, probably in the mid-1830s, and had four children, of whom at least two were boys. One of these became an actor, and another went to sea. Mrs O'Brien, who survived her husband, stood by her man loyally through all his vicissitudes, bravely sharing his poverty and the humiliation of being evicted, with her children, from house and home when creditors 'put the brokers' men in', as they did on more than one occasion. She was with her husband when he was arrested in the street in October 1839, and she tried to bring blankets and a pillow to him in prison. She seems to have been a woman of character; self-respecting, and possessing a certain independence of spirit. Throughout the country and in London there were many active female Chartists and not a few associations of female Radicals, such as the East London Female Patriotic Association. There were even circulating female lecturers, like 'Miss Jones of Hampton'.[2] It is not beyond the bounds of possibility that Bronterre O'Brien may have met his future wife when attending a meeting or a soirée organized by one of these associations. Perhaps she sprang from one of the many Radical families of those days. But this is pure conjecture.

Although Bronterre's ambitious literary programme was never carried through, he did much to spread and keep alive on this side of the Channel the ideas and influence of the French revolutionists. It is unlikely that a great number of working men actually read his books, which were undoubtedly much too long, detailed, and solid to be popular. It would have been far better, for example, if, instead of his full-length annotated translation of Buonarroti's work on Babeuf, O'Brien had written in his own words a short, vivid outline of the Babouvists' conspiracy and the fundamentals of their faith. Yet the few devoted enthusiasts who did read O'Brien's writings no doubt talked to others, and in so doing contributed more than they knew to that slow seepage

[1] O'Brien, *Dissertation and Elegy on Maximilian Robespierre* (1859), p. 5.
[2] *The Times*, 1st July 1839; *Charter*, 20th October 1839.

of democratic thought and feeling which later became a swelling flood. This certainly happened with other authors. There must have been, for example, many thousands of ardent single-taxers who never read Henry George,[1] and probably millions of convinced Communists who never waded through even the first volume of Karl Marx's monumental *Das Kapital*. Bronterre's writings were certainly influential in his own time and in the decades immediately following, albeit well-nigh forgotten before the end of the century.

[1] For H. M. Hyndman's views on Henry George, see his *Record of an Adventurous Life* (1911), pp. 290–3.

Chapter V

PRELUDE TO 1839

IN THE autumn of 1836, when Chartism was in embryo, O'Brien, sensible of the need for much more propaganda, decided to bring out a cheap journal of his own in which to expound the true nature, principles and aims of democracy and Radical reform. The voteless masses urgently needed a teacher to prepare them for the day when the franchise would be theirs. O'Brien claimed that since his arrival in London in 1830 he had made such 'immense progress in Radical reform . . . that were a professorship of Radical reform to be instituted tomorrow in King's College (no very probable event . . .) I think I would stand candidate for the office'. He was sure he had Radical blood in his veins, and felt as if his food underwent 'at the moment of deglution, a process of radicalization'.[1] And when he said 'Radical reform' he did not mean 'reform after the Whig humbug fashion', but the real thing, going deep down to the very roots of the social system.

O'Brien was now so well known under his pen-name, 'Bronterre', that he decided to call his paper *Bronterre's National Reformer*, and to price it at a penny a copy in the (highly optimistic) hope that its circulation might reach 50,000–100,000 copies weekly.[2] There was to be little news in the *Reformer* for that would mean paying a tax upon every copy. John Bell of the *London Mercury* had offered to print in his paper Bronterre's observations upon current events, thus freeing *Bronterre's National Reformer* to concentrate upon the discussion of questions relating to social reform which derive their interest not from ephemeral occurrences, but from their own intrinsic importance.[3] But as O'Brien soon realized, 'it is hard to write politics without glancing at the "goings on" around us' and, he might have added, still harder to interest the man in the street. After five years in Radical journalism he should have known, beyond a doubt, that the use of space in the *London Mercury* would not save his own journal from failure if it lacked an attractive

[1] *Bronterre's National Reformer*, 7th January 1837.
[2] *London Mercury*, 8th December 1836.
[3] Cf. *Bronterre's National Reformer*, January 1837; *London Mercury*, December 1836–January 1837.

variety of matter. Indeed, as early as 1832, a speaker at the Third Co-operative Congress had pointed out that William Carpenter's *Trades Free Press*, although ably conducted and strenuously fighting for the rights of the working class, 'was compelled to be abandoned for want of subscribers, while at the same time *The Weekly Dispatch*, with its dog-fights, cock-fights and man-fights', had a weekly circulation of nearly 30,000.[1]

In the first number of his *National Reformer*, which appeared on 7th January 1837, O'Brien set forth his aims:

'. . . the end I have in view is social equality for each and all, to obtain this we must first have political equality for each and all. To obtain political equality, we must have a more extensive and effective organization of the working classes, and of that portion of the middle class which is immediately dependent on their custom, than has hitherto been even thought of, much less accomplished. It will, therefore, be an object of mine to promote such extensive and effective organization, and as the best means of promoting it, I will never cease to recommend and encourage, among those classes, knowledge and union; a full and accurate knowledge of their wrongs and of their rights; and a steady union of purpose to redress the one and obtain permanent enjoyment of the other.'

Bronterre's National Reformer is chiefly characterized by a series of lengthy letters to the editor signed 'Philo-Bronterre' (rather obviously the work of O'Brien himself); some criticism of Daniel O'Connell, whose Whig leanings and anti-trade union attitude had become, in O'Brien's eyes, a betrayal of true democracy and a stain upon the honour of Irishmen; and several vigorous attacks upon the new Poor Law, which, he declared, was designed to benefit the masters, not the men. The object of the new measure should have been to amend the conditions of the poor; but instead it had made them even more desperate and had 'awarded to poverty the privations and penalties due to felony'.

The reference here, is, of course, to the Poor Law Amendment Act, 1834, which drastically changed the old system of poor relief, by abolishing outdoor relief for able-bodied persons and substituting indoor relief governed by two principles; 'deterrence' and 'less eligibility'. This meant that once the new Act came into force, relief

---

[1] *Proceedings of 3rd Co-operative Congress*, 1832, p. 39. The owner of the *Weekly Dispatch* was James Harmer, son of a Spitalfields silk weaver, who became a City Alderman in 1833. A. B. Beaven, *Aldermen of the City of London* (1913), II, p. 204; Broughton, *Recollections of a Long Life* (1909), IV, p. 327.

would be available to able-bodied poor persons and their families only in workhouses, and that the lot of such persons must be made 'less eligible' than that of the most poorly paid independent labourer outside, so that the poor would be deterred from seeking relief except as a very last resort. 'The discipline of the workhouse,' said a Radical critic, 'is to be such as to be held *in terrorum* of all paupers. Applications for relief are to be discouraged by hard labour, coarse fare, degrading attire, and other contrivances of pain and ignominy.'[1] Many weighty arguments were, of course, marshalled against the old system and in favour of the new. But people on the poverty line cannot be expected to concern themselves with probable long-term effects upon the national economy. They can think only of the immediate effects upon themselves and their families. In the industrial districts the old 'outdoor' system had, in effect, given a sort of unemployment 'benefit' in periods of trade depression, seasonal recessions, and individual misfortune. It certainly prevented starvation in bad times. The new Act cut off all outdoor relief and offered instead the 'workhouse test', which meant loss of personal liberty and segregation of the sexes, so that husbands, wives and children were parted and put into different sections of the horrid, inhuman 'Bastilles'.

Furthermore, in their hatred of everything and everybody identified with the new Poor Law, the workpeople included the three newly-appointed Commissioners – Thomas Frankland Lewis, J. G. Shaw-Lefevre, and George Nicholls, with their secretary, Edwin Chadwick – who were seen as a cabal of heartless despots sitting at Somerset House with full powers to decide from a distance whether honest workmen should survive or starve. All who administered or supported the new Poor Law were deemed to be disciples of the Reverend T. R. Malthus, whose famous *Essay on Population* (1798) had asserted that population tends to increase faster than the means of subsistence unless checked by famine, pestilence or war, or by 'prudential restraint' (i.e. birth control). When they grasped its full significance, the 'lower orders', infuriated by this doctrine of despair, saw in the new workhouse rules a dastardly attack on personal freedom and the sanctity of marriage and the family. O'Brien had no time for 'Parson Malthus', whose theory he described as one of the most eccentric doctrines ever taught. The Reverend J. R. Stephens, Richard Oastler, John Fielden, and many other Radical humanitarians strongly denounced Malthusianism as contrary to Scripture, Christianity, and decent human feeling. The country, they said, was *not* overpopulated: poverty and hunger were caused by bad

---

[1] Appendix to the *Black Book* (1835), p. 42. For reports on arson and other forms of violent resistance to the new Poor Law see *H.O. Papers* 64 (4–6).

75

government and an evil social system, not by surplus population. In his *Legacy to Labourers*, written in 1834, the year before his death, Cobbett was among the first to deliver a full-scale attack upon the new Poor Law and its tendency, as he thought, to beat down English workers to 'Irish wages and Irish diet'. O'Brien, who had never forgotten what this meant in Ireland when he was young, added his voice to Cobbett's. Much of the money raised by the poor rates was, he said, 'wasted in parochial guzzlings' before any of it reached the pockets of the poor. It was scandalous that 'a married man or woman of decent feelings' should be obliged to live on the terms of those 'upstart adventurers, Chadwick and Co.', in a 'Whig union workhouse', completely under the thumbs of 'these central Bashaws'.

These vehement and persistent humanitarian protests were not without effect, for they helped to widen the rift between Chadwick, who wanted to press on regardless of protests and objections, and the three Commissioners, who evinced considerable caution (some said 'to the point of cowardice') in exercising their powers. In 1839, five years after the passing of the Poor Law Amendment Act, 'the number of paupers in workhouses was about 98,000, those receiving out-door relief over 560,000, and no effective effort had been made even to exclude able-bodied men from the latter category'. The protesters had been so successful in creating and spreading a hostile atmosphere that renewal of the Act, which would have expired in 1839, was opposed not only by the Chartists, but by influential men like Thomas Wakley, the proprietor and editor of the *Lancet*, and John Walter, proprietor of *The Times*. In 1839, 1840, and again in 1841, the Act was renewed for one year only; in 1842 it was renewed for five years, but before the end of the period a new amending Act was passed which brought the Poor Law Commission to an end [1] by transferring its responsibilities to a Minister.[2]

Another legitimate grievance was the heavy burden of the poor rates upon the humbler rate-payers. This, said O'Brien, ought to be lightened. Assessment of the rate upon the value of houses was often inequitable, for a man's dwelling-house does not necessarily vary in value in proportion to variations in his income and family responsi-

---

[1] *The Times* (4th February 1847), printed some satirical valedictory verses entitled 'The Last Dying Speech and Confession of the Poor Law Commissioners'.

[2] For an interesting discussion of 'the distortion of the Poor Law between 1793 and 1834 and its over drastic reorganization', see D. Marshall, *English People in the 18th Century* (1956), pp. 248–9; G. Slater, *Poverty and the State* (1930), pp. 92–112.

bilities. O'Brien advocated 'a proportional rate' levied on income as well as property, with a proviso that income derived from property should pay a higher proportion than that derived from the professional or industrial occupation of the rate-payer.[1]

Bronterre's National Reformer not only slated the new Poor Law and the system of taxation, but gladly gave space to the early drafts of the petition and 'People's Charter' which William Lovett, with the advice and assistance of several well-known Radical politicians, was struggling to perfect on behalf of the L.W.M.A. Substantial portions of these documents were, of course, not new. Modern democracy in England had a long gestation period reaching back, certainly, to the protracted and earnest debates in Cromwell's army and to the contemporary 'contagion of the democratic movement' among the rank and file of many of the craft gilds during the Civil War and Commonwealth period.[2] Thus *The Case of the Commonalty of the Corporation of the Weavers of London truly stated*, printed in 1649 or 1650, argues that

'All legal jurisdiction over a number of people or society of men must either be primitive or derivative. Now primitive jurisdiction is undoubtedly in the whole body and not in one or more members, all men being by nature equal to other and all jurisdictive power over them, being founded by a compact and agreement with them, is invested in one or more persons who represent the whole and by the consent of the whole are impowered to govern . . . without the performance of which mutual contract all obligations are cancelled and the jurisdictive power returns unto its first spring – the people from whom it was conveighed.'

Nothing lasting was achieved by such advanced theories at the time, and after the Whig-Tory reaction and the restoration of the monarchy in 1660, the infant spirit of democracy slept for many years, though occasionally it stirred restlessly, to awake reinvigorated during the last quarter of the eighteenth century. In 1776, the year of the American Declaration of Independence, Major John Cartwright (1740–1824), brother of a famous inventor of textile machinery, published his booklet, *Take Your Choice*, which contained four of the 'six points' that were put into the Chartists' programme sixty years later. Then, in 1780, the Duke of Richmond sponsored in the House of Lords a Bill designed to introduce annual Parliaments and to give the right to vote to 'every man not contaminated by crime, nor incapacitated for want of reason';

[1] Cf. *London Mercury*, 12th February 1837; T. Macconnell, *Prize Essay on the Present Condition of the People of this Country* (1838), p. 20.
[2] G. Unwin, *Industrial Organization in the 16th and 17th Centuries* (1904), p. 207.

and in the same year a committee of the electors of Westminster, with Charles James Fox in the chair, produced a report recommending Annual Parliaments, Universal [Manhood] Suffrage, Equal Voting Districts, Voting by Ballot, Payment of Members of Parliament and No Property Qualification to be required of them. Here we have the famous six points which, after much consideration by the L.W.M.A. and its friends during 1836–7, were eventually incorporated into the Chartists' Petition to the House of Commons, and, in much greater detail, in 'The People's Charter', which was drafted in the form of a Parliamentary Bill 'to provide for the just representation of the people of Great Britain and Ireland in the Commons House of Parliament'.[1] And, as Mark Hovell pointed out,

'. . . when the salvation promised by the Whig reform of 1832 had proved illusory, it was perfectly natural to raise once more, in the shape of the "People's Charter", the ancient standard of popular reform. By this time, however, the six points acquired a wholly different significance. In the minds of the early Radicals they had represented the practical realization of the vague notions of natural right . . . an end in itself, the realization of democratic theory. By 1838 the Radical programme was recognized no longer as an end in itself, but as the means to an end, and the end was the social and economic regeneration of society.'[2]

From the outset Bronterre O'Brien won recognition as a vigorous champion of Chartism. He was one of the first of the few friends of the working men to be elected an honorary member of the newly-formed London Working Men's Association on 24th July 1836, at the same time as Francis Place, Dr John Roberts Black, Augustus Harding Beaumont, and William Carpenter. Towards the end of the same year Robert Owen, Feargus O'Connor (who was seeking a foothold in English Radical politics) and John Bell were also elected. Such 'honorary members not of the working classes' were deemed to be 'sufficiently identified' with the working-class members, and had the right to attend all meetings and take part in all debates and discussions; but they were

[1] Some reformers wished to enfranchise women, but this proposal was dropped for fear that it might hold back the extension of manhood suffrage.
[2] *Add.MSS.* 37,773, L.W.M.A. Minutes, October 1836; *Add.MSS.* 27,819(46); *Bronterre's National Reformer*, 11th February 1837; W. Lovett, *Life and Struggles* (1876), Ch. VIII and Appendices A and B; E. and A. G. Porritt, *The Unreformed House of Commons* (1903), *passim*; G. S. Veitch, *The Genesis of Parliamentary Reform* (1913), *passim*; M. Hovell, *The Chartist Movement* (1918), Ch. I; E. P. Thompson, *The Making of the English Working Class* (1963), p. 84.

not permitted to hold office or to take any part in the management of the Association.[1] The L.W.M.A. sought to spread an understanding of democratic political ideas among the 'useful classes' and to unite them in support of a single comprehensive plan of reform.[2] O'Brien, who was in complete sympathy with these aims, declared in his *National Reformer* that the only way of felling the 'money-monster' without being buried beneath his ruins would be 'to smite him with the authority of the law, having first got the law on the people's side'. He deplored the paralytic apathy of the submissive masses and appealed for the immediate creation of a dynamic national democratic movement.[3]

Within a few weeks it seemed to O'Brien that the masses were responding, for on the last day of February 1837 the London Working Men's Association was able to hold a successful public meeting. O'Brien was there and reported enthusiastically upon the proceedings and prospects. 'The immense room of the Crown and Anchor Tavern was crowded to overflowing'; hundreds thronged the corridors and stairs, dozens waited outside in the Strand or went away disappointed. The platform, too, was crowded. William Lovett, in an able and sincere speech, introduced the 'Petition to the House of Commons', which he had drafted with such admirable patience during the preceding months, and which contained the nucleus of the People's Charter. The meeting was unanimous and orderly, and, according to Lovett, the Petition was signed by some three thousand persons. O'Brien described Lovett's speech as 'one of the most eloquent addresses I ever heard . . . the speaker never lost sight of the great moral to be inculcated, which was, that the end and object of all despotism being to uphold monopolies, there can be no escape from it, so long as the *exclusive power of law-making* shall be suffered to abide with the monopolists'. The meeting, O'Brien declared, had set an example to the Radicals of all England: 'now is the time to strike a blow for universal suffrage'.[4]

His own public affirmation had already been made in 'Bronterre's Letters', printed in Hetherington's *Twopenny Dispatch*:

'I am for Liberty and Equality, meaning by the terms . . . an equal opportunity to every man of obtaining all the advantages of society; no one having a monopoly, and each exclusively enjoying the produce of

---

[1] *Ad.MSS.* 37,773(8). The minute book shows that the L.W.M.A. was 'established' on 26th June 1836. See also Place Collection (Brit. Mus.), Vol. 56, Lovett to Place, 4th August 1836; Lovett, *Life and Struggles* (1876), pp. 92–7.

[2] Place Collection (Brit. Mus.), Intro. to Vol. 56, written by Francis Place; see also *Add.MSS.* 27,819(21).

[3] *Bronterre's National Reformer*, 7th January 1837.

[4] *London Mercury*, 5th March 1837; Lovett, *Life and Struggles*, pp. 102, 444.

his own industry and intellect. The first step towards this equality is the extension of the franchise to all classes alike. . . . Therefore, the first article in my creed is Universal Suffrage, *alias* the equal participation of all in forming the laws and institutions of the country. As to the ballot, short parliaments, etc., they are mere contrivances for securing the valid use of the franchise. They are not rights, but arrangements for the due exercise of rights.'

Unfortunately *Bronterre's National Reformer*, notwithstanding its low price and the quickening public interest in Radical reform, failed to attract sufficient support. One correspondent said that O'Brien should have 'stated at the outset of his paper, that he was "late Editor of the *Twopenny* and *London Dispatch*, and the *Poor Man's Guardian*", etc., etc. Great numbers would then have hailed the publication as that of an old friend with whom they had long been acquainted, and to whose writings they were much indebted'.[1] Perhaps the workmen's pence were too few and the Radical journals too many to allow of success in every case; and a paper like *Bronterre's National Reformer*, which contained propaganda without news or any 'light relief', was certainly under a heavy handicap.[2] In the eleventh and last number of the *Reformer* O'Brien ruefully announced that the circulation was but 4,000 copies weekly – not sufficient to justify its continuance: 'I have spent the little money I had upon it. . . . This is a bad world for an honest Radical.'[3]

Soon after this failure O'Brien became associated with John Bell and an eccentric egomaniac named J. B. Bernard in another politico-journalistic venture. Bell was one of the proprietors and editors of the Radical *True Sun* and editor of the *London Mercury*.[4] J. B. Bernard, the principal financier of the project, was a Cambridgeshire farmer and currency reformer. In company with Bell and Feargus O'Connor, he tried to form a new society to be called the Central National Association, designed to link up under its auspices all the bodies working for Radical Reform, and to use the *London Mercury* as its organ. But, according to Place, they failed because 'they quarrelled with all other associations and almost everybody who came their way'.[5]

---

[1] *Bronterre's National Reformer*, 28th January 1837.

[2] John Cleave's *Penny Gazette of Variety and Amusement* was designed to appeal not only to working men, but to their wives and children.

[3] *Bronterre's National Reformer*, 16th March 1837.

[4] Francis Place had a poor opinion of John Bell and his wrong-headed, 'vulgar notions'; see Place Collection, Vol. 56, p. 4.

[5] *Ibid.*, Place's Introduction to Vol. 56. See also *Add.MSS.* 37,819(88), and *London Dispatch*, 2nd April 1837.

Bernard's chief concern at this time was the state of the legislature. Neither the Lords nor the Commons as then constituted were, in his opinion, competent to legislate for the country as a whole because both Houses were 'swamped by property in the mass' – the landowners in the Lords and the 'money-mongers' in the Commons – while the interests of the real producers, the working class, were ignored. Therefore, Bernard concluded, 'a new and altogether differently constituted legislature was indispensably necessary to save the country from bankruptcy and revolution'.[1] In 1835 O'Brien had condemned Bernard's 'scheme for the regeneration of society' because it failed to give pride of place to universal suffrage. Could not Mr Bernard understand 'that without *political* reform we can have no *social* reform?'[2] This argument seems to have convinced Bernard of the fundamental importance of universal suffrage, which he soon began zealously to advocate, although he continued to regard himself as a Tory. He was also a 'currency crank', with his own special scheme for 'restoring' the currency, removing debts in a flash and making everybody rich.[3] Equally staggering was his suggestion that the London Working Men's Association should unite with the Cambridgeshire farmers! It is true that in 1836 many of the farmers were in economic difficulties, caught between their debts and high fixed rents, on the one hand, and falling corn prices on the other. But did this justify such a strange proposal? The London working men, for their part, were luke-warm and refused to discuss anything except 'the principle of universal suffrage'.[4] At O'Brien's suggestion a provisional committee was set up comprising Bernard, Bell, O'Connor and Stephens, with two of O'Brien's friends and followers, Murphy and Rogers, and 'the élite of the London Working Men's Association'. They met on 17th March 1837 at the *London Mercury* office and unanimously adopted resolutions stating that their aims were universal suffrage, reform of the existing laws relating to manufactures, commerce and agriculture, and the total repeal of the New Poor Law.[5] John Bell was to be the secretary of the new 'Central National Association', while the *London Mercury* (with Bell and O'Brien as joint editors) and the *London Dispatch* were to be its official organs. But disagreements arose even before the committee had emerged from the 'provisional' stage. Before the end of March 1837, Hetherington, Vincent and Hartwell (among others) had been

---

[1] *London Dispatch*, 13th and 27th November 1836.
[2] *Poor Man's Guardian*, 25th July and 12th September 1835.
[3] *Add.MSS.* 27,819(41).
[4] *Add.MSS.* 37,773(8–12, 17).
[5] *London Mercury*, 26th March 1837.

added to the committee; but Hetherington withdrew almost immediately, ostensibly on account of his objection to the inclusion of a certain Mr Watkins, and on 2nd April the *London Dispatch* published an article, probably from the pen of Dr Black, condemning the Central National Association as 'a new attempt at political delusion'.

The replies from O'Brien and Bell make it clear that a serious breach had opened between O'Brien and his old comrade, Hetherington, and that the *London Dispatch* (which referred slightingly to Bell, Bernard and O'Brien as 'the triumvirate') would be neither organ nor ally of the new association. As the weeks passed the rift widened.[1] The London Working Men's Association became involved in the quarrel on Hetherington's side and called upon O'Brien and Bell to explain, justify or retract certain 'abusive epithets'. The L.W.M.A. minute book (20th June 1837) records that

'Mr O'Brien denied having at any time said anything abusive of the Association, whatever he might have said of some of its members . . .. Mr Bell was called upon to retract the abusive language he had used towards the Association, as he had failed to substantiate it – he refused to do so, and the meeting separated without coming to any conclusion on the subject.'[2]

Yet another rift appeared at Cambridge where the farmers, who wanted the franchise for themselves, objected to its extension to the agricultural labourers. O'Brien saw at once that this difficulty would need careful handling, but hoped to convince the farmers by a fair presentation of the labourers' case.[3]

Meanwhile, the *London Mercury* was losing money. It had been appearing weekly in four editions; on Thursday for remote parts of the kingdom; on Friday for the Midlands, and on Saturday and Sunday for London. On 23rd April 1837, O'Brien and Bell announced that this could no longer be done at the price of fourpence a copy (including the penny newspaper stamp). At this juncture Bernard, unwilling to see the infant Central National Association lose its mouthpiece, acquired the *Mercury* and raised its price to fivepence. No change in policy or opinion was contemplated; the editors were to be left free to conduct the paper as before.[4] But the increase in price caused a sharp fall in circulation to

---

[1] *London Mercury*, 2nd, 9th, 16th and 30th April 1837; *London Dispatch*, 2nd and 9th April 1837; see also Birmingham Ref. Lib., 'Working Men's Association, Newspaper Cuttings, etc.'; Lovett Papers, I, pp. 62, 72–3.

[2] *Add.MSS.* 37,773(52, 56), L.W.M.A. Minutes.

[3] *London Mercury*, 9th April 1837.

[4] *Ibid.*, 23rd April 1837.

barely 5,600 copies weekly, and on 14th May 1837 the price was reduced to 3½d.

During May 1837, the meetings of the provincial committee were thrown open and working men were invited to attend. Finally, on 12th June 1837, the Central National Association was formally launched at a public meeting at the Crown and Anchor Tavern, Strand. Bernard and O'Connor extolled the possibilities of the Association, while O'Brien seized the opportunity to outline what afterwards became known as his election or hustings plan. Petitioning, he said, was no use unless it had some real force behind it. The new association could be a means of calling up throughout the provinces a mighty force with a rallying-point in London. Let them see to it that in every borough at the next general election Radical candidates were ready to go to the hustings: the unenfranchised masses should not *ask* for the vote, they should *take* it. Given adequate arrangements, something like four hundred democrats might be elected by universal suffrage *in spite of the existing electoral law*, and *these true representatives of the people should then go to St Stephens and take their seats*. This would show the tyrants 'the difference between a Parliament nominated by nine or ten millions, and one elected by three or four hundred thousand monopolists'; and would benefit their cause more than all the petitions of the last forty years. If strongly supported the Central National Association would be able to play a useful part in this scheme.[1]

O'Brien subsequently elaborated his election plan, asserting that if every man had a vote and used it, the true leaders of the people would be elected up and down the country by large majorities.

'Would not Oastler have the show of hands at Huddersfield? Would not Feargus O'Connor have ten to one in the West Riding, or almost anywhere? . . . Is there a single one of the seven metropolitan boroughs in which two respectable Chartist candidates would not have an overwhelming majority of hands against the present Whig representatives? There is not one. . . . I tell you that 400 delegates, elected by an average majority of, say, from five or six to one, at all the principal elections throughout Great Britain, would be the real *bona fide* representatives of the country.'

Once this had been done, it would be impossible for the Whigs and Tories to argue that the Chartists were but a small, unimportant fraction of the population, or to deny the working people's interest in the suffrage question, or to use repressive measures against them. 'Could the money-

[1] *Ibid.*, 18th June 1837.

83

mongers' house refuse to negotiate with such a body? . . . Would it be safe to refuse? . . . the moral power of an assembly so chosen would be tremendous.' As a petitioning body it would be irresistible.[1]

It so happened that shortly after the formation of the Central National Association O'Brien was invited to test his election plan at an imminent general election by standing for Manchester as a Radical candidate seeking the suffrages of the citizens at large, whether electors or non-electors. Accepting the challenge eagerly (indeed, he could hardly refuse!), he went to Manchester where he addressed five public meetings and claimed to have received so much support that had he been legally nominated he would surely have been elected. But for legal nomination a deposit of £150 was required; a sum which it was impossible to collect at short notice. Nevertheless, O'Brien appeared on the hustings, made a speech to a large crowd of electors and non-electors, and, according to Radical reports, he obtained, on a show of hands, an 'immense majority' in favour of the proposition that all the other candidates were unfit to represent the constituency.[2]

The general election was hardly over before Bernard sold the *London Mercury*, complaining that he had not met with the support he had expected and that the money he was willing to devote to the paper was exhausted. O'Brien now gave up his joint editorship, leaving Bell to carry on single-handed,[3] and seems to have been, once again, at a loose end until January 1838 when O'Connor's *Northern Star*, then rising in Leeds, triumphantly announced that it had 'at length' secured the 'valuable services' of Bronterre, and to prove it printed a leading article by O'Brien on the Canadian rebellion, in which he supported the 'rebels' against the Government and roundly asserted that Canadian affairs had been misrepresented by the whole press – liberal as well as anti-liberal. The core of the dispute was not, as they pretended, the right of control over the Canadian revenue, which after all was a relatively small sum, but the Canadian people's legitimate desire for a radical revolution as a step towards national independence and self-government.[4]

---

[1] *Add.MSS.* 27,819(55); *Southern Star*, 23rd February 1840. The National Charter Association approved of O'Brien's election plan, but the Edinburgh Chartists were not agreed upon its merits. *Leeds Times*, 28th March 1840; *Northern Star*, 1st August 1840; cf. *English Chartist Circular*, Vol. I, No. 15.

[2] Similar calls came from Newcastle, Derby and Norwich. According to Hovell, 'the Chartists later made considerable use of the opportunity which these bogus nominations offered to air their views at election times'.

[3] *London Mercury*, 13th August 1837; a few months later the *Mercury* was incorporated with the *London Dispatch* under the editorship of Arthur James Beaumont.

[4] *Northern Star*, 27th January and 3rd February 1838.

O'Brien's second article opened with a broadside denouncing all despotic measures, actual or threatened, aimed at the extinction of the workers' civil rights, and urging that 'at a time of horrors like these . . . every moment that the producers can steal from their tasks and meals ought to be religiously consecrated to plans of mutual defence against the enemy . . .', he warned the trade unionists against Government enquiries into union affairs, for their enemies were the property owners who live on tolls, tithes, rents, interest and commissions, and have, therefore, 'a direct interest in putting down your Combinations; because each and every one of them wants the produce of your labour to be dirt cheap, in order to swell their own incomes at your expense . . . your interests as producers are perfectly irreconcilable with those of the parties alluded to'.[1]

During 1838 O'Brien wrote many similar outspoken and challenging leading articles for the *Northern Star* upon a variety of topics, including colonial affairs, Radicalism and Socialism, the so-called 'reformed' parliament, universal suffrage, 'that stalking pestilence' the new Poor Law, poverty and hunger in Ireland, and the treatment of pauper children: all of which attracted a good deal of attention, especially in Radical circles.[2] 'Tell O'Brien to put the *Poor Man's Guardian's* soul into the *Star*,' wrote Richard Oastler to J. R. Stephens, the ex-Methodist minister.[3] Francis Place, a less enthusiastic commentator, after seriously misrepresenting O'Brien's policy on private property, had to admit that O'Brien's articles increased the sales of the *Northern Star* (which achieved a peak circulation of 40,000 copies a week early in 1839), 'helped to make O'Connor a great man in his own conceit', and 'enabled him to pay Hill [his editor] and O'Brien money enough to induce them to go on vigorously . . . no doubt can be entertained that these men fully expected to see all that they promised accomplished'.[4]

The friendship and co-operation between O'Brien and O'Connor (who was the elder by ten years) – the two Os, as they were sometimes called – was certainly fruitful while it lasted. Its starting point was doubtless their common Hibernian hatred of tyranny, oppression and undeserved misery. Both were sincerely set upon casting out the social

---

[1] Northern Star, 10th and 17th February 1838. For Francis Place's somewhat similar strictures upon the government see *Add.MSS.* 27,819(5) and 27,789(227).

[2] O'Brien received from two to three guineas for each article.

[3] Richard Oastler and Joseph Rayner Stephens had stood out as leaders of the agitation against the new Poor Law.

[4] *Add.MSS.* 27,820(154–5). After 1839 the *Northern Star's* circulation decreased. The stamp returns show: 1840, 18,780; 1841, 13,580; 1842, 12,500; end of 1843, 9,000. M. Hovell, *op. cit.*, pp. 173n., 269n; R. D. Altick, *The English Common Reader* (1957), p. 393.

devils of their time. But on the other hand lay their marked dis-similarities, making them a balanced two-man team while they worked in harmony, but fierce enemies when they fell out. O'Connor's intel-lectual ability was poor; his limited stock of ideas a jumble; he was capable of colossal incoherence and lack of logic, and he was quite unable – and, indeed, thought it unnecessary – to create, or cope with, advanced political and social theories. His ideal was a simple agri-cultural society of happy peasants; a vision which enabled him to 'speak comfortably' to all the victims – and they were legion – of economic progress: displaced half-starved labourers, under-employed handloom weavers, ragged and famished stocking knitters, sweated nailmakers and the like. O'Connor's genuine sympathy for them 'made the wretched and oppressed all over England look on him as their friend, and go on forgiving and loving him whatever he did amiss'.[1] A natural tribune of the people, he could always command the allegiance of the masses, especially in the industrial Midlands and the North. In London, too, strong support might well have been expected from the journeymen handloom silk weavers of the Spitalfields district, formerly renowned for their readiness to rise and riot, who had suffered two severe blows since 1824 – the repeal of the Spitalfields Acts which, for fifty years, had given legal force to the piece-rates negotiated in the industry; and the reduction of the protective tariff on foreign-wrought silks by the ruth-less free-traders. But by 1838 the London silk weavers were, for the most part, in deep poverty, terribly dispirited and too ragged to wish to be seen among their fellow-men.[2]

Feargus O'Connor's special flair for winning over 'his fustian jackets' in the northern towns and villages brought, for a time, circula-tion and success to his *Northern Star*. Also he was shrewd enough to spot men capable of doing work which he was unable or unwilling to do himself. In his heyday he was a demagogue of a high order, he controlled capital resources and had a certain business acumen; he fully realized (as O'Brien did not) that a newspaper, whatever the social status of its potential public, must offer variety in its columns to appeal to variety of tastes, and that this would boost circulation and so attract advertisers, and this, in turn, would increase revenue. Since the back-bone of his paper must, of course, be the political articles arising from current affairs, he enlisted Bronterre, late editor of the *Poor Man's Guardian*; for who was better known as a fearless advocate of popular

[1] G. D. H. Cole, *Chartist Portraits* (1941), pp. 301, 307.
[2] *Add.MSS.* 35,245B: Report by 'A Weaver', *viz.* Richard Cray, a Spitalfields silk weaver and a member of the L.W.M.A. See also *Northern Liberator*, 10th February 1838.

rights and a free press; who better to present important ideas hammered home by trenchant arguments; who more highly qualified to be 'the Chartists' schoolmaster'?

O'Connor was not far wrong. O'Brien's substantial articles in the *Northern Star* constitute the first attempt to formulate for Chartism a philosophy and a programme. They were a prelude or curtain-raiser to the Chartist Convention of 1839. Bronterre's forward-ranging, fertile mind saw that great technical advances, which were inevitable and must be accepted, could bring in their train widespread wealth and leisure for all, provided that the working class could grasp political power, through universal suffrage, and learn to use it wisely through reformed, democratic Parliamentary institutions. His views on the use of machinery in production were far more enlightened and penetrating than those commonly held among Chartists at that time. Machinery, he argued, is evil only when owned by a capitalist employing class: in other words, the evils of machinery are not inherent in the machines themselves, but in the existing social system. The familiar fact that machines 'economise or supersede the necessity of human labour' is no argument against the use of machinery. On the contrary,

'... what could be a greater blessing to man? ... Is not his primeval curse to be obliged to live by the sweat of his brow? And would not he be the greater benefactor of man who would deliver him from this curse and make his life one of comparative ease and abundance? ... If, instead of working to enrich a few avaricious task-masters at the expense of their slaves, machinery were made to work for the general good by being employed as an auxiliary to, instead of as the antagonist of, human labour, there is no fixing a limit to the blessings that might be derived from it.' [1]

And when, a few years later, he prophesied that a three-hour working day would not be impossible 'in a just state of society', he seems to have caught a glimpse of a future age of automation.[2] But such visions did not blind him to the hard facts of the present: in 1838 even the first objective – universal suffrage – had yet to be achieved.

About the middle of October 1838, O'Brien became editor of the *Operative*, a journal 'established *by* the working classes *for* the working classes, to defend the rights of labour from the aggressions of Capital',[3] and to support the People's Charter, universal suffrage, and every other

---

[1] *Poor Man's Guardian*, 13th April 1833; *Destructive*, 12th October 1833; *Political Herald*, No. 1, 1835.

[2] O'Brien, *Life of Robespierre*, p. 12.

[3] *Operative*, 2nd December 1838; *Penny Satirist*, 26th January 1839.

measure 'that can tend to raise the moral, social and political condition of the Working Man'. Its capital was divided into 4,000 shares at five shillings each 'so that any working man might possess a share', and it had a committee of management consisting of twelve London trade unionists: two printers, two tobacconists, a compositor, a smith, a whitesmith, a goldsmith, a currier, a joiner, the secretary of the London Union of Compositors, and the secretary of the Friendly Society of Operative Carpenters. As soon as 500 shares had been taken up, the *Operative* was launched, although the treasurer had barely £100 in hand. O'Brien declared that he stood for universal suffrage and a fair day's wages for a fair day's work – two closely connected aims, for fair wages would never be obtained without a complete change of system brought about through universal suffrage, from which he expected many other important changes such as alterations in the 'laws of landed property', beneficial use of public credit, reduced taxation, the appropriation of tithes and Crown lands to useful purposes, and protection for trade unions, 'native industry', and the poor.[1]

Unfortunately for O'Brien and his supporters the *Operative* had a rival, the *Charter*, an organ of the London Working Men's Association, which took up a hostile attitude to O'Brien's paper largely because of the *Operative*'s militancy and the bad feeling generated by the *London Mercury* and Central National Association episode. This hostility, when reciprocated in the *Operative*, killed the possibility of merging the two journals, which would have been the sensible thing to do. Soon the *Operative* began to decline. Early in 1839 an open letter from members of the management committee appealed to the working men for support; [2] but the rot could not be stopped, and the *Operative* ceased to appear after the middle of May 1839. The *Charter*, too, was unable to pay its way, and on 22nd March 1840 it was incorporated with the *Statesman and Weekly True Sun*, a pro-Chartist weekly.[3]

Meantime the 'People's Charter' had been printed and published. William Lovett, acting for the London Working Men's Association, had drafted it, with much valuable help from Francis Place and John Arthur Roebuck. Four months later on the initiative of the same Association, a public meeting was held on 17th September 1838 in Palace Yard, Westminster – opposite Westminster Hall where Parliament was then

---

[1] *Operative*, 4th November 1838, 24th February 1839. For Francis Place's hostile comments see *Add.MSS.* 27,821(22, 29, 259).

[2] *Operative*, 2nd December 1838, 24th February 1839; *Add.MSS.* 27,821(326).

[3] *Charter*, 1st and 15th March 1840. This merger angered William Carpenter who wanted the *Charter* to amalgamate with the *Southern Star*.

sitting – to consider the propriety of urging Parliament to pass a law
based upon the People's Charter. Francis Smedley, the High Bailiff of
Westminster, took the chair, and speeches were made by Feargus
O'Connor, William Lovett, Henry Hetherington, John Cleave, Richard
Hartwell, and Ebenezer Elliott, famous for his *Corn Law Rhymes*. P. H.
Douglas had come from Birmingham, and Robert Lowery from
Newcastle. Two representatives of the Edinburgh Radicals were
present. Bronterre O'Brien was there but did not make a speech.
Francis Place and John Roebuck had refused to attend, despite a
persuasive letter from Lovett. Place tells us that the 'Householders
Inhabitants of Westminster took no part in the proceedings', and the
young Scotsman, Samuel (Self-help) Smiles, then on his first visit to
London, was not at all favourably impressed by O'Connor and thought
that most of those in the audience were 'not working men at all, but
merely idlers and loafers'. Cannily, he kept clear of them and looked
after his pockets! But he may have been mistaken. Hovell, in his history
of Chartism, says that the meeting was packed with L.W.M.A. supporters and sympathizers; the resolutions were all cut and dried; and
Radical delegates from all parts of the kingdom – Sheffield, Birmingham, Edinburgh, Colchester, Carmarthen, Brighton, Ipswich, Wor-
cester – were present.[1]

According to Lovett, who occupied a pivotal position at that time, the
'General Convention of the Industrious Classes', generally referred to
as the Chartist Convention, to which the Palace Yard meeting was a
prelude, 'originated with the Birmingham Political Union, as did also
the National Rent Fund . . . the plan of Simultaneous Meetings, and the
first National Petition'.[2] The idea of a national convention was circulating in London as early as 1831, for it was then proposed that the
National Union of the Working Classes should have numerous branches
from each of which delegates could be sent.[3] In May 1833, large bills
headed 'A National Convention the only proper remedy' were distributed in Westminster, while O'Brien announced in the *Poor Man's
Guardian* that, a national convention having been decided upon by the
N.U.W.C., the whole country was 'on the move'. 'All parties must
move on,' he said; 'some will move *in*, some *out*. . . . Unless we be

[1] *Morning Advertiser*, 18th September 1838; *Northern Liberator*, 22nd
September 1838; Brit. Mus., *Add.MSS*. 37,773(118, 122) and Place Collection,
Vol. 56 (1838), p. 3; A. Smiles, *Samuel Smiles and his Surroundings* (1956),
pp. 43–4; M. Hovell, *op. cit.*, p. 76; G. Wallas, *Life of Francis Place* (rev. edn
1918), p. 367.
[2] Lovett, *Life and Struggles* (1876), p. 201.
[3] *Poor Man's Guardian*, 10th September 1831.

89

greatly deceived, we shall have in England before twelve months, not only a new Government, but a *new form* of Government.'[1]

Tension continued to build up in the Midlands, especially in Birmingham, and in the North. Slack trade and bad harvests in 1837 and 1838 increased the hardship and bitter discontent. The explosive situation in and around Newcastle-on-Tyne is vividly described by Thomas Ainge Devyr, a dedicated Irish Radical, who, from humble and unpromising beginnings, had become a reporter on the staff of the Radical *Northern Liberator*, by dint of courage, natural ability, persistence, and a modicum of luck. Devyr was a native of Donegal town, where his father was a baker in a small way of business. Although Devyr senior was an Irish Catholic, his wife, strangely enough, was English and a Methodist. They were poor, but they kept their son, Thomas, 'closely, and in winter very cruelly, to school', to and from which the children walked (a mile each way) barefoot, even in snowy weather. They attended a parish school provided by the Hibernian and Kildare Place Societies, somewhat similar to the Granard parish school to which O'Brien went. As his father's son, Thomas Devyr was nominally a Catholic, but never slavishly so, for he always retained a certain independence of thought and judgment on religious, as on political, matters. He was distinctly a bookish boy, so much so that his companions thought him an oddity because of his unusual use and command of language: 'my language taking shape from my thoughts [he says] often exposed me to the ridicule of those around me, all very poor and wholly illiterate'.[2] Such a setting could not hold him indefinitely. For a few years he traded as a chapman and small shopkeeper, but in 1836 he left Ireland to try his fortune in journalism in London, where Samuel Laman Blanchard, who edited the *True Sun* from 1832 to 1836, and was sometime editor of the *Court Journal*, tried him out on his new Radical morning paper, *The Constitutional*. Here he felt on top of the world, earning an adequate salary by work he greatly enjoyed. Unfortunately a serious policy disagreement with Blanchard led, all too soon, to his resignation, and he found himself out of employment, with a wife and two children to keep, and no immediate prospects. In sheer desperation he joined the Metropolitan Police, but, obsessed by the feeling that he was working on the wrong side of the fence, he grew to loathe the job, fell sick in mind and body, and eventually left the Force. After a short spell with the *Greenwich, Woolwich and Deptford Patriot*

[1] H.O. Papers 64 (19); *Poor Man's Guardian*, 11th May 1833; *Working Man's Friend*, 18th May 1833.

[2] T. A. Devyr, *The Odd Book of the Nineteenth Century* (New York, 1882), pp. 32–40.

90

he secured a post in Newcastle on the weekly *Northern Liberator*
(newly-founded by Robert Blakey, a prosperous furrier, in collaboration
with Augustus Beaumont and Thomas Doubleday), which stood for
freedom of the press and universal suffrage, and in Devyr's time
developed into one of the best Radical-Chartist newspapers of the
period.

Devyr left London without regret and says that he was delighted to
find himself in Newcastle,

'. . . among a body of Reformers remarkable indeed for their zeal,
activity and singleness of purpose. Shortly after my arrival the Northern
Political Union, which had been discontinued when the Reform Bill
became law, was revived, and I was elected its corresponding Secretary.
This was in the spring of '38. It was a time of great depression and
scarcity of money, caused mainly by the great collapse of '36 in America,
and all round . . . the multitudes were in great distress. . . . The workers
crowded everywhere to hear the new evangel, and after stirring up the
adjacent villages for a fortnight or three weeks, a demonstration was
advertised on Glasgow Green. It was a success far beyond our expecta-
tion. The movement thus vigorously commenced rolled southward.
Sunderland, the two Shields, the collieries, were . . . stirred up. As
reporter, I was present at most or all of them, till they culminated in a
"demonstration" at Newcastle on coronation day. . . . The workers met
on the Town Moor, covered over by 500 banners, and intervaried with
fourteen bands. . . . The agitation was now fairly commenced, and what
the flunkies called a "Political Methodism" seized upon the leaders. At
six o'clock, throwing down their implements of toil, those true – not
mock – noblemen would hasten home, lunch [on] bread and cheese and
a glass of ale, and off on foot to a meeting generally one or two, sometimes six or seven miles off. . . .

'Foreseeing what approached, the forward reformers all round were
steadily exchanging a little silver for a little steel and lead. There were
some neutrals, not very many, and whatever neutral had an unused
"shooting stick" found a sudden market for it. . . . In obedience to the
law of "demand" one case of fifty muskets and bayonets came along
from Birmingham in answer to a message of bank notes.' [1]

One man had 'a gun about a yard long, encased in wood' to look like a
stout walking stick. The most popular and widespread weapon, however,
was certainly the pike, which, unshafted, was commonly spoken of as the
'Chartist dagger'. At a pinch, two of them could be made by taking

---

[1] T. A. Devyr, *op. cit.*, pp. 157–71. For an obituary and memoir of Augustus
Beaumont see *Northern Liberator*, 3rd February and 21st April 1838.

apart a pair of sheep shears. 'We computed,' says Devyr, 'sixty thousand pikes made and shafted on the Tyne and Wear between August and November 1838.'[1]

It is not easy to imagine or describe the pitch to which political excitement rose among the working class during the second half of 1838. In the principal industrial districts of England and Wales there were demonstrations and processions with bands and banners; moonlight meetings on the moors; secret and not-so-secret arming; and the exchange of fraternal messages designed to produce or increase a sense of solidarity between the Chartists of widely separated regions. Chartist speeches delivered in London were reported and read in Newcastle, more than 270 miles away. 'The hills of Monmouthshire are alive with meetings of Cambrians determined to set Britain free,' said the Welshmen of Newport in a message to the Sunderland Chartists. At such gatherings signatures to the National Petition were collected. 'More than 30,000' had already been obtained, said the *Northern Liberator* on 28th July 1838, but a great many more were required. Then there was the 'National Rent' to be collected to finance the Movement, and meetings to be held to choose delegates to the National Convention soon to be held in London. Bronterre O'Brien was elected a delegate for Manchester at a great meeting on Kersal Moor, near Manchester, towards the end of September 1838.[2] The Chartists of Newcastle were so keen that even on Christmas Day they had a 'great public demonstration' followed by a soirée.

The dangers inherent in large meetings, crowd psychology, and the possession of arms gave rise to a rift between those who thought that the use of 'physical force' might become both necessary and justifiable, and those who were for peaceful pressure or 'moral force', fearing that out of the marching of crowds might spring spontaneous, unpremeditated acts of violence which might give the Government a good excuse to suppress the whole Movement. Bronterre was alive to these potential dangers and early in December 1838, he ventured to offer some advice to his 'Brother Radicals':

'At a moment like this, avoid disunion. Let not the men of Birmingham quarrel with the men of the North. . . . We cannot afford to lose a single man in our ranks . . . in order to command both force itself and the fear of force you must be united as one man and you must observe strict legality in all your proceedings. You must not attack, but you must be

---

[1] T. A. Devyr, *op. cit.*, pp. 63, 171, 177; J. A. Langford, *A Century of Birmingham Life* (1868), II, p. 640; *The Times*, 31st December 1838.

[2] *Northern Liberator*, 1st and 29th September 1838.

prepared to defend. You must not exhort another to get armed . . . but . . . you have, each and all, the indubitable right to be armed in defence of your personal rights and liberties. . . . In short, you must consider your position to be a strictly defensive one, so that if a fight is to come, you may be able to throw upon your enemies the *onus* of commencing it, and, as a consequence, all the responsibility.' [1]

Little more than a fortnight later, the Government issued a Royal Proclamation against torchlight assemblies which had, they said, 'by loud shouts and noises, and by the discharge of fire-arms and the display of weapons of offence, greatly alarmed the [neighbouring] inhabitants . . . and endangered the public peace'.[2] So, in an atmosphere tense with threats and warnings, the curtain came down on 1838.

[1] Printed in *Northern Liberator*, 8th December 1838.
[2] *Newcastle Chronicle*, 22nd December 1838.

Chapter VI

SHARP ARGUMENTS

DURING the year 1839 the Chartist movement reached a peak of intense political agitation such as it never achieved again. And so it was with Bronterre O'Brien, who made his maximum effort in that year, devoting himself utterly to the Cause, and sacrificing, ultimately, both his health and his liberty in so doing. The story presents us with a vivid picture of the ups and downs of a Radical agitator's life, tough and strenuous to the last degree, yet yielding little reward except the plaudits of the multitude and the inward satisfaction of fighting a good fight for freedom and the deserving but helpless poor. Chartism had different meanings for different people according to their current circumstances. It was seen by the well-to-do as a serious threat to 'property', but to the starving hand-loom weavers it held out the hope of food and clothing for their famished families. To Bronterre O'Brien it meant the achievement of political freedom and social justice through universal suffrage and a socially-conscious legislature. With this vision before him, he threw himself whole-heartedly into all departments of the agitation.[1] He was already its most influential journalist. Besides editing the *Operative* he stumped England and Scotland, making three or four speeches a day and giving 'sermons' on Sundays. Crowded audiences in civic assembly halls; monster demonstrations on the moors 'Walled by wide air and roofed by boundless heaven'; gatherings on village greens; a knot of folk around a parish pump: no meeting was too large, none too small, for the National Petition needed every signature it was possible to get. When he was not on tour he sat in the Chartist National Convention (which opened in London on 4th February 1839), representing no fewer than six separate localities.[2] Here, too, he made frequent speeches, served upon committees, and drafted resolutions and 'addresses'. All this at a period when speeches were expected to be much longer than they are

[1] Brit. Mus. Place Collection, Vol. 56 (1838), pp. 1, 6.
[2] The Metropolitan districts (except Marylebone), Leigh, Bristol, Norwich, Newport (I.W.), and Stockport. *Add.MSS.* 34,245B(318).

today and when travelling, much of it still done by stage-coach, was slow, comfortless, and exhausting.[1]

Although O'Brien's appeal was rather more rational than emotional, he did not fail to stir his audiences by the flash and fire of his oratory. His grasp of facts and figures won their admiration, his Hibernian humour made them laugh, and his devastating denunciations of the rich and privileged classes reflected and expressed all the workmen's own fierce resentments. Robert G. Gammage, a contemporary, the first historian of Chartism, and a life-long admirer of O'Brien, declared that O'Brien's oratory, judged by its effects upon his hearers, was of the first order, 'for when in health and spirits and favoured by a numerous audience, his principal difficulty was not that of exciting his hearers to a sympathy with his sentiments, but it consisted in keeping down the tumultuous applause with which he was greeted'.[2] The newspaper reports of O'Brien's speeches, and the fact that he could hold his audience for three, four, and even five hours at a stretch, sometimes even into the small hours, confirm Gammage's observation. Referring to one of O'Brien's orations, delivered at Glasgow during 1839, the same writer remarks that 'the effect produced on the meeting it were almost impossible to exaggerate. At nearly every sentence the speaker drew forth a burst of laughter or cheering, or both, according to the nature of his remark and the style in which it was delivered'.[3] The Reverend Henry Solly, who was present at the first Complete Suffrage Conference in 1842, said that O'Brien, tall and slim with a slight scholarly stoop, 'as he leaned over the railings of the platform, fairly swept the crowd of stalwart Birmingham artisans below him into ecstasies of delight and admiration'.[4] And Frank Peel, who gleaned much of his information from old men who could remember the doings of the decade 1838–48, wrote:

'It would be unjust to represent the leaders of this new political crusade as mere violent demagogues whose sole aim was disturbance and sedition. . . . Amongst them were able writers, and great orators like Bronterre O'Brien, who could sway large crowds with impassioned

---

[1] *Chartist*, 21st April 1839. In December 1842, Henry Solly travelled from Tavistock to Birmingham. 'It was [he says] a desperately tedious journey of two days . . . by an omnibus to Exeter, then by coach to Taunton, rail to Bristol, coach to Gloucester, rail to Birmingham.'

[2] Gammage, *op. cit.*, pp. 77, 119–20.

[3] *Ibid.*, p. 121. R. G. Gammage, a native of Northampton, worked as a cartwright and a shoemaker before finally becoming a medical practitioner. He was a staunch O'Brienite.

[4] H. Solly, *These Eighty Years* (1893), I, p. 381.

oratory as the corn is swayed by the autumn wind. . . . Bronterre O'Brien was one of the most eloquent of perhaps the most remarkable band of orators that ever stood on a political platform in this country.' [1]

Once the decision had been taken to open the National Convention, O'Brien intensified the urgency of his appeal to the 'Real Radical Reformers of the United Kingdom'.

'We have now [he wrote towards the end of January 1839] only a few days left for filling up the National Petition and bringing up the National Rent. . . . There is, therefore, no time to be lost if we are to meet Parliament strong in numbers and strong in the "sinews of war".'

His target was three million signatures on the Petition, and from £10,000 to £20,000 in 'National Rent' (i.e. subscriptions) in hand before the presentation of the Petition. This sum, he thought, would be ample; for forty-nine delegates at £2 a week each 'is less than £100 for the whole'. General expenses should not exceed £300 a week, or a total of £10,000 if the Convention sat twenty-five weeks.[2]

O'Brien's first speech in the Chartist Convention was made on the apparently harmless proposal that Lovett should be appointed secretary. There could be, said O'Brien, no doubt of Lovett's secretarial ability but, in his opinion, the person selected should be a man of no party or sect of Radicals. It was well known that the London Working Men's Association, to which Mr Lovett belonged, differed considerably from large masses of people in the North as to the means by which the object of the Convention should be carried out. Therefore, he proposed Alderman Hadley or Mr Salt. But when they both declined nomination, O'Brien hastened to disclaim any personal hostility to Lovett, saying that if the delegates thought Lovett the right person for the office, he would withdraw his amendment. After further discussion the motion was put from the chair and Lovett was elected, much to the annoyance of Feargus O'Connor.[3]

Lovett had certainly not been voted into a soft sinecure. Quite the reverse, for besides recording the minutes of the Convention's proceedings, which often involved listening to long-winded and confused speeches, extremely difficult to summarize, he was soon inundated by a voluminous correspondence with Chartists in all parts of the country. From the provinces flowed a swelling stream of requests for the services

[1] F. Peel, *The Rising of the Luddites, Chartists and Plug-drawers* (1888), pp. 323–6.
[2] *Operative*, 27th January 1839. On the extortion of 'National Rent' from Leeds shopkeepers by Chartist threats, see A. Briggs (ed.) *Chartist Studies*, p. 78.
[3] *Charter*, 10th February 1839; Lovett, *op. cit.*, p. 201.

of delegates as speakers at local meetings and demonstrations, which called for prompt and tactful attention. All minutes, letters and other documents had to be hand-written; yet there is no evidence that the Secretary was given any clerical staff. He seems to have had no helpers at all except Matthew Crabtree, who was employed by the Convention as doorkeeper and messenger at thirty shillings a week.[1] Small wonder, then, that the secretaries of political unions and working men's associations in various provincial towns and districts complained that although they had collected and sent both money and signatures, the Convention seemed to ignore them; their letters were not answered; copies of important documents, such as the Manifesto on ulterior measures, failed to reach them; and when they had taken the trouble and *incurred the risk* of organizing meetings, they were not told who the speaker(s) from London would be, or when they would arrive, or, indeed, whether anybody at all would come. Month after month this spectre of poor communication haunted and hindered the Movement's progress. Nor was the pressure wholly from without. From day to day, the Secretary had to cope with unreasonable demands from certain eccentric or extremist members of the Convention, such as Reginald John Richardson's proposal 'that the Committee of General Purposes be authorized to ascertain the number of associations in Great Britain having for their object the attainment of universal suffrage'.

The success of the Anti-Corn Law agitation has been attributed mainly to five factors: the organization of 'the Platform'; ample financial resources; singleness of aim; unanimity of leaders; and the justice of the Cause. The Chartists, unfortunately, had none of these keys to success except the last. They tried to organize and administer a nation-wide political movement on less than a shoestring. To have organized efficiently, on a national scale, a programme, or series of programmes, of public meetings addressed by capable speakers would have required the full-time services of a staff of specialist organizers, to say nothing of a section to deal with the 'National Rent', the Convention's sole source of income, without which it could not remain in being. This money came in fairly well in the early months of 1839, when hopes of a speedy success were high; and it is certain that many poor families went without necessaries in order to contribute their mites. In particular, the agricultural workers and the handloom weavers (including the Spitalfields silk weavers) found it very hard to spare a contribution. A letter from Halstead in Essex, dated '5th Mo., 3rd., 1839', evidently written by a Quaker, says: 'Having had a traitrous Rent Collector, I fear we

[1] J. West, *History of the Chartist Movement* (1920), p. 109; *Add.MSS.* 34,245A and B, *passim.*

shall not be able to do much, if any, more on that head at present . . . [the men] are much tyrannized over by the agricultural employers, and we rarely see any of them at our meetings.' Gloucester, too, was sorry to be 'behind in this great Object [the Petition]. However, the few persons who have signed, I think are staunch. Still we regret we have no Money worth sending at present'. Later, as the Convention achieved no tangible results, both enthusiasm and contributions tapered off. This in itself would have been serious enough, but when, in the second half of 1839, the Government began to arrest Chartists in various parts of the country, the need to defend the accused persons presented the Convention with a financial problem of frightening proportions. W. P. Roberts, the famous Radical solicitor, gave his services freely, but other lawyers did not, and in many a case defence costs of upwards of fifty guineas had to be faced. Local Chartists and sympathizers raised a little money, and a number of appeals for help were made to the Convention in London. A Defence Fund was started, but the available resources were never enough to meet all the demands. For instance, on 13th August 1839, George Julian Harney wrote from Warwick Gaol saying that he could not obtain bail and had no funds to pay the expenses of lawyers and witnesses. When, two days later, bail had been found and he was released, he could not return to London as he was still 'completely pennyless'. This is but one case among many, and the pressure upon the Convention's secretary and treasurer can easily be imagined. Doubtless they did the best they could, but inevitably the upshot was a terrible tangle, and when, eventually, a committee, under O'Connor's chairmanship, was appointed to investigate and report upon the Defence Fund, it encountered such 'insurmountable difficulties' in obtaining accounts and vouchers from people in various parts of the country by whom or to whom payments had been made, that the attempt to bring order out of chaos had to be abandoned.

A few members thought the Convention's methods unsystematic and wished to see some tightening-up. To begin with we have O'Brien's notice of motion in April 1839, 'That it be an instruction to the Petition Committee to ascertain the various shops and places in the Metropolis where petition sheets are lying for signature, and that they do forthwith advertise the same in the *Times*, *Chronicle*, and *Weekly Dispatch* and that the proprietors [of] Metropolitan Chartist papers be requested to advertise the same weekly . . . until the petition is ready for presentation.' Early in July 1839, Peter Murray McDouall was much concerned that the Convention should create 'a more perfect co-operation amongst the people' of England, Scotland and Wales, including the trade unions, and at about the same time there was a request 'that the delegates be furnished with a chart for their guidance, distinguishing the several places which have been agitated from those places which have not been so generally agitated, in order that ample justice may be done to public opinion'.[1] These, however, are the voices of a small minority in the Convention. The majority, it seems, gave little or no thought to problems of organization and administration. Chartists, both leaders and led, were in a hurry, for their grievances were great and in many districts their plight was desperate. And, when all is said, no such agitation, on such a scale, had ever been attempted before by the working people of Britain.

Behind the incipient opposition to Lovett's nomination lay the reluctance of the 'physical force' group to have a 'moral force' man as secretary. Thus, in the Convention's first hour the symptoms of disunity made their sinister appearance. Bronterre O'Brien was on the militant left of the Movement at this time. At least as early as October 1836 he had declared that 'the rich are now what they have ever been . . . merciless and irreclaimable. . . . Against such an enemy it is a farce to talk of moral force. It is the overwhelming fear of an overwhelming physical force which alone will ever conquer them into humanity.' [2] O'Brien continued to hold this position throughout the 1830s. From the close of 1838, Bronterre's *Operative* carried many approving references to public meetings, torchlight demonstrations and arming; and an assortment of quotations from authorities such as Blackstone and Locke in support of the proposition that the law allowed every citizen to acquire and possess arms for his own protection, but it was unlawful to advise or urge another man to arm. O'Brien told his readers that *he* always kept arms of some sort for his own protection, and he left the rest to them. Moral force arguments he dismissed as so much 'twaddle'; and on the eve of 1839 he wrote:

'At present the people may arm, both legally and constitutionally. It may not be so legal to arm after the meeting of Parliament [February 1839]. The Parliament once assembled, and the people *unarmed*, the National Convention will be about as powerful as forty-nine babes in their swaddling clothes.' [3]

---

[1] *Add.MSS.* 34,245A (ff.118, 349, 394) and 34,245B (ff.101, 135, 151, 235–6, 250). On the 'alarming distress and destitution of the Spitalfields weavers', see *Northern Liberator*, 10th February 1838.

[2] *London Dispatch*, 30th October 1836.

[3] *Operative*, 30th December 1838; cf. T. A. Devyr, *Odd Book*, p. 167. In an editorial published during the Reform Bill agitation, the *Morning Chronicle* (14th November 1831) had said:—'We are all by law entitled to arm ourselves, and we ought to avail ourselves of the privilege.'

The unrestrained speeches and dark hints of the physical force faction aroused antipathy not only outside the working class, but among the moderate groups, such as the London Working Men's Association and many of the Scottish Chartist bodies, who disapproved of violence and feared that irresponsible talk of armed force might stultify rather than strengthen the Chartists' chances of success.[1] Thomas Attwood, the Birmingham Radical M.P. and merchant banker who presented the Chartists' first petition in the House of Commons, always repudiated physical force.

'Undoubtedly,' he wrote to a friend, 'the wild nonsense about *physical force* has done much mischief. . . . I assert with confidence that if the bitterest enemies of the people had sat down in an infernal conclave to devise the means of injuring the people's cause, they could not, by any possibility, have devised more efficient means than by recommending the people to have recourse to *physical force*.' [2]

But when this letter was read at a public meeting in Birmingham in April 1839, *it was received with derision and dissatisfaction*.[3] The opposite, physical force, point of view was put bluntly by the Cobbett Club which asked, 'is it at all likely that a *remonstrance* from the people, accompanied with a declaration that they will not, under any circumstances, have recourse to arms, will induce the Government to relax in their refusal of their demands?' [4] Barbara Hammond has shrewdly remarked that although physical force might have been useful 'as an ally in the background. . . . The more violent Chartists made the mistake of parading their ally till his weakness was apparent to everyone.' [5]

Two days before the Convention opened at the British Coffee House in Cockspur Street, the first number of the *Chartist* (a newspaper 'for those who produce – for the mighty many') contemplated the approaching assembly with feelings of hope mingled with anxiety. If the people's delegates pursued a timid and over-cautious policy, the confidence and ardour of the working people would be damped and their opponents would treat them with contempt. On the other hand, intemperate rashness and impatience would probably involve the delegates in the

---

[1] *Northern Star*, November–December 1838, *passim*; 9th February 1839; cf. *Add.MSS.* 34,245B(291), a gentle remonstrance from the Montrose Chartist Association.

[2] Attwood to Salt, 28th March 1839.

[3] Wakefield, *Life of Thomas Attwood* (1885), p. 344.

[4] Cobbett Club of London, *Political Tract No. 1* (1839), p. 49.

[5] B. Hammond, *William Lovett*, p. 18.

meshes of the legal net, besides creating a powerful opposition by exciting the fears and prejudices of large numbers of persons. An immense responsibility rested upon the Convention, and its failure to take the right course might retard for years the progress of the movement.[1] These comments, however, went unheeded by the physical force members, who continued to urge an early appeal to the 'resistless power' of the people, as the only way to sweep their oppressors from the path. And this policy they pursued despite clear evidence that the authorities were very much on the alert. On 4th January 1839, for example, just one month before the opening of the Chartist Convention, a London police report stated that a public meeting in support of the Charter assembled at 8 p.m. in the Assembly Rooms in Theobalds Road and went on for three and a half hours. Four hundred people were present and the meeting 'passed quietly off'. But in March the London police reported that 'Chartist spearheads' made by country blacksmiths were selling at 2s 3d and 2s 6d each. After a meeting in Finsbury on 11th May, the police seized five pikes in a house on Clerkenwell Green, and at a 'council' or committee meeting held on the same evening in a room in Ship Yard, Strand, thirteen persons were arrested, one of whom thrust at a police inspector with a pike.[2] Such incidents, however, were not typical of the situation in London where, during the Movement's first phase, it seems that moderate counsels prevailed and there were no disturbances like those in the Midlands and the North of England, or the rising in Wales. London was not Paris; and although London Chartism gained in strength and militancy between 1842 and 1848, the possibility of a successful Chartist Revolution was always remote.[3]

So far as the City of London – the central square mile – is concerned, it is not generally known that the Lord Mayor in 1838–9, Alderman Samuel Wilson, was a man with liberal leanings. Although, as a magistrate, he could never countenance any unlawful activities, his sympathies were certainly with the deserving poor 'whose only crime was their poverty', and with those who wished to bring about a further substantial extension of the franchise by peaceful means. Therefore he believed in freedom of speech and writing, and the right of peaceful assembly. On 30th May 1839 the Court of Common Council of the City, with Lord Mayor Wilson in the chair, had a brisk debate on a motion supporting an extension of the liberties and franchises of the people; recognition of 'equal civil rights without distinction of sect or party'; improvement of the condition of the working classes, and promotion of the cause of universal

---

[1] *Chartist*, 2nd February; cf. 9th March; 7th July 1839.
[2] H.O. Papers 61 (22).
[3] Cf. Hovell, *op. cit.*, p. 144.

education 'which by purifying and reforming our institutions wherever abuses exist, may secure to the Throne the only safe and permanent basis for a constitutional Monarchy, the sincere affection and support of a free and contented people'. Although this motion was lost by 121 votes against 75, it is clear that a substantial minority – nearly two-fifths of those voting – of the members of Common Council, favoured further parliamentary reform and a national system of education for all.[1]

After a five-months' vacation, Parliament reassembled on 5th February 1839 (the day after the first meeting of the Chartist Convention) and Bronterre at once attacked the Government because the Speech from the Throne, while it censured 'disobedience and resistance to the laws', made no reference to the distress of the working class nor any proposals for their relief. This was deplorable, since hope alone, he said, was keeping the people quiescent for the time being. Shortly afterwards, in an eloquent and cogent speech, he returned to the urgent need to collect a mighty multitude of signatures to the National Petition; because 'ministers could make no reply to a petition having three millions of signatures . . . and could not be so forward to display physical force against three millions as against half that number'. Furthermore, the same 'ulterior measures' to be adopted if the Petition were rejected, namely (a) withdrawal of deposits from banks and the conversion of all notes into gold, (b) a general strike, (c) refusal to pay rents, rates and taxes, (d) the purchase of goods exclusively from shopkeepers known to be Chartists, (e) refusal to read hostile newspapers and (f) abstention from excisable commodities, would be much more effective if backed by three millions of people than if supported by only one million and a half.[2]

In many parts of the country, especially the southern and western counties, nothing had been done to procure signatures.[3] How was this mass of potential petitioners to be approached? How could the enthusiasm of the centre be communicated to the circumference? The convention's answer was an instruction to its committee for extending political information to examine and report upon a proposal to send out and maintain a team of 'missionaries'; and when the committee reported favourably, a dozen members of the Convention were chosen to go on tour for three weeks from 26th February. Eight were assigned to Buckinghamshire, Berkshire and the South and West; Bronterre O'Brien was one of three chosen to go into Kent, Sussex and Surrey;

[1] *The Times*, 1st–3rd and 7th January 1839; *Minutes of the Proceedings of the Court of Common Council 1839*, pp. 144–5.
[2] *Operative*, 27th January; 17th February 1839; *Charter*, 17th February 1839.
[3] Lovett, *op. cit.*, p. 202.

while the twelfth man was sent to South Wales 'for a few days'. All were enjoined to notify immediately places they meant to visit; they were supplied with maps, copies of the Charter and the National Petition, signature sheets, and credentials from the Convention. Each missionary received a salary of £2 a week and an advance of £10 to cover expenses; he was required to keep an account and refund any unspent balance upon his return. The Convention charged them not to use 'violent or unconstitutional language, and not to infringe the laws in any manner by words or deed'; but to collect 'National Rent' and be economical in their expenditure.[1]

Their reception was mixed. Some wrote to Lovett reporting well-attended, enthusiastic meetings and good collections; others sent deeply pessimistic accounts of apathetic workpeople and hostile authorities.[2] At the end of a fortnight O'Brien reported to the Convention that he had addressed meetings in Brighton, Cuckfield, Chichester, Southampton and Portsmouth, on the mainland, and at Newport and Yarmouth on the Isle of Wight; attendances had been good and signatures to the Petition numerous, although at Portsmouth the signatories seemed somewhat furtive while in the act of signing. At Brighton, which had not only a regal but a Radical quarter, and where a Regency façade half hid some dreadful slums, O'Brien made a fighting speech:

'Chartist petitioners [he said] do not intend to pray for anything, nor to fall low on bended knee, but will stand erect as men in the attitude of demand. The National Petition is like a bill of exchange and if the House of Commons dishonours it, Chartists must have recourse to ulterior proceedings, *which are generally compulsory*. The Petition can be regarded as a notice to quit, to be followed up, if necessary, by what is called a writ of ejectment. The Convention has not yet decided whether the ejectment shall be through the door or out of the window – whether it shall be on the Westminster Abbey side of the House or on the side next to the River Thames! – but one thing is certain: an empty house is better than a bad tenant. . . . Only let the Petition be signed by two million and it will be a matter of very little moment whether it is received or rejected.'

Had it not been, he continued, for the restraining hand of 'certain enlightened friends and leaders', the men of the North would even then be marching to London, there to constitute a parliament of their own. But the South, East and West had still to be organized. This done, 'the

---

[1] *Ad.MSS.* 34,245A(61); 34,245B(224); 27,821(40); see also *Northern Star*, 13th July 1839.
[2] *Add.MSS.* 34,245A(107, 120, 128, 148, 154, 157, 162).

irresistible array of a consolidated people' would secure all their objectives.

'What a farce the present system is! The present House of Commons does not represent the people, but only the fellows who live by profits and usury – a rascally crew who have no interest in the real welfare of the country. Pawnbrokers are enfranchised, and two thousand brothel-keepers in London all have votes, but honest working folk have none. Not a single stockbroker is without a vote, yet there is not a man among them who does not deserve the gallows. Every lawyer in the country can vote – every thief of them – yet when did any one of this gang add a stiver to the wealth of the nation? . . . Votes have been given to all the parsons, who live by explaining those things which they tell us are inexplicable, who preach abnegation of the lusts of the flesh while losing no opportunities of greasing their own rosy gills. . . . Then you have those slaughtering, soldier-flogging, billiard-playing creatures called officers of the army, and the cotton-lords who possess all the skill and trickery and daring and effrontery of the pick-pocket, the burglar and the highwaymen rolled into one – *they* all have votes, but not the working people. It is, indeed, disgusting to see how much of the honey is appropriated by the drones, and what a pittance is left to the bees of the hive; and how the parliamentary franchise is monopolized by one-tenth of the popularion – and that tenth *the worst* tenth.' [1]

Bronterre O'Brien's efforts were energetically backed up and continued by Osborne and Good, the two Brighton delegates, while unexpected illumination came from a Shoreham innkeeper, an ex-naval man who said his pension had been stopped because he supported the Chartists. He reported that ships' crews from Newcastle, Seaham and Sunderland, then ashore in his town, and some 'excavators on our railroad' were all helping to 'stir up the Spirit of Liberty that has lain Dormant in the breasts of our townsmen'. O'Brien's visit evoked appreciative letters to the Convention from the working men of Gosport and Alverstoke pledging their full support, and a similar letter from the Southampton Working Men's Association ends with a reference to 'open intimidation' in that town, intended to deter people from joining the Chartists.[2]

Shortly after his return to London, O'Brien received invitations to visit other southern counties and also to go north to his 'constituents' at

[1] *Charter*, 14th April 1839; *Sun*, 1st May 1839; *Add.MSS.* 27,821(77). On the readiness of the labourers in Devon and Somerset for pikes, pistols and fighting, see Morley, *Life of Cobden* I, pp. 156–7.

[2] *Add.MSS.* 34,245A(264, 318, 346); 34,245B(21, 27); S. Pollard, art. on 'Dr William King', in *Co-operative College Papers*, No. 6, April 1959.

Leigh in South Lancashire. As he had so recently visited the South he now turned to the North, leaving London on 20th April and returning nine days later, having spoken at nineteen public meetings and an even greater number of small gatherings, usually in or outside public houses. Everywhere he asked his hearers whether they were 'up to the mark' and 'prepared with arguments of a pointed and forcible description'. In some places where the Petition had been signed there was, he told them, 'a pike for every signature', and once he could see several million of such signatures on the Petition he would be ready 'to try any means from marbles to manslaughter' to carry it into effect.[1]

In Manchester on 23rd April, Bronterre O'Brien was billed as principal speaker at a public meeting in the building where normally Batty's 'Circus Royal' provided the working man with 'a night's rational and delightful amusement for 6d'. But now they were interested in activities more serious than the clever tricks of performing animals. O'Brien's speech, at first characteristically humorous and informative, became distinctly inflammatory towards the end. Only twenty members in the whole of the present House of Commons, he said, would vote for what working people wanted; the rest were unfit to represent the people and must be ejected. The other speakers that night were Peter Murray McDouall and William Benbow. McDouall, a contemporary and friend of O'Brien, whose political opinions he shared, was a 'respectable surgeon in decent practice in the manufacturing district of Ramsbottom, near Bury, in Lancashire'. Although 'Dr' McDouall was strongly in favour of physical force if there was no other way, and did not hesitate to say so, William Benbow, the veteran revolutionist, outshone him in the violence of his speech, 'ranting like a mad fool . . . about pikes, guns and swords', and about the army and the police. The meeting went on from 8 p.m. until midnight. The *Manchester Times* acidly remarked that such physical-force blusterers could scarcely injure the Chartist cause more if they were paid to do so, adding that if the Whigs and Tories wished to fasten a rural police force upon the country, they could not be better served by their own hired spies and *agents provocateurs* 'than they are by the McDoualls and the O'Briens'.[2]

Only four days later O'Brien was back upon the same platform, this time with Feargus O'Connor, who was beginning to ride a great wave of popularity, and Reginald J. Richardson, a Salford Chartist with a 'physical force swagger' often to be seen at local meetings and monster demonstrations; 'a wordy pedantic logic-chopper of the worst descrip-

[1] *Northern Star*, 27th April 1839; *Add.MSS.* 27,821(54, 118).
[2] H.O. Papers 40(43); Reports of Constables John Oakes and James Irwin. *Manchester Times*, 27th April 1839; *The Times*, 1st July 1839.

tion'. Richardson, like Bronterre O'Brien, represented Manchester in the first Chartist Convention, but he resigned because his 'constituents' failed to pay him a salary of £5 a week. He was a fluent public speaker capable of holding forth for 1½ to 2 hours at a stretch, and at this second meeting in Batty's Circus it appears that the trio administered to their eager audience what Dr McDouall might have described as 'the mixture as before'.[1]

By this time the authorities were watching developments carefully, resolved to prosecute the more militant Chartist leaders as soon as enough evidence could be collected. The newspaper reporters, however, fought shy of making the necessary depositions, being reluctant to destroy the fountain heads whence flowed such streams of good 'copy', and equally unwilling to waste their time acting as witnesses.

In London again at the end of April, O'Brien reported to the Convention that he had visited Leigh, Chorlton, Manchester, Salford, Bolton, Bury, Ashton-under-Lyne, and Rochdale, and had met little coteries of the leading men at a number of other towns. Support for the Convention was strong, and almost everywhere he had been greeted by bands and processions. The people, however, resented the disharmony among the members of the Convention and other leaders. In Manchester he had found two contending parties – 'the out-and-outers, and the broad-cloth men' – and had striven to close the breach between them.

Meanwhile, the weeks were passing and little ice was being cut in the Metropolis, so O'Connor and O'Brien suggested that the Convention should remove from 'the deadening atmosphere' of London to Birmingham, where they could sit 'under the shelter of the guns of the people', for when the time came for 'ulterior measures' it would be far better to be based upon Birmingham or Manchester.[2] A notice of motion over O'Brien's signature declares 'That . . . in the event of the legislature rejecting our demands, this Convention is of opinion that its sittings ought forthwith to be removed to Birmingham or Manchester, and we do hereby accordingly resolve to make Birmingham or Manchester the scene wherein we will enter upon the discussion of ulterior measures.'[3] But a formal debate was deferred for the time being.

About this time, Madame Flora Tristan, the French authoress, ardent feminist and advanced social reformer, was in London collecting

[1] Lovett, *op. cit.*, p. 181; Gammage, *op. cit.*, p. 52; Hovell, *op. cit.*, 91; L. C. Wright, *Scottish Chartism* (1953), p. 129; *The Times*, 31st December 1838, quoting *Manchester Guardian*, 29th December 1838; *The Times*, 3rd and 5th January 1839; H.O. Papers 40(43): Report of J. R. Holt.

[2] *Northern Star*, 4th May 1839; *Operative*, 5th and 12th May 1839.

[3] *Add.MSS.* 34,245B(255).

material for a new book. She had, of course, heard of the National Convention and, characteristically, she wished to see for herself and form her own opinion. The result is a vivid and obviously authentic vignette. It seems that a friend who was 'intimately linked with one of the Chartists' leaders' offered to help, and conducted her one day 'to the room off Fleet Street where the National Convention held its meetings . . . in a beer house reached by a narrow passage'. As the two ladies entered they were promptly challenged by a pot-boy who, having received the password, led them through a back parlour, across a small courtyard and then along a corridor to the door of the meeting-room. 'My friend,' Madame Tristan continues, 'asked for Mr O'Brien and Mr O'Connor. They came out, and after I had been introduced to them they took me into a large room, where nobody was admitted except after being vouched for by two known members. These wise precautions prevented spies from slipping inside. The first thing that impressed me was the expression on the faces of the delegates . . . each head had a striking individuality of its own. There were about thirty or forty members of the National Convention present and about the same number of young working-class sympathisers. I was pleased to find five French working men and two women of the same class among them. Everyone present followed the discussion with alert attention. Feargus O'Connor spoke with passion, appealing to the emotions. O'Brien's speech was controlled, lucid, well-reasoned, showing thorough knowledge of past events. He was followed by Doctor Taylor, who had a brisk delivery and glowed with enthusiasm.'

But Madame Tristan, although an experienced and acute observer,[1] could survey only the surface. The fermentation underneath was uncovered by Alexander Somerville, a shrewd Scot of working-class origin and Radical leanings, who had served as a cavalry trooper in the Scots Greys in 1832, and as a volunteer in the British Legion in the savage Spanish Civil War during 1835-7. He was in touch with certain members of the Convention at this time and knew about the private conferences held by the physical force faction. They believed, he says, in 'the propriety and practicability of a revolution which should level the entire fabric of our political constitution and existing orders of society'. He was actually introduced to two members of a Chartist 'Secret Committee of War' as an experienced soldier 'who could give

[1] For the life of Flora Tristan (1803–44) see Eléonore Blanc, *Biographie de Flora Tristan* (Lyons 1845); J-L. Puech, *La Vie et L'Œuvre de Flora Tristan* (Paris 1925); C. N. Gattey, *Gauguin's Astonishing Grandmother* (London 1970). Her plan for a world union of workers, *L'Union Ouvrière*, was published in 1844, four years before Karl Marx's *Communist Manifesto*.

107

a practical opinion of the feasibility of their intended insurrection'. Somerville, who had returned as recently as the autumn of 1837 from active service in Spain under Lt General Sir George De Lacy Evans, a Peninsular veteran, threw cold water upon the extremists' foolish plans. He told the secret committee that he had seen, besides the horrors of bloodshed and death in battle, 'fertile fields trodden under the hoofs and wheels of the artillery . . . vines cut down . . . the houses of rich and poor . . . of political and non-political inhabitants, battered to atoms'. Whether Bronterre O'Brien was a member of this committee we do not know, but he must have known of its existence, for his friend, the loquacious McDouall, was one of its leading lights. Indeed, according to Somerville, who despised him, McDouall had cast himself for the rôle of commander-in-chief of the Chartist forces, and on one occasion, although he had no knowledge of weapons and warfare, he went 'with another person who knew as little . . . to walk through Woolwich Arsenal to see how it could be captured and to report thereon', to watch 'the artillerymen at exercise', and to ask many questions of their bombardier-guide. Somerville, much disturbed by certain inflammatory speeches he had heard at Chartist meetings, and by the even 'more absurd, though not less dangerous, warlike notions of the doctor [McDouall], as propounded by him to me', decided to write, and publish, as rapidly as possible, a series of weekly penny 'Letters to the People' under the general title, *Dissuasive Warnings to the People on Street Warfare*, in which he refuted the potentially mischievous 'instructions' offered by the revolutionary Colonel Francis Maceroni in his *Defensive Instructions for the People in Street Warfare*.

Maceroni (or Macerone) had at one time moved in exalted circles, having been aide-de-camp to Joachim Murat, King of Naples, Napoleon's brother-in-law and one of his marshals; but in 1830 he was living in London, very much down on his luck. When, in 1831, he wrote his little military manual – extracts from which appeared on 11th April 1832 in the *Poor Man's Guardian* – he had in mind, not the Chartist Movement, but the intense Reform Bill agitation which preceded it by six or seven years. By 1838–9, however, many a Chartist had managed to obtain a copy of Maceroni's *Defensive Instructions* 'containing the new and improved combination of arms, called Foot Lancers, miscellaneous instructions on the subject of small arms and ammunition, street and house fighting, and field fortification'. In its pages a method of making ball and buckshot cartridges was explained and illustrated, and so was 'the mode of defending a house, a church, or [other] public edifice', a village or town, including the way to use moveable barricades, hand-grenades and 'burning acids'. Coloured plates purported to show

108

SHARP ARGUMENTS

the advantage of the ten-foot lance in repelling a charge by either cavalry or infantry against 'Foot Lancers'.[1] The gallant colonel having stressed the importance of good organization and discipline, claimed that 'a body of determined men, armed with my lances or with pikes, must undoubtedly overthrow their opponents, whether infantry or artillery, of the present army, if they have the opportunity and courage to close on them with alacrity'.[2] Dangerous stuff, indeed, in the hands of desperate revolutionary civilians. Somerville's opinion was that by 1839 'the agitation in the manufacturing districts is high enough for immediate action, and from a too well grounded discontent – but that agitation is not yet national, nor from the mingled indifference and opposition of the middle classes will it soon become general – therefore an armed movement must be defeated. . . .'[3] On 27th July 1839 the popular weekly *Penny Satirist*, which claimed to have some 50,000 subscribers, nearly filled its front page with a copy of an engraving, taken from Somerville's letters, which purported to show the effects of artillery fire 'on a town in a state of insurrection'. Some contemporary observers said that Somerville's *Dissuasive Warnings* did much to avert a rising in the summer of 1839.

An even greater contribution to civil peace was probably made by the skill and humanity of Major-General Sir Charles Napier, a seasoned professional soldier, yet full of sympathy for the working people, who commanded some 5,000 to 6,000 regular troops, with eighteen guns, in the Northern District, ably assisted by two trusted officers, Sir Hew Ross and Colonel Wemyss. In March 1839, General Napier made the following remarkably wise and broad-minded comment in his journal:

'. . . it is said arms are being provided for insurrection; this is the result of bad government, which has produced want, and the people are rather to be pitied than blamed. . . . As matters stand, I am for strong

[1] A recent authority has said that one of the chief lessons of the great Irish Rebellion in 1798 was that 'cavalry were useless against pikemen if they held their ground'. T. Pakenham, *The Year of Liberty* (1969), p. 203.
[2] A. Somerville, *History of the British Legion and the War in Spain* (1839); A. Somerville, *Autobiography of a Working Man* (1848), pp. 423–9, 441–3, 455, and Appendix III; also *Conservative Science of Nations* (1860), p. 213; Extracts from Maceroni's *Defensive Instructions*, with fanciful pictures of workmen armed with pikes resisting attacks by cavalry and infantry were published in the *Poor Man's Guardian* as early as 11th April 1831; cf. *Add.MSS.* 27,821(85), and *Weekly True Sun*, 14th April 1839; F. Maceroni, *Memoirs of the Life and Adventures of Colonel Maceroni* (1838).
[3] A. Somerville, *Public and Personal Affairs* (1839), p. 14; *Penny Satirist*, 25th May, 1st June 1839. In 1849 Cobden suggested that Somerville might undertake the writing of a history of Chartism. Morley, *Cobden*, II, pp. 54–5.

police; but the people should have universal suffrage – it is their right. The ballot – it is their security and their will, and therefore their right also – and the new poor law should be reformed; but while doing these things, I would have a strong police force to stand between the soldiers and the people.' [1]

Realizing that a small spark might detonate a big explosion, he 'forbade the soldiers to be marched out of barracks for fear of encountering a body of Chartists and having a collision, which must be carefully avoided'.

On 22nd April 1839, he

'Went to a meeting. . . . There were nearly three thousand people, most of them spectators taking no interest in the proceedings; no cheer followed the orator's expressions, it was like a religious meeting. Was this deep attention or not? In my mind not, for numbers came and went the whole time, and plenty of a Chartist description walked about wholly inattentive to the speakers. Feargus O'Connor and Bronterre O'Brien were advertised to be the orators but did not come.'

And to Sir Hew Ross he wrote:

'We shall have a rough time, all my reports point to the middle of May as the time when a rising will be attempted. I hate a well-fed traitor, but in Lancashire the hand-loom weavers are in terrible distress and I pity them from my heart. Poor fellows, they know not the wild work that O'Connor, O'Brien and Oastler – said to be madmen – are leading them to.' [2]

The state of the framework knitters was equally desperate. At Sutton-in-Ashfield fifty families had no beds, only straw to sleep on, and no bed coverings but 'the few battered clothes they wear in the day time'. Yet although a knitter's earnings were but seven shillings a week, the dedicated Sutton folks had raised £20 for the National Rent. [3]

At the end of April 1839, O'Brien was asked to represent the Perth Chartists in the Convention until they could provide another delegate in place of one who had resigned. A few days later he went to Bolton where he spoke at a meeting for upwards of three hours. He referred,

---

[1] Quoted by W. N. Bruce, *Life of General Sir Charles Napier* (1885), Ch. 4.

[2] Sir W. Napier, *Life and Opinions of Sir Charles Napier* (1857), II, pp. 11, 16, 19–23; cf. *H.O. Papers* 40(43), Letter from Colonel Wemyss to Sir Charles Napier.

[3] *H.O. Papers* 40(53), Letter to Dr Wade, Vicar of Warwick.

first of all, to the circulation of certain sinister statements falsely describing him as a man who wanted to cut the throats of the rich and to divide their property among the poor. The walls of Chichester had been placarded with such lies. The real robbers, of course, were the parsons, aristocrats, fundholders, placemen and sinecurists who persisted in denying to the productive classes their just rights. In the days of their ancestors, the working man had roast beef, plum pudding and a tankard of ale every day, and before another year had passed the golden age of plenty would be restored, by means of a parliament, *elected by the productive classes*. This done, there must be a commission to enquire into land tenure, and if it should be found that some of it had been acquired for nothing, it should be taken back for nothing! Finally, as to arming, he said that it would be illegal to advise them to arm; but he was armed himself, and they all knew that the law allowed every man to possess arms for his own defence.

In May 1839 the Convention set up a special committee to prepare a draft address to the people. O'Brien not only served on this committee with Feargus O'Connor, Robert Lowery, Matthew Fletcher, and John Frost, but when the draft was agreed and ready, he was chosen to introduce it. Its object, he told the Convention, was to teach the people their duty at that critical time, so that they should not submit to any kind of oppression, nor, on the other hand, be led by spies or irresponsible fanatics to resort to physical force. He then read the address, which began by accusing the Government of setting the upper and middle classes against the working class with the object of provoking an outbreak in which the latter could be crushed.

'What course then, do we advise? Our advice is that you *rigidly obey the law*; but at the same time be prepared to make your oppressors likewise obey it. Be upon your guard against spies or madmen, who would urge you to illegal practices, but at the same time bear in mind that you have the same right to arm that your enemies have, and that if you abandon that right your liberties are gone for ever.'

The people must temper courage with caution; they should not parade arms at public meetings, lest this should give the enemy an excuse to invade their rights of assembly and discussion; but at the same time they should not fail 'to be prepared with those arms to resist any and every unconstitutional attempt to suppress . . . peaceable agitation by physical violence'. Feargus O'Connor, seconding the address, commended the 'able document' prepared by Mr O'Brien. But some members did not like it. Obviously it was ambiguous – perhaps intentionally so, and in the end, after a long, heated discussion, the dangerous

111

phrase 'with those arms' was struck out. The address, so amended, was carried by 32 votes to 7.[1]

The time had now come for the Convention to move to Birmingham, where the members arrived on 13th May, not in a cavalcade of coaches, but 'by the one o'clock train' on the recently-opened London to Birmingham railway. *The Times* correspondent, quite unimpressed, reported with a sneer that, 'Taken as a whole, the members of the "People's Parliament" presented a most wretched spectacle; they appeared for the most part half-starved, and certainly did little credit to the metropolitan pasture in which they have recently been feeding.' [2] But they received a much warmer welcome from the Birmingham Chartists. Within two hours of his arrival Bronterre O'Brien was carried off to address a great crowd at Holloway Head, a popular meeting place only a short walk from the famous Bull Ring. They were assembled, he said, to tell the Government that if they would make just laws the people would obey them; but if, instead of passing measures to benefit the working class, they tried to govern by the sword, the workers would put them down by the pike. He spoke contemptuously of a warrant issued against him six weeks before, and said that he had been given to understand that further action would depend upon his present conduct. If the authorities thought that such threats would make him a 'good and dutiful sort of boy' they were much mistaken. O'Brien then moved that an address be sent to the Queen, and O'Connor rose to speak to the motion but became unwell and had to retire. However, several other members of the Convention made speeches. The same evening, in a relaxed atmosphere, they dined together, and 'the cloth having been removed, strangers were admitted, and in a short time the room was crowded to excess. Several toasts were proposed and responded to by Mr O'Connor, Mr O'Brien . . . and others, and the festivities . . . were kept up till twelve o'clock'.[3]

The next day we see the Convention discussing a fiery, long-winded Manifesto which embodied O'Brien's election or hustings plan, 'ulterior measures', including a general strike, and the arming of all Chartists – dangerous topics indeed. At a serious of 'simultaneous meetings' to be held throughout the country before 1st July, the people were to be asked (*inter alia*):

'Whether they will provide themselves with Chartist candidates, so as to be prepared to propose them for their representatives at the next general

[1] *Add.MSS.* 27,821(121, 126–30; *Charter*, 12th May 1839; *Northern Star*, 18th May 1839; *Hull Saturday Journal*, 18th May 1839.
[2] *The Times*, 14th May 1839.
[3] *Birmingham Journal*, 18th May 1839.

election; and if returned by a show of hands, such candidates to consider themselves veritable representatives of the people – to meet in London at a time hereafter to be determined on?'

O'Brien, of course, approved of this question, but he was much less enthusiastic about the Manifesto as a whole. In principle he favoured ulterior measures, but he feared that if, at that juncture, the Convention tried to induce other persons to refuse to pay taxes, members of the Convention might become liable to charges of conspiracy and so give the Government a pretext – for which they were eagerly waiting – to swoop down and suppress the Chartist Movement. Therefore he suggested that 10,000 copies of the Manifesto should be privately printed and circulated in order to take the sense of the country before the Convention committed itself to the document. But the Convention, although far from unanimous, rejected O'Brien's buck-passing proposal, and resolved upon prompt public issue of the Manifesto.[1]

The Chartists' leaders and their militant Manifesto were, so it seems, rather too much for the Birmingham magistrates who, despite the fact that Stephens, Lovett, Collins and Vincent were already marked down for prosecution, decided to arrest two or three more 'revolutionary orators' as a further salutary warning to others. Accordingly, on 17th May, constables were sent to the 'Red Lion' P.H., the Chartists' rendezvous at this time, where they found 'the celebrated vindicator of Robespierre, Mr O'Brien', with Dr John Taylor, a young Scottish ex-naval surgeon who has been described as 'one of the most romantic figures in nineteenth-century Scots history'; tall and swarthy, with jet black hair hanging in curls to his shoulders, and large eyes 'dark as coal'. He had lived in France in his youth, moving in Jacobin and Babouvist circles (a fact of great interest to O'Brien) and could boast that he had spent his twenty-first birthday in a French prison! The constables' visit, it appears, caused no surprise to O'Brien who 'supposed that he was wanted . . . [and] said he was quite ready'. But it so happened that he was not their quarry: they were looking for Joseph Fussell and Edward Brown, two Birmingham Chartists, and for George Julian Harney, who had formerly worked with O'Brien on the *Poor Man's Guardian*.[2]

---

[1] Hovell, *op. cit.*, pp. 148–50; Lovett, *op. cit.*, pp. 206–15.
[2] *The Times*, 18th May 1839; Gammage, *op. cit.*, p. 28; L. C. Wright, *op. cit.*, p. 26 and Appendix D. Dr John Taylor had served as a naval surgeon as did many young men of moderate means who wished to enter the medical profession, for at that period the qualifications required for appointment as a surgeon in the Army or Navy were lower than for the ordinary diploma of the College of Surgeons, but after three years' service a military or naval surgeon could enter civil practice on the same terms as other members of the College; see W. J. Reader, *Professional Men* (1966), p. 35; J. Burn, *Autobiography* (1882), p. 166.

113

By this time, O'Brien and O'Connor had begun to hedge on the subject of arms. Indeed, on 18th May 1839, O'Connor publicly deprecated the practice of carrying arms to meetings and suggested that the Convention should ask O'Brien to draw up a declaration of policy. This was agreed to, and on the next day O'Brien produced a series of four resolutions:

'1st   That peace, law and order shall continue to be the motto of this Convention, so long as our oppressors shall act in the spirit of peace, law and order towards the people; but should our enemies substitute war for peace, or attempt to suppress our lawful and orderly agitation by lawless violence, we shall deem it to be the sacred duty of the people to meet force with force, and repel assassination by justifiable homicide.

'2nd   That in accordance with the foregoing resolution, the Convention do employ only legal and peaceable means in the prosecution of the great and peaceable objects of the present movement. Being also desirous that no handle should be afforded to the enemy for traducing our motives, or employing armed force against the people, we hereby recommend the Chartists who may attend the approaching simultaneous meetings to avoid carrying staves, pikes, pistols, or any other offensive weapon about their persons. We recommend them to proceed to the ground sober, orderly and unarmed . . . also to treat as enemies of the cause any person or persons who may exhibit such weapons, or who by any other act of folly or wickedness, should provoke a breach of the peace.

'3rd   That the marshals and other officers who may have charge of the arrangements for the simultaneous meetings, are particularly requested to use every means in their power to give effect to the recommendation embodied in the preceding resolution. We also recommend that the aforesaid officers do in all cases consult with the local authorities before the meetings take place.

'4th   That in case our oppressors in the middle and upper ranks should instigate the authorities to assail the people with armed force, in contravention of the existing laws of the realm, the said oppressors . . . shall be held responsible in person and property for any detriment that may result to the people from such atrocious instigation.'

When these resolutions had been passed the Convention adjourned until 1st July 1839.

During the recess a number of monster meetings and demonstrations were organized, usually upon a piece of open ground conveniently situated within marching distance of several large industrial centres of population. Peep Green (Hartshead Moor) in the West Riding was such a spot, for it was approximately equidistant from the chief towns of the Riding, while the land formation made a huge natural theatre. From Bradford, Huddersfield, Halifax, Dewsbury and other smaller towns the Chartists marched in formation, several thousands strong, with banners flying and bands playing. Many wives and families accompanied their menfolk. As the columns converged upon the moorland meeting-place the gathering crowds, refreshed by the air, spread themselves over the grass, creating a scene resembling a fair ground, with banners and music and even huts erected by enterprising traders for the sale of food and drink.[1] A large concourse of this kind gathered at Peep Green on 21st May. Although the magistrates had posted placards warning all 'well-disposed persons' to keep away, a large crowd, perhaps 20,000–30,000 strong assembled to hear speeches by Feargus O'Connor and Bronterre O'Brien, who travelled across country from Manchester. O'Brien's speech emphasized the advantages of his election plan and stressed the need to force the Government to choose between conceding universal suffrage or, alternatively, setting up an out-and-out despotism.

'If they choose the latter [he said] we shall be dissolved from our allegiance, and that will be the signal for a general rising. . . . I cannot avoid putting it to you whether you will much longer submit tamely to be governed by imposters and robbers.'

The resolution 'carried unanimously' at the end of the meeting ran:

'That this meeting, seeing the determination of the Government to resist the just demands of the people, consider it an imperative duty on every lover of freedom and his country to rally round and stand or fall by that Charter, which will ultimately be the conservator of their rights and liberties. . . . If this government persist in resisting their just demands, they cannot be answerable for the deeds of men driven to desperation by insult and oppression.'

Another monster meeting was held four days later (25th May 1839) on Kersal Moor, about three miles from Manchester, and again O'Connor and O'Brien were the principal orators. The actual attendance will never be known. The *Northern Star*, with its customary exaggeration, said that 500,000 people were there; the *Morning Advertiser* guessed 300,000,

---

[1] *The Times*, 21st May 1839; J. F. C. Harrison, 'Chartism in Leeds', in Briggs (ed.), *Chartist Studies* (1959), p. 75n; see also J. F. C. Harrison, *Society and Politics in England, 1780–1960* (1965) for an eye-witness account by the Chartist, Benjamin Wilson.

while Sir Charles Napier, who went to see for himself, estimated no more than 30,000 'very innocent people' for the most part, including many women and children. The Chartists' speakers seemed to him to be expressing 'orderly, legal political opinions very like my own', which suggests that the General must have missed or misunderstood O'Brien's most virulent passages.[1]

It would be wrong to assume that all Chartist meetings were well-attended even at the height of the agitation. In some places enthusiasm was lacking and the anti-Chartists were in hopes that the movement would die of inanition. On the other hand, we know that various Chartist groups were preparing to spread yet more propaganda. Some of the Scottish Chartists, for example, invited Bronterre to embark on a lecture tour in Scotland. 'The plan,' said a writer in the *True Scotsman*, 'is the result of a long conversation . . . in Birmingham.' It was proposed that the course of lectures should include such intriguing subjects as: 'The Cause and Consequence of Popular Revolutions', 'The Influence of Accumulated Property upon the Value of Labour', 'The Extent to which Taxation can be Extended with safety to the State'. The itinerary, approved by the Convention,[2] took O'Brien from Glasgow through Renfrewshire and Ayrshire to Edinburgh. Speaking at Glasgow he declared that the meetings of the Convention were strictly legal and that he had never advised people to violate the law, not because he cared a fig for it, but because he had a precious regard for his own carcase and for those of the working men. He also recommended his election plan and strongly stressed the injustice of withholding the franchise from the productive classes.[3] Dr John Taylor, Robert Lowery and Peter Bussey also addressed the meeting, and on the same evening O'Brien and Taylor went together to speak at Barrhead.[4] Later, at Kilmarnock, Bronterre told his audience that during the past three months he had made innumerable speeches to some $2\frac{1}{2}$ millions of people and the

---

[1] The Chartists usually over-estimated the numbers of their supporters. Richard Carlile said that O'Connor and 'the *Northern Star* (and not only the *Star*) most outrageously exaggerated the popular feeling. Every beer-house was a Chartist Legislature, a minor or local convention, and every expression a resolution to be printed in the *Northern Star;* the end of which was *nothing done*'. On O'Connor's deliberate exaggerations in Ireland in 1832 see D. Read and E. Glasgow, *Feargus O'Connor* (1961), p. 27. John Brown and John Clough, government agents, were at the Peep Green meeting and reported to the Home Office; *H.O. Papers*, 40(51).

[2] *Add.MSS.* 34,245B(218).

[3] *Add.MSS.* 27,821(235). O'Brien's election plan was tried out in Scotland and Wales, see L. C. Wright, *Scottish Chartism* (1953), pp. 126–9; A. Briggs (ed.), *Chartist Studies* (1959), p. 243.

[4] *True Scotsman*, 15th June 1839.

strain was beginning to tell.[1] Nevertheless, he went on with his tour. On 15th June, he was in Paisley and towards the end of the month he reached Edinburgh where, at Whitefield Chapel, he gave a short series of lectures under the auspices of the Edinburgh and Midlothian Universal Suffrage Association, on 'The Grievances under which the People Labour, and the Best Remedy for these Grievances'. At the time appointed for his first lecture he was ushered into the pulpit, but 'finding himself rather ill at ease there, he descended to the platform amidst the reiterated cheers of the meeting, which was very numerous'. 'I like to be on a level with you,' he remarked. 'I believe Providence never intended me for the pulpit.' During the past two months, he said, he had addressed meetings all over the North of England; he had also been in the South – at Portsmouth 'under the very frown of cannons', and at Southampton. In Scotland he had visited Ayr, Maybole, Girvan, Kilmarnock, Glasgow, Paisley and Leven. In some of these places the people had arms; in nearly all they were determined to have their rights, peaceably if they could, or any way if they must. The paramount needs of the time were universal suffrage and a thorough reform of the existing iniquitous system of land ownership.[2]

The *True Scotsman*'s leading article on 6th July throws some light upon the maner and matter of O'Brien's speeches, discribing them as highly interesting, instructive and impressive in style, and marked by 'admirable powers of reasoning', so that he not only evoked enthusiasm but carried conviction to his audience. But, asked the *True Scotsman*, 'why does he insult the religious feelings of his audience by repeated oaths in his lectures? The people of Scotland are not accustomed to this kind of treatment.'

Nor did the *True Scotsman* agree with O'Brien on physical force:

'No man can doubt, on hearing O'Brien, that he has little faith in the efficacy of moral agitation; and that he looks to a revolution to overturn the present government. . . . Therein we differ. We think moral agitation is quite adequate to gain the Charter; and . . . we do not believe they [the people] will ever be got to act in sufficient numbers to gain it by force.'

Notwithstanding the defects to which the *True Scotsman* objected, O'Brien drew large audiences in Scotland in 1839. 'If God sent the rich into the world with combs on their heads like fighting cocks,' he exclaimed, when addressing a great assembly on Monkton Moor,

'. . . if he sent the poor into the world with humps on their backs like

---

[1] *Ayrshire Examiner*, 14th June 1839.
[2] *True Scotsman*, 22nd June, 6th and 13th July 1839.

117

camels, then I would say that it was predestined that the rich should be born booted and spurred, ready to ride over the poor; but when I see that God made no distinction between rich and poor – when I see that all men are sent into this working world without silver spoons in their mouths or shirts on their backs, I am satisfied that all must labour in order to get themselves fed and clothed. . . . Unfortunately, those who have not worked themselves, whose ancestors have never worked, have all the good things, while those whose fathers and mothers have worked hard and who themselves have all their lives worked hard, endure all the privations and sufferings which can be inflicted in this world. . . . You produce annually 450 millions of wealth, and the idlers take 4s 6d a pound of it. They take nearly one-fourth, though they are only one in two thousand of the people. Next come the profit-mongers – those who make their fortunes by grinding the poor and cheating the rich . . . who buy cheap and sell dear, who spoil [i.e. steal] the wholesome articles you have made and distribute them to others – they take 7s 6d a pound of what you produce. Thus 12s is gone before you have a pick. They promise you a paradise hereafter. You pay 1s to the clergy for that, on condition they preach to you to be content with your lot and to be pleased with what divine providence has done for you. . . . Then they take 2s 6d a pound for their military forces – to keep you down. This leaves 4s 6d. . . . By God's help this system shall be changed before the year's end.'

It is not unlikely that the inspiration for O'Brien's many speeches and lectures on the injustices of the distribution of the national income and the burden of taxation came from a cartoon entitled 'The Tree of Taxation', which was first printed in the *Northern Liberator* in Newcastle in October 1838. The tree is depicted as a sort of vegetable vampire, its roots sucking life from the poor and industrious classes to provide golden windfalls for the rich and the privileged, who catch the falling fruits with gleeful dexterity. This engraving, said the editor,

'may be taken from the paper and framed, as no useless ornament to the house of a working man. . . . It is so distinct and plain . . . that a child may be taught to apprehend its general meaning, and this meaning, we trust, will be taught to the children . . . by their parents'.

The cartoon was subsequently printed separately and sold at six shillings for 100 copies.

Although he offended some, Bronterre O'Brien became very friendly with several of the Scottish Chartists. There was, for example, Dr John Taylor, only a year younger than O'Brien, with whom he had much in

118

common. Having returned from France, Taylor served in the Navy for a time as a surgeon. In the early 1830s, he founded the *Ayrshire Reformer* and, shortly after, the *Liberator*, a Radical-Chartist journal, published in Glasgow, in which the Cotton Spinners' union invested £1,000. As a result of a libel action, he was forced into bankruptcy by Kennedy of Dunmure, whom he challenged to a duel, and for so doing he was imprisoned for two months. He was Chairman of the West of Scotland Radical Association in 1836, and played a prominent part among the Scottish physical force Chartists. The 'ablest man among the extreme revolutionists' in the Chartist Convention of 1839, he was strongly prejudiced against William Lovett and the L.W.M.A., while Lovett reciprocated by expressing his contempt for all such 'blood-and-thunder heroes'. Another of O'Brien's friends, a man very different in many ways from John Taylor, was John M'Crae, who was a preacher-teacher in a 'Christian Chartist church and school' in Kilbarchan; work for which he received a salary of twelve shillings a week. In 1841 M'Crae stood as a hustings candidate at Greenock, where he claimed a victory on the show of hands. Unlike O'Brien, he never parted company with Feargus O'Connor, but continued to support him, with reservations, even after the failure of 1848. An even closer personal friend of O'Brien for many years was Robert Cranston (1815–92), a leading Edinburgh Chartist. The son of a mason, he had attended a Lancasterian school in Edinburgh and was afterwards trained as a tailor. In 1843 he opened, in High Street, Edinburgh, a coffee-house which quickly became one of several regular meeting places of the Chartists and other Radicals. Cranston was a 'genial, warm-hearted and kindly man', a pacifist, a member of the Edinburgh Total Abstinence Society, and a pioneer of temperance hotels. In 1848 he opened the Waverley Temperance Hotel in Princes Street, Edinburgh, which proved so successful that he was encouraged to launch similar enterprises in Glasgow and London. These hotels 'became models for the unlicensed premises then coming into vogue', and in Scotland they were often chosen as the venue of trade union meetings. In the political field he edited the *North British Daily Express* in which he stood for Radicalism, Chartism, and Temperance. Surprisingly, he was arrested in 1848 by a nervous police force and accused of 'preaching treason under the guise of temperance'. Some twenty years later, when he was quite well-to-do, he became a Liberal and an active and prominent town councillor. He built what were then regarded as model workmen's dwellings, which included washhouses and a library. Mrs Luisa St John Duff, one of Bronterre O'Brien's daughters, was employed for a time as manageress of Cranston's New Waverley Hotel in Edinburgh, and later became his housekeeper. When he died, in 1892, he left her an annuity of £25, which was inherited by her daughter, Isabella. Robert Cranston's son remembered O'Brien well and often spoke of him.[1]

As for the rank-and-file Chartists, Bronterre O'Brien certainly reached the peak of his popularity with them in the summer of 1839. At the beginning of May, James ('Shepherd') Smith's *Penny Satirist*, always sensitive to the thoughts and feelings of its working-class readers, published on a twopenny sheet five 'Portraits of Living and Dead Advocates of the Principles of the People's Charter', namely Feargus O'Connor, Richard Oastler, Bronterre O'Brien, Henry Hunt and William Cobbett. And just two months later, on 6th July 1839, the same paper filled the top of its front page with portraits of 'Four Political Lions' – Richard Oastler, Joseph Rayner Stephens, James Bronterre O'Brien, and Feargus O'Connor.

At the time of the serious 'Bull Ring' riots in Birmingham early in July 1839, Bronterre O'Brien, much in demand, was fulfilling several speaking engagements in Newcastle and Sunderland. Dr John Taylor was also expected to speak in Newcastle during the same week, but, with Dr McDouall, he became entangled in the riots in Birmingham where he was arrested on the night of 4th–5th July. When this news reached Newcastle, O'Brien was called upon, at short notice, to deputize for him as principal speaker at 'a great public Meeting of the Radical Reformers of Newcastle' on Sunday, 7th July, and was 'received with tremendous cheers' by an audience all agog to hear hot news of the recent riots and the hated police imported from London to put down the workpeople of Birmingham. Bronterre began by reading a newspaper report of what took place in Birmingham on Thursday, 4th July, adding his own pungent comments as he went along and concluding with a vehement attack upon the Government's intolerable interference with the people's right to peaceable assembly to discuss their great grievances. The time had come, he said, for the people to defend themselves as best they could, and had they taken his advice many years ago they would long since have been prepared for the worst. At this the audience roared, 'We are now ready!' Then O'Brien's compatriot, Thomas Devyr of the *Northern Liberator*, seized the moment to propose the following resolution:

[1] E. Mein, *Through Four Reigns* (n.d.); *Glasgow Herald*, 10th February 1934: Article by W. H. Marwick on 'Some Scottish Chartist Leaders'. Other details kindly given by Miss Elizabeth Mein, Robert Cranston's great-granddaughter. L. C. Wright, *op. cit., passim*; T. Johnston, *History of the Working Classes in Scotland* (1922), p. 246; G. Wallas, *Life of Francis Place* (rev. edn 1918), pp. 373–4.

'That in case the Government shall persist in dispersing the constitutional meetings of the people by physical force, we, the men of Newcastle, putting our trust in God, and resting upon our rights and the constitution, are determined to meet illegal force by constitutional resistance.'

This was promptly seconded and carried 'amid loud cheers' and the meeting ended with a hearty vote of thanks to Bronterre O'Brien.[1] For his speech at this meeting he was tried at Newcastle Assizes in February 1840.[2]

During the previous evening O'Brien had addressed the members of the Durham Charter Association in the Assembly Rooms at Sunderland. In a speech lasting three hours he said that his object was to get universal suffrage as quickly as possible. The working people's burdens and all the pressing evils of society were rooted in private ownership of the land and the banking system, and the object of the present régime of robbery and plunder was to increase the value of capital and decrease the value of labour. But he had no doubt at all that the men of Durham County would not be found wanting when the time came to destroy this plundering, murdering system.

On the morning after the Newcastle meeting O'Brien was up betimes to catch the five o'clock coach for Leeds, where he delivered two lectures, and later that week, at Bradford and Barnsley, he spoke in terms decidedly truculent. At Dewsbury, on the Sunday, he was billed to speak in the large room of the Wellington Tavern, but the landlord became panicky, fearing hostile action by the magistrates, and in the end O'Brien 'preached' from the cross in the Market-place a 'sermon' which took 'nearly three hours in its delivery'. Rooms had been reserved for the speaker at the Red Lion Inn, Dewsbury, 'but during the time Mr O'Brien was preaching, the landlord sent word that the person could not be allowed to stop at his house that night'. This gave a lead to the landlord of the Wellington Tavern and several other innkeepers, who also turned him away. 'Mr O'Brien then went with a friend to Batley Carr, to which place he was followed by a very large number of friends and disciples. This state of things must be nearly at an end or else something worse must and will follow.'[3] O'Brien's next engagements were at Batty's Circus, Manchester (with the veteran Richard Carlile as the other principal speaker) and at Stockport. Although a charge was made for admission to the Manchester meeting

[1] *Northern Liberator*, 6th and 13th July 1839; *The Times*, 6th July 1839.
[2] See below, Chapter 8.
[3] *True Scotsman*, 13th July 1839; *Northern Star*, 13th and 20th July 1839.

121

(Boxes 6d, Pit 4d, Gallery 2d), the building was packed and many could not get in.[1] At Stockport 'an immense concourse of men and women' gathered and waited to hear O'Brien, who was delayed and did not arrive until 9 p.m. Greeted by tremendous cheering he at once launched into his speech, saying that he had recently addressed no fewer than sixty meetings in Scotland and Cumberland, and he was convinced that the people of Scotland were preparing to have the Charter, peaceably if they could, but any way rather than be without it. Seeing that the rich had already 108,000 armed men to protect them, who would dare to deny that the working classes were entitled to have arms to protect *their* lives and liberties?

'Let the government dare to hang one Chartist – and for every one there would be ten of the other class hung up to their own doors [Applause]. The question was, were they up to the mark and provided with the appliances wherewith to bring the accursed profit-mongers to their senses? [*Yes!*] He would not and durst not say anything illegal, because he heard that there were already 29 warrants of one sort or another out against different members of the Convention; but he bade the labouring classes to . . . prove by hanging something bright and shining over their chimney pieces that they were prepared for the crisis.'[2]

And if the Chartist Convention should decide to call a general strike,

'let not the anvil be struck within the breadth and length of the land. Let not a spade be used unless to dig some tyrant's grave. Let not a shuttle move, unless to weave the winding sheet of some monster robber, some profit-monger, who dared to attack the people's Parliament. All will then soon be over'.[3]

---

[1] *H.O. Papers*, 40(43).
[2] *Manchester Times*, 20th July 1839; *Northern Star*, 20th July 1839.
[3] Quoted by Jephson, *The Platform: its Rise and Progress* (1892), II, p. 281.

Chapter VII

BENBOW'S BANTLING

WHEN the Chartist Convention paused for breath at Whitsuntide 1839, two related questions lay oppressively upon the minds of its more thoughtful members: would armed risings in the industrial districts be likely to impress Parliament and overawe the Government; and would a general strike, if called, be an effective weapon, either as a prelude to, or in place of, armed insurrection? [1] The idea of resorting to nation-wide strike action for important political ends was not entirely new. A proclamation addressed to all the inhabitants of Great Britain and Ireland by workers on strike in Glasgow and neighbouring towns in April 1820, earnestly requested that

'. . . in the present state of affairs, and during the continuation of so momentous a struggle . . . all [will] desist from their labour . . . and attend wholly to their Rights, and consider it is the duty of every man not to recommence until he is in possession of those Rights which distinguish the Freeman from the Slave; *viz.*, that of giving consent to the laws by which he is governed. . . .

> *By order of the Committee of Organization,*
> *for forming a Provisional Government.*

The weavers of Glasgow and Paisley struck work on 1st April 1820, the colliers of the district followed two days later and were soon joined by the cotton-spinners, machine-makers and founders; [2] but the stoppage did not become more general than this.

On many occasions and in various places during the heat and ferment of the 1830s the political general strike was seriously suggested. Francis Place, writing in 1834, recalled that

'Four years ago a proposal was made (by some desperate rascals in London who had imposed upon many better men) to the working people all over the country to have what was called a holiday. They were to live sparingly and carefully for some time to accumulate the means of

---

[1] Gammage, *op. cit.*, p. 127.
[2] Cobbett's *Political Register*, 15th April 1820, pp. 360–2.

existence for a fortnight and they who had most means were to assist those who had the least and then on a certain day they were to leave off work and have a fortnight's holiday, during which time they were to attend public meetings all over the country – thus stop all manufacturing business and commerce, all farming, anything in fact but the buying and selling of provisions among themselves. No man was to do more work as a baker or butcher or other food salesman than would be sufficient to feed the working people, the rest were to starve or to live how they could, and such was the infatuation of numbers that they believed the scheme was practicable. The same notions have recently been revived and much diligence is employed to persuade the people to take "a month's holiday"!'[1]

This plan was published in 1832 in a pamphlet entitled *A Grand National Holiday and Congress of the Productive Classes*. Its author was William Benbow, a stockily built, tough, tireless, irrepressible character, who used to go about in a cart making speeches and selling pamphlets; also, on and off, he helped to make pikes and heavy cudgels capable of breaking an arm or cracking a skull. This man trod the revolution road for half a century, grappling with the Government and exerting considerable influence within the working-class movement. Born in 1784, he was a native of Birch, a hamlet near Middleton in Lancashire, where he worked as a shoemaker – a craft noted as a nursery for Radicals. Self-educated and a free-thinker, he was always powerfully attracted by politics. As early as 1816 he joined the Manchester Hampden Club and in company with Joseph Mitchell, also a physical-force Radical, he went on a political mission into Yorkshire and the Midlands, stirring up the 'lower orders' with flights of fiery rhetoric. In 1817 Benbow set up as a bookseller in Manchester, working at the same time with men like Richard Carlile on the extreme left wing. He met Henry Hunt in the same year, while in London as a delegate from the Manchester Hampden Club to a Radical parliamentary reform meeting. As suspected preachers of armed insurrection, Benbow and Mitchell went in imminent danger of arrest and detention after the suspension of the Habeas Corpus Act on 4th March 1817, and had to keep 'on the run . . . scarce ever resting two nights in one place'. Eventually, Benbow was caught, clapped into prison, and kept there for nearly a year: a gross injustice, stormed the furious prisoner, perpetrated by that evil 'public robber', Lord Sidmouth. When William Cobbett, then a political refugee in America, wrote his two 'Letters to Benbow' (outlining his plans for a popular English grammar and other writings) which were printed in the

[1] *Add.MSS.* 35,154(203–4).

Political Register towards the end of 1817, Benbow was still in prison. After his release, he moved to London and became at first agent and then publisher of Cobbett's *Political Register*. About this time, too, he issued under Cobbett's auspices his popular pamphlets, *A Peep at the Peers* and *Links of the Lower House*, in which he attacked without mercy the corruption of the governing classes. At the end of six months as Cobbett's publisher, Benbow ended the arrangement after a furious quarrel over some £400 which Cobbett said Benbow had failed to account for. Thereafter Benbow not only tried to carry on bookselling and publishing on his own account, but opened a coffee-house near Temple Bar which became a favourite meeting place for working-class Radicals. Here the National Union of the Working Classes used to meet and enrol new members in its early days, from May 1831 onwards. Benbow assiduously attended every sort of Radical meeting where he saw any chance of airing and spreading his political notions. In the early 1830s he was a frequent speaker at meetings of the N.U.W.C., but many members found his extreme opinions unacceptable. William Lovett, for one, refers to 'some very improper language used by Benbow at a meeting in the Rotunda . . . which language, however, was strongly deprecated by the Committee and members generally'.[1] Benbow supported Owenite co-operation, especially the idea of exchanging labour for labour; but, like Bronterre O'Brien, to whom he became well known during the 1830s, he was for positive political action and attached the greatest importance to forms of government. His hatred of 'despotism under every form' was implacable, and his efforts to 'do everything in his power to destroy it' were unceasing and lifelong.

Benbow enhanced his popularity in London in March 1832 when, with William Lovett, James Watson and Henry Hetherington, he helped to organize and lead a procession of protest against the sheer hypocrisy and futility of a day of fasting (21st March) prescribed by the Government during a serious outbreak of cholera; an epidemic so severe, indeed, that out of 11,020 cases recorded in 1832, mainly in London's riverside parishes and the Spitalfields district, no fewer than 5,275 were fatal. The Fast Day, said the Radicals, was in fact a *farce day*, because the poor, who were the chief victims of cholera, needed more food, not less.

'We resolved, therefore,' said William Lovett, 'from the first, that we would not comply with this piece of hypocrisy, but that we would enter into a subscription to provide the members of our union [the N.U.W.C.]

[1] *Add.MSS.* 27,822(24).

with *a good dinner on that day*; those who could afford it to provide for those who could not.'

Lovett, who was present as one of the leaders, also tells us that the 'farce day' procession assembled in Finsbury Square – perhaps 100,000 people all told – and marched four abreast peacefully enough through the City, intending to go *via* the Strand and Piccadilly to Hyde Park, returning by way of Oxford Street and Holborn. But the authorities, unwilling to have the Radicals in the West End, obstructed their progress 'by the new police drawn across Temple Bar armed with staves and drawn cutlasses'. The procession turned aside up Chancery Lane, only to meet one police cordon barring the westward route along Holborn, and yet another drawn across Tottenham Court Road. At this point tempers flared. Benbow and a few other extreme Radicals tried to thrust the police aside; scuffles ensued and the police used their staves; but after a dangerous minute or two the crisis passed. Lovett and his friends, fearing further disturbances if they continued the procession, 'drew up in the North Crescent, and there, we having addressed a few words to the people . . . they, by our advice, broke up, and retired to their respective classes to dine. . . .'

But this did not conclude the business. Within a day or two Benbow, Lovett, and Watson were arrested, and, in due course, tried at the Middlesex Sessions, Clerkenwell Green, on 16th May 1832, on a charge of 'riotously assembling and contriving together for the space of five hours against the peace of our lord the King'. The trio pleaded not guilty and were triumphantly acquitted by the jury, after Benbow had made a long political speech in court – a golden opportunity which, come what might, he simply could not miss![1]

Always a tireless agitator, Benbow supported the public protest against flogging in the army, saying that every man who failed to lift up his voice was, in effect, an accessory to these barbarities.[2] He opposed the new Poor Law, of course, and passionately took the side of the poor Dorchester labourers – the Tolpuddle martyrs. The working men of England, he declared, ought to put themselves into such a position that

---

[1] Lovett, *op. cit.*, pp. 78–80; C. Creighton, *A History of Epidemics in Britain* (1965 edn), II, pp. 796, 820–1; N. Longmate, *King Cholera* (1966), p. 86; M. C. Buer, *Health, Wealth and Population in the Early Days of the Industrial Revolution* (1926), pp. 226–7.

[2] Flogging in the Army was not abolished until 1881. An eye-witness account of savage floggings in Wellington's army during the Peninsular War is given in G. Bell, *Soldier's Glory* (1956), pp. 96–7; and in his *Autobiography of a Working Man*, pp. 284–91, Alexander Somerville tells how he received one hundred lashes when serving in the Scots Greys in 1832.

they could 'speak to their rulers in a voice of thunder' to demand the labourers' release, and they should not be daunted by the risk of violence. Meantime they were in duty bound to support the victims' families.

During the Reform Bill agitation of 1831–2 Benbow was every bit as sceptical as O'Brien about its probable benefits for the working man, and even more keen to try out 'ulterior measures', including, of course, the general strike. It was at the end of September 1831, when a resolution in favour of universal suffrage, annual parliaments and vote by ballot was under discussion by the N.U.W.C., that Benbow, seconding the resolution, called attention to his 'bantling', or as others would call it, 'a spoiled child of his own rearing', saying that he wished again to impress upon the workers' minds the necessity of taking a holiday for a month, for he had a peculiar desire to see a festival of that kind, emanating from a grand and solemn national conference, which would give such a lesson to their taskmasters as would teach them to sing another song. Three weeks later, Benbow again recommended his project to the working classes, saying that 'he would tell them how easily they could humble their taskmasters without resort to anarchy, confusion, revolution and blood'. The last clause does not sound like Benbow; perhaps he inserted it to avoid alarming the moral force section of his audience. He did not believe that alliances with shopkeepers and the middle classes would help forward the workers' cause, but the national holiday would start such a transformation that afterwards working men would 'all live well and have three clean shirts a week' (tremendous cheering).[1]

As the excitement generated by the Reform Bill agitation mounted, the debates of the National Union of the Working Classes became more bellicose. The Union was organized in small units of 30–40 members, called classes, and, in November 1831, Benbow, now a 'class leader', urged all old soldiers to go to their classes and teach their brethren military evolutions.[2] At the same time, he never ceased to advocate the general strike and the organization of the working masses in one great 'general union'. The cautious Committee of the N.U.W.C. managed to persuade him to defer publication of his plan, but he flatly refused either to abandon it or to keep quiet. At a meeting on 12th December 1831, he declared that it was better to be idle than to work and starve. The men of the North had some notion of his holiday; but they must await the appointed time, for all must act together; let the holiday be unanimous and general, and in one month the people would obtain their rights.

[1] *Poor Man's Guardian*, October, November and December 1831, *passim*.
[2] *Ibid.*, 26th November 1831; Lovett, *op. cit.*, p. 68.

The 'great plan', published as a twopenny pamphlet in January 1832, was introduced by Benbow in three short pithy sentences:

'Plundered fellow-sufferers, I lay before you a plan of freedom. Adopt it and you rid the world of inequality, misery and crime. A martyr in your cause, I am become the prophet of your salvation.' [1]

Organization and control, he explained, would be entrusted to local committees in every parish and district, whence representatives would come to the national congress.[2] Carefully co-ordinated preparations would be essential. The strikers must provide themselves with food for the first week, after which the 'sovereign people', acting through their local committees, would requisition whatever they needed. In the past, Benbow argued, the workers had been too honest, too conscientious, too delicate; but now was the time to take boldly what was rightfully theirs.

Moderate opinion, fear of consequences, shortage of funds, lack of essential organizational links on the workers' side, and energetic counter-measures by the government, robbed Benbow's 'inert conspiracy of the poor against the rich' of all momentum in the early 1830s; but it was certainly not forgotten. Towards the close of the decade the Chartists, casting around for ways and means of putting pressure upon

---

[1] *Poor Man's Guardian*, 14th January 1832. The Glasgow Radicals believed that Benbow's plan would destroy the existing social system because 'every link in the chain which binds society together is broken in a moment by this inert conspiracy of the poor against the rich'; *Glasgow Liberator*, 1st February 1834.

[2] The proposal was for a population of 8,000, 'two wise and cunning men'; for 15,000, four; for 25,000, eight; for London, fifty. So it seems likely that the membership of the proposed congress would have reached 1,500 at least. In addition to those given above, many references to William Benbow's activities are to be found in: *Add.MSS.* 27,791(317–347); 27,827(15 *et seq.*); Cobbett's *Political Register*, 29th November, 6th December 1817; *Poor Man's Guardian*, 18th June, 6th and 20th April 1831, 24th March, 7th April, 14th July 1832; *Morning Chronicle*, 9th November 1831; *Destructive*, 2nd February 1833; *Working Man's Friend*, 9th February 1833; *Republican*, 6th April 1834; *Northern Star*, 17th August 1839; 25th April 1840; *Statesman and Weekly True Sun*, 19th April 1840; Wm. Benbow, *Censorship Exposed, or Letters to Lord Sidmouth* (?1818); *Proceedings of the 3rd Co-operative Congress held in London in April 1832*, pp. 51–3; *The Trial of William Benbow and Others . . . May 6th 1832* (1832); S. Bamford, *Passages in the Life of a Radical* (1893 edn), II, pp. 18–21; Henry Hunt, *Memoirs* (1820–2), III, pp. 411–12, 473, 519; R. Huish, *Life of Henry Hunt* (1835), II, p. 122; M. Beer, *History of British Socialism* (new edn 1929), I, pp. 286, 314–18, II, pp. 82–3; G. D. H. Cole, *Life of William Cobbett* (1927), pp. 245–6, 270–1, 351, 373; Dolléans, *Le Chartisme* (1912–13), I, pp. 122 *et seq.*; F. F. Rosenblatt, *The Chartist Movement in its Social and Economic Aspects* (N.Y. 1916), p. 28; E. P. Thompson, *The Making of the English Working Class* (1963), pp. 642, 650–1.

a contemptuous government, began to consider the possibility of a general strike as one of some half-dozen 'ulterior measures'. Speaking in the Chartist Convention on 11th February 1839, Feargus O'Connor argued that the best way to make an impression on Parliament would be to go with the Petition in one hand and ulterior measures in the other. But Bronterre O'Brien, in a moderate mood for once, thought that courtesy was the best policy, for 'no set of men like to be bullied'.[1] In April, O'Connor again spoke in support of the strike, saying that the workers could 'meet the cannon with the shuttle'; but definite action was deferred.[2] Eventually it was decided to put the following question (*inter alia*) to 'the people' at the Whitsuntide meetings which were to be held while the Convention was in recess:

'Whether, if the Convention shall determine that a sacred month will be necessary to prepare the millions to secure the Charter of their political salvation, they [the Chartists] will firmly resolve to abstain from their labours during that period, as well as from the use of intoxicating drinks?'

Lovett, who thought this question savoured too much of irresponsibility, wanted to fix a day 'for one or two trades to cease from labour', calling simultaneously upon the rest of the workers in all parts of the country to raise a fund to support the strikers. This, he argued, would provide a practical test, for if those not on strike would not, or could not, contribute to the fund, they certainly would not strike *en masse* at the bidding of the Convention. Perhaps he expected the fund to prove a failure and secretly hoped that this would put an end to the general strike project with all its difficulties and dangers.[3] If so, his hopes were not realized, for early in July 1839, shortly after the Convention had reassembled, the more impatient members again raised the question of ulterior

---

[1] *Add.MSS.* 27,821(31); Beer, *op. cit.*, I, p. 316.

[2] *Charter*, 28th April 1839. In his novel *Sybil* (1845) Benjamin Disraeli indicates the part Benbow and Chartists like him hoped to make the general strike play in their campaign for political reform; 'there are to be no leaders this time, at least no visible ones. The people will do it themselves. All the children of Labour are to rise on the same day, and to toil no more, till they have their rights. No violence, no bloodshed; but toil halts, and then our oppressors will learn the great economical truth as well as moral lesson, that when Toil plays, Wealth ceases. . . . The Benefit Societies, the Sick and Burial Clubs, have money in the banks which would maintain the whole working classes, with aid in kind that will come, for six weeks, and that will do the business. And as for force, why there are not five soldiers to each town in the kingdom. It's a glittering bugbear, this fear of the military; simultaneous strikes would baffle all the armies in Europe'.

[3] Lovett, *op. cit.*, p. 217.

129

measures and pressed for quick action, arguing that the numerous meetings held in the past six weeks had shown that the rank and file were ready.[1] Discussions dragged on, however, until 12th July, when the Convention (now returned to London from Birmingham) at last published a manifesto in favour of ulterior measures, but with the sacred month in very small type at the bottom of the list. On the same day the Chartists' first petition to Parliament was decisively rejected in the House of Commons by 235 votes against 46.[2]

Three days after this contemptuous rebuff the Convention, with its ranks already much diminished by a series of resignations, reconsidered the general strike idea. Peter Murray McDouall, leading the left-wing, favoured July – 'a celebrated month for revolution and reformation' – when they would probably have a good harvest before them. A stormy debate developed, in which many of the speakers were obviously ill at ease. James Taylor, a Unitarian minister from Oldham, felt that food supplies would not last a month if all work ceased. Marsden, a poor weaver, who earlier had been wholly in favour of a general strike, now stressed the importance of forming a correct estimate of their resources, and refused to vote for the strike until he was satisfied that the people were prepared for it and the Convention had matured a proper plan of action. Even Harney was against it, for although he advocated a rising, he did not want it to be premature. Carpenter said that there were certain delegates who ought to have been there to give advice and to take their share in the responsibility. 'Where was Mr O'Connor? Where was Mr O'Brien?'[3]

After two days of discussion the momentous – indeed, desperate – decision to call a general strike was carried by 13 votes against 6, with 5 abstentions.[4] During these proceedings Bronterre O'Brien had been absent on a speaking tour in the north, but as soon as he returned he realized that the Convention was on the brink of a precipice, and saw the urgent need to procure a drastic alteration of the Convention's decision. He was, indeed, in an awkward dilemma. If, hitherto, his belief in the strength of the Chartist Movement had been genuine, the moment had come to confess his mistake; but if, on the contrary, he had been playing a game of bluff, he must now admit that his bluff had been called and the game was lost. The task went much against the grain, but it had to be done. On 22nd July, he told the Convention that

[1] *Add.MSS.* 27,821(283, 292).
[2] *Hansard*, 3rd Series, Vol. XLIX, pp. 220 *et seq.; The Times*, 9th July 1839; *Charter*, 21st July 1839.
[3] Gammage, *op. cit.*, p. 127; *True Scotsman*, 27th July 1839.
[4] Hovell, *op. cit.*, p. 165.

while he still saw the general strike as a potent weapon, it was his opinion that the present members of the Convention were not at that moment competent to wield it. If they willed the end, they must also will the means. But desertions and arrests had so greatly reduced the Convention's numbers that, in view of the awful suffering inseparable from a *partial* strike, the people themselves ought to make the decision, for they were, after all, the best judges of their readiness and resources. His own opinion, after his speaking tours in many parts of the country, was that the people were *not* prepared. Moreover, many would regard it as the beginning of a revolution, and to a certain extent that was his own view, but he did not wish to act rashly. He wished to say to the people, 'if you strike universally, you strike successfully; but if partially, fatally'. The strike, if general, would mean the salvation of the country; if partial, it would result in misery for the masses and the sacrifice of all the best friends of the cause: a disaster for which the Convention would be morally responsible. He moved, therefore, 'that the vote of the Convention which fixes the 12th of August for the commencement of the Sacred Month be reconsidered with a view to a more general and mature investigation of the subject . . .'.[1] This motion was carried by 12 votes to 6, seven members abstaining.[2]

The plunge over the precipice was thus narrowly avoided; but this belated moderating effort of O'Brien's did nothing to allay the Government's suspicions about his real aims. His movements were being watched and his speeches noted by the authorities. The Whig Home Secretary, Lord John Russell, keeping an ear to the ground to detect any sinister moves, such as arming, secret meetings, drilling contrary to the Royal Proclamation of May 1839, or preparations for a general strike, placed O'Brien's correspondence under surveillance.[3] This meant that his letters could be intercepted, opened by the Post Office and sent to the Home Secretary for inspection, before being copied, carefully re-sealed and delivered to the addressee.[4] A number of Chartist leaders – O'Connor, Dr Wade, Frost, Richardson, Vincent, Hetherington,

---

[1] *Add.MSS.* 34,245B(266); 34,245A(175); 27,821(71).

[2] *Northern Star*, 27th July 1839. *The Weekly True Sun* anticipated that when the general strike began, the starving Irish would come over in their thousands to do the work. For other arguments against the general strike see A. Somerville, *Dissuasive Warnings*, Letter vii; and James Burn, *Autobiography* (1882), pp. 176–7.

[3] *H.O. Papers*, 79/4, fo. 235; Warrant dated 3rd August 1839, cancelled 23rd November 1839; *H.O. Papers* 40(46), Letter, 26th August 1839, from the Senior Magistrate, Newcastle-upon-Tyne, to the Home Secretary; *State Trials* (New Series), Vol. IV, p. 1428.

[4] F. Mather, *Public Order in the Age of the Chartists* (1959), pp. 218–21.

Hartwell and others – were subjected to similar treatment in 1839 and at other times.[1] There are, in fact, no intercepted letters to or from O'Brien in the bundles (*H.O. Papers*, 40/53 and 33/4) preserved at the Public Record Office.

The early days of August 1839 found Bronterre O'Brien serving on a committee set up by the Chartist Convention to collect evidence on the attitude of working men throughout the nation to the general strike project. The information received quickly convinced the committee of the futility of pursuing the matter. Since a substantial majority of the letters and reports from a wide area were not in favour of the 'sacred month', it is probable that the response to a general strike call would have been meagre and, therefore, ineffective. The Greenwich Working Men's Association shrewdly noted that 'the Delegates are as much divided' on the strike issue 'as are the tens of thousands whom they represent'.[2] Newspaper reports of Chartist meetings tell the same tale. For instance a special mass meeting was held early in August 1839 at Rochdale whence, barely three months earlier, had come a report that the

'. . . Chartists still continue to purchase arms in the town and neighbourhood. There is a village not far from Rochdale which contains only 55 male adults, 45 of whom have each a rifle, and many of them pikes besides. The Chartists have [also] commenced a run on the savings banks in Rochdale, which still continues to an alarming extent: they will have nothing but gold.' [3]

By August, however, although the workmen were attentive when the sacred month was mentioned, they were neither enthusiastic nor united. John Deegan of Stalybridge, a bookseller and a militant local leader, wanted the general strike to start on 12th August, and a journeyman tailor from Heywood assured the meeting that all was ready in his town; but another speaker shared with the chairman of the meeting a contrary opinion. Finally, it was resolved that Rochdale would not lead, but would join in if other towns started a general strike on 12th August. After the meeting Deegan was arrested.[4]

On 6th August 1839, the Convention's committee of investigation published, in the form of a resolution moved by O'Brien and seconded by O'Connor, their unanimous conclusion, based upon the evidence

[1] *H.O. Papers*, 79/4, fo. 233; Lovett, *op. cit.*, pp. 297–8.

[2] *Add.MSS.* 34,245B(38, 53, 70, 110, 119, etc.); Gammage, *op. cit.*, pp. 145–8, 154–5.

[3] *The Times*, 21st May 1839.

[4] *Northern Star*, 17th August 1839; *The Times*, 12th August 1839.

received, that a general strike was impracticable. The same evidence, they continued,

'. . . convinced us that the great body of the working people, including most of the trades, may be induced to cease work on the 12th inst., for 2 or 3 days, in order to devote the whole of that time to Solemn Processions and Solemn Meetings for deliberating on the present awful state of the country, and devising the best means of averting the hideous despotism with which the industrious orders are menaced by the murderous majority of the upper and middle classes, who prey upon their labour.'

On the heels of this pronouncement O'Brien published in the *Northern Star* an open letter to the Chartists of the United Kingdom, telling them that although the arrests and imprisonments of the last fortnight were acts of unmitigated despotism, the Chartists must not rise, for such a rising would surely fail and result in the final triumph of the upper and middle classes. No resistance must be offered 'for the present'; peaceful propaganda, quiet organization and arming must be the order of the day 'until the whole industrious strength of the country is ready to come to your relief'. He concluded with the hope that 12th August would see them 'peaceably and legally assembled together to protest against the landlords' and money-mongers' usurpation of the sovereignty of this nation'.[1]

So the projected month-long nation-wide general strike dwindled by degrees to a few local demonstrations lasting but an hour or two. In London, on Sunday afternoon, 11th August, a body of about 500 Chartists met in West Smithfield and walked in procession to St Paul's Cathedral, which they occupied for some time in a perfectly decorous manner. At Manchester, too, the Chartists assembled in the Cathedral, but they left abruptly when the preacher announced his text taken from Luke 19. 46: 'My house is the house of prayer: but ye have made it a den of thieves.' Even in and around Newcastle nothing serious happened and the Mayor was able to send a reassuring report to the Home Office. A few collieries stopped, but all except one were at work again by 15th August.[2]

The *Northern Star* now denounced the decision to call a general strike as 'a most ill-judged and suicidal act', adding that 'any attempt to bring about the sacred month before a universal arming shall have taken place, will ruin all'. Feargus O'Connor, swinging round like a well-

[1] *Northern Star*, 10th August 1839; *The Times*, 12th August 1839.
[2] *H.O. Papers*, 40(46); C. Webb, *Modern History of the City of London* (1896), p. 182.

oiled weathercock, addressed a long letter, full of inaccuracies, to the 'working millions', declaring that he had always disapproved of the general strike, and had, indeed, exposed the fallacy of the project. Moreover, said he, 'O'Brien, the schoolmaster of public opinion for eight long years of undeviating practice', was also against it.

Before the end of August 1839 it had become obvious that the first Chartist Convention had shot its bolt, and it fell to O'Brien to make a face-saving speech, during a debate early in September, stressing the useful results achieved. Signatures to the National Petition had been increased from 400,000 to over 1,280,000, and, after Parliament's rejection of the Petition, the Convention had embarrassed the Government by recommending resort to ulterior measures.[1] It could hardly have done more. The Convention, he went on, should now dissolve and all the Chartist Associations in the kingdom should form themselves into 'election clubs' so as to be free from Government interference. He then drew up a valedictory address for the appropriate committee, from which it was passed to the Convention with a favourable report.[2] But the Convention, after a prolonged discussion, rejected O'Brien's draft and chose a new committee. According to O'Brien, the 'Closing Address of the General Convention of the Industrious Classes', published on 22nd September 1839, was a blend of his draft and one prepared by Dr John Taylor: an Anglo-Irish-Scottish mixture concocted on the day of dissolution by a mere 'rump' of nine or ten members who had not yet gone home.

Although, for the most part, the fires of agitation and incipient insurrection died down during the summer of 1839, they continued to smoulder dangerously in certain places. In mid-July, for example, a cache of fire-arms and a copy of Colonel Maceroni's pamphlet on street warfare were seized in the home of Timothy Higgins, who was secretary of the Chartist Association of Ashton-under-Lyne, J. R. Stephens's stronghold.[3] It would have been strange indeed if all the militant propaganda poured out by O'Brien and his fellow agitators had failed to produce some results. In fact there were still a few clandestine com-

[1] *Charter*, 8th September 1839; cf. *Northern Liberator*, 6th July 1839; *Add.MSS.* 27,821(292). It is interesting to note that on 17th June 1839, Joseph Parkes, a right-wing Radical, wrote to Francis Place: 'This year has been productive of the gain of the penny post – of some shove on of the Ballot question, and of a deep foundation being laid in the Chartist agitation, whereon at some future day to build a further change of the vile Representative System.' *Add.MSS.* 27,949(403).

[2] *Northern Liberator*, 21st September 1839.

[3] *The Times*, 15th July 1839. For biographical articles on Joseph Rayner Stephens see *The Times*, 31st December 1838, 2nd, 3rd and 5th January 1839.

mittee meetings which spies tried to infiltrate; some surreptitious drilling; and much angry muttering about a widespread armed revolt. There are distinct signs of the continued existence of a secret central 'committee of war', now based not in London but in Birmingham, and of plans for sending out a pre-arranged signal to start simultaneous risings throughout the country as soon as news was received of one successful revolt in any district.[1] Lovett's enquiries, made after his release from prison in July 1840, convinced him that the people of Yorkshire and Lancashire were ready to rise in 1839 in support of a Welsh revolt, and he mentions a meeting of some forty Chartists from Heckmondwike and district at which 'the intended rising in Wales was discussed'. Feargus O'Connor and Peter Bussey received assurances that the Chartists were 'all well provided with arms', and were asked to 'come and lead them on'. But the valiant Feargus played a double game and was conveniently called away to Ireland on urgent business; while Peter Bussey 'was very suddenly taken ill', yet could not be found by the Bradford Chartists when they searched for him![2]

Without doubt, the acquisition of arms by the Chartists was both widespread and persistent, nor was it confined to the factory and mining districts. For example, the *Suffolk Chronicle* reported that as early as February 1839, and as far east as Norwich,

'The People's Charter-men . . . have commenced arming in right good earnest . . . no less than 68 pikes have been sold among them. They are about 18 inches long, so that they can be carried in the bosom, with a sort of knife-hook at the end, for the purpose of cutting horses' reins, anticipating, we suppose, that they will come in contact with the military. A club is established for the purchase of these, to which every member pays one penny a week. The price [each] is about eightpence or ninepence, and . . . a raffle takes place to see who is to be first supplied.'

From the West Country the Anti-Corn Law lecturers reported that the Devonshire labourers, barely existing on 'a compost of ground barley and potatoes', were 'just as ready for pikes and pistols as the most excitable people of the factory towns', and were actually enquiring of travellers 'where the fighting was to be'.

But no serious attempt at insurrection was made except in South

---

[1] Edward Thompson has shown that early in 1817 there existed a 'sketchy system of national organization' in preparation for a rising intended to be controlled by secret committees from four centres in the Midlands, Lancashire and Yorkshire. E. P. Thompson, *The Making of the English Working Class* (1963), pp. 651–2.
[2] Lovett, *op. cit.*, pp. 239–41.

Wales, which had long been a seething cauldron of discontent. In May 1839 *The Times* reported that Chartists were known to be going round all the pawnshops in Bristol buying up pistols and other arms; and when two men, Henry Fawkner and Thomas Jones, 'who stated they were from Newport', were arrested, they had upon them 'a quantity of Chartist publications, eight or nine sovereigns in gold, nine pistols and three powder flasks'.[1] Doubtless other emissaries were collecting arms in other towns over a period of many months, probably down to the eve of the so-called Newport Rising in the winter of 1839, when a body mainly composed of colliers, perhaps between 1,000 and 3,000 strong, set out to march on Newport in three converging columns in the middle of the dark, wet night of 3rd–4th November, aiming to join forces near the town just before dawn. This would have been no simple operation even for professional soldiers; for the Chartists the scheme was far too ambitious and, as we now know, ended in dismal failure. But the first tidings to reach England told a very different story. In a message dated 'Newport, Monday, 11 o'clock a.m.' and published in the second edition of *The Times* on 5th November, that paper's correspondent reported:

'The Chartists have almost entire possession of the town. 7,000 or 8,000 have marched in from the hills, and attacked the Westgate Inn, where the magistrates are sitting. I have heard 30 or 40 shots fired, and learn that several of the Chartists as well as the soldiers are killed. What the end will be God only knows; they are firing now.'

In Newcastle the effect of this message was electrical. According to Thomas Devyr, who, as we know, was in the thick of things there,

'. . . delegates from 65 armed districts were [soon] assembled in Newcastle waiting for the expected Proclamation by Frost. . . . The two Shields, Sunderland, and the more distant districts of Durham and Northumberland were not present, but they were . . . prepared to rise at the expected signal. . . . We expected the gallop of a horse every instant [for] the proclamation was to radiate by horse express from the centre, Birmingham, all round.' [2]

In fact, the first tidings were false. The rising had failed miserably; and when this was made known in Newcastle by a private letter sent urgently *via* Sunderland, and by a correction in *The Times* of 6th November, exultation, turning sour, gave way to despair and desperation. But had they received confirmation of a success in Wales, or else-

[1] *Northern Liberator*, 2nd March 1839; *The Times*, 21st May 1839.
[2] Devyr, *op. cit.*, p. 200.

where, the Chartists of the north-west region would have risen *en masse*, as would those in many other districts of the North and Midlands. Speaking at Manchester in December 1841, Bronterre O'Brien asserted that John Frost 'had been led to expect that in case he was forced' into a rising, 'he should have the sympathy and support of other parts of the country'; a statement confirmed, quite independently, by Alexander Somerville who said he was 'solicited' to join in the proposed

'Welsh insurrection of 1839, which was to have taken place several times during several months, before it was actually begun by Frost and those Chartist chiefs, not less criminal than he, who misled him by the reports of what they would do in Yorkshire and Lancashire, while he raised the standard of revolt in Wales.' [1]

Immediately after the Newport Rising, 125 persons were arrested, of whom 29 were committed for trial, 21 of them, including the chief leaders, John Frost, Zephaniah Williams, and William Jones, charged with high treason. The defence of Frost, Williams and Jones, who stood in imminent danger of execution if found guilty, now took the centre of the Chartists' stage. It was imperative to arouse and focus a strong public opinion in favour of the accused men and to raise funds to pay the legal expenses. Bronterre O'Brien, of course, went to it with a will, as did Feargus O'Connor and many other Chartist leaders and associations throughout the country. On 12th January 1840, for example, O'Brien took the chair at a public tea-meeting of the Surrey Political Union, at which many women were present, to raise contributions for the defence fund. In the course of an over-long address from the chair, O'Brien spoke hopefully of the prisoners' prospects of securing an acquittal, although as a former law student he must have realized in his own mind that the chances were slender indeed. In fact, on 16th January the three prisoners were found guilty of high treason and the ancient, barbarous sentence of death by hanging, drawing and quartering was passed upon them.

When this horrifying bombshell burst, and the execution had been fixed for 1st February 1840, the Chartists redoubled their desperate efforts to save the condemned men; but the time – a bare fortnight – was terribly short. A legal appeal was lodged, and O'Connor, O'Brien, Hetherington, Cleave, Carpenter, Rogers and many other leading Radicals organized a meeting at the Crown and Anchor Tavern in the Strand to get up a petition praying for remission of the sentences, while the leading provincial political unions also did what they could in the

[1] A. Briggs (ed.), *Chartist Studies* (1959), p. 49n; Somerville, *Autobiography*, p. 422.

remaining few fleeting hours. The Surrey Political Union, for example, worked day and night to collect over 4,600 signatures on a petition for a free pardon, and 'seven voluminous petitions from various parts of the kingdom' were actually presented to Queen Victoria by Dr Wade at a royal levee. Hope, however, nearly died on 28th January when the legal appeal was dismissed; but at the last moment the death sentences were commuted to transportation for life, and by the end of February the prisoners were on board a convict ship bound for Tasmania, half a world away.[1]

Even after the Newport débâcle, certain groups of Chartists still clung obstinately to the idea of insurrection. From Halifax a magistrate reported to the Home Secretary that a Chartist group in that town still favoured a rising, but conducted better than at Newport, 'where they considered it to have been badly mismanaged'.[2] Early in 1840 the *Statesman and Weekly True Sun*, a pro-Chartist paper, reported that it had received private information 'of an intended rising of Chartists' at Sheffield in the small hours of a Sunday morning. Forewarned, the 1st Dragoon Guards, with police and constables, 'succeeded in taking seven or eight of the ringleaders and . . . an immense quantity of firearms of all descriptions, ball-cartridges, iron-bullets, hand-grenades, fire-balls, daggers, pikes – some 12 or 14 feet long – swords and an immense quantity of crow-feet, a most formidable weapon for disabling horses'. Long before the constables had finished searching the houses of suspected persons 'the police-office was literally filled with implements of warfare, and astonished the soldiers themselves'. At the same time, Thomas Devyr tells us, warlike preparations were being made in Newcastle and its neighbouring villages for a rising which was intended to spread throughout the north-east [3] like a forest fire. So bitter was the people's mood, especially in the industrial districts, that they were loath to abandon even the most desperate schemes.

[1] *State Trials* (New Series), Vol. IV (1892), pp. 85 *et seq.*, The Queen *v.* John Frost for high treason, 31st December 1839 and following days. Between pp. 1428 and 1429 in this volume is a map of Newport and district, and a plan of the Westgate Hotel, Newport, showing the position of the soldiers, fields of fire, etc., at 8.45 a.m. on Monday, 4th November 1839. *Charter*, 15th December 1839, 12th and 27th January, 2nd February 1840; Hovell, *op. cit.*, pp. 185–6.

[2] *H.O. Papers*, 40(43); cf. A. J. Peacock, *Bradford Chartism 1838–1840* (Borthwick Papers No. 36, 1969).

[3] *Statesmen and Weekly True Sun*, 19th and 26th January 1840; see also Appendix A.

Chapter VIII

COUNTER-ATTACK

TOWARDS the end of his connection with the *Operative*, which was
absorbed by the *London Dispatch* in June 1839, Bronterre O'Brien, in
the midst of the clamour and turmoil of the Chartist agitation, tried to
start another journal 'upon sound, honest, Radical principles'. On 25th
May 1839 the *Northern Star* announced a fund-raising lecture tour in
these words:

'*Direction of the Movement*

Nothing at the present moment is more important, than that the continuous flow of agitation should be kept up; while at the same time its
irresistible current is properly directed. Our readers will have learned
from the letter of Bronterre O'Brien, in our last week's paper, that it is
the intention of that indefatigable patriot to do a great deal towards the
effecting of this desirable purpose, by lecturing in all the large towns,
especially of the North. The people and the people's cause probably owe
more to Bronterre than to any other man living. . . . The people will . . .
receive much valuable instruction; and . . . he will confer a double
obligation upon his respective audiences – present gratification, and
future battling for their rights.'

While this was in the press O'Brien had already begun to break
ground at Leeds – 'a magnificent meeting' – and at Nottingham. From
Darlington the Operative Tailors' Society sent a subscription and called
upon all Chartist Associations to do the same. The money, however,
trickled in but slowly, and it was late September before the number of
quarterly subscriptions reached three hundred. O'Brien, over-sanguine
as always, was hoping to emulate in the South the success enjoyed by
O'Connor's paper in the North, but failed to realize that he lacked
comparable business flair and financial resources. His optimism was
built up by a group of enthusiasts in Brighton who, stirred by his
oratory, talked confidently of support in the chief towns throughout
Sussex and Hampshire, and commended the new *Southern Star* to all
democrats as the 'most determined Radical journal ever published in
England'. But the project still hung fire. Unable to go forward alone,

O'Brien enlisted the help of his old friend and fellow-agitator, William Carpenter, and towards the end of 1839 they ventured to announce that No. 1 of the *Southern Star and Brighton Patriot* (price 6d) would appear on 22nd December and would go 'the whole hog' on behalf of the plundered and oppressed classes. But the *Southern Star* was never a lucky star. At the very last moment publication was blocked because the Commissioners of Stamps – who had their reasons for disliking the ex-editor of the *Poor Man's Guardian* – refused to accept one of O'Brien's sureties. Feargus O'Connor's name was then substituted, only to be rejected by the Commissioners, whose obstructive tactics so incensed O'Brien and Carpenter that they threatened to put the clock back by bringing out an *unstamped* paper. O'Brien angrily protested that his first surety, Alderman Scales, was 'worth at least £40,000', and the other, Feargus O'Connor, had freehold and leasehold property worth at least £600 a year, and was actually paying the Government £13,000 annually in stamp duty. After taking their time to 'reconsider', the Commissioners accepted O'Connor as second surety, and the first number of the *Southern Star*, produced in 'circumstances of haste and embarrassment', was eventually published on 19th January 1840. But its initial circulation was barely 2,000 copies, and it never flourished. For one thing, the new paper had made its appearance too late upon a scene already over-crowded with Radical journals of all sorts. Moreover, many readers complained that the price of 6d a copy was sure to defeat its avowed primary aim – the wide diffusion of political knowledge among the masses. In April 1840 the price was brought down to 4d and the paper was reduced in size, but by dint of condensation and smaller type a proportionate reduction in reading matter was avoided. By this time, however, the Government had caught up with Bronterre and many of his fellow-agitators also. His skirmish with the Commissioners of Stamps was no more than a prelude to the big battles soon to be fought out in the County Assize Courts.[1]

To the reactionaries with privileged positions to preserve it must have seemed, by the summer of 1839, that the Government had been more than patient with such militant agitators as Bronterre O'Brien, and that further forbearance would be interpreted by the Chartists as a sign of weakness and fear. The time seemed ripe, therefore, to give them a sharp salutary lesson in governmental power by making a clean sweep. And this, indeed, was done. Wholesale arrests of Chartists were made – members of the Convention, local leaders, and scores of the

---

[1] *Penny Satirist*, 5th October 1839; 18th January 1840; *Northern Star*, 28th September, 28th December 1839; 4th January 1840; *Southern Star*, 19th January, 23rd February 1840; *Charter*, 2nd October, 24th November 1839.

rank and file – on charges ranging from unlawful assembly to high treason. Several leaders of the Manchester Political Union and the Northern Political Union of Newcastle were roped in.

'Wholesale trials followed. At Liverpool some seventy or eighty Chartists were brought up together; at Lancaster, thirty-five; at Devizes, twelve. At Welshpool thirty-one Llanidloes rioters were tried, the sentences ranging from fifteen years transportation to merely binding over to keep the peace.[1]

The Assizes and county gaols of the North and Midlands – Newcastle, York, Lancaster, Chester, Warwick – became choked with Chartists. Among the popular national leaders, Henry Vincent was tried at Monmouth at the beginning of August 1839 and sent to prison for conspiracy and unlawful assembly. Four days later, at Warwick Assizes, William Lovett and John Collins were each sentenced to one year's imprisonment for publishing a 'seditious libel' which, in fact, was nothing worse than a blunt criticism of the Birmingham magistrates and the London police they had called in to suppress the Chartists' meetings in the Bull Ring. About a week later J. R. Stephens was tried and sentenced at Chester Assizes for 'seditious words, riot, and unlawful assembly'.[2] The eclipse of Stephens, who had become extremely eccentric, was no great loss to Chartism; but to deprive the Convention of its Secretary, Lovett, for a year from August 1839 was a shrewd, severe blow at the already overloaded nerve centre of the Movement.[3] John Collins, too, was a considerable loss, for he had won popularity among the workers as a plain, sensible, earnest and colloquial speaker, and 'with a magazine of facts on the shelves of his memory', he everywhere drew great crowds 'to hear the new evangel'.[4] So great was the increase in the numbers of meetings and trials to be reported that papers such as the *Northern Liberator* were forced to use smaller type for many of their pages.

'It has come at last!' O'Brien told the Chartists. 'The Government of law has all but ended in England; the Government of the Sword has already begun. In one more brief month every gaol in England will be crammed. In one month more there will not survive a vestige of liberty in the land, except for those usurpers and murderers of society who call *you* "mob", and style themselves as the "higher and middle Orders".'

[1] Hovell, *op. cit.*, pp. 170–1.
[2] *State Trials* (New Series), Vol. III, 1831–40 (1891); *Charter*, 25th August 1839; *The Times*, 12th August 1839.
[3] Lovett, *op. cit.*, pp. 218–28.
[4] Devyr, *op. cit.*, Part I, p. 160; James Burn, *Autobiography* (1882), pp. 178–9.

141

It was, he exclaimed, the last extreme of irony that all over the country Chartists were being arrested by 'the armed cannibals who prey upon their labour', equipped with weapons bought with taxes wrung from the workman's toil and misery! He advised them, however, to repress their natural impulse to retaliate, and not to play into the hands of their enemies.

'The object of the rich is to drive you, unarmed, unorganized and un-prepared, into rebellion, in order that they may cut down the bravest of you in small sections, strike terror into the rest, then bring up your leaders, and thus crush the movement altogether.' [1]

The Government's counter-attack was certainly pressed home relentlessly on a broad front. At the end of May 1841, Peter McDouall printed in his *Chartist and Republican Journal* a 'List of 46 Chartist Victims',[2] which included the names of such leaders as Feargus O'Connor, William Benbow, and Bronterre O'Brien. But this is little more than one-tenth of the total number. An official return of prisoners confined in Great Britain for 'political' offences during the eighteen months between 1st January 1839 and 30th June 1840 shows a total of 444 – 380 in England, 63 in Wales, and 1 in Scotland – including 13 committed for high treason, and 6 for high treason and sedition. Three-quarters of a century later, an American scholar, Dr Rosenblatt, calculated that, during the same period, the number of individual convictions was 543.[3]

It goes without saying that the Government did not overlook Bron-terre O'Brien when it struck back. He was, in fact, twice brought to trial: at Newcastle Spring Assizes at the end of February 1840, and at the Lancaster County Assizes a month later. These trials were the normal sequels to various happenings during the summer of 1839. The charge brought against him at his first trial was based upon the speech he made in Newcastle-upon-Tyne on 7th July 1839, when he deputized for Dr John Taylor, who had been arrested and detained in Birmingham. On 29th July, a grand jury at Newcastle brought in a true bill against O'Brien and three others who were accused of unlawful and seditious assembly and conspiracy, but he was not arrested until a fortnight later. The prosecution relied especially upon a passage in which O'Brien was reported as having said to the assembled Chartists:

'If the Government do not accede to your demands, I advise the people

[1] *Northern Star*, 10th August 1839.
[2] No. 9, 29th May 1841, p. 67.
[3] *Parliamentary Papers 1840*, p. 600; Hovell, *op. cit.*, p. 190n.

to arm to a man to put down by force the traitors who dare to use force.
. . . I call upon you to arm with all possible means. . . . A large proportion of the Convention is in gaol already. Many of them have been
arrested for riots which the authorities have caused themselves, as they
did in Birmingham.' [1]

On 12th August, the day fixed for the Grand National Demonstrations, O'Brien, speaking at a meeting on Kennington Common, maintained that he had not exhorted his working-class friends and followers
to arm until Lord John Russell had called upon the other classes to do
the same. The workers might be subdued or enslaved, but they could no
longer be duped.[2] Feargus O'Connor was in the chair at this meeting,
and Carpenter, Cardo, Hartwell and Beniowski, the Polish refugee and
agitator,[3] were also present. On his way home from this meeting O'Brien
was served with a judge's warrant and taken to Bow Street.[4] As to what
happened next we have only O'Brien's uncorroborated word that he

'. . . was locked up all night and till one o'clock next day in a dark cell at
the station-house . . . I was not allowed a pillow . . . nor any covering to
wrap round me . . . I was not suffered to see or communicate with anybody, not even my wife. . . .' [5]

On the morning of the 13th, he appeared before a magistrate at Bow Street,
attended by his friends, Dr John Taylor and William Carpenter, and by
certain other members of the Convention. When the magistrate asked him
if he had anything to say, he replied that he would reserve his defence for
a higher and more important tribunal. Bail was not opposed; two householders came forward as sureties, and the prisoner was released.[6]

For a time O'Brien went on with his speaking engagements. Agitation, he said, must be kept up at all costs until the workers had gained
the right to elect the nation's legislators, and until power over the land
and the system of money and credit had been wrested from the aristocratic and middle classes. The day would surely come when peaceable
agitation would sway public opinion in the people's favour.[7]

---

[1] *Northern Star*, 3rd August 1839; *True Scotsman*, 3rd August 1839.
[2] *Sun*, 14th August 1839; *Northern Star*, 17th August 1839; *Northern
Liberator*, 17th August 1839.
[3] See Hovell, *op. cit.*, p. 177. In 1838 Beniowski had wanted the London
Working Men's Association to have medals cast with 'our six principles on
them'. *Add.MSS.* 37,773(123).
[4] *The Times*, 13th August 1839; *Sun*, 14th August 1839.
[5] *The Times*, 23rd October 1839.
[6] *Northern Star*, 17th August 1839.
[7] *Champion and Weekly Herald*, 25th August 1839.

All Bronterre O'Brien's movements were now closely watched by the authorities, who were again preparing to pounce. Early in October 1839, O'Brien was arrested, taken to Bow Street, and brought before the magistrate on a second charge. On this occasion he was required to find bail in £200 himself, and two sureties of £100 each: sums which were exactly double those previously required, and in O'Brien's view excessive. He protested that he had never acquired much property, and, indeed, he had at that very moment an execution in his house. He compared his bail with that required of Feargus O'Connor, arguing that £50 from him was more than £150 from O'Connor. 'I am,' he said, 'already held to bail, and have found sureties . . . for my appearance to answer another charge.' But the magistrate was deaf to these arguments. Fortunately, before the magistrate left the Court, two sureties, named M'Connell and Brooks, agreed to enter into the necessary recognizances for O'Brien's appearance at the Assizes, and he was liberated.[1]

A few days after this second arrest O'Brien made a formal complaint to the Bow Street magistrate about his treatment on the evening when the police took him into custody, alleging that he had been forced, while in ill-health, to lie all night on bare boards, and that his wife was not permitted to provide him with a pillow or a blanket. He also addressed a long, indignant letter to the editor of *The Times* complaining that his treatment by the police at the time of his first arrest had been nothing short of barbarous, and on the second occasion it was no better.

'I was arrested between the hours of 11 and 12 o'clock on Tuesday night, while returning from a friend's house, where I had passed the evening, accompanied by my wife. The arrest took place at the entrance to Palsgrave-place . . . and was effected by Sergeant Kerr "assisted" by two constables . . . to my astonishment, I found, upon arriving at the station house, that the inspector on duty there would not hear a word. . . . He would neither accommodate me himself nor suffer my wife to do so, but beckoning with his hand (without uttering a word), pointed to the passage which leads to the cells in the yard! I was immediately hustled off, and as before, locked up for the night in one of those dens of infamy to which pickpockets, prostitutes and persons accused of felony are taken before committal. . . . A convicted felon is allowed a bed or a rug to lie down upon, and is not debarred from all intercourse with his friends. I have been denied these common necessaries . . . and . . . be it observed, the accusations against me come from two Whig corporations, the leading members of which (including Fife, the Mayor of Newcastle, and Potter, the Mayor of Manchester) have uttered more

[1] *Sheffield Iris*, 15th October 1839.

144

"sedition" . . . in one week during the Reform Bill agitation than I have uttered all my life. . . . Your reporter . . . makes it appear that Sergeant Kerr had some difficulty in finding me, that he had "attended five or six public meetings for that purpose, and at last succeeded in capturing me". All this, Sir, is incorrect. Sergeant Kerr knew well where to find me . . . in my own home . . . had his employers thought proper to send him. . . . But it suited their base purpose, instead of arresting me in the morning, and at my own home, to arrest me at night, and away from my house, in order to have me locked up in a dungeon for 13 hours. . . .'[1]

Exactly seven months elapsed between the true bill against O'Brien at Newcastle and his trial, which opened at Newcastle Spring Assizes on 29th February 1840. He was indicted, together with four active members of the Northern Political Union – Thomas Devyr of the *Northern Liberator*, and three craftsmen, James Ayre, John Mason, and William Thomason – on three counts, *viz.*, first, unlawfully assembling in Newcastle on 7th July 1839; second, seditiously meeting to raise discontent and breaches of the peace, and by inflammatory speeches to obstruct the execution of the laws; and third, conspiring with the like objects. The number of persons alleged to have been subjected to these evil influences was estimated at one thousand.

No sooner had proceedings begun than O'Brien asked the judge, Mr Justice Coleridge, whether he could be tried separately, on the ground that he had attended the meeting independently of the other accused persons, and, in his submission, experience proved that where persons, against each of whom the evidence was different, were mixed up in one charge, there was a risk of injustice because the jury might easily confuse the evidence against one with that against the others. After consultation with Mr Justice Erskine, the judge refused O'Brien's request as there was no precedent; no injustice would be done by proceeding; and the state of the business of the Assize demanded all possible despatch compatible with justice.[2] 'I will offer no further objection,' said O'Brien, 'if I may be allowed to defer addressing the jury until after counsel for the other prisoners.' To this the judge raised no objection.

Briefly, the case for the crown was that on 7th July 1839, at a meeting held in the Music Room in Nelson Street, Newcastle, to protest against the use of a force of soldiers and London police to break up a Chartist meeting at Birmingham on 4th July,[3] O'Brien had made a speech in

---

[1] *The Times*, 23rd October 1839; cf. *Northern Star*, 2nd November 1839. On John Fife's violent anti-Tory activities in 1832, see Schoyen, *op. cit.*, pp. 42–3.

[2] *State Trials* (New Series), Vol. IV, 1839–43, pp. 1341–5.

[3] Hovell, *op. cit.*, p. 156, says that the Birmingham meeting was certainly illegal, but the magistrates acted hastily and recklessly.

145

which he had used such expressions as 'to put down by force the traitors who dared to use force'. This speech had been reported for the *Tyne Mercury* by one Henderson, who was called as witness for the Crown. There were, said Henderson, other speeches besides O'Brien's, after which the meeting carried a resolution: 'That the Government have committed high treason against the Queen and Constitution by attempting to disperse the people of Birmingham while discussing their mighty grievances.'

O'Brien, conducting his own defence, was greatly helped both by his legal studies and his inside knowledge of journalism. He cross-examined Henderson and made him admit that newspaper reports of political speeches, including even those of Members of Parliament, were often 'coloured' and garbled. O'Brien then pointed out that the report in the *Northern Liberator* differed materially from Henderson's report written for the *Tyne Mercury*, and forced the witness to agree that one of them was probably wrong. O'Brien next proceeded to 'refresh' the witness's memory on various points of detail concerning incidents at the meeting, until the judge said to Henderson, 'You seem to have left out a great deal of important matter.' After hearing further cross-examination by O'Brien and re-examination by counsel for the prosecution, the judge suggested that, while there was certainly some evidence to go to the jury, it was insufficient to enable the Court to ascertain the actual tendency of the speeches. Counsel for the Crown, however, decided to go on with the case. J. P. Cobbett, counsel for Thomason, then addressed the jury at considerable length, after which Bronterre O'Brien rose to speak in his own defence.

He began by saying that the report in the *Tyne Mercury* was false. Although he was prepared to admit he often used strong language, he was always careful to keep within the law. At the meeting in question he had said that the people had good reason for their great excitement, but at the same time he had counselled obedience to the laws so long as the magistrates acted legally. The learned counsel on the other side had defined sedition as language calculated to alarm Her Majesty's peaceable subjects, and language calculated to provoke a breach of the peace, riots, tumults, and so forth. Now, although during the past eight or nine months he had addressed two millions of people, in not a single instance had a breach of the peace resulted. Moreover, the audience at the Newcastle meeting were evidently not alarmed, for they applauded him most vociferously. The chairman of the meeting should have vacated the chair if he heard any seditious language. Why was this not done? Simply because the chairman – one of the most amiable men in Newcastle – had felt that there *was* no sedition. O'Brien then read, from several news-

146

paper articles, passages which were, he suggested, more violent than anything in his speech, and closed his defence with a confident assertion that the evidence was obviously valueless, and he believed the jury would share his opinion. He had spoken for an hour and a half.

Mr Justice Coleridge, summing up, remarked that Henderson was the only prosecution witness, and although he had doubtless acted 'honestly', it was clear that he reported for a paper hostile to the Chartists, and that he did not go to the meeting with the object of making a *full* report such as would serve the purposes of a Court of Law, but only to take such notes as would suit his own immediate object. A person indicted for a printed libel had a right to have *the whole* of it read, and the same principle applied to what a man said. Had the jury before them sufficient of O'Brien's speech?

'The language he admits using is very strong, even intemperate [said the judge], but he cannot be punished for that. The real question is whether, upon the whole, it was calculated to produce the effects charged in the indictment. . . . The procuring of fire-arms is not an unlawful act, the people have a right to have arms; but the question is whether they were to get these arms for the purpose of using them against the public peace. . . . But I must here remark what a dangerous thing it is to incite the people to arm, and to make them the sole judges of whether they had a right to interfere.'[1]

Subsequently the *Northern Liberator* remarked with approval that the judge had '. . . discountenanced minute criticism of particular expressions. He told the jury to judge only from an entire speech of the honesty and good intentions of the speaker; wisely observing that an extempore speaker might easily drop, in the heat of speaking, objectionably or imprudently-worded sentences, which the tenor of the whole might contradict and neutralize'.

After a hearing lasting twelve hours the jury took only fifteen minutes to bring in a verdict of 'not guilty' in favour of all the accused, except Thomas Devyr who was absent. Spontaneous cheers shattered the dignified atmosphere of the closely packed court, and when O'Brien and his elated fellows appeared to the huge crowd waiting in the street 'the air was rent with exclamations of gratulation and joy'.[2] The acquittals were hailed as a brilliant popular victory, and that night a celebration dinner was held at which George Julian Harney, Robert

[1] *State Trials*, Vol. IV, *op. cit.*, pp. 1344–5.
[2] *Northern Star*, 7th and 28th March 1840; the *Northern Liberator*, 6th March 1840, carried a leading article and a full report on O'Brien's trial.

Lowery, and other Chartist leaders made congratulatory speeches 'amid wild enthusiasm and cheers for Bronterre O'Brien,[1] who must have felt on top of the world at that moment, for he had achieved a considerable personal triumph by repulsing so decisively the Government's attack upon himself and the Newcastle Chartists. The *Southern Star*, of course, was jubilant, attributing the collapse of the case for the Crown to O'Brien's astute cross-examination of Henderson. The *Charter* reacted more soberly, expressing the opinion that despite the indiscreet language undoubtedly used by that 'somewhat crotchety politician', Mr O'Brien, the verdict constituted a 'direct censure' upon a vindictive Government actuated by 'passion and class prejudices'. Why, asked the *Charter*, had Vincent, Lovett, and Collins not been similarly acquitted: 'may it not be said that they were punished upon a false pretence?'[2] To his old comrade, William Carpenter, then trying to run the *Southern Star*, O'Brien wrote exultantly: 'I have beaten the Philistines . . . as dead as Mark Antony! . . . Should I meet with similar success in Lancashire, it will be a glorious triumph indeed.' In a similar strain he wrote to the Chartists and Radical Reformers of London, Brighton, the Isle of Wight, and the southern counties, claiming that, as a result of the Newcastle trial, every one of the impending prosecutions for sedition and conspiracy in the County of Durham had been 'virtually abandoned'. 'Give me Mr Justice Erskine, or Coleridge, in Liverpool, and a jury to correspond, and I think I may safely promise you . . . one more triumph over the Philistines.'[3]

Thomas Devyr of the *Northern Liberator*, who should have been in court side by side with Bronterre O'Brien and the others, had neither part nor pride in these rejoicings, for on the eve of the trial he had jumped his bail and fled in panic with his wife and family and a druggist named John Rucastle to the United States, where he eventually arrived with only fifteen pence in his pocket. In his autobiography he says that

'Twenty minutes before I started for America, I had not the remotest idea of ever crossing the Atlantic. . . . I left it [the Chartist Movement] when I saw myself without means of resisting the Government. I had no disposition to submit to its vengeance.'

He ought to have been utterly ashamed of his dishonourable conduct, for not only had he failed to put up a fight for Chartism, but he had badly betrayed his sureties.

'I was,' he wrote, 'under two separate bonds on charges of sedition.

[1] Howell Collection (Bishopsgate Institute), News Cuttings, fo. 44.
[2] *Charter*, 8th March 1840; *Northern Liberator*, 13th March 1840.
[3] *Southern Star*, 8th and 15th March 1840.

My employers were securities on one, and John Blakey, clogger, and I think Richard Ayr, publican, on the other. The latter two, fearing to lose the amount of the recognizance, had us pursued to Liverpool, whence we narrowly . . . got away. The former retained an amount of my salary which they were, indeed, entitled to retain to cover the risk. The Government did exact the penalty, but returned it again at the intercession of the then member for Gateshead.'

No word here of apology or contrition: a poor showing throughout. Devyr got a job in journalism and settled in Williamsburg, Long Island; but apparently he found the republican United States little more to his liking than the monarchical United Kingdom, and soon he realized, as did Charles Dickens: 'This is not the Republic of my imagination.' [1]

From the platform of the new lecture room in Nelson Street, Newcastle, two days after the trial, O'Brien addressed the Tynesiders. According to the *Northern Liberator*, an enthusiastic audience crammed the room to suffocation to hear a lengthy discourse 'in his usual style of oratory' denouncing the Government's attack upon him and many other Chartists, and setting forth the principles of true democracy. Eventually, he drew to a conclusion by referring to his approaching trial in Lancashire, which, he said, with almost prophetic insight, would probably not be such a triumph as the first one. Nevertheless, he was determined to persevere in the cause of 'the poor oppressed against the rich oppressor' so long as he was able and at liberty to do so. At this the audience sprang to its feet and, led by George Julian Harney, gave three resounding cheers for Bronterre O'Brien. [2]

A few days later O'Brien traversed the extreme North of England from Newcastle to Carlisle, where the local Chartists and Radicals packed the theatre to hear him. Having referred with characteristic humour and sarcasm to his trial at Newcastle, he went on to deal in forthright terms with the existing misery and discontent, and the remedy – universal suffrage. 'Mr O'Brien reminds us,' said the editor of the *Northern Star*, 'very much of the late Mr Cobbett, in his manner of going into the subject of which he treats. . . .' The next day O'Brien went about five miles into the country to preach one of his Sunday political 'sermons' at the small town of Dalston where lived many active Chartists. This was the place where Harney had been met by two men accoutred with sword and musket, who marched about playing a fife and drum to call out the inhabitants, many of whom carried heavy

[1] Devyr, *op. cit.*, Part I, pp. 208–11; Part II, *passim*; A. Wilson, *The World of Charles Dickens* (1970), pp. 153–70.
[2] *Northern Liberator*, 7th March 1840.

sticks and knives.[1] There is nothing to suggest that O'Brien was simi-larly honoured: perhaps weapons were not carried in Dalston on Sundays.

Although O'Brien's defence and acquittal had enhanced his popu-larity among the workpeople, he was by no means out of danger from the Government and the law, for a second trial was imminent. At this time, too, Feargus O'Connor and several other Chartist leaders were facing similar charges, and in order to raise money to meet their legal expenses, a great Radical meeting was held in Manchester on 23rd March 1840. The two Irishmen were both billed to speak, but for some reason or other O'Brien failed to arrive. O'Connor, however, filled the gap with a long speech, the audience rose to him, and the meeting was proclaimed a huge success.

O'Brien's second trial took place at the Lancaster County Assizes in Liverpool at the end of March 1840, when he, together with three Man-chester Chartists, the Reverend William Vickers Jackson, R. J. Richard-son, and William Butterworth, stood indicted not for a single seditious speech, but for a seditious conspiracy (with various 'intents', such as malicious and illegal excitement of discontent, riots, and routs; induce-ment of arming, and intimidation of the Government), and with having committed certain overt acts in furtherance of such objects during a tour of Lancashire in the summer of 1839. There were four counts to the indictment: two charging the defendants with seditious conspiracy, and two charging them with unlawful assemblies and seditious speeches. Mr Justice Coleridge was again the judge. Sergeant Atcherley appeared for the prosecution; Butterworth and Jackson had counsel; O'Brien and Richardson defended themselves. In his opening speech Sergeant Atcherley said that the first political meeting at which the alleged offences were committed was held at Batty's Circus, Manchester, on 23rd April 1839. All the defendants were there.[2] The chairman had spoken of 'ulterior measures' and O'Brien said that he was glad to find them 'up to the mark', as were the people of Leigh, Chowbent, and other places, where everyone had signed the petition and was pre-pared with 'a sharp argument' – a pike for every signature – and if all the men in England acted similarly, England would soon be free. The National Petition was a notice to quit to the House of Com-mons; and if they would not go, resort should be had to a writ of ejectment.

Witnesses were examined and after counsel for Butterworth and

[1] *Northern Star*, 14th March 1840; Schoyen, *op. cit.*, p. 47.
[2] It appears from the *Northern Star*'s report that William Benbow, too, was present; cf. *H.O. Papers*, 40(43).

150

Jackson had addressed the jury, O'Brien opened his defence. He was not aware, he said, that the meeting in question was illegal, for the object was merely to petition Parliament. As for the speech attributed to him, 'it was as the grinning skeleton to the living form'. His influence had always been exerted against illegal and seditious practices, and in support of obedience to the law until the demonstration of the public mind in favour of change had become so general that there could be no illegality. The unoppressed minority, on the other hand, were openly advised to arm in order to put down the majority. The people had, he argued, a right to meet peaceably to discuss their grievances; a right not to be oppressively arrested; a right to *habeas corpus*; a right to trial by jury – *a right which was undermined because poor men were not tried by men of their own class*. He also emphasized the Englishman's undoubted right to arm in self-defence. The *Manchester Guardian's* reporter was not, he contended, a disinterested witness and the more sincere he was in his politics, the more he would be likely to misrepresent him (O'Brien) and to garble his speech. Nobody had more right to use strong language about the Government than he had, for he had been treated unjustly many times; notices of his meetings had been repeatedly torn down by the police; when he had tried to start a newspaper, the Government had refused for four months to accept his sureties. The true cause of public disaffection lay not in his speeches but in widespread starvation, low wages, and various acts of oppression, such as harsh police action. If the prosecution secured a verdict against him, it would be but a mean triumph over a man already broken in health and fortune; it would certainly not be a victory over the cause he had espoused.

After Richardson had addressed the jury, the judge summed up. Reviewing the evidence he said that although the meetings were peaceable and no disrespectful language had been used of the Queen, the expressions used by O'Brien and the others about 'sharp arguments', pikes, and so forth, were, in his opinion, tantamount to a determination to obtain an object by force; therefore, they were illegal. When the judge went on to mention the general strike, O'Brien interjected that he had himself prevented it.

The verdict was 'guilty' against all the accused; but the business of the court was so congested with the trials of other Chartists that sentences were not passed immediately. Instead, O'Brien and the others were released temporarily on bail to await sentence in due course.

Mr Justice Coleridge must have fallen heavily in O'Brien's estimation when, on 9th April, he sent him to prison for eighteen months, at the same time requiring him to give a £500 bond and to find two sureties of

151

£150 each to guarantee that he would keep the peace for three years. [1]

This trial clearly shows that at the end of March 1840 O'Brien was not half the man who had won his case at Newcastle a month earlier. Evidently the strain of his exertions during 1839 had begun to impair his mental and physical health. His defence at his second trial was marred by many irrelevancies and lacked the moderation which told so strongly in his favour in the previous trial. On the other hand, the case against him at the Lancaster Assizes was prepared with greater skill and care, for this time the Government was taking no chances. The net was much stronger, but the captive certainly was not.

After sentence O'Brien was taken to the gaol in Lancaster Castle, and on 18th April 1840 the *Northern Star* printed a notice:

'It is Mr Bronterre O'Brien's particular request that all letters, parcels, and other communications intended for him, shall, till further notice, be addressed to the care of Mr J. G. Smith, Bookseller, Scotland-place, Liverpool, or to Mrs O'Brien, 3 North Place, Kennington Road, Lambeth, London, by whom they will be forwarded to him, or their contents made known, as far as the prison regulations allow. It is also Mr O'Brien's particular request that no communications intended for him shall be addressed to the *Southern Star* office, as Mr O'Brien has no longer any connection with that or any other journal.'

When John Finch, one of Robert Owen's most ardent lieutenants, heard of O'Brien's conviction, he suggested to his 'Dear Social Father' that the time was ripe to persuade Bronterre O'Brien and others like him to abandon Chartism and embrace Owenism.[2] Finch, however, had mistaken his man and nothing came of his bright idea. It is true that O'Brien was utterly exhausted both mentally and physically, and deeply depressed during many bitter days of disillusion by the tremendous force of the Government's blow at Chartism and by the length of his sentence, coming as it did, so soon after his complete acquittal at Newcastle. The prison regulations restricted his reading matter to the Bible and the Book of Common Prayer, and his writing was severely limited to a few personal letters, and even these had to be left open for scrutiny by the prison censor. To a man of Bronterre O'Brien's tastes

---

[1] *Manchester Times*, 11th April 1840; *Northern Star*, 11th April 1840; *Statesman and Weekly True Sun*, 12th April 1840; *State Trials*, Vol. IV, *op. cit.*, p. 1345; *H.O. Papers* 18, Bundle 52.

[2] John Finch to Robert Owen, Letter dated 8th April 1840, in Manchester Collection of Owen's Correspondence. On John Finch (1784–1857) and Owenism, see J. F. C. Harrison, *Robert Owen and the Owenites* (1969), pp. 122–6.

and way of life such narrow restrictions on his reading and writing must have been punishment indeed. But, on the other hand, his enforced idleness gave him a sorely-needed rest of body and mind, and ample time and opportunity for thinking. Samuel Daniel, the Elizabethan poet and tutor, somewhere sagely remarks that

> '... the best way unto discretion is
> The way that leads us by adversity.
> And men are better showed what is amiss
> By the expert finger of calamity,
> Than they can be by all that Fortune brings,
> Who never shows them the true face of things.'

O'Brien now had leisure to reflect, deeply and at length, upon 'the true face of things'. In his mind's eye he was able to review the course of the Chartist movement so far, and to consider its future – and his own. The end product was his abandonment of physical force: henceforth, if measured by the standards of his earlier days, he was to be a moderate. But although his opinions about methods were changing, his zeal for the Chartist cause and his genuine desire for its success remained unquenched.

Meantime, O'Brien's imprisonment had left his wife and young family almost penniless, and when this became known several local Chartist bodies rallied to their support. Early in June 1840, for example, the Metropolitan Charter Association decided 'to take into consideration the best means of effectually and permanently providing for the family of that incarcerated patriot, Mr O'Brien'.[1] The Brighton Chartists also came to the rescue, while the *Northern Star* increased its price by one halfpenny, to fivepence a copy, in order to raise extra revenue to assist the families of imprisoned Chartists. The usual allowance was £1 a week per family, and O'Brien stated publicly (at the height of his quarrel with Feargus O'Connor) that Mrs O'Brien had, in fact, received from the *Northern Star* £1 a week throughout the whole period of his imprisonment; a total of £80. But Mrs O'Brien's relations with the *Southern Star* were very different, for in the spring of 1840 she became involved in a dispute with Thomas Smith (who had put money into the *Southern Star* after O'Brien left it) because she objected to the publication of statements that the paper was being continued for her benefit. On 2nd June 1840 *The Times* printed a dignified denial from her,[2] to which the editor of the *Southern Star* retorted, with more

[1] *Northern Star*, 6th June 1840.

[2] *Southern Star*, 26th April 1840; *Statesman and Weekly True Sun*, 26th April 1840; *Northern Star*, 30th May 1840; *The Times*, 2nd June 1840. It seems unlikely that the *Southern Star* was making a profit at this time.

vehemence than gallantry, that 'it has been said and proved that the paper was conducted for the benefit of Mr O'Brien and his family, and any assertion or insinuation of Mrs O'Brien to the contrary is a calumny and a falsehood'.[1]

The southerners did not forget Bronterre during his imprisonment. When Peter McDouall went down to Sussex in June 1841 he found, in one of the secluded valleys among the South Downs near Brighton, 'a rural Chartist tea-party, got up for the benefit of James Bronterre O'Brien'.

'I observed,' he wrote, 'several hundreds of Chartists enjoying themselves with all kinds of games, and the various groups of cricket players, dancers, &c., formed a picturesque sight on the green grass. After tea the drums and fiddles beat and played for the gathering. I mounted the bank of one of the reservoirs and addressed the audience. I found a glorious spirit pervading the minds of the majority, at the same time that I perceived a strangeness of look and fidgety bearing on the part of those to whom the principles were new. . . .'

Later in the day the meeting adjourned to a large room at an inn where McDouall was introduced to

'. . . the unadulterated democrats – the real grain and no chaff. There all was energy, enthusiasm and principle. John Good, once a delegate to the General Convention, now an earnest advocate of the Chartist cause; always a democrat bold, and to be the M.P. for Brighton, filled the chair, [presiding over] a whole roomful of noble-hearted men. . . . The public meeting [also] did honour to the Brighton Chartists, first because it was in the Town Hall and, secondly because the room was completely filled.'[2]

After Bronterre had lain isolated and almost *incommunicado* in Lancaster Castle for six months, much of his normal optimism revived, stimulated, almost certainly, by the prospect of access to books and writing materials during the remainder of his sentence. In October 1840 he wrote a somewhat jaunty letter to the editor of the *Northern Star*.

'*Lancaster Castle,*

Monday, 11th October 1840.

Dear Sir,

To save me the trouble of writing to a great many friends, will you be kind enough to insert this, informing our brother Chartists that, at last,

[1] *The Times*, 3rd June 1840.
[2] McDouall's *Chartist and Republican Journal*, No. 13, 26th June 1841, p. 97.

154

after six months' memorializing and battling with the Visiting Magistrates of this gaol, myself and fellow-prisoners will be henceforward allowed the free use of books, writing materials, correspondence, &c., subject only to the Government's controul and inspection, which we have reason to believe will not be needlessly or captiously exercised.

Our friends in the good cause may therefore expect to hear oftener from us in future; and meanwhile Mr O'Connor ought to be informed of this, that he may take such steps as may induce the Yorkshire magistrates to allow him similar privileges, if he have them not already.

Thanks to the good air of Lancaster Castle – which stands on very high ground – to our own good consciences . . . as well as prayers eight times a week in chapel, . . . we are in tolerably good health and spirits, notwithstanding our long and close confinement. You will guess that it is close enough, and that though we confess with Parson Rowley eight times a week that we are erring and straying like lost sheep, there is no danger of our straying very far from here. When I tell you that there are two great iron doors to each of our cells, a solid and massive one, and a grated one – that our day-room is separated from our yard by three other doors of *the right sort*, while the only window attached to it is ornamented with four rows of strong iron bars . . . which, with the aid of a high dead wall close behind, not only saves us from a superfluity of light, but are equally effective, with our worthy Chaplain's prayers, to correct our tendency to err and stray like lost sheep.

Add to this, that our yard or play-ground (which is just *five* yards by *ten*, one-half of it occupied by tubs, chamber-pots, skilly noggins, and a score of the like ornaments) is on all sides surrounded by high walls . . . and without saying aught of the dozen other doors and gates between us and the profane public, our friends will at once see that . . . Parson Rowley's flock is, at any rate, *dead safe* – aye even from sedition, privy conspiracy, and rebellion.

Yours, &c.

James Bronterre O'Brien.'

Apparently the promise of books was greater than the performance, for the *Morning Chronicle* called public attention to the 'astounding absurdity' of the fact that, after much demurring and discussion, O'Brien had only been allowed a copy of Blackstone's *Commentaries on the Laws of England*, 'a few works of classical literature having been refused him'. Writing materials, however, were not severely limited after October 1840, and a number of articles from O'Brien's pen, such as those written for McDouall's *Chartist and Republican Journal*, were published during his imprisonment.[1] He was able, also, to write to the *Northern Star*, re-establish contact with his friends in the Chartist movement, and exchange views with them on future policy. Unfortunately, hardly any of these letters have survived, but the one to his friend, John M'Crae of Kilbarchan, a leader of the Ayrshire Chartists, is probably typical.

'*Lancaster,*

12th December 1840

My dear M'Crae,

I have duly received your kind letter through Mrs O'Brien, and beg to transmit her and my best thanks to our good friends the females of Kilbarchan, for the repeated proofs of sympathy and good will I have experienced from them since my imprisonment. . . .

I am delighted to hear that the "good cause prospers" in your quarter, and I am happy to say that I receive, almost every day, similar gratifying accounts from other parts of the kingdom. From what I can collect, however, I incline to believe that there is far more zeal and perseverance on your side of the border than on ours . . . really I have seen so much jealousy, so much petty squabbling and slander, and so little of charity and friendly feeling amongst the leaders, generally, wherever I have been, that I have been tempted sometimes to abandon the cause altogether in despair, and even now can see little hopes of success while such feelings predominate. I never visited Manchester or Brighton, or several other places I might name, that I did not find most of the leaders at loggerheads, and though I generally succeeded in making peace amongst them, and keeping it while I remained, yet no sooner was I gone than the old feuds broke out again. . . . Is there no remedy for this evil? If there be not, I fear we shall never succeed . . . how can we expect those, who look upon us as leaders, to be united if we be not united amongst ourselves? Have you not observed that the moment dissensions began in the Convention, that moment the country became divided also, and then also began the system of arrests and persecution by the Government. . . . My accounts from Manchester, Brighton and the Isle of Wight, and several other places are, on the whole, cheering. In Manchester great numbers are being every week enrolled in the Association and, what is still more gratifying, a majority of the new members are Irishmen! . . . If the Irish resident in England will but go on as they have begun, you will hear of glorious sport on both sides of the Channel before long, for when the Irish take any thing up they go the Whole Hog at once, and go it right gallantly into the

[1] L. C. Wright, *op. cit.*, pp. 115, 121.

bargain. . . . I find, in spite of all that false friends and open enemies and jealous calumniators have done to ruin and depopularize me (in order to render me useless to the cause) . . . that I possess the confidence and affections of thinking Chartists in all parts of the country, where my name and public conduct are known. . . .

Yours very sincerely,

James B. O'Brien.'

Although O'Brien had written cheerfully about his health in the autumn of 1840, a rumour got abroad in the following spring that his life was in danger. In May 1841 several petitions praying for his release were sent to the Home Secretary from meetings of working men in London, Salford, Bristol, Brighton, Bradford, and Newport (I.W.). The Londoners sent a deputation to the Home Office, while the Brighton petition, bearing thirty signatures, sounded a note of warning:

'Your memorialists beg to urge on your Lordship the fact that the great mass of the industrious classes would deem the decease of James Bronterre O'Brien as a national calamity, and in the event of this happening prematurely in a felon's dungeon, your Memorialists are apprehensive that the industrious clases generally would regard it as premeditated on the part of the Government.'

These appeals, however, availed nothing, for the prison surgeon promptly certified that O'Brien's life was not in danger; on the contrary, his health had improved since he had been in prison.[1] So, with what patience he could muster, O'Brien had to remain in Lancaster Gaol until the autumn of 1841. But now that he had pen, ink, and paper he was no longer inactive.

Lord Melbourne's Whig administration was brought down in May 1841 by a defeat in Parliament on its budget proposals, and after some procrastination, Parliament was dissolved in time for a summer general election. The Chartists' Election Committee at Newcastle-upon-Tyne immediately went into action by inviting Bronterre O'Brien to accept nomination as their candidate.[2] Despite his imprisonment and consequent remoteness from the scene of action, O'Brien accepted the invitation and issued an election address, dated 'Lancaster Castle, 23rd

---

[1] *H.O. Papers* 18, Bundle 52(4). O'Brien appears in the Criminal Register and the Register of Petitions as 'James Bronterre O'Brien; aged 35; degree of instruction – superior'. No remarks upon his character appear in the column provided; *H.O. Papers* 27, Vol. 61, fo. 470; *H.O. Papers* 19, Vol. 9.

[2] *Northern Star*, 19th June 1841; David Cecil, *Melbourne* (1955), pp. 356–7.

June 1841',[1] 'To the Electors and Non-Electors of the Borough of Newcastle-on-Tyne'. After appealing for a frank, hearty union between the electors and non-electors, O'Brien set out a summary of his political beliefs and economic policies. He described himself as a 'Conservative Radical Reformer' standing for peace, liberty, justice, and order for all, 'founded upon the freely expressed will of the majority, and for the radical reform of 'all that is unsound in our institutions', while conserving 'all that is sound'; and in particular for Parliamentary Reform 'upon the plans and principles of the People's Charter'. He declared himself in favour of liberty of the press and of opinion, and against all privileged monopolies, 'whether of wealth, power, or knowledge', and all restrictions upon trade and industry designed to favour particular vested interests. He also strongly urged a thorough revision of the system of taxation and a reduction of its burdens.[2] Although the glint of pikes and the smell of gunpowder are conspicuously absent, and the candidate skates over several patches of thin ice, the address ably outlines an advanced Radical programme designed to win the support not only of convinced Chartists, but all others holding genuine progressive opinions. It clearly shows that O'Brien's thinking was far ahead of most of his contemporaries, and as Hovell remarked, it stirs the imagination to think of him taking part in important parliamentary debates on subjects such as the Corn Laws. 'How he would have laid about him.' [3] Certainly he would have done greater credit to Chartism in the Commons than did Feargus O'Connor, who quite failed to impress the House either in 1833 when he sat for County Cork, or in 1847 when he was returned for Nottingham.[4] In point of fact, O'Brien's supporters claimed that he *had* been elected by 'an overwhelming majority of the electors and non-electors', and the *Northern Star*, under the headline 'Bronterre O'Brien, M.P. for Newcastle', argued that a petition to the House must result in the seating of O'Brien, for the other candidates, Ord, the Whig, and Hind, a Peelite Tory, had been decisively rejected! O'Brien maintained that he had been elected by a show of hands, and *as no poll was taken to reverse the decision thus given by the electors, he was one of the chosen representatives*. It was proposed to levy a shilling a head upon all members of the National Charter Association to meet the legal expenses. Indeed, an O'Brien Petition Fund was actually opened in Newcastle, but the task was beyond the slender means of the wage-

[1] See Appendix B below.
[2] *Northern Star*, 10th and 31st July 1841. Copies of this election address were subsequently printed and sold as penny pamphlets.
[3] Hovell, *op. cit.*, p. 240.
[4] Cf. Read and Glasgow, *op. cit.*, pp. 32, 124.

earners. Nevertheless 'from his felon's cell' O'Brien did not forget to send them his thanks, for their conduct in the election had, he said, 'outshone everything hitherto known in the history of elections. You have flung into the shade wealth, rank, station, local connections – everything that ignorance worships and that commands the homage of slaves and parasites'.[1] The men of Newcastle, he told a Birmingham audience, in 1842, had elected him to the House of Commons, but 'such was the love the ruling powers had to him that nothing but a castle was thought fit for his residence; instead of sitting with the big thieves in London, he was compelled to herd with the small thieves at Lancaster'.[2]

The general election of 1841 was the first to be held since the emergence of the Chartist Movement and the formation, at about the same time, of the Anti-Corn Law League which, with ample funds, able leaders, singleness of purpose, and solid middle-class support, quickly became a powerful rival of Chartism. Many Chartists were uncertain about the policy they ought to pursue. Feargus O'Connor told his followers that they should support the Tories so that the Whigs might be crushed; for if the Whigs were re-elected they would have another seven years in which to ride roughshod over the working class. But if they were defeated, adversity would make them more willing to listen to the Chartists' claims.[3] Bronterre O'Brien's vehement repudiation of this policy marks the beginning of his ultimate break with Feargus O'Connor.

Hitherto the agitation for the repeal of the Corn Laws had been regarded by nearly all Chartists, including O'Brien, as a counter-stroke organized by their middle-class enemies. The anti-Corn Law movement was, in O'Brien's eyes, an attempt to side-track the Chartist agitation for political rights by holding before poor, ill-fed working people the alluring prospect of cheap food; 'a bait which would crumble to powder in their grasp', because if food prices fell, money

---

[1] *Northern Star*, 10th, 17th, 31st July, 21st August, 20th November 1841. Seven other Chartist 'hustings' candidates presented themselves in 1841 in constituencies as far apart as Carlisle and Marylebone, Leeds and Tynemouth. Peter McDouall claimed that he had been elected at Northampton in 1841 'by the largest show of hands ever given to any former candidate'; but he came bottom of the poll; McDouall's *Chartist and Republican Journal*, No. 16, July 1841, pp. 121–2. G. J. Harney gave Lord Palmerston a face-to-face thrashing on foreign policy at Tiverton in 1847 and won easily on the show of hands, but not, of course, when the poll was taken, because the large crowds contained few legal voters. Schoyen, *op. cit.*, pp. 150–2; see also G. D. H. Cole, *British Working Class Politics 1832–1914* (1941), *passim*.

[2] *Northern Star*, 21st May 1842.

[3] *Northern Star*, 19th and 26th June, 3rd July 1841; Hovell, *op. cit.*, p. 239.

159

BRONTERRE

wages would be reduced, and the real income of the workers would be no greater than before. The anti-Corn Law agitation 'was got up to put down Chartism' by catching Chartists in a dangerous trap. The Charter, O'Brien argued, would be less difficult to obtain and *its* benefits would be not illusory, but real. He would stubbornly resist and reject repeal unless concurrent measures were passed to secure the benefits for the working people; but the Whigs did not propose to bother about this. Therefore he was opposed to what he called 'Whig repeal' of the Corn Laws.[1] John Mason put the position as the Chartists saw it, clearly and bluntly, in 1840:

'When we get the Charter we will repeal the Corn Laws and all the other bad laws. But if you give up your agitation for the Charter to help the Free Traders, they will not help you to get the Charter. . . . "Cheap Bread!" they cry. But they mean low wages.'[2]

In his own forthright fashion O'Brien had expressed similar views in 1836:

'The cry of "cheap bread" is the cry of knaves and fools who would benefit all the world at the expense of England. It is the cry of cotton-lords and iron-masters, who would beat down the quartern loaf only to beat down human labour. . . . It is the cry of the usurers and profit-mongers, who tell us through their mouth-piece, Joe Hume, that "it would be an incalculable blessing for the country, if the cultivation of all kinds of grain were to be abandoned in Great Britain!"'

As for the 'Sham-Radicals' who favoured the repeal of the Corn Laws,

'the only answer to these fellows is, "vote for our enfranchisement before you vote for cheap bread, or by all the Evangelists we will have nothing to do with you, though your accents were as sonorous and solemn as those of Great Tom of Oxford. It is true . . . that the landlord is a robber, but it is equally true . . . that you, the capitalist, are a stronger robber. . . ."'

If the Corn Laws were repealed, the industrial workers would find themselves still 'at the old starvation point', while the farmers and agricultural labourers would be ruined. But if the working people were

[1] *Add.MSS.* 27,821(33); *Northern Star*, 23rd October 1841.
[2] Quoted by Dolléans, *Le Chartisme*, II, p. 24. Two Sunderland Chartists, Williams and Binns, put the point succinctly: 'Chartism aims at something higher than the repeal of a tax. It aims at the stoppage of Tyranny and slavery at their sources.'

160

enfranchised *first*, they would be in a position to protect themselves 'against any or all changes'.[1] As matters stood, they were worse off than their ancestors had been at the end of the fifteenth century; they had gained nothing since England became the world's workshop, nor would they, so long as the capitalist system lasted, Corn Laws or no Corn Laws.[2] On 12th February 1839, when the first Chartist Convention was but a week old, O'Brien had tabled a motion calling upon all true Radicals to oppose the Corn Law repealers because their agitation was an insidious attempt to divert the people's attention from the real cause of their wretched condition. The Convention must not forget, said he, that the anti-Corn Law agitation was contemporaneous with the Chartist movement; there was something very suspicious in that. The repeal of the Corn Laws without parliamentary and currency reform would be injurious to the poorer classes and would 'throw three-fifths. of the property of the country into the hands of the Jews and jobbers'. The much vaunted reduction of prices would certainly be offset by reduced wages, while some £350,000,000 would be added to the burden of the National Debt. He therefore urged implacable opposition to the Corn Law repealers 'until the fate of the National Petition, and the People's Charter shall have been determined, so far as the legislature is competent to determine it'.[3] But all this did not mean that O'Brien was willing to support the Tories against the Whigs. It would be, he said, the height of folly to vote for a villain who wanted to put down Chartism by brute force, in order to keep out 'another villain who has tried the same game and failed'. Let there be no pandering to either party. O'Connor's advocacy of such a course was contrary to all his recorded opinions and previous policy.

'Our business as Chartists,' O'Brien proclaimed from Lancaster Gaol, 'is to disavow both factions alike. . . . As to the *hocus pocus* policy of promoting Chartism by inundating the next House of Commons with Toryism, I cannot find language capable of expressing my contempt for it.'

For neither Tories nor Whigs would ever swallow the Charter: on the contrary, they would certainly aid and abet each other 'in every liberticidal act'.

'I would,' O'Brien wrote, 'tell my own father he was mad, if he tried to persuade me that the present race of Whigs will ever be democrats, or

---

[1] *London Mercury*, 25th December 1836 12th February 1837.
[2] *Operative*, 30th December 1838; 13th January 1839.
[3] *Ayrshire Examiner*, 15th February 1839; *Add.MSS.* 27,821(33).

even make common cause with the Chartists. . . . I care not what private information you may have to the contrary.'

The sickening Whig-Tory see-saw would go on, interrupted at intervals by 'paroxysms of public exasperation', until the Chartists could create power enough of their own to 'extinguish both parties together'. Feargus O'Connor with his *Northern Star*, Thomas Cooper with his Leicester Chartists, and all other supporters of the stupid pro-Tory policy seemed to have gone 'stark staring mad'. But, he wrote to O'Connor,

'I will not be angry with you. So pray don't be angry with me . . . [but] we must tie you down rigidly to principle. We must show you that while we honour you as our undoubted chief and champion, we are ready to throw *even you* over-board, the moment you attempt to substitute expediency for principle.'

Such serious blunders might lead to a disastrous disintegration of the democratic movement.[1] Although neither protagonist would yield an inch, an open breach between the two Irishmen had, apparently, been avoided; but their relations gradually became less cordial and co-operative after 1841.

As the date of O'Brien's release from prison approached, proposals were put forward to give him an ovation and to raise money to place him once again in an editor's chair. On 19th June 1841, the *Northern Star* carried an appeal for funds to furnish Bronterre with a press, types, and other materials 'that he may not only preserve himself and family from the jaws of starvation, but give a full, free and uncontrolled expression to his opinions', for such men ought not to be silenced either by the power of tyrants or the weight of poverty.[2] O'Brien refused the proposed demonstration in his honour, saying that Chartists could ill afford to spend between 40 and 100 guineas in this way. When, on a previous occasion, the people of Leigh in Lancashire had organized a great demonstration he had been grieved to learn that 'fifteen poor fellows' had lost their employment in consequence. Others must act as they thought fit, but he regarded triumphal entries as mere tomfoolery.[3] This was a slap at Feargus O'Connor, who loved to play the central role in a triumphal procession, as he did when he was released from York Castle, and again at Huddersfield in 1841 and at Nottingham in 1842.

---

[1] *Northern Star*, 19th and 26th June, 3rd and 10th July 1841; Read and Glasgow, *op. cit.*, p. 95.

[2] *Northern Star*, 19th June, 24th July, 25th September 1841.

[3] *Ibid.*, 14th August 1841.

At Huddersfield in December 1841 many hundreds of Chartists marched 'sixteen abreast' in a great procession thick with flags and banners; then came the breath-taking climax:

'*THE CARRIAGE* drawn by four greys; postilions in scarlet jackets, black velvet caps and silver tassels; containing the People's Champion, *FEARGUS O'CONNOR, ESQUIRE*, along with . . . friends. Transparent lamps and Green silk flags on each side of the carriage,'

which was followed by more 'operatives sixteen abreast'. Bronterre O'Brien, however, preferred soirées (if celebrations there must be) because they were less costly than processions or public dinners, they did not cause loss of work, and women could more conveniently attend them. Accordingly, in September 1841, a well-attended soirée to mark O'Brien's release was held in Lancaster, at which, despite certain signs of physical weakness, he made a lengthy speech. His re-appearance at a number of other places, such as Manchester and Edinburgh, was warmly greeted by the local Chartists. There was 'a magnificent meeting in the Guildhall in Newcastle, with the Mayor in the chair' – the same Guildhall in which, just two years before, he had been tried and found 'not guilty' – and an equally impressive gathering at Liverpool, 'the scene of his enemies' triumph'. Such demonstrations of working-class appreciation of his efforts gave a welcome boost to O'Brien's morale. 'His spirit,' said the *Northern Star*, '. . . is unbroken, and his scholars are threatened with the terror of his tongue if they do not progress rapidly in their education.' [1]

[1] *Ibid.*, 2nd October 1841; *Reynolds's Political Instructor*, 30th March 1850; Hovell, *op. cit.*, pp. 226–7; Read and Glasgow, *op. cit.*, pp. 96–8.

Chapter IX

BECKONING MIRAGE

DURING 1841 the Chartist Movement was in a sorry plight. Scores of its national and local leaders were, as we have seen, in gaol; others had fled to America; the Scottish Chartists had broken away in the summer of 1839; the Government, fed with reports from its ubiquitous spies, was known to be still very much on the alert and some Chartist splinter groups had gone underground. The whole atmosphere in the Movement was highly charged with bickering and recrimination. Clearly a great work of revival, regeneration, and reconstruction needed to be done. Equally clearly, as Bronterre O'Brien saw, success would depend upon the achievement of unity. But events were to frustrate this. Again and again, all attempts to weld the fragments into a single whole were thwarted by policy disagreements and personal animosities impossible to overcome.

O'Brien, of course, could not know this in the autumn of 1841, and very soon after his release from prison he was once again pulling his weight in the cause of Chartism, writing trenchant newspaper articles and lecturing in London and the North. Early in October 1841 he addressed Chartist meetings at Ashton-under-Lyne (where he spoke for three hours), Bolton, Hyde, Stalybridge and Stockport; and by the middle of the month he had reached Oldham, Rochdale and Bury. Shortly afterwards he was reported at Sheffield and Whitechapel. At every meeting collections were taken for the Bronterre O'Brien Press Fund, and all contributions were acknowledged in the *Northern Star*.[1]

Early in 1842, when the *Scottish Patriot* ceased publication, the Chartists of Hamilton suggested that O'Brien might fill the gap by bringing out a *Scottish Star*, but nothing came of this idea.[2] Although he continued active in the Cause, O'Brien must have realized that the future outlook for Chartism was, to say the least, 'unsettled'; for it was

[1] *Northern Star*, 25th September – 27th November 1841; See also Arthur O'Neill's appeal on behalf of O'Brien's Press Fund in *Northern Star*, 9th April 1842.
[2] *Northern Star*, 29th January 1842.

about this time that he thought of emigrating. But, after long and anxious consideration, his rooted reluctance to abandon the Chartist Movement (which was showing signs of recovery and expansion, especially in London), reinforced by the inevitable upheaval and expense of transporting himself, his wife and four children, induced him to await the result of the press fund effort.[1] At length, on 9th July 1842, the *Northern Star* advertised Bronterre's new venture in journalism:

'WHOLE HOG CHARTISM

J. Bronterre O'Brien respectfully announces to the Chartist public that he is now sole Editor and Part Proprietor of the *British Statesman*; which paper shall, henceforward, under his management, advocate genuine Chartism, and no mistake! No factious Politics – but real Democracy!'

When the *British Statesman*, a Radical weekly, first appeared in March 1842 it was primarily an Anti-Corn Law paper; but after O'Brien took it over, four months later, it strove to spread the Chartist gospel according to Bronterre. A broad hint of this change was given on 19th June 1842, when the *British Statesman* announced that it

'. . . appears today under new auspices. Some improvements will, we trust, be visible already in its pages. Many more are contemplated; but they need time for their development. . . . In the ideal character indicated by the noble name of this Journal, we shall review the politics of the day, maintaining strenuously the rights of the many – claiming for them impartial justice, and admission within the pale of the constitution, with such protections as shall make the franchise a reality, and not, as it now is, a mockery and a degradation.'

The next Number carried on its front page an open letter from Bronterre O'Brien, 'To the Unenfranchised Millions, their friends of the Middle Classes, and more particularly to the subscribers to the O'Brien Press [Fund]', bearing the *British Statesman's* office address, 170 Fleet Street:

'*My Dear Friends* – I hasten to announce to you that after this day's publication, the *British Statesman* will be edited by me. I have . . . concluded . . . an arrangement which places the entire Editorial management of the Paper under my control, together with such an interest in the copyright as renders me, to all intents and purposes, a Co-pro-

---

[1] *English Chartist Circular*, Vol. I, No. 43.

prietor – liable to sink or swim with the fortunes of the paper. . . .
The politics of the paper shall be the same that you have ever known
me to advocate. . . . Genuine democracy . . . shall be the order of the
day. . . .'

This news was well received in Radical-Chartist circles. Among the
goodly number of letters which came in, congratulating Bronterre on
his return to the Radical press, was one from William Thomson, a
leading Scottish Chartist who edited the *Chartist Circular*, and another
from a former regular reader of the *Poor Man's Guardian*. On 2nd July
1842, the *British Statesman* carried a long editorial from O'Brien's pen –
three full columns – in which sheer joy at finding himself in an editor's
chair 'after a three years' exile from the press' beams from every line.
He lost no time in re-affirming his adherence to all six points of the
People's Charter, for he was 'more than ever convinced that all attempts
to stop short of Universal Suffrage, and the details necessary for carrying it out, will but aggravate existing evils and diminish the chances of
a peaceable change'. He was also concerned to defend the Complete
Suffrage Conference 'lately held in Birmingham', for it was to be part
of his editorial policy to build a bridge between the Chartists and 'their
friends of the Middle Classes'. This aim is further emphasized by the
inclusion, in the remaining two columns on the front page, of a 'Sketch
of our Political Creed', which turns out to be a re-print of Bronterre's
address to the electors and non-electors of Newcastle, which he wrote
in prison in June 1841. This document he reprinted a second time in the
Social Reformer on 6th October 1849.

The *British Statesman* was a substantial weekly, printing a considerable variety of news and political matter, the main features being foreign
news, extracts from parliamentary debates, police news, items from
Ireland, Scotland, and the English provincial towns, reports of Chartist
meetings held in various places, usually printed under a general heading
such as 'State of the Country' or 'Progress of the Movement'. There
were, also, miscellaneous snippets grouped as 'Gossip of the Week'.
Setting the tone, of course, there were O'Brien's weekly editorials on
subjects such as 'Administration of the Poor Laws – unholy alliance
between the Landlords and Parsons to rob the Poor'; 'Politics in the
U.S.A.'; 'Free Trade'; 'The Anti-Corn Law Movement'; 'The
Horrible Spy System'; 'The Reign of Truncheons and Terror'.
Several editorials were devoted to the current riots in the manufacturing districts, said to be 'in a state bordering upon civil war', where the
working people were treated worse than galley-slaves. In one article
(27th August 1842), Bronterre supported his statements by quoting

from Dr Cooke Taylor's eye-witness descriptions of the appalling conditions in industrial Lancashire in the first half of 1842.[1] At Colne Cooke Taylor visited

'. . . 88 dwellings, selected at hazard. They were destitute of furniture save old boxes for tables or stools, or even large stones for chairs; the beds were composed of straw and shavings. The food was oatmeal and water for breakfast; flour and water, with a little skimmed milk for dinner; oatmeal and water again for a second supply . . . [yet] all the places and persons . . . were scrupulously clean. The children were in rags, but they were not in filth. In no single instance was I asked for relief. . . . I never before saw poverty which inspired respect, and misery which demanded involuntary homage.'

At Burnley, the weavers 'were haggard with famine', but they asked for employment, not charity. They were all Chartists, 'but with this difference, that the block-printers [of fabrics] and hand-loom weavers united to their Chartism a hatred of machinery which was far from being shared by the factory operatives'. Only 100 of Accrington's 9,000 inhabitants were fully employed. Some, like the Irish peasants remembered by O'Brien, tried to keep alive by collecting nettles and boiling them; some had but one scanty meal a day; others, still worse off, had a meal only on alternate days.

During the first half of 1842, while he was awaiting the outcome of the Press Fund appeal, O'Brien went again on tour. January saw him in Newcastle, where he was sure of a welcome, and early in February we find him in Glasgow inspiring a meeting with such zeal that it went on until one o'clock in the morning! At the end of March he was in Bath discoursing upon the manifold defects of the social system and stressing the paramount importance of unity, reminding his hearers that a cable is composed of many thousands of tiny, weak fibres, which become strong only when they are entwined together; and pointing the moral that the Charter would be won not by 'pot-house politicians', but by the solidarity of the people. At Birmingham, in May, he claimed that since his release from gaol he had visited no fewer than ninety-three towns.[2]

Meanwhile, the Chartist Convention of April 1842 had opened at Dr Johnson's Tavern in Bolt Court (Fleet Street), and O'Brien, elected to it by the Newcastle Chartists, took his seat in due course. But this Con-

[1] See *British Statesman*, July–December 1842, *passim*. W. Cooke Taylor, *Notes of a Tour in the Manufacturing Districts of Lancashire* (1842), and *Factories and the Factory System* (1844).
[2] *Northern Star*, 12th February, 9th April, 21st May 1842.

167

vention could do little more than arrange for the presentation of a new Petition, [containing, it was claimed, over three million signatures) and after three weeks of desultory discussions it dissolved itself.[1]

About this time a stir was caused among the Chartists by the emergence of the short-lived Complete Suffrage Movement, which was 'a kind of middle-class Chartism' led by Joseph Sturge, a well-to-do Quaker-Radical who deemed it a Christian duty to help the oppressed working folks to secure 'a just and permanent control over their own affairs'. Hence the formation of the Complete Suffrage Union which, during a meteoric career of little more than a year, attracted as members many of the leading figures among the Chartists and middle-class Radicals, including Sharman Crawford and Francis Place, sundry ministers of religion like Henry Solly, Thomas Spencer (Herbert Spencer's uncle), Edward Miall, and the indefatigable Dr Wade; and Chartists such as Bronterre O'Brien, William Lovett, Henry Vincent, John Collins, and Arthur O'Neill.[2] Branches of the C.S.U. were formed in forty or fifty big towns, the six points of the Charter were adopted in all but name, and the Union strove to unite middle-class and working-class citizens upon a common platform. Joseph Sturge, its tireless and respected leader, nearly defeated a strong Whig candidate in a parliamentary by-election at Nottingham in the summer of 1842. Although Sturge flatly refused to resort to any form of bribery, he polled no fewer than 1,801 votes against 1,885 cast for his opponent; a remarkable result which won the sincere admiration of Bronterre O'Brien, who wrote:

'Sturge was too honest, too high-minded for these [middle-class] trimmers. He would sooner have sacrificed fifty seats than [have] abandoned a single pledge he had given. . . . He has lost his election. But he has gained an imperishable wreath of glory in exchange. His purity and patriotism have enshrined him in the hearts and affections of millions.' [3]

As a man of peace, Sturge was much disturbed by the prevalent hostility between the middle and working classes. Edward Miall, a vigorous advocate of civil and religious equality, thought it his duty to

[1] *Ibid.*, 16th April – 7th May 1842; *British Statesman*, 24th April, 1st May 1842; Gammage, *op. cit.*, p. 208.

[2] A. Miall, *Life of Edward Miall* (1884), Ch. V; S. Hobhouse, *Joseph Sturge* (1919), Ch. VI.

[3] Hobhouse, *op. cit.*, pp. 74–7; *British Statesman*, 6th August 1842; also 13th August 1842, p. 5, for letters from Joseph Sturge, and from Thomas Biggs of Nottingham, author of *Three Lectures on the Moral Elevation of the People* (1848).

strive for a reconciliation of the two classes upon the principal point in the People's Charter – extension of the franchise. A series of excellent editorials in the *Nonconformist*, which Miall had founded in 1841, met with complete approval from Sturge who helped to have them reprinted as a pamphlet for which he wrote a preface arguing that the principles of Christian equity were incompatible with class legislation. Typical of the C.S.U. was the attitude of the Reverend Thomas Spencer, who differed profoundly from those

'Church of England priests who think their duty consists in performing, ceremonies, conducting praises, offering prayers, and uttering such injunctions as do not offend the influential members of their flocks – his conception of the clerical office was more like that of the old Hebrew prophets, who denounced the wrong-doings of both people and rulers. He held that it came within his function to expose political injustices and insist on equitable laws. Hence it happened that he took an active part in the agitation for the repeal of the Corn Laws – attending meetings, giving lectures, writing tracts. . . . This was not his only endeavour to further political equity. He entered with energy into the movement for extending the franchise. He was a member of the first conference held at Birmingham to initiate the Complete Suffrage, movement, and was a delegate to the subsequent conference, also held there, to frame, if possible, a basis of agreement with the Chartists – a futile experiment.'

Herbert Spencer speaks of Joseph Sturge's 'unyielding pursuit of his benevolent aims', and of the Chartists, Vincent, Lovett and Collins, as 'much to be admired', but he does not mention Bronterre O'Brien.[1]

O'Brien and Lovett were invited to join a committee to arrange for the convening of the first Complete Suffrage Conference in Birmingham in April 1842, and we have a record of a preliminary meeting in February of that year at which the honest Lovett made it quite clear that the Chartist members intended to 'hold firmly to the Charter'.[2] O'Brien certainly agreed with this, but he now admitted that Chartists might well link hands with certain worthy middle-class Radicals, such as Joseph Sturge and his friends. He was completely at one with Sturge's criticism, in the so-called 'Sturge Declaration', of the

'. . . essentially unsound condition of our present parliamentary representation . . . the evils arising from class legislation and . . . the suffering

[1] H. Spencer, *Autobiography* (1904), I, pp. 29–30, 251.
[2] *Northern Star*, 19th February 1842. The main Conference met first in the Waterloo Rooms from 5th to 8th April 1842, and afterwards in Birmingham Town Hall.

thereby inflicted upon our industrious fellow subjects [who are] unjustly excluded from that full, fair and free exercise of the elective franchise to which they are entitled by the great principle of Christian equity and also by the British Constitution'.

And the following passage in a letter written by Joseph Sturge to Richard Cobden in 1841 might have been penned by Bronterre himself.

'I have been driven to the conclusion that it is not only hopeless to expect justice for the labouring population from the representatives of the present constituencies but that the infatuated policy which now guides our rulers will be persisted in, until they plunge millions into want and misery if [they do] not bring them into a premature grave.' [1]

Sturge and O'Brien, however, never came to know each other well; if they had, their exchange of views on many other questions would certainly have been interesting, to say the least. O'Brien, always an avowed Chartist, was now willing to accept the reluctance of others to adopt the name, so long as they would help him to agitate for the substance, especially if such tolerant co-operation promised to put the essence of the Charter more speedily upon the statute book.[2]

Feargus O'Connor's attitude to the new movement was, on the contrary, extremely hostile. 'The Sturge move,' he stormed, 'is to include the Whigs generally – the Attwoodites,[3] the Corn Law Repealers, the Christian Chartists . . . and certain other scabby sheep that will but infect the flock.' Complete Suffrage was complete humbug. Sturge would be used by the 'Malthusian starve-beggar faction. . . . They will milk [him] and then send him to grass. They could not have hit upon a better milch cow for their purpose'. William Hill, editor of the *Northern Star*, embroidering his master's theme, concluded that Complete Suffrage would leave the working class, in the end, still prostrate to capitalists and speculators. O'Connor's counter-move to Sturge's Birmingham Conference in April 1842 was to call a conference

[1] Hobhouse, *op. cit.*, p. 71.

[2] Cf. *Northern Star*, 29th January and 21st May 1842; *British Statesman*, 9th July 1842. In the House of Commons on 21st April 1842, a motion to consider the 'complete suffrage' proposal, including vote by ballot, equalization of electoral districts on the basis of population, payment of members, and annual elections, was lost by 220 votes against 67; *Hansard* (Third Series) Vol. LXIII, pp. 907–984. See also National Complete Suffrage Union Minute Book, 10th May 1842 (Birmingham Reference Library).

[3] Currency reformers, followers of Thomas Attwood, M.P., a Birmingham banker, who advocated, in advance of his time, full employment secured and maintained by a managed currency system geared to industrial and agricultural production.

170

of his own to meet in Birmingham on the same days, thus forcing the moderate Chartists to choose which conference they would attend. Bronterre O'Brien took up the implied challenge and somehow contrived to attend and speak at both conferences![1]

During the Complete Suffrage Conference, O'Brien, having been 'frequently called for', addressed the members several times. He spoke against the idea of basing parliamentary representation upon the payment of taxation, since it might be possible to argue that 'he who paid most taxes should have most rights'; the true democratic basis, in his opinion, should be subjection to the law. He denounced the property qualification because it 'was like giving sparrows the right of choosing their protectors, but circumscribing their choice to hawks', and he went on to point out that an essential corollary to abolition of the property qualification must be payment of members of parliament and election expenses from the public purse. Praising the democratic spirit of the Conference, he noted with satisfaction that the Charter's six points had been 'admitted' in the preliminary committee; and now, he continued,

'I look upon the middle-class members as baptized in the waters of Chartist righteousness; as redeemed from the original sin of class legislation; as regularly born again. It now remains to confirm them in the faith, and I hope they will show that faith by their good works.'[2]

The smouldering hostility between the two Irishmen now blazed up.[3] Feargus O'Connor's character and conduct, his unquenchable thirst for popular acclaim, his increasing arrogance, and his personal and political instability had become such that 'no man of independence, talents, and integrity could long co-operate with him'.[4] The files of the *Northern*

---

[1] *Northern Star*, March–April 1842; Read and Glasgow, *op. cit.*, p. 95. William Hill had been a schoolmaster, a Swedenborgian minister, and a political lecturer. He edited the *Northern Star* ably. In 1842 he was arrested in connection with the 'plug plot' strike of that year. Later, when the *Northern Star* was waning, he left it and went to Edinburgh where he published lists of business failures, protested bills of exchange, applications for sequestrations and the like. He was so successful with his Scottish lists that in 1853 he added the English lists of weekly mercantile defalcations and opened offices in London, Dublin, and several large towns, with an enquiry department for the use of his subscribers. Hill was an early pioneer of the present system of mercantile agencies. Burn, *op. cit.*, pp. 555–6; Hovell, *op. cit.*, pp. 96, 262.

[2] *Report of the Proceedings at the Conference of Delegates of the Middle and Working Classes, held at Birmingham* . . . (1842); *The Great Suffrage Meeting at Birmingham* . . . (reprinted from the *British Statesman* and sold as a penny pamphlet).

[3] *Northern Star*, 16th and 30th April 1842.

[4] Hovell, *op. cit.*, p. 255; Read and Glasgow, *op. cit.*, pp. 26, 95–6, 147.

Star and the lesser Chartist journals for 1841 and 1842 reveal O'Connor's mounting quarrels with the leaders of Scottish Chartism, and with Richardson, Vincent, Harney, and many others. He looked with disdain upon O'Neill's Christian Chartism, and affected to despise O'Brien's ability, conveniently forgetting the many articles from Bronterre's pen that had enhanced the *Northern Star*'s reputation and promoted the cause of Chartism. O'Connor even used O'Brien's developing social theories in an attempt to denigrate him in the eyes of the rank and file. In 1841 O'Brien began to stress not only the political power of the privileged aristocracy and wealthy middle classes, but also the political importance of their pervasive social influence; i.e. the pressure they exerted upon and within the body politic through their wealth, position and functions in society, and especially in the national economy. This influence or power, O'Brien argued, was enjoyed 'to a great extent independently of Acts of Parliament' and was used to the detriment of the political rights and social comforts of the people.[1] But O'Connor, who had no time for such theorizing, hinted darkly that behind it there must be something sinister and traitorous to the Cause.

The first Complete Suffrage Conference brought this quarrel to a crisis. The *Northern Star* insinuated in a garbled report that for supporting the Complete Suffrage Movement, O'Brien deserved the censure of all Chartists. This threw O'Brien into a fury, and when Complete Suffrage came up for discussion in the Chartist Convention early in May 1842, he went into action with all guns blazing, accusing the *Northern Star* of deliberately and grossly misrepresenting his conduct and denying him the right to correct its false reports. By their denunciations, O'Connor and his henchmen were fomenting deep dissensions among Chartists which, he feared, would make it quite 'impossible to maintain their existence as a party. Although such 'denunciations were couched in honeyed language [and] given as a surmise . . . suspicion was set afloat . . . character was traduced, while the real author was allowed to escape'. Month after month, so O'Brien declared, 'this fleeting spirit of division [had] been fostered in every town' until it had 'raised up two antagonistic parties'. He had himself been called 'a middle-class adulator' and made to appear as 'one of the devils of the Birmingham Conference', while the Sturgeites were held up to scorn as 'a regular set of knaves'. At this point, Peter McDouall

---

[1] *Northern Star*, 17th April 1841. In the 1860s reformers like Richard Monckton Milnes (created Baron Houghton in 1863) were stressing the 'real danger to England . . . from the alarming increase in the political, and still more in the social, power of wealth'.

rose and interrupted O'Brien, bluntly asserting that the quarrel had gone far enough: it was harmful to Chartism, and, sincere though they might be, if the two Irishmen were to be always at loggerheads, 'the Movement would be better without them'.[1] O'Connor, of course, denied misrepresentation and still maintained that O'Brien was completely in the wrong: nevertheless, to end all bad feeling he was willing to bury the past and extend to O'Brien 'the right hand of fellowship'; a gesture which O'Brien accepted, without enthusiasm, 'on public grounds'.

Notwithstanding his talk of fellowship, O'Connor did not cease to denounce the Complete Suffrage Movement,[2] and the uneasy truce lasted barely a week. Towards the end of May, Bronterre, still boiling with indignation, published a pamphlet entitled *Mr O'Brien's Vindication of his Conduct at the late Birmingham Conference containing his 'Blackguard Letter' to the Editor of the 'Star' which that personage suppressed*,[3] in which he repudiated the suggestion that his support of the Conference had been in any way reprehensible; on the contrary it had been 'eminently calculated to benefit the cause of Chartism'. In the same pamphlet he explained his revised attitude to the middle classes:

'I have never . . . proposed a union or alliance with the middle classes; and that for this obvious reason, that it is impossible to unite with men who will not unite with us. The middle classes, as a body, have shown no disposition whatever to recognise the justice and wisdom of our principles. . . . But there is a considerable and growing minority of the middle classes with whom I deem a union not only possible but probable. . . . This portion is composed partly of good and wise men, whose probity and love of justice raise them above class-prejudices; and partly of tradespeople and others in embarrassed circumstances who see no hope . . . while the laws are made only by, and for, the opulent portion of society.'[4]

In 1834–7, said O'Brien, addressing the working men through the columns of the *British Statesman*, 'it was necessary to rouse you, as with a rattling peal of thunder. The case is different now.' Then the middle classes treated all working-class Radicals with scorn, but this was no

---

[1] *Ibid.*, 7th and 14th May 1842.

[2] See e.g., *Northern Star*, 21st May and 16th June 1842.

[3] Birmingham Reference Library, Cat. No. 223638; see also *British Statesman*, 10th September 1842.

[4] *O'Brien's Vindication of his Conduct etc.* (1842), pp. 21–3; see also a letter from O'Brien to the *British Statesman*, 15th May 1842.

longer so among a certain section of the middle classes. Therefore, said O'Brien,

'... our business [in 1842] is to deal with them as we find them – to accept their advance and proffered aid in a frank and friendly spirit, to reciprocate such acts by every means at our disposal that involve no compromise of principles'.[1]

Usually, he pointed out, the Chartist leaders were preaching to the converted; but at such gatherings as the Complete Suffrage Conference, men like Lovett, Collins, Parry, and Vincent were in a position to render real service to the Chartist cause by appealing to a wider audience, and

'... had O'Connor ... acted as we did, the impression would have been still better and far more durable, owing to his greater popularity and influence ... while I differ essentially from Mr Lovett and his friends, as regards the practicability of a union with the middle classes *generally*, I differ still more from those heartless and factious politicians who ... confound the honest middle-class man, that would give me my rights, with the knave who would not. ...'

O'Brien's final breach with O'Connor and the *Northern Star* proved extremely damaging to him as a leader and to the prospects of Chartism itself. Even in Brighton and Newport (I.W.), towns where he had been most popular, he began to lose support.[2] At Leicester, Thomas Cooper told his 'Shakesperian' Chartists that Sturge, a rich corn-dealer, could not possibly be honest and that O'Brien was his tool. Cooper later admitted his mistake and came to value Sturge's friendship,[3] but the immediate result of his blunder was a serious split in the ranks of the Leicester Chartists. When O'Brien went to lecture in Leicester, the O'Connorite section rushed the doors and on the second evening there were hostile disturbances culminating in a vote of 'no confidence' in O'Brien, despite his plea that his support of Sturge's movement meant no disloyalty to Chartism, and that he still stood for the complete Charter, 'details, name and all'. Thomas Cooper recalled these incidents many years after in a letter to Robert Gammage:

'*26th February* 1855.

... The people taught me this attachment [to O'Connor]. I did not teach it to them. I was assured they had no hope in Chartism but in him.

---

[1] *British Statesman*, 9th July 1842.
[2] *Northern Star*, 4th June, 16th July, 3rd–17th September 1842.
[3] Gammage, *op. cit.*, pp. 202–4, 408; cf. *Brief Sketches of the Birmingham Conference* (1842), published by John Cleave.

He won me also, by his letters, and by his conversation in the few interviews I had with him during my Leicester chieftainship. I saw reason in the after time to alter my opinion of him; but during the period I am referring to, I held that *union* was the absolute requisite for Chartist success; and as the people cleaved to O'Connor as their leader, I became a foe to all who opposed him as the fomentors of *disunion*. For this reason I opposed O'Brien. And I regret that my opposition was not enacted in the fairest spirit. I have apologized to him; and have also publicly intimated to the Leicester people that I considered we did wrong towards him. Whether O'Brien can forgive a wrong when it is acknowledged, I am not sure ... the truth is, I was the People's instrument, rather than their director, even in the stormy contests with O'Brien and others.'

The second, and last, complete Suffrage Conference, held at the end of December 1842, was ruined largely by the O'Connorites. Feargus, who had decided to change his tactics, actually attended the Conference with a number of his faithful followers, and their very presence, of course, blasted the last frail hope of forming a united Chartist-Complete Suffrage front. The Sturgeites would not use the term 'Charter'; the Chartists recoiled from the alternative title, 'Bill of Rights': differences which were less trifling than appears at first glance. Although 'The People's Charter' was repugnant to some, it aroused strong, even passionate, feelings of loyalty in many; for Chartism, with something of a fighting tradition already, appeared strong enough to continue the struggle. Despite several setbacks, it was still a going concern with a numerous following. The Sturge Movement, on the other hand, was quite new and had but a tenuous hold upon a relatively small public. To the Chartist leaders it appeared essential that the newer movement should join on to the older, otherwise Chartism might become merged and lost in a small-scale, mainly middle-class agitation. No *rapprochement* was ever reached between 'the respectables' and the Chartists,[1] although personal relations between individual members did not always reflect the party alignment. Many Chartists, O'Brien among them, held Sturge in high esteem; while the Reverend Henry Solly, who had been converted to Chartism by the craftsmen of Yeovil, refers to O'Brien as 'a remarkable and generous hearted man' who 'gave cordial and effective help'.[2] But there was no genuine unity, even among

---

[1] H. Richard, *Memoirs of Joseph Sturge* (1864), pp. 316–18. For a criticism of the Complete Suffrage party and Joseph Sturge's rejoinder, see *English Chartist Circular*, Vol. II, Nos. 66 and 85.
[2] H. Solly, *These Eighty Years* (1893), I, pp. 348, 377.

the Chartists, at the second Complete Suffrage Conference. By standing uncompromisingly for the Charter, Lovett succeeded momentarily in drawing together the O'Connorites and the O'Brienites, but the brief alliance scarcely survived the meeting.[1] Bickering and discord broke out between O'Connor's followers and the other Chartists, and between the Sturgeites and the Chartists.[2] The O'Connorites' dislike of Sturge and his friends was fully reciprocated. 'It is not your principles we dislike' declared Lawrence Heyworth when matters had come to a crisis, 'but your leaders.' Men like Heyworth and William Johnson Fox could neither suppress nor conceal their contempt for professional agitators, who 'toil not with their hands but with their tongues. . . . The loom and the plough know them not; yet they always affect to speak in the name of the working classes. Their harangues glitter with pikes and smell of gunpowder, although they generally contrive to keep out of harm's way.'[3] Even the patient, charitable Sturge allowed himself to remark, with evident sadness, that 'from the mad and wicked conduct of some of the Chartists, Chartism is viewed by many with the same horror as Abolitionism is in America; so much are good principles often damaged by bad advocates'.[4]

Unlike his friend, Peter McDouall, who had much closer contacts with the trade unions, O'Brien kept clear of the meetings, strikes and riots which swept through the Midlands and the North, with Lancashire as the storm-centre, in the summer of 1842. Bodies of strikers went through Lancashire and parts of Yorkshire stopping the mills that were still working by removing the plugs from the boilers so as to cut off the source of power. Chartist speakers addressed meeting after meeting, and Chartist resolutions were passed declaring that work would not be resumed until the People's Charter became law. Thus, with McDouall's connivance, that menacing monster, the general strike, again raised its head, only to be quickly knocked down by a thoroughly-scared Feargus O'Connor.[5]

Bronterre O'Brien, now approaching forty, and probably feeling a good deal older – 'a tall, stooping, quiet man, with dignified bearing' – continued to edit the *British Statesman* until its demise in January 1843. Throughout the summer and autumn of 1842, he had worked hard to make it a commercial success. He had nearly doubled its circulation by

[1] Cooper, *op. cit.*, pp. 220–7.

[2] Solly, *op. cit.*, I, pp. 405–6.

[3] R. Garnett, *Life of W. J. Fox* (1910), p. 257.

[4] Hobhouse, *op. cit.*, pp. 74, 78.

[5] Hovell, *op. cit.*, pp. 261–2; G. D. H. Cole, *Short History of the Working Class Movement* (1925), I, pp. 163–4; Rudé, *The Crowd in History* (1964), p. 187.

achieving an increase of 1,500 copies weekly, selling at fivepence a copy. Nevertheless, by mid-October, the familiar symptoms common to so many struggling Radical journals in those days, began to appear: circulation too small despite the considerable volume and variety of the contents; expenses too heavy; a consequent loss, averaging £10 a week, which could not be borne indefinitely.[1] The last issue of the *British Statesman* is dated 21st January 1843, after which the paper, but not its editor, was taken over by the *British Queen and Statesman*.

We next hear of Bronterre in the autumn of 1844, when he removed from London to the Isle of Man to run a printing and stationery business and a circulating library at No. 40 Duke Street, Douglas. Here he launched another journal: *The National Reformer and Manx Weekly Review of Home and Foreign Affairs*. No doubt it was inconvenient for the editor of a Radical paper aiming at a wide circulation to be so far from the centre of things; but publication in the Isle of Man enabled O'Brien to avoid the hated newspaper taxes and at the same time to use the privilege of free postage then enjoyed by the island's inhabitants.[2] Another advantage, doubtless appreciated by the impecunious O'Brien, was the low cost of living in the island at that time, fish, in particular, being extremely cheap. From 1845 to 1847 he used his *National Reformer* to preach Chartism, land nationalization, reform of the currency laws, and 'equitable exchange through national marts'. The People's Charter, of course, had first place in his programme, for he was still convinced that until all the people gained political power other radical reforms would be impossible.

'Universal suffrage,' he told the struggling workers, 'is, after all, a grand test of Radicalism. . . . Without the franchise, you can have nothing but what others choose to give. . . . Knaves will tell you that it is because you have no property that you are unrepresented. I tell you, on the contrary, it is because you are unrepresented that you have no property. Every industrious man who produces more [in value] of the goods of life than he needs for his own or his family's use, ought to own the difference in property. You are almost all in that condition. . . . Why are you not masters of the difference? . . . Because certain laws and institutions give it to the law-makers. But if you were represented as well as they, you would have quite other laws and institutions, which

[1] J. McCabe, *Life and Letters of G. J. Holyoake* (1908), I, p. 134; *British Statesman*, 15th October 1842; cf. *The Charter*, 29th December 1839.
[2] *National Reformer*, 3rd October 1846; 13th March 1847; see also W. J. Linton, *The English Republic*, with Introduction by K. Parkes (1891), p. viii. Linton brought out the *Cause of the People* in the Isle of Man in 1848.

would give the wealth to those who earned it, and consequently, the best share to the most industrious. Thus your poverty is the *result*, not the *cause* of your being unrepresented.'

Trade improved between 1843 and 1845, the spectre of starvation retreated, and interest in political agitation waned for the time being, This was bad for O'Brien's *National Reformer*, which ran into such financial trouble that publication had to cease in April 1846, after seventy-five numbers had appeared. Then we hear nothing until the beginning of September when the silence is broken by a letter from Bronterre O'Brien to his old comrade and publisher, James Watson.

> '*40 Duke Street,*
> *Douglas, Isle of Man.*
> *4th Sept.* 1846

My dear Watson,

You will see by the enclosed that the *National Reformer* is about to be revived. I write this to request that you will get my friend Holyoake to insert the enclosed as an advertisement, or as a paragraph in the next two or three Nos of the *Reasoner* [1] or any other publication you may have as a substitute, and I will return him the favor with interest in the *National Reformer*. . . .

I will send you Bills or placards in a few days – and meanwhile I will thank you to make known the revival of the *National* as extensively as you can. I have sent advertisements to the *Northern Star*, [to] Douglas Jerrold's paper, &c.

Hoping Mrs W. & yourself are well,

> *I remain,*
> *Very sincerely yours,*
> *James B. O'Brien.*' [2]

In the following month the *National Reformer* reappeared. Reduced in size and price, but not in optimism, it announced that important public events were 'conspiring with truth and reason' in favour of Radicalism. But, unfortunately, this favourable trend did not benefit the rejuvenated *Reformer*. Early in the new year (1847) O'Brien crossed to England in search of additional agents and correspondents, and on this mission, which took him to London, Birmingham, Edinburgh and Glasgow, he gave a number of lectures, some of which were very poorly attended: all so different from 1839. He was greatly worried, also, by his

---

[1] *The Reasoner* was an Owenite-rationalist periodical, republican in politics, edited by G. J. Holyoake from 1846 to 1861.

[2] Owen Collection, Co-operative Union, Manchester.

financial difficulties, for in two years he had lost £290 and was once again seriously in debt.

'A portion of my loss,' he said, 'exists in the form of a debt which I must either find the means of paying, or sell my goods to discharge. While this liability hangs over me I expect my political friends to make allowances. . . . And if I succeed in the arrangements I am about, I promise they shall have ample compensation in the future numbers of the *Reformer*.'[1]

At this point the paper was, in fact, just clearing its expenses, and although O'Brien was making a profit on his printing and stationery business, it was not sufficient to discharge the debt incurred in 1845–6. When his creditors increased their pressure (although various advertisers and newsagents owed him between £130 and £150) he was forced to make an urgent appeal for £90 to save the *National Reformer* from final disaster.

'Were I to accept an appointment tomorrow,' he wrote, 'at ten or twelve guineas a week, on a Metropolitan Whig or Tory paper (and time was when I could have got the larger sum) the great bulk of the Chartist body . . . would call me "renegade", "apostate", "traitor". . . . Yet, for being true and faithful to your interests for 16 long years, to the deep injury of myself and family, they would appear to have no better reward for me than the prospect of . . . positive and ruinous loss.'

The evil day was postponed for two months, but at the end of May 1847 the *National Reformer* was forced to close down. In a farewell note O'Brien assured his readers that his views upon the franchise, land nationalization, currency and exchange would yet influence the future destiny of society.[2]

★　　　★　　　★

Another source of Chartist disunity was the land question. The land monopoly, as they called it, was one of the Chartists' chief grievances, but their leaders could never agree upon a land policy. On the contrary, in course of time a deep chasm opened between those who advocated nationalization of all land coupled with a system of tenancies held directly from the State, and those who favoured private peasant proprietorship widely spread. O'Brien led the former school, O'Connor

[1] 'No. 76: No. 1 – New Series', cost ½d postage free. *National Reformer*, January–April 1847, *passim*.
[2] *Ibid.*, 13th March, 29th May 1847. Three years later we find George Julian Harney closing his monthly *Democratic Review* because he could not make it pay.

the latter; which meant that O'Connor appeared to have aligned himself with the forces of individualism, conservation and reaction, while O'Brien was for an advanced, forward-reaching policy backed by the power of the State. Like Charles Hall, O'Brien held that the private ownership of the land by the rich, and the widespread dispossession of the poor, lay at the root of many prevalent social ills,[1] He knew what Thomas Spence and William Ogilvie had written on the subject half a century before, and he had read Tom Paine's *Agrarian Justice* in which the 'contrast of affluence and wretchedness . . . like dead and living bodies chained together' is attributed to the 'landed monopoly'. Like Hall, Thompson, Gray and Hodgskin, O'Brien maintained that the 'productive classes' produced much more than they consumed, but the surplus was taken from them by those who produced nothing. On the farms and in the factories alike, he said, it was a case of – work, work, work, and be defrauded. In Gloucestershire, Worcestershire and the south-west of England men were working for 6s or 7s a week, 'while 8s 6d were necessary to supply their families with bread alone'. Therefore, 'at this rate no amount of industry could make a man independent, though he were to live as long as Methuselah; in fact at the end of his 997th year he would be poorer than when he began . . .'.

'What a chain of evil follows upon the usurpation of the soil! What a rapid striking off of the links of the chain would follow upon the nationalization of landed property! Only prevent one set of men from making God's "gift to all" [the land] their private property, and that moment you open the door to unlimited improvement.'[2]

Early in 1837 O'Brien was hammering home the doctrine that the absolute dominion of the soil belongs to the nation, which alone should have the power of leasing the land for cultivation and using the rents. The right to allocate land to individuals and families, and to administer the system, ought to be vested in the nation; and since every citizen was in theory a part-proprietor of the soil, every citizen would benefit

---

[1] In his work *On the effects of Civilisation on the People in European States* (1805), Charles Hall proposed that the state should possess itself of the whole land of the nation, and parcel it out in allotments, taking into account the size of the cultivator's family in each case. Such allotments were to be indefeasible unless the family became extinct, when they were to revert to the state. Cf. H. M. Hyndman, *The Nationalization of the Land in 1775 and 1882* (London 1882). See *Add.MSS.* 34,245A, *passim*, for many appalling details of low wages and living conditions which were sent to the Secretary of the first Chartist Convention.

[2] *National Reformer*, 17th April 1847; cf. *English Chartist Circular*, Vol. I, No. 17.

indirectly from increased land values.[1] He had no time for 'Redemption Societies, Land Lotteries . . . Co-operative Leagues, and Harmony Halls'; all of which he described as mere nibbling and bubble-blowing.[2] It was essential to get down to bed-rock and work from the proposition that there should not be, and should never have been, *private* ownership of land. If mankind 'in the origin of society' had refused to recognize such ownership 'they would have prevented ninety-nine parts out of a hundred of all the woes and crimes that have hitherto made a pandemonium of the world'. Even within living memory, during the reigns of the four Georges, the upper and middle classes – the very people who pretended to abhor encroachments upon the right of property – had filched from the working class, by means of Enclosure Acts, millions of acres of common land. And so it had been throughout the ages. By means of fraud and brigandage the people's rights to the national territory had been usurped by sinister private interests, by 'usurpers and tyrants of the soil'. In truth and justice the 'whole people or State is the only legitimate landlord in every country', and so long as the masses of the people were debarred from using the land on their own account, 'not as vassal-tenants or serf-labourers, toiling for mere wages', but as proprietors or freeholders, liberty remained but an empty name. Once the soil of a country has been bought up or otherwise monopolized, the community becomes a society of tyrants and slaves.[3] Over the years, landlordism had driven masses of men into the towns, there to become the 'hired slaves of middle-class demons', and no mere tinkering could effectively alter 'a system based on so hideous a foundation'.[4]

---

[1] *Bronterre's National Reformer*, 25th February 1837.

[2] *National Reformer*, 24th April, 1st May 1847.

[3] *Operative*, 25th November and 9th December 1838; *National Reformer*, 10th, 24th October 1846; O'Brien, *Rise, Progress and Phases of Human Slavery*, p. 126; cf. H. Solly, *What says Christianity to the present Distress?* (1842), Chs. III and IV. Many years before, Francis Place had written to James Mill: 'All they (the landlords) cry out against is the high wages of labour, and they exult at every opportunity to reduce them. They (as Paine said some years ago) depend more on breaking the spirit of the people by poverty, than they fear goading them into insurrection by oppression. Thus the value of all the improvements in agriculture goes to the landowners, and the price, so far as it is advanced by the increased rent, is levied by them upon the people, who are unable to purchase necessaries with the miserable pittance they receive for their labour.' Francis Place to James Mill, 17th October 1814, quoted by Wallas, *Life of Francis Place*, p. 166.

[4] O'Brien in *The Power of the Pence*, 21st April 1849; cf. also *National Reformer*, 3rd and 17th October 1846; *Rise, Progress and Phases of Human Slavery*, p. 127.

181

Influenced by William Ogilvie's *Essay on the Right of Property in Land* (1782), O'Brien urged that the land ought to be put into a separate category and marked for special treatment.

'Read Paine, Locke, Puffendorf, and a host of others,' he said to a meeting in Edinburgh, 'and they will tell you that labour is the only genuine property. . . . I hold that the object of property is to give a stimulus to human labour. . . . Labour betters the land, but does not create it. . . . Why then does a band of villains dare to say, "the land is ours"? . . . I hold that the land has three values –

1 The original value of land;
2 The improvements on land;
3 The capabilities of land for yielding value.

The first and third belong for ever to the nation. The second may be claimed by the improver.' [1]

Since the land was the 'free gift of the Creator to all his creatures' and not the produce of human labour, it could never, in O'Brien's view, become the legitimate subject of property as could food and other commodities.[2]

The land, then, must become State property: 'You cannot have honest laws, i.e., laws founded upon first principles,' said O'Brien, 'without making land public property.' [3] But this great end must be attained gradually and justly, not by revolutionary confiscation, the State assuming eminent domain by purchase of land, mines, turbaries, fisheries, etc., as they came into the market. No landlord would suffer; the law would leave him in full possession of his present rights during his lifetime, and would secure to his family or representatives at his death the full market value of his estate, to be paid by annual instalments out of future rents. Thus, in the fullness of time, the State would become the sole landlord and trustee in perpetuity of all the land, which could be divided by a steady, gradual process into small farms let to cultivators assisted by the 'mighty engine' of public credit. Every citizen would have the right, if he cared to exercise it, to become a tenant farmer directly under the State and to receive from the State loan

---

[1] *True Scotsman*, 6th July 1839. O'Brien included a similar passage in the speech for which, *inter alia*, he was convicted and imprisoned in 1840; M. Beer, *History of British Socialism* (new edn 1929), II, p. 100n.

[2] O'Brien applied the same reasoning to minerals and other forms of *natural* wealth 'because they are of God's and not Man's creation'. *Power of the Pence*, 27th January 1849.

[3] *National Reformer*, 20th February 1847.

capital to enable him to stock and crop his farm. Ultimately, the rents would form a great national revenue sufficient to defray current expenses, including the education of the whole nation, and to finance necessary public works, without recourse to taxation.[1]

O'Brien also wanted to extend public ownership to various public utilities and kindred enterprises, arguing that

'Railroads should not be private property; neither should canals, docks, fisheries, mines, the supplying of gas, water, etc. Works of this sort, designed for the use of the public, should be constructed or executed only at the public cost . . . and the public only should have the advantage. They should not be suffered to fall into the hands of private speculators, for whom they are only a legal disguise to enable them to rob the public. . . . The mercantile middle classes are everywhere organizing chartered companies to give themselves perpetual vested interests in the labour of the working classes, and mortgage the latter to posterity, through public loans and state indebtedness.'

His views on credit, which were linked with his land proposals, began with the proposition that the labourer's capacity to produce more than he consumes during the period of production is the true basis of all credit. Yet the very man whose surplus production enables others to obtain loans and to repay both principal and interest, cannot get a loan for himself; 'the Credit as well as the land of the country is hermetically sealed against him'. O'Brien suggested a chain of district banks into which the rents of the nationalized land in each district would be paid. From these funds loans could be made to every deserving man able to bring proof of good character, fitness to be entrusted with an advance, and ability to turn it to productive account. Both the banks and the funds would be public, and the 'stock and labour of every such man would be mortgaged, as it were, to the public, for the repayment of the loan out of the future proceeds of his industry'.[2]

The Chartist Programme of 1851, embodying most of O'Brien's proposals, drew hostile criticism from *The Times*, which objected that the expenditure proposed could not possibly be met from the low rents likely to be paid by poor small-holders farming nationalized land. The whole 'magnificent' scheme was impractical, and the Chartists had, in the opinion of *The Times*, 'failed in their first budget'.[3] But George Julian

[1] *Bronterre's National Reformer*, 25th February 1837; *Operative*, 25th November 1838; *National Reformer*, 20th February, 8th May 1847.

[2] *National Reformer*, 16th January 1847.

[3] *The Times*, 22nd April 1851.

Harney, at the other extreme of opinion, thought that O'Brien's proposals should be boldly extended by the nationalization of manufactures.[1]

O'Brien linked his views on the land question with his suggested
solution of the unemployment problem, asserting that it was the duty of
the Government to use surplus revenue and the income from 'national
and public property' to purchase land upon which to settle the unemployed poor. This scheme, soon to be called 'home colonization', was
to be financed initially by loans raised upon the security of the local
rates. With more optimisim than agricultural knowledge, he estimated
that in a year or two the new cultivators would be able to live in comparative comfort out of their resources, while the rents paid by them
could be devoted, first to the repayment of the loans raised on the
security of the rates, and afterwards to the purchase of other land, 'till
all who desired to occupy land, either as individual holders or industrial
communities might be enabled to so do'.[2] When it was objected that his
proposals would benefit the poor only, he replied that the lands purchased would belong not to the poor but to the whole nation – rich and
poor; and the whole nation would benefit by the consequent reduction
of rates and taxes.[3]

To many Chartists, however, O'Brien's plan seemed to offer, at best,
only a painfully gradual transformation. Some, whose roots had but
recently been severed from the land, listened nostalgically when
Cobbett and O'Connor called them away from the slums and smoke and

[1] *Reynold's*, 30th March 1851. See also John Gray's *Efficient Remedy for the
Distress of Nations* (1852), Chs. II and III, on state factories and currency
reform. John Francis Bray (1809–97) was opposed to private ownership of
the land, and he may have been indebted to some of O'Brien's earlier articles.
O'Brien himself recommended Bray's book as 'the best we know on the relative
rights of capital and labour'; *National Reformer*, 24th October 1846, p. 9.
Patrick Edward Dove, writing a decade later, adopted O'Brien's views on the
special nature of land and the feasibility of raising a substantial portion of the
national revenue from the rents of state-owned land; *Science of Politics*, Part II,
1854. For biographical and bibliographical details of J. F. Bray see H. J. Carr's
article in *Economica*, November 1940, pp. 397–415.

[2] O'Brien, *The Rise, Phases and Progress of Human Slavery*, Ch. 18.

[3] *Ibid.*, p. 118. It is interesting to notice a certain similarity between the
views of O'Brien and those of Francis Place upon the question of land nationalization. Place was originally opposed to nationalization of the land, but his
opinions changed until he came to hope and believe that when men were wiser
and the rate of increase of population had been brought within 'proper' limits,
private property in land would end and the people would be 'the sole landlord
and receive all the Rent'; see *The Traveller*, January 1821; Wallas, *Life of
Francis Place*, p. 173. For arguments in favour of home colonization see
Reynold's Political Instructor, 9th and 16th February 1850.

grime of the new machine industry based on coal and iron, back to the clean, spacious countryside.[1] O'Connor had an Irishman's natural preference for the small farm, and, impatient of the slow political progress of the Chartist Movement, he put forward in the Chartist Convention of 1843 a scheme to form a National Land Company to buy large private estates and divide them into small holdings, upon which he proposed to settle working men who had subscribed for a certain number of shares in the company. O'Connor's skill as an agitator stood him in good stead in the rôle of company promoter. He gave a glowing account of the produce and profits a man could earn if he had four acres under the spade,[2] commending his scheme as a quick way of escape from capitalism, and the only means whereby individual labour could be properly valued.[3] What other occupation was so healthy, remunerative and independent as 'a man's working on his own land for his own self?'.[4] A small holder upon his little farm with his foot upon his spade, would be, in very truth,

'. . . a man standing on his own resources. . . . It is his pride to rise betimes, according to his strength, rejoicing in the reflection that upon his industry the whole family must depend; while, in return, he looks for that contentment which a happy home alone can bestow. . . . If he should be overworked, or even drowsy, he dreads not the awful sound of the factory bell. He is not deprived of the comfort of the society of his wife; he is not degraded by living as a prostitute upon her and his children's labour. He is not reduced to the humiliating necessity of shaking his slumbering babe into a kind of artificial life, in order that she may obey the capitalists's morning summons. He sees no cripple at

---

[1] Cf. Dierlamm, *Die Flugschriftenliteratur der Chartistenbewegung*, p. 19; Engels, *Conditions of the Working-Class in England in 1844* (ed. 1920), pp. 235–6; Cole, *A Short History of the Working Class Movement*, II, p. 12; Bachmann, *Die Agrarreform in der Chartistenbewegung* (1928).

[2] Robert Owen, also, had urged the superiority of spade husbandry. In his Report to the County of Lanark (1820), he wrote: 'It is also known to all practical agriculturalists, that to obtain the best crops, the soil ought to be well broken and separated; and that the nearer it is brought to a garden mould, the more perfect is the cultivation. These facts no one will dispute; nor will they deny that the spade is calculated to prepare a better recipient than the plough for an excess of water in rainy seasons, and to return it to the seed or plant afterwards, in a manner most favourable to vegetation.' See also *The Economist*, 25th August¦and 15th September 1821.

[3] O'Connor and Ernest Jones jointly edited *The Labourer*, a periodical designed to boost the land scheme.

[4] But cf. A. W. Ashby, *Allotments and Small Holdings in Oxfordshire* (1921), p. 95.

his board, no dwarf in his family. . . . He is master of himself and his time. . . He seeks no refuge for his wounded feelings in the beer shop or gin palace.' [1]

And in response to the many enquiries evoked by this lyrical voyage to Arcadia he wrote:

'I am asked by several parties if four acres of land would not be preferable to two? I should much prefer four acres myself, especially for persons with large families; and we shall have . . . a large majority of that class. I am asked what the rent of a cottage and four acres would be? At a "guess" I should say about £7 10s I am asked what size the cottage should be? I should say a good four-roomed cottage, with spacious porch to wash in, and for shelter, all on the ground floor, windows in front, and back-wall of house shedded and divided for out-offices. The houses should be built so that each occupant could add to them at pleasure. Each cottage should stand, as near as practicable, in the centre of the land.' [2]

O'Connor's National Land Company had a nominal capital of 100,000 shares of £1 6s each, which could be bought by weekly instalments of 3d, 6d, 1s, or larger sums. Subscribers of £2 12s (two shares) became entitled to a cottage, a two-acres holding and an advance of £15 (i.e. £7 10s per acre); for three shares, a cottage, three acres and an advance of £22 10s could be had, and for four shares, a cottage, four acres and an advance of £30. The response was striking. Within ten months of the provisional registration of the Company the 'land fund' reached £50,000.[3]

O'Brien, having disagreed profoundly with O'Connor about tactics in the 1841 General Election, and quarrelled with him on the Complete Suffrage issue, now attacked Feargus's land scheme root and branch,

---

[1] O'Connor, *A Practical Work on the Management of Small Farms*, pp. 9 et seq.

[2] The bungalows at Minster Lovell, near Witney, are on this plan. The estate of 300 acres, bought by the National Land Company in 1847, was divided into eighty-one holdings of 2-4 acres. Sturdy bungalows (three rooms and a kitchen) were built, roads made, and the land ploughed up, at the outset, at the Company's expense. *Northern Star*, 19th July 1845; cf. the defence of O'Connor's scheme in *People's Paper*, 18th September 1852, and the letter from Thomas M. Wheeler of O'Connorville in *People's Paper*, 13th November 1852.

[3] *Accounts and Papers*, 1847-8, XIX. William Prowting Roberts, 'the Miners' attorney general', acted as treasurer and solicitor to the Company. Gammage, *op. cit.*, p. 285.

condemning it and all similar palliatives as certain to split the working class into separate sections each intent upon small selfish objectives, and to destroy all chance of united action before the people had gained their true political rights. Such paltry ephemeral projects, which did infinite harm by luring the working class away from the pursuit of substantial reforms, were threatening to side-track the Chartist Movement, Even if the National Land Company proved a success, it could benefit no more than a minute section of the workers, and that at the cost of detaching them from all sympathy and co-operation with their less fortunate fellows. The operations of the Company were, moreover, a practical recognition of those existing laws and institutions of property which every honest Chartist ought to repudiate. Every man who joined the National Land Company was enlisting on the side of the Government against his own class by trying to acquire as private property that which ought to be the private property of no man. O'Connor's 'land-lottery' had no more connection with the people's rights to the soil than had a friendly society or a burial club. It was a misguided agitation 'to get land for about one in every thirty or fifty who can and will unite to buy it! But no land at all for those who cannot buy, and who most need it – the vast majority of the population.' [1] This pitiful, futile, delusive scheme was draining away funds which should have been devoted to the agitation for the Charter; a point which O'Brien drove home by showing that for the week ended 13th May 1847, the subscriptions to O'Connor's Land Company were £641 18s, while the National Charter Association had received only £1 2s. How *could* working men, with their gaze turned to the future, be so stupid as to rate investment in O'Connor's Land Company so much higher than investment in Universal Suffrage?

Lastly, Bronterre did not fail to remark upon

'. . . the strangest thing of all . . . that the philanthropic Feargus should have dragged millions of people after him to torch-light meetings, demonstrations, etc., all attended with great sacrifice of time and money, and caused the actual ruin of thousands through imprisonment, loss of employment, and expatriation, when all the while he had only to establish a "National Chartist Co-operative Land Society" to ensure social happiness for us all, and when, to use his own words . . . he had discerned that "political equality can only spring from social happiness". Formerly, he taught us that social happiness was to proceed

[1] *National Reformer*, 9th January, 17th April 1847; cf. Alexander Somerville's articles in the *Manchester Examiner*, December 1846–January 1847.

187

from political equality; but doubtless when his land-bubble has burst, he will have the old or some other new creed for us.'[1]

A shrewd thrust!

O'Brien's hostility to O'Connor's land scheme was shared by all sorts and conditions of men. Thousands of trade unionists would not touch it.[2] Charles Kingsley thought it quite reactionary. William Lovett disliked and distrusted both O'Connor and his scheme; but he was equally opposed to O'Brien's land nationalization plans. Robert Gammage, on the other hand, strongly favoured land nationalization, and even Ernest Jones came into line with O'Brien within a year or two of the collapse of the National Land Company,[3] declaring that

'There is nothing more reactionary than the small freehold system. It is increasing the strength of landlordism.[4] . . . Let the Government divide the waste lands among the people – they would support the entire pauper population and thus relieve the artificial labour market. . . . Instead of building workhouses, erect Colleges of Agriculture: instead of emigration promote home colonisation. . . .'[5]

[1] *National Reformer*, 15th and 22nd May 1847. Thomas Frost, on the other hand, thought that the formation of local branches of the National Land Company did something to re-unite the Chartists; see his *Forty Years' Recollections* (1880), p. 96. James Burn was 'convinced that O'Connor was perfectly honest in his intentions, and that he was sanguine of the entire success of his strange abortion of a plan for the redemption of the people . . . . The idea of possessing land . . . is a pleasing one. When we know that Sir Walter Scott plunged himself and others into irredeemable difficulties from an insane desire to possess landed property, we cannot wonder at the alacrity with which numbers of the people seized upon the agrarian bauble'; Autobiography, p. 178. For a defence of the National Land Company by 'An Unlocated Member' see *Reynold's Political Instructor*, 9th March 1850.

[2] Webb, *History of Trade Unionism* (1907), p. 161.

[3] *Accounts and Papers*, 1847–8, XIX (398), p. 50; *Notes to the People*, Vol. I, pp. 54–6, 104–14, 120, 185–6, 256; *People's Paper*, 5th, 12th and 19th June, 25th September, 25th December 1852. See also letters headed 'The Two Irish Os and the Land', and 'Land and Building Associations', in *Lloyd's Weekly Newspaper*, 15th June and 31st August 1845. The fact that Ernest Jones was a trustee of the National Land Company, coupled with his co-operation with O'Connor to produce the *Labourer* chiefly in the interests of that Company, might lead one to set him down as a staunch supporter of small holdings. But further enquiry shows that by 1851–2 he had changed his views, and although he held that a system of small-scale farming by occupying owners was preferable to landlordism and capitalistic large-scale farming, he thought that the way of *real* progress lay through nationalization of the land, after which, he said, 'such a thing as pauperism, in its real sense, could hardly exist'.

[4] See J. Saville, *Ernest Jones, Chartist* (1952), p. 138 and Appendix 3.

[5] Ernest Jones, *Open letter to Chief Justice Wilde* (1848); Saville, *op. cit.*, pp. 24, 152–7.

Meanwhile, rumours having spread that the National Land Company was mismanaged, questions were asked in Parliament and on 23rd May 1848 the House of Commons ordered an investigation by a Select Committee.[1] From a muddled mass of vouchers, memoranda and other loose papers it was estimated that the subscribers numbered approximately 70,000, of whom less than one-third had paid in full for their shares. A total sum exceeding £90,000 appears to have been received by the Company, which at one period was enrolling 5,000 new members weekly. Nor had the Company been idle: it had bought five estates and had built some 250 substantial cottages and four school-houses, while much of the land had been prepared and planted,[2] and 229 subscribers, chosen by ballot, were already settled upon it.[3] Unfortunately these industrial workers were soon in serious difficulties for they were, for the most part, ignorant of agriculture. On 1st August the Committee reported that since the Company could not be classified as a friendly society, it was illegal. The accounts, such as they were, showed that O'Connor had advanced several large sums of his own money, so that the Company appeared to owe him between £3,300 and £3,400.[4] As there had been no fraud, but rather the reverse, the Committee recommended that the scheme should be ended quietly before more serious consequences ensued.[5] The costly and complicated winding-up proceedings which followed, dragged on for more than ten years.[6]

The Chartist Movement was now showing signs of intensified activity, stimulated mainly by another trade recession at home and revolutionary happenings abroad. The improvement in trade and employment after 1842 had been short-lived, and by 1847 a complex tangle of economic and financial factors and forces, such as famine and

[1] *Hansard* (Third Series), Vol. XCVIII, p. 928.
[2] Finlaison found that 19,331 men had subscribed £74,406.16.0 in full payment for 57,236 shares. Part-payments amounted to £16,348.2.0 by 50,669 subscribers on 150,025 shares; *Accounts and Papers*, 1847–8, XIX (557), p. 1–3 and Q.1371; (398) pp. 73 *et. seq.*
[3] On four-acre holdings – 103 settlers were established; on three-acre holdings – 35; and on two-acre holdings – 91.
[4] *Accounts and Papers*, 1847–8, XIX (577), iii; *Labourer*, Vols I-IV, *passim.*
[5] For a detailed study see *Chartist Studies*, Ch. X, 'The Chartist Land Plan' by Joy MacAskill; cf. also A. Plummer, 'Spade Husbandry during the Industrial Revolution' in *Journal of South West Essex Technical College*, Vol. I, No. 2 (1942).
[6] *National Union: A Political and Social Record and Organ of the Political Union for the Obtainment of the People's Charter*, 1858, pp. 20, 28, 33, 43–5; *Star and National Trades Journal*, 10th April 1852, Letter from Martin Jude, the Newcastle miners' leader.

unrest in Ireland, wild speculation in railway development in England, and a short cotton crop in America, produced yet another crisis and 'great depression in nearly all branches of trade and industry'.[1] 'Tens of thousands of workers were . . . out of employment and starving', while unemployment continued to increase.[2] Early in 1848, a lean year on the whole, the revolutionary events in France, the displacement of Louis Philippe's regime by a republic with leanings towards Socialism, added fuel to the fires of discontent in England. Riots flared up in Glasgow and Manchester, and disturbances broke out elsewhere. Assembly halls in London were packed to capacity with excited workmen, and a meeting called to protest against the income tax, and banned by the police, was turned into a Chartist demonstration which the police were powerless to break up. Disorderly clashes erupted in Trafalgar Square and Camberwell. Meantime, Feargus O'Connor had astonished everybody and heartened the Chartists by winning a seat at Nottingham in the General Election of 1847 – thus becoming the first Chartist to sit in Parliament – while ten other seats were won by Radical candidates sympathetic to Chartist principles.[3] A new Chartist Petition was prepared, and as crowds flocked to sign it the *Northern Star* hopefully proclaimed that 'as France has secured for herself her beloved Republic, so Ireland must have her Parliament restored, and England her idolized Charter'.[4]

In the midst of this mounting political tension O'Brien (now living in London again) ranged himself with the right-wing Radicals, speaking at several meetings in moderate terms.[5] At the same time Hetherington and Holyoake came out strongly against any form of violence, even if the police were provocative; and O'Connor and Ernest Jones, despite the growing disapproval of many of their followers, took the same line.

A new Chartist Convention composed of forty-four members from thirty-six towns assembled at the John Street Institution in 3rd April 1848, and the very next day the old familiar cleavage appeared between those who were for strictly legal action and others disposed to be less cautious. O'Brien was a member of the Convention and, remembering the lessons of 1839–40, he 'poured abundant cold water' on the

---

[1] Richard Cobden, *The Three Panics, An Historical Episode* (1884), pp. 16–19.

[2] H. M. Hyndman, *Commercial Crises of the Nineteenth Century* (1892), p. 59.

[3] P. W. Slosson, *The Decline of the Chartist Movement* (1916), pp. 94–5; M. Beer, *op. cit.*, II, p. 165; G. D. H. Cole, *British Working Class Politics* (1941), pp. 21–2, 258.

[4] *Northern Star*, 25th March 1848. The Budget which had proposed to increase income tax from 7d to 1s in the £ had to be 'withdrawn for amendment'.

[5] McCabe, *op. cit.*, I, p. 136.

grandiose schemes of the (O'Connorite) executive,[1] pointing out that the forty-four members represented but a small fraction of the whole nation. But the Convention, with its head in the clouds, ignored O'Brien's advice and decided in favour of the convocation of a National Assembly empowered to present a memorial to the Queen and to stay in session until the adoption of the Charter should open the way to a Chartist Commonwealth.

Parliament was more practical. Feargus O'Connor, eccentric and unstable, failed to reassure the Commons as to the Chartists' peaceful intentions; a great force of police, special constables and troops, with four batteries of field guns to cover the approaches to the bridges, was at hand; and on 7th April the Commissioner of Police issued a proclamation declaring illegal the procession to Westminster which the Chartists planned for 10th April.[2] Queen Victoria, with her family left London on the following day. As flash-point loomed up, O'Brien decided to secede from the Convention, and on the day before the procession he publicly announced his resignation to a meeting of Chartists in Lambeth; a withdrawal due to the revision of his views on physical force, dating from the time of his imprisonment. He had made his decision, he said, because the Convention was for the most part composed of men from districts where the people were in the most dreadful condition, and 'in times of stirring excitement as the present, a Convention elected under such circumstances was likely to go too fast' and collide with the Government. Since he had given no pledge when elected to the Convention, he felt free to refuse his support to a scheme which, in face of the strength of the Government's preparations, could not possibly succeed.[3] The members of the Convention were, he believed, actuated by the noblest feelings, but their convictions had from the first been different from his. This pacific statement was frequently interrupted by hostile shouts and groans. A motion introduced in the Convention on 13th April: 'that the secretary write to James Bronterre O'Brien to request him to assign a reason for his long absence, or to attend to his duty', found a seconder but was eventually lost. Next day the Convention received a formal report that O'Brien had resigned, and Harney, turning angrily against his erstwhile hero, moved

[1] Hovell, *op. cit.*, p. 287–9.

[2] *Hansard* (Third Series), Vol. XCVII, pp. 1353 *et seq.; Fraser's Magazine*, May 1848; *Annual Register*, Vol. 90, p. 124; *Gentleman's Magazine*, May 1848, p. 536; Thos. Frost, *op. cit.*, Ch. VIII; H. Solly, *James Woodford*, II, p. 200; E. Longford, *Victoria R.I.* (1964), p. 196; See also an anti-Chartist pamphlet, *What the Chartists are*, by 'A Fellow-labourer' (London 1848).

[3] *The Times*, 10th April 1848.

a motion censuring O'Brien for having acted with great disrespect to the Convention by the irregular manner in which he had vacated his seat. This was carried.[1]

Thus it was that O'Brien publicly and permanently renounced physical force and took no part in the monster procession and demonstration which ended on Kennington Common in the so-called 'fiasco' of 10th April 1848.[2] It seems likely that he knew much more about the intentions of the militant elements among the London Chartists, which included many Irishmen, than he was prepared to divulge in public. Recent research shows that Chartism in London, after hesitant beginnings, gained in numbers and improved in organization from 1842 to 1848, when a peak of turbulence was reached. In the shadows, McDouall, true to form, was busily egging on a revolutionary 'Ulterior Committee' towards an armed rising in the centre of government. Fighting between police and Chartists actually flared up at Clerkenwell Green in May, and the watchful and well-informed authorities, expecting a great 'popular commotion' at Bonner's Field in Bethnal Green on Whit Monday, 12th June, had police and troops standing by in considerable numbers.[3] Easy penetration by government spies now caused the hasty dissolution of the Ulterior Committee, after which the insurrectionary movement collapsed and, with the marked improvement in national economic growth during the decade 1849–58, the fortunes of Chartism sank to a new 'low'.[4] Its many weaknesses became more obvious; the whole Movement more seriously split; the leaders more at loggerheads. Strong allies had not been found, while unity and harmony in the pursuit of a single supreme objective continued to hover, alluring yet unattainable – a beckoning mirage always out of reach.

---

[1] *Northern Star*, 15th and 22nd April 1848. Mathew Arnold attended a meeting of the Convention of 1848 and was struck by the ability of the speakers; but he thought he would not like to be governed by them; Russell, *Letters of Matthew Arnold*, I, p. 7.

[2] For an account of the procession from the John Street Institution to Kennington Common by a writer hostile to Chartism, see Charles Mackay, *Forty Years' Recollections* (1877), II, pp. 52–8; see also *Illustrated London News*, 15th April 1848, pp. 241–3; Malmesbury, *Memoirs of an Ex-Minister* (1884), I, pp. 208–38.

[3] *Punch* (1848, p. 172), depicted a special constable 'laying down the law' to a Chartist: 'Now mind . . . if I kill you, it's nothing; but if you kill me, by Jingo it's Murder.'

[4] Society for the Study of Labour History, *Bulletin No.* 20, Spring 1970, pp. 10–18.

Chapter X

A CENTRE IN SOHO

During the summer and autumn of 1848 O'Brien suffered a partial eclipse, but he reappeared in November as editor of *The Power of the Pence*, a Chartist weekly 'intended for those who know the look of a penny better than that of a pound'.[1] In this penny journal O'Brien carried on, for six months, a genuine attempt at adult education by means of well-written full-length articles on many aspects of current affairs, such as universal suffrage, nationalization of land and minerals, banks for the people, the church establishment, financial reform, and the gold discoveries in California. Most ambitious, perhaps, was a series of articles on the Constitution of the United States: thorough and detailed, but almost certainly too 'stiff' for all but a few of the working people; and a number of penetrating essays on direct and indirect taxation also written by O'Brien, whose views on the use of taxation as a leveller of wealth and an instrument of 'social equilibrium' were well ahead of his time. Four-fifths of the public revenue, he said, came from the pockets of the poor through indirect taxation: a situation which ought to be reversed.

On 14th April 1849 the editor announced that 'a severe illness' prevented him from writing much that he wanted to say, and a week later *The Power of the Pence* was brought to an end.

'This journal,' O'Brien wrote, 'has now been established some six months. . . . From its great size (being the largest political serial of the day) and the consequent great expense attached to the typographical department, it would require a circulation of not less than 15,000 to meet its expenses. A circulation of ten times 15,000 might possibly be obtained for a weekly publication devoted to light reading . . . for people of all ages and all creeds, but we have been unable to secure a sufficiently large one to warrant the continuance of the present undertaking.'

During the same winter (1848–9) O'Brien gave weekly lectures at

[1] The first number appeared on 11th November 1848, and the last (No. 24), on 21st April 1849.

the John Street Literary and Scientific Institution, as well as other lectures elsewhere, and in the spring of 1849 he presided over a series of discussions 'on all the engrossing questions of the day'. He also had under consideration a tour of the Midlands and North, as far as Glasgow, to begin after Easter 1849. But, said he, in a revealing statement,

'I will not go anywhere to oppose Owenism, or Fourierism, or Communism, or any other *ism* that is not in itself opposed to the rights of the people. . . . I will not embroil myself with sectarians of any kind, political or religious (including Chartist sects or factions) . . . I will discuss only these questions with them, *viz*:

(1) What are the rights which the people of this country are entitled to demand from their government?

(2) Would the concession of these rights suffice to secure for us a real and permanent prosperity?

(3) What are the means to enforce a concession of these rights by the parties now opposed to them?'[1]

About this time, too, O'Brien probably wrote (or re-cast) his essays on 'The Rise, Progress and Phases of Human Slavery: How it came into the World and how it shall be made to go out'. In this series of twenty-one articles,[2] the first of which appeared in No. 2 of *Reynolds's Political Instructor* on 17th November 1849, O'Brien developed the thesis that slavery, on one form or another, exists, and has always existed, the world over. Nothing appears more common and widespread than the subjection of man by force or fraud in human societies, ancient and modern, barbarous and civilized, Christian as well as pagan. But there is one important difference. In ancient pagan societies slavery was open and avowed, while in nearly all modern Christian societies it is hypocritically masked, and is, therefore, all the more galling and unbearable. Working-class people are, in truth, the slave populations of modern capitalist societies. Few pause to notice, said O'Brien, that in countries such as England and France, the working class constitutes

---

[1] *The Power of the Pence*, pp. 24, 242, 257.

[2] These articles, which appeared over a new *nom-de-plume*, 'A National Reformer', were reprinted and published in book form, with some alterations and additions, postumously, in 1885 by William Reeves, 185 Fleet Street, in association with Martin Boon and G. Standing, as a book of twenty-one chapters and 148 closely printed pages. 'It seems to us,' said one reviewer, 'as the rising from the dead, after a long sleep, of the mighty great who electrified his audiences with his eloquence.'

194

'a separate and distinct race',[1] deprived of the fruits of true liberty – independence, self-reliance, security and happiness.

'The working classes . . . in modern society are . . . bequeathed to us by the ancient world under the name of Proletarians. By the term "Proletarians" is to be understood, not merely that class of citizens to which the electoral census of the Romans gave the name, but every description of persons of both sexes, who, having no masters to own them as slaves, and consequently to be chargeable with their maintenance, and who, being without fortune or friends, were obliged to procure their subsistence as they best could – by labour, by mendicity, by theft, or by prostitution. The Romans used the term to denote the lowest, or lowest but one, class of voters – those who, being without property, had only their offsprings (*proles*) to offer as hostages to the State for their good behaviour, or rather as guarantees for not abusing their rights of citizenship. We use the term in the more enlarged sense of its modern acceptation, to denote every description of persons who are dependent upon others for the means of earning their daily bread, without being actual slaves.'

Bad as the system of slavery was in the ancient world, it exhibited nothing so abominable as the development and progress of modern proletarianism; an evil which had grown alarmingly, especially in recent times. The ancients did not regard slavery as an unnatural and inhuman institution.[2] The doctrine of human equality had not at that time made its way into the world. Livy, Aulus Gellius, Tacitus, and other Roman historians mention between them about ten revolts of slaves, but none of these had as its chief cause the desire for real liberty or equality.[3] The openly avowed slavery of the ancient world was, in O'Brien's opinion, 'less destructive of life, morals, and happiness to the majority than the present system of indirect or disguised slavery, as effected in most civilized countries by unjust agrarian, monetary, and fiscal laws'.

O'Brien saw no essential difference between treating men, women and children as chattels, and employing them for a mere pittance in a slop-shop under a sweat-master.[4] There is, he declared, no law of the Twelve Tables giving Irish landlords direct power over the bodies of

[1] Cf. Disraeli's *Sybil, or the Two Nations* (1845).
[2] Cf. Zimmern, *The Greek Commonwealth* (1911), (5th edn 1931), pp. 385n., 387n.
[3] O'Brien, *Rise, Progress and Phases of Human Slavery*, pp. 27–30.
[4] Cf. J. F. Bray, *Labour's Wrongs and Labour's Remedy* (1839), p. 69; 'the working classes are no less owned than their ancestors were'.

195

their tenants, but laws exist which authorize landlords to evict their tenants and drive them 'homeless and breadless, to find a shelter and a crust where they may'. The slaves of ancient Rome, knowing little or nothing of real liberty, were, in fact, better off than the so-called 'free and independent labourers' of nineteenth-century Britain, who were without arms, votes, land, money or credit.[1] The superficial conversion of the Roman pagans to Christianity, and the abolition of chattel-slavery had the effect, in the long run, of turning 'well-fed, well-housed, comfortable slaves into ragged, starving paupers' and filling Europe 'with a race of Proletarians by far more numerous and miserable than the human chattels of the ancients, whose place they occupy in modern civilization'. Even the Negro slaves of America were, on the whole, in a better position than the 'proletarian wage-slaves' of Britain, for 'emancipation enables the master to get more labour and pay less for it'. Let the British people look at the *Morning Chronicle*'s investigations which revealed that there were in London at that time over 28,000 needlewomen whose average earnings were only 4½d a day, and there were 'many others whose earnings hardly exceeded three shillings a week all the year round'. While the American Negro slave had a considerable value in the eyes of his master, the same could not be said of the Irish peasant, for in the dreadful famine winter of 1846–7, two millions of the Irish people were 'condemned as surplus', and it was actually considered worth while to spend money to get rid of them.[2]

The rescue of the greater part of the human race from proletarian wage-slavery would require, said O'Brien, a great social revolution. Whether this deliverance would come peaceably, 'in the way of social reformation', or emerge from the chaos of a violent convulsion, nobody knew. His mature opinion in the late 1840s was that the times seemed favourable to a peaceable solution; a bloodless revolution 'in the political and social mechanism of society' which ought naturally to follow the amazing revolution in the arts and sciences. Fully alive to the enormous productive potentialities of the new machines, he declared categorically that 'no portion of the human race needs the subjugation of any other portion for the gratification of its utmost legitimate wants and desires'. In such an age of plenty every vestige of every description of slavery ought to disappear, as indeed it would, if only a proper spirit were abroad. It seemed incredible that the so-called Christians who were straining to secure the abolition of chattel-

[1] O'Brien, *Human Slavery*, p. 39.
[2] *Ibid.*, pp. 48–50; cf. Royden Harrison, *Before the Socialists* (1965), p 60.

slavery abroad, had made no attempt to abolish wage-slavery at home.[1] Yet wage-slavery was neither inevitable not indestructible, for it was a man-made product of tyrannical laws imposed by fraud and force by one social class upon another, and while it gave 'monstrous hell-begotten opulence' to the few, it meant slow starvation for the many. The agricultural labourers, the very men without whom England would be a wilderness, were driven by low wages and starvation, to the brink of rebellion. These were the men who had raised and earned, many times over, the food now denied to them. The root causes of all this misery were private property in land and unjust 'money laws'. The land and the raw materials which it contains should belong to all men; 'to assert the contrary would be to assert that God, like a capricious despot, dispenses His favours regardless of justice or of the wants of His creatures.

'We defy all the learning and ability in the United Kingdom to show how we can be extricated from poverty and premature death in this country without a radical reform of our land and money laws.'

Was Parliament, admittedly so powerful in other matters, powerless in this? Not at all. Broadly stated, the problem was how

' . . . to supersede old worn-out institutions by new and life-giving ones, suited to the wants of the age, and capable of giving the utmost possible development to liberty and progress, without avenging the past or doing violence to existing rulers or interests. . . . It only needs a sense of justice in rulers and ruled'.

'Why should violence and destruction be called in 'to do what good sense and justice should alone suffice to accomplish? . . .'

'We assert emphatically that the repeal of unjust laws and the enactment of a few just and salutary ones, upon Land, Credit and Equitable Exchange (the latter including Currency), is all that is needed to terminate poverty and slavery for ever.' [2]

It was during the second half of 1849 that O'Brien was encouraged by a group of his friends and followers to bring out yet another penny

[1] George Beaumont tells us that, at the age of seven, he started to work a fourteen-hour day in a mill, to which, every morning, he helped to carry his five-year-old sister. 'Those who advocate the abolition of colonial slavery,' he declared at a public meeting in Huddersfield in 1831, 'ought not to be considered as sincere unless they advocate the extinction of slavery in factories. . . . Should children be worked 14 or 16 hours a day, merely because their parents are poor?'
[2] O'Brien, *Human Slavery*, pp. 54–5, 98–100, 108, 112, 121–2, 126–8.

weekly paper – the *Social Reformer*, aimed at preparing 'the public mind' for political and social reforms which would 'emancipate the labouring classes'. Besides publishing articles and reviews on such familiar, current topics as Chartism, Free Trade and 'the Manchester School', the state of Ireland and the Irish peasants, the diseases of the poor, revolutionary happenings in France, and the Hungarian patriots' fight against the Austrians, this well-printed little paper, which ran for only eleven weeks (11th August to 20th October 1849), was the organ of the newly-formed Eclectic Club, from which it received a modest subsidy. The names of seventy-eight members of the Club were printed in the issue for 1st September 1849, and a fortnight later it carried an announcement that a 'ball and concert would be held for the benefit of the funds of the Eclectic Club'. At the end of September 1849 a member of the Club suggested the formation of a new propagandist body to press forward the cause of political and social reform. G. W. M. Reynolds and several other keen Radicals favoured the proposal, and so there emerged, in outline, the 'National Reform League for the Peaceful Regeneration of Society', one of the splinter groups, such as the People's Charter Union, William Lovett's short-lived People's League, and G. J. Harney's Society of Fraternal Democrats, all formed as boosters during Chartism's final phase.[1] Feargus O'Connor's prophecy, made in 1841, that the triumph of Chartism 'was on the swiftest wing of fast-flying time'[2] had proved utterly false. 'The old Mechanics' Institutes have failed to accomplish their purpose; the political associations of the Working Classes have become almost lifeless' so wrote Thomas Cooper in 1850, when he thought the time had come to form a 'Progress Union' to 'combine efforts for the spread of intelligence with a united struggle for the franchise, and for the general amelioration of our political and social condition'.[3] Even Ernest Jones had to admit, early in 1852, that Chartism was *in extremis*;[4] while the veteran revolutionist, William Benbow, was at last forced to the conclusion that if they were to have any chance of success, Radicals 'must lop off everything but the principle', manhood suffrage, leaving all other 'points' and details to be dealt with by 'a Manhood Suffrage Parliament'.[5]

[1] When Henry Hetherington died, in August 1849, O'Brien wrote an obituary article in the *Social Reformer*. G. W. M. Reynolds was a successful writer and publisher. For some details of his sales of cheap fiction, see R. D. Altick, *The English Common Reader* (1957), p. 384.
[2] *Northern Star*, 17th July 1841.
[3] *Cooper's Journal*, 5th January 1850.
[4] *Notes to the People*, II, p. 876.
[5] *Star of Freedom*, 16th October 1852.

Early in January 1850, *Reynolds's Political Instructor* printed an open letter (dated 19th December 1849) signed by Bronterre O'Brien and John Rogers, one of his staunchest friends and followers, which outlined the aims of the National Reform League and appealed for support.[1] Briefly, it stood for more than the People's Charter, but less than the full programme of the Owenite Socialists. In addition to a 'full, fair and free representation of the whole people in the Commons House of Parliament', the N.R.L. proclaimed that seven fundamental reforms 'are necessary to ensure real political and social justice to the oppressed and suffering population of the United Kingdom, and to protect society from violent revolutionary changes':

1 Abolition of the existing poor law system and its replacement by a just and efficient system 'which would centralize the rates and dispense them equitably and economically for the beneficial employment and relief of the destitute poor', so as to render poor people 'self-sustaining and self-respecting'. The rates should be levied upon the owners of every description of 'realized property'.[2]

2 In order gradually to diminish both the burden of the rates and the growing mass of pauperism', the government should buy land and settle the unemployed poor upon it either as individual tenants or as 'industrial communities'.[3]

The burdens of taxation and public and private indebtedness should be 'equitably adjusted in favour of the debtor and productive classes . . . upon a scale corresponding with the general fall of prices and of wages'.

4 The State should gradually resume (after paying fair compensation) the ownership of all land, mines turbaries, fisheries, etc. in the United Kingdom and the colonies. As trustee in perpetuity, the State should let the land, mines, etc. 'on such terms as the law and local circumstances shall determine'. Ultimately the rentals so collected by the State 'would form a national fund adequate to defray all charges of the public service, execute all needful public work, and educate the population, without the necessity for any taxation'.

---

[1] *Social Reformer*, 6th October 1849; *Reynolds's Political Instructor*, 29th December 1849 and 5th January 1850.

[2] 'Realized property' is not defined.

[3] This proposal, called 'home colonization' by the O'Brienites, contained more than a modicum of Owenism.

5 It should be the duty of the State to provide a sound system of national credit, to enable approved applicants to rent and cultivate land on their own account instead of being subjected to the injustice and tyranny of wage-slavery. 'The same privilege of obtaining a share of the national credit to be applicable to . . . individuals, companies and communities in all other branches of useful industry'.

6 The national currency should be based upon 'real, consumable wealth, or on the *bona fide* credit of the State, and not upon the variable and uncertain amount of scarce metals'.

7 It is an important duty to set up, in every town and city, public marts or stores, 'for the reception of all kinds of exchangeable goods, to be valued by disinterested officers appointed for the purpose, either upon a corn or a labour standard; the depositors to receive in exchange symbolic notes 'which should be legal currency throughout the country, enabling their owners to draw from the public stores to an equivalent amount'.

The statement ends by disclaiming any attempt to prescribe *all* the reforms needed in society; 'doubtless, we want a sound system of national education for youth, made compulsory upon all parents and guardians . . . doubtless, we require a juster and more humane code of civil and penal law, to say nothing of the nationalization of public utilities such as railways, canals, bridges, docks, gas-works and water-works. But these reforms may be expected to follow, once the basic reforms have been carried through.

The League's first headquarters were at 72 Newman Street, off Oxford Street, and here 'social re-unions' were held every Sunday evening, O'Brien's week-night lectures being given at the John Street Institution. The new body was recognized by the National Charter Association, with G. W. M. Reynolds acting as a link, and by the Fraternal Democrats. In March 1850, its proposals for the peaceful reform of society were 'passed by a crowded meeting held in the large theatre of the Literary Institution, Leicester Square, London, on the motion of J. Bronterre O'Brien, seconded by Richard Hart'. Supported by members of the National Charter Association and the Fraternal Democrats, the proposals were subsequently 'carried at various public meetings'.[1] O'Brien, still anxious to promote a sense of unity among

[1] James Bronterre O'Brien, *State Socialism* (1850), p. 1. In 1856, Richard Hart stood as a Chartist 'hustings candidate' at Newcastle-upon-Tyne, but he did not go to the poll; see G. D. H. Cole, *British Working Class Politics* (1941), p. 259.

Chartists, Owenites, and all other sympathetic Radicals, attached importance to such expressions of agreement and mutual support. At a banquet sponsored by the Fraternal Democrats to mark the first anniversary of the French Revolution of 1848 he spoke in favour of a union of Chartists and Socialists, and, incidentally, effected a personal reconciliation between himself and Harney, his erstwhile pupil. O'Brien's N.R.L. confined its activities mainly to the Metropolis, and, although its membership was never very large – probably about 500 – its influence in the realm of ideas was considerable over many years. O'Brien was elected the League's president and principal leader; he lectured twice a week under its auspices, and he was largely responsible for the preparation of its programme.

This programme forms the first and principal part of Bronterre O'Brien's ten-page pamphlet entitled *State Socialism* (1850).[1] The second part consists of the 'principles and practice of the Rational Religion as developed and promulgated by Robert Owen', and the third part sets out the object of the National Rational League based upon the social system of Robert Owen and the political programme of Bronterre O'Brien.[2]

On 30th March 1850 *Reynolds's Political Instructor* carried a brief biography of Bronterre O'Brien illustrated by a portrait printed on the front page, from a recent daguerreotype photograph taken by Mayall of 433 Strand. Evidently the biography was either written by O'Brien, or compiled from material supplied by him. Although several details

---

[1] O'Brien, *State Socialism* (1850), pp. 1–6; *Reynolds's Political Instructor*, 4th May 1850; Gammage, *op. cit.*, p. 401; State Socialism assumed that power would be won by parliamentary means and then used to nationalize industries. But it offered to the working class only the state and state-appointed managers in place of private employers or companies under the managers appointed by them. This appeared to be no great improvement, if any, in the eyes of many working men.

[2] The essence of Robert Owen's 'rational religion' seems to be contained in two propositions: (1) that 'the contemplation of Nature will create in every mind feelings of high adoration, too sublime and pure to be expressed in forms or words, for the Incomprehensible Power which acts in and through all Nature, everlastingly composing, decomposing, and recomposing the material of the universe, producing the endless variety of life, of mind, and of organized form; and (2) that the practice of the Rational Religion consists of promoting, to the utmost of our power, the well-being and happiness of every man, woman and child, without regard for their sects, party, country or colour; and its, Worship, in those inexpressible feelings of wonder, admiration and delight, which . . . naturally arise from the contemplation of the infinity of Space, of the Eternity of Duration, of the Order of the Universe, and of that Incomprehensible Power by which the atom is moved and the aggregate of Nature is governed'. O'Brien, *State Socialism* (1850), pp. 7–9.

relating to his school days are inaccurate or exaggerated, the account is, on the whole, a fair one, and it is specially interesting to find a claim, later in the article, that O'Brien's political and economic ideas were already becoming well-known not only in the United Kingdom but in the United States also, 'owing, in America, to the great number of his disciples that the persecutions of 1839–42 and subsequent years forced to exile themselves'. Five weeks after this, the *Political Instructor* (No. 26) printed an article (unsigned) on Robespierre, as well as the final instalment of Bronterre O'Brien's series on 'Human Slavery'.

We have now struck the keynote of O'Brien's career after 1850. On paper and from the platform he strove to disseminate his political, economic and moral theories and to keep alight the flickering flame of Chartism; activities which occupied his time but yielded only a scanty income. Although, after 1848, he was a less prominent – and in some quarters, less popular – figure in the Chartist movement, which was dominated in its few final years by Ernest Jones, he remained always a staunch Chartist. On 10th June 1850, with a flash of his old fire, he told a gathering of Greenwich Chartists that no measure of reform short of the People's Charter could ever rescue the oppressed working class from the tyranny of the upper classes.[1] In company with Harney and Ernest Jones he was against the formation of yet another splinter group, the National Charter League, because it would further divide and weaken the movement. Although he declined to seek election to the executive of the National Charter Association, he remained a prominent member and opposed all attempts to draw people away. At the John Street Literary and Scientific Institution during 1850, O'Brien and Reynolds gave a series of lectures, under the auspices of the N.C.A., on political questions, which drew from the executive committee of the N.C.A. a resolution of thanks to O'Brien for his zeal and devotion to the Association and to the cause of democracy in general.[2] He attended nearly all the large democratic meetings and demonstrations held in London, including those connected with democracy and socialism on the Continent, and everywhere his contributions to the discussions were well received. When the Society of Fraternal Democrats celebrated Robespierre's birthday by a supper on 5th

[1] *Reynolds's*, 16th June 1850; cf. *Notes to the People*, II, pp. 822, 843, 971.

[2] *Reynolds's*, 5th and 26th May; 30th June; 1st and 8th December 1850; *Northern Star*, 21st December 1850; Hovell, *op. cit.*, p. 298. The John Street Institute, opened in 1840, was 'a kind of club or mechanics' institute for advanced thinkers among workmen, and especially for the followers of Robert Owen'. The name was changed to the 'Literary and Scientific Institution' in 1846; it was closed in 1858.

April 1850, Harney presided and 'Citizen' Bronterre O'Brien's 'vindication of the character of the victim of Thermidor was enthusiastically applauded'.[1] A month later he spoke at a celebration to mark the success of Eugene Sue and the six Republican candidates at the French elections, and in June he was the principal speaker at a meeting convened by the Fraternal Democrats to discuss the suppression of electoral reform in France. Hitherto, apart from a letter in praise of Kossuth, Mazzini and Ledru-Rollin, published in the *Political Instructor* in December 1849, he had said and written little about international affairs, but now, in his old style, he attacked the 'moneyclass' in France 'who sought to keep the people poor by robbing them of the fruits of their labours', declaring that these lying, cheating tyrants who had filled Paris with 150,000 hired assassins, deserved nothing short of death. In June he made a long speech at a meeting held to protest against the treatment of his namesake and contemporary, William Smith O'Brien (1803–64), the Irish Nationalist, who was transported to Tasmania in 1848 after his conviction on a charge of high treason for a pitiable attempt at insurrection in Ireland. At other times Bronterre helped to raise relief funds for Polish and Hungarian political exiles. When Holyoake, Harney and others wanted to found a society to unite all social reformers, to propagate a knowledge of associative and co-operative doctrines, and to press for unsectarian education, O'Brien promptly offered his support.[2] At the same time his lectures on politics, economics, ethics and religion, given under the auspices of the National Reform League,[3] were eagerly listened to by the younger men, small in numbers but ardent in spirit, some of whom were to become Labour leaders in the years ahead, finding their way into all the important progressive movements – franchise extension, trade unionism, education, public health, temperance, and social insurance.

O'Brien now became connected in some way with *Reynolds's Weekly* newspaper (price 4*d*), a more ambitious venture which superseded the *Political Instructor* in May 1850, G. W. M. Reynolds, its owner, describing it as 'a Journal of Democratic Progress and General Intelligence'. The exact nature of O'Brien's connection is obscure; he certainly wrote for it, for about three months, probably as a leader

---

[1] *Democratic Review*, May 1850, pp. 463–4. O'Brien also proposed a toast to 'the chairman, George Julian Harney', and later in the evening other toasts included 'Health and long life to Bronterre O'Brien'; 'The memory of Robert Emmet and the health of . . . Smith O'Brien and all other true Irish patriots.' Tom Paine, George Washington and Ernest Jones were similarly honoured.

[2] *Reynolds's*, 12th and 19th May, 2nd and 9th June, 28th July, 20th and 27th October 1850; *People's Paper*, 6th November 1852.

[3] *Reynolds's*, 19th May and 23rd June 1850.

writer, and he may have helped, briefly, in an editorial capacity. At any rate, the choice of O'Brien to reply to the toast of 'The Democratic Press' at the festival held to celebrate Ernest Jones's release from prison suggests that his past services were not forgotten and that he was still respected among Radical journalists in the middle of 1850.

In August O'Brien travelled once again over familiar ground when he went on a lecture tour through N.W. England, during which – perhaps somewhat nostalgically – he made several speeches in Manchester and Bury. Ernest Jones and Feargus O'Connor were also touring in the north of England at that time.[1] Early in the following month O'Brien was back in London, and on 1st October, when he attended a Chartist meeting convened to celebrate the opening of a Working Man's Hall at Church Fields, Greenwich, police 'interference' twice caused the adjournment of the meeting to another place; but the Chartists persisted and finally came to rest at the Globe Tavern, where O'Brien told the gathering that during the twenty years of his active political life he had had many experiences of police persecution. He urged all working men to co-operate in building halls for themselves, adding that the large numbers of unemployed men could not be better employed.[2]

About this time, with the advice and assistance of several members of the National Reform League, O'Brien founded and opened the Eclectic Institute in a disused chapel which could be entered either from Dudley Court (now called Denmark Place) or from No. 18 Denmark Street, Soho, not far from the Parish Church of St Giles-in-the-Fields. Dudley Court was a somewhat obscure alley linking Crown Street (now much widened and re-named Charing Cross Road) and St Giles High Street. The existence of a nonconformist meeting house or chapel here can certainly be traced back to 1776 when the occupiers were a small Scottish sect known as Bereans or Barclayites;[3] and it may have 'belonged originally to the French Protestants'. But no sect

---

[1] *Ibid.*, 25th August, 1st and 8th September 1850.

[2] *Ibid.*, 15th September and 6th October 1850.

[3] Founded by John Barclay (1734–98), M.A. (St Andrews), a Scottish minister and a powerful preacher, whose doctrinal views shocked the more narrowly orthodox elders at that time. He established 'Berean' churches – so called because their congregations, like the early Christians of Berea, 'received the word with all readiness of mind, and searched the scriptures daily' (Acts XVII, 10–11) – in a dozen cities and towns in Scotland, and during a visit to London in 1776 he founded a similar church and a debating society in Dudley Court, Soho. See D.N.B.; Ency. Brit. (1964 edn), III, p. 156; W. Wilson, *Dissenting Churches and Meeting Houses in London, Westminster, and Southwark* (1814), IV, pp. 37–9; *Gent. Mag.*, Vol. 68 (1798), p. 724.

or denomination seems to have remained in possession for very long. During the late 1820s and early 1830s the Baptists held services in the Dudley Court Chapel, and in the 1840s the Reverend Richard Bevill Isaac, a Congregational minister, used it temporarily. Therefore, it seems not inappropriate that eventually the building came to be used by a body dedicated to eclecticism. When Bronterre O'Brien took it over in 1850, the owner of No. 18 Denmark Street and the chapel at the rear was a Mr Taylor, and the tenant, from 1850 to 1853, was Egbert Griffith, a carpenter, from whom Bronterre O'Brien seems to have taken a sub-tenancy of the chapel premises. The rent charged was probably quite small, for at that date the rateable value of the chapel, as a separate building, was only £13 per annum.[1] The entrance to the chapel or hall during O'Brien's occupancy was through a passage from No. 18 Denmark Street, which was designated, unofficially, '18A'. It appears that in the mid-1850s Griffiths, the carpenter, moved out and was succeeded by John Flexman, who, by an arrangement with O'Brien, turned No. 18 into a coffee and reading rooms, which served as a useful annexe to the Eclectic Institute.

On 7th January 1851, at the first public meeting of the Institute, Bronterre O'Brien explained that the new club would not be pinned to any party, but would take what was good from all parties. He stressed the importance of the principles and purposes of the National Reform League, commending especially a proposal to make a thorough study of public credit and currency. Manufacturers, he said, could easily get loans, but the working man, the true basis of all credit, was denied at the banks and defrauded by the pawnbrokers. Clearly it was imperative to go on instructing the people as to their rights, both political and economic. Henceforth O'Brien's regular week-day lectures as well as his Sunday discourses were delivered at the Eclectic Institute instead of the John Street Institution.[2] Classes in English grammar and

---

[1] L.C.C. *Survey of London*, V, p. 121; R. Dobie, *History of the United Parishes of St Giles-in-the-Fields and St George Bloomsbury* (1829), p. 70; *V.C.H. London*, I, pp. 391–2; Parish Rate Books, St Giles-in-the-Fields; London Directories, 1849–56; *Congregational Year Book*, 1867, p. 291. Additional information has been supplied by the London Borough of Camden, the Baptist Union of Gt Britain and Ireland, Dr Williams's Library, and the Rector of St Giles-in-the-Fields. In 1850, Karl Marx and his family occupied two second-floor rooms at 28 Dean Street, Soho, only a short walk from O'Brien's Eclectic Institute.

[2] The Literary and Scientific Institution was in John Street (now Whitfield Street), off the Tottenham Court Road. Before long it became well known as a forum for lectures and a centre of Owenism in London, offering adult education and social amenities and recreation.

composition, French and mathematics were also offered at the new centre, and, from 1852, 'The Eclectic Young Men's Educational Classes' in English, French and Science, were held at 8.30 p.m. on Tuesdays and Thursdays. This courageous piece of pioneering was one of the small originating cells from which there has grown in London today's vast and varied part-time non-vocational institutes and classes; a provision of adult education quite unsurpassed, in both quantity and quality, anywhere in the world.

To those who attended his lectures O'Brien gave the distilled essence of his reading, thinking, and writing, and of his experience in the political mêlée for more than twenty years. He was careful to point out that although universal suffrage was of paramount importance, it would be 'a great error to suppose that when the vote is gained all is gained. All the real work will then remain to be done'. But, he told them,

'. . . you will [then] stand on the threshold of good government. Whether or no you will enter the banquet hall and partake of the feast will depend entirely upon the intelligence and integrity brought to bear on the work. At least the people will stand on vantage ground, and, for the first time in history, govern themselves'.

Their ability to do this well would depend upon the provision of a national system of free secular education, which would be the democratic path to political, intellectual, and economic freedom and power. 'Education is like wealth or machinery or manure or the air of heaven. . . . It is good if widely diffused.' He poured scorn upon the pernicious, bogus education which merely taught people to be 'content with their station, that is to say, remain passive paupers and slaves'. But once the producers had become 'as wise as their taskmasters', their 'misery and poverty would . . . be replaced by riches and good living'. Therefore, let the people begin without delay to 'educate themselves in a thousand ways' by taking advantage of all forms of voluntary adult education through both the printed and the spoken word, 'and thus endow themselves with greater power to enforce concessions from the legislature'. These two planks, Franchise and Education, 'form the platform to be attained before we can hope to reach loftier elevations, and become truly great and excellent as a nation and a people'.[1]

Two topics always proved especially attractive – money and religion. From the beginning of Bronterre O'Brien's career, the currency question was much to the fore. William Cobbett thundered on the subject for

[1] McDouall's *Chartist and Republican Journal*, Nos 14 and 17 (July 1841), pp. 110, 132.

years;[1] Thomas Attwood, a professional banker, persistently advocated an expanded and managed paper currency; while a host of other writers made up a loud, discordant chorus, for no subject attracts more cranks than currency and credit. The disastrous financial panics and trade slumps of 1825, 1836–9, and 1847 could still be remembered; and in the early fifties, while O'Brien was giving his lectures, a torrent of new-found gold was gushing into Europe from the diggings of California and Australia.[2] As one would expect, O'Brien approached the problem from the standpoint of the poor man, who was commonly the innocent – and ignorant – victim of the actions of governments and bankers, merchants and industrialists; actions which he was powerless to control. When the bankers over-issued notes, prices rose and real wages fell, thus depriving the working man of 'a great portion of his hard earnings'. On the other hand, when prices fell employers reduced wages and discharged workmen; so that while the workmen did not share in the so-called 'general prosperity', he was the first to suffer in times of depression.

'It matters not to him which party prevails – the Banking, the Trading, or the Agricultural interest – whoever may succeed in obtaining most of the spoil, *he is sure to be the victim.*'

What the majority of the newspapers, with their eyes upon the revenue returns, were pleased to call 'the increasing prosperity of the country', O'Brien saw as nothing more that 'an increasing consumption of excisable luxuries . . . by the plundering and gormandizing classes'.[3] Of course, he did not make the elementary error of confusing money with real wealth.

'It is not [he said] gold and silver, nor yet bank notes, *as the paper money schemers would have us believe*, that have given the prodigious impulse we have witnessed to improvements in America. It is the abundance of food produced by its agricultural population, that enables so great a number to be employed in constructing canals, bridges, railroads, etc.'[4]

Paper money, he argued, is as 'real' or 'good' as gold money if its purchasing power is the same; but neither a Bank of England note

[1] See e.g. W. Cobbett, *Paper against Gold*, a series of thirty-two *Letters* published between July 1812 and September 1815, purporting to show 'that Taxation, Pauperism, Povery, Misery and Crime have all increased and ever must increase' as a result of the issue of inconvertible paper money.

[2] H. M. Hyndman, *Commercial Crises of the Nineteenth Century* (1892), Chs. II–IV.

[3] *London Dispatch*, October 1836, *passim.*

[4] *Bronterre's National Reformer*, 7th January 1837.

207

nor a gold sovereign would be worth anything in a country where there was nothing to buy. If paper money represents *bona fide* wealth given in exchange for it by the holder, it is not only inconvenient, but unnecessary, to convert the paper into gold. Money is required merely as a 'token of value' and 'whether the token be of gold or of paper ought not to make a pin's difference'.[1] In O'Brien's view, it was not essential that the medium of exchange should have 'intrinsic value'.[2] Reformers in the past had seen one class of men thriving unduly at the expense of another class through the instrumentality of paper money, and had mistakenly concluded that all systems of paper currency were bad. It was quite possible to make a paper currency work for the benefit of the poor, and to this end O'Brien, strongly influenced by Owenism, shaped his plan, for a 'symbolic currency'.

The national currency should be based, he argued, not upon the variable and uncertain quantity of scarce metals, but upon real consumable wealth or upon the *bona fide* credit of the State. A currency based upon the so-called precious metals, however suitable in past times, or in the present for purposes of international trade, had become 'inadequate to perform the functions of representing and distributing' the growing volume of national wealth 'thereby rendering all commodities liable to perpetual fluctuation in price, as those metals happened to be more or less plentiful in any country'.[3]

'In no country have the working classes been allowed any of the advantages of paper money. In no country has there been allowed a symbolic currency to represent the products of their labour, and to enable them to interchange, at sight, with one another, their respective productions on the equitable principle of equal labour for equal labour. Till this is done the inestimable value of symbolic money, as an instrument of exchange must remain unknown.'[4]

Having indicated his objective from a hilltop, O'Brien plunged into the thickets in the valley between; but here he became unsure of his path; uncertain of the respective merits of wheat or labour as standards of value. On the whole he was more strongly attracted towards labour as the best standard of value in his ideal system; the currency consisting of stamped paper notes representing the labour of so many hours, days, weeks or months. 'This is the currency Mr Robert Owen has advo-

[1] *National Reformer*, 15th May 1847.
[2] O'Brien, *Human Slavery*, p. 139.
[3] *National Reformer*, 30th January 1847; O'Brien, *Human Slavery*, p. 134, written on the eve of the gold discoveries in California and Australia.
[4] *National Reformer*, 24th October 1846.

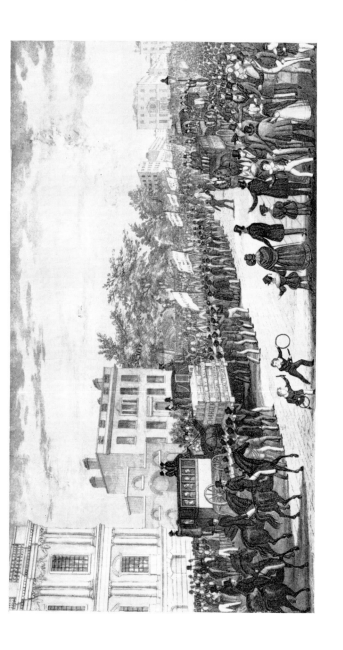

5. The Chartists march through London carrying their National Petition to the House of Commons in 1842.

6. A physical force Chartist arming for the fight, 1848. By courtesy of
Punch.

cated.'[1] Money ought to be a symbol 'exactly expressive' of the labour-content of each article or commodity; and 'under a proper commercial system nothing could be easier than to value goods according to the *average* labour expended in making them'.[2] This anticipation of the nub of Karl Marx's theory of value[3] is clearly a statement of an ideal. Bronterre was telling people not how value was currently being determined, but how he wished it to be determined under the new economic system he was trying to outline. (But by talking of 'average' labour in terms of time alone, he sidestepped the immensely important question of variety of *qualities* of labour, dependent upon education, training, and inborn natural ability.) Actual legal tender, he thought, should be issued solely by the government, but individuals might be allowed to issue 'mercantile paper' against exchangeable wealth (including the precious metals) provided that they gave ample security

'. . . to the local administration . . . such paper to be then stamped and made a legal tender from all parties but the issuers, by whom it must be always convertible, on demand, into Government paper, or into the precious metals at the market price. And on the issuing of such mercantile paper, no privilege of any sort to be allowed.'[4]

O'Brien, living in a period of recurrent booms and slumps, was well aware of the dangers of over-issue and inflation, for in those days money earnings were markedly less mobile than the cost of living. For the working man, therefore, inflation meant decreasing real wages and increasing deprivation for him and his family. Inflation, moreover, reduced the value of the small man's savings. The fact that deflation, on the other hand, could cause a great increase in the real burdens of taxation and indebtedness was realized, and is referred to in Item 3 of the programme of the National Reform League. It was fear of inflation and its consequences for the poor man which led O'Brien to reject Thomas Attwood's proposals for a so-called 'action on the currency'. Up to a point their plans had much in common, *viz.*, a currency and credit policy closely related to prevailing economic conditions, designed to encourage productive activities, and not dependent upon the world supply of gold. 'Attwood wanted to make

---

[1] Cf. F. Podmore, *Robert Owen* (1906), pp. 273–4 and Ch. XVII; the *Northern Star* (29th March 1845) was hostile.
[2] *National Reformer*, 20th February 1847.
[3] For an exposition of the Marxian meaning of 'value' see G. D. H. Cole, *What Marx really meant* (1934), Ch. VII.
[4] *National Reformer*, 16th January 1847.

it easy for country bankers to lend, and for business men to borrow, in order to increase production and employment.'[1] O'Brien, too, wanted to see similar results, but feared that, under Attwood's scheme, strong inflationary factors would, in practice, prove uncontrollable. Fresh swarms of middlemen would spring up, and a wild bout of over-speculation would pour 'sudden and fraudulent' riches into the capacious pockets of crafty speculators, 'aristocratic drones and vampire money-mongers'.[2]

In order to facilitate the interchange of wealth locally, O'Brien proposed the setting up of state marts or stores in every town, 'for the reception of all kinds of exchangeable goods to be valued by disinterested officers . . . either upon a corn or labour standard'. In exchange for their products the producers were to receive legal tender symbolic notes which would give to the holder, whoever he might be, the right to draw a corresponding quantity of goods from the State stores. O'Brien was optimistic enough to hope that such an expansion of Owen's hitherto unsuccessful 'labour exchange' scheme to national proportions would gradually displace the competitive system.[3]

The National Reform League's programme (Item 5) refers, as we have seen, to the state's duty to provide 'a sound system of national credit' to facilitate productive activities in agriculture and 'all other branches of useful industry'. O'Brien wanted to create a nation-wide, integrated banking system, nationalized from top to bottom, and to abolish all private banks of issue. These sweeping reforms were to begin with the Bank of England which, as then owned and operated, was, in O'Brien's opinion so heavily tainted by the ruthless commercial system that had produced it, as not to be a true national bank. His alternative was a fully nationalized central Bank of England, maintaining branches in all the principal cities and towns, linked or integrated with a widely-spread network of people's banks; the whole system to be kept 'under the surveillance and control of a legislature chosen by the people'.

O'Brien's Sunday lectures and commentaries 'illustrative of the real character of Christ's Mission on Earth, and of the frauds and delusions with which the various sects and churches have mystified this important subject in the interest of tyranny and crime',[4] were a compound of theology, religion, and social ethics which owed a good deal to his early upbringing and education, and even more to his later

---

[1] G. D. H. Cole, *Chartist Portraits* (1941), p. 115.
[2] *London Mercury*, 11th June 1837.
[3] O'Brien, *Human Slavery*, pp. 134–5.
[4] *People's Paper*, 8th May, 26th June, 25th September 1852.

thinking and experiences. As a youth he was, at least nominally, a Roman Catholic,[1] but in manhood he showed little respect for the Catholic Church or any other. In religion, as in politics, his thought was always independent, shying away from doctrines offered, ready-made, by some 'superior authority'. Like many other Chartists he regarded contemporary 'organized religion' with distrust and contempt. He is on record as a forthright critic of Catholic clericalism in his native Ireland, roundly condemning it as a type of despotism subversive of every human right;[2] and on occasion he did not hesitate to comment unfavourably upon certain Papal encyclicals. This independence, however, did not lead him to infidelity. He rejected atheism and agnosticism 'emphatically', and he never wavered even when, young and inexperienced, he came into close contact with various strong-minded Radical free-thinkers and atheists, such as Henry Hetherington. For this steadiness the influences of his early years were largely responsible. The spiritual anchors then forged and fixed remained always a stable element at the centre of his religious beliefs and opinions. It is remarkable that although he spent his whole child-hood and adolescence in early nineteenth-century Ireland, he was nurtured and educated in an atmosphere, not of bigotry and religious strife, but of Christian teaching and tolerance; an atmosphere to which both Catholics and Protestants appear to have contributed. Surprising as it may appear, this is true of the whole of O'Brien's early life, from primary school to university. In religion, as in politics, his beliefs were deep-rooted.

By the time he had reached man's estate he had worked out for himself both his personal position and his attitude to organized religion. Like Joseph Priestley before him, O'Brien saw that he must take his stand between 'spurious Christianity on the one hand, and infidelity on the other'. He retained his faith in the fundamentals of Christianity, his admiration for Christ's teaching, and his belief in prayer, both public and private, whether said in churches or the open air.[3] Above all, he was caught up, heart and mind, by the social message and implications of Christianity; the *true* gospel. He agreed with Cobbett that 'Religion is not an abstract idea . . . not something metaphysical. It is to produce effects upon men's conduct . . . a good influence in the affairs and on the conditions of men', otherwise it is 'good for nothing'. O'Brien was convinced that no sincere Christian could live his life in a vacuum. For him religion and radicalism were harmonizing

---

[1] *Alumni Dublinenses*, p. 627.
[2] *National Reformer*, 7th November 1846.
[3] *Ibid.*, 8th May 1847; O'Brien, *Human Slavery*, pp. 56, 80.

211

colours in the same grand social design. The evils linked with religion, like those connected with commerce, lay in 'the tyrannic institutions by which both have been governed and conducted. . . . Religion, which was designed to deter the strong from tyrannizing over the weak, had only served as a cloak to screen the tyrant in the exercise of his tyranny. . . . The beauty of wealth,' he said, quoting St Ambrose of Milan, 'is not to reside in the money bags of the rich, but to serve as an aliment to the poor. . . . Christians ought to know that they should employ money to seek not what is of them, but what is of Christ, in order that in his turn Christ may seek them.' [1] For the labours, sacrifices and zeal of the early Christians in their fearless preaching of 'the sublime dogmas of the Gospel', O'Brien had nothing but veneration and praise, because he believed that the very essence of the Gospel was fraternity and equality; and true Christianity, as he understood it, made power 'a trust for the governed . . . not a profitable monopoly for the governors'. It also taught that this life was a probationary state for another, eternal, life. Therefore, those who robbed and enslaved their fellow men imperilled their own eternal salvation; a professing Christian who sweated his employees must be either a hypocrite or an idiot. In the eyes of the early Christians, who exemplified in their lives the charity, the purity, and the selflessness enjoined by the Gospel, the life of Christ was a divine protest against the abasement of the human race by tyranny and slavery. But all the labour and martyrdoms of three centuries had been nullified by the 'establishment' of the Christian religion under Constantine. This, said O'Brien, was not a triumph for Christianity, but a disastrous defeat. 'What churchmen call its final victory, its crowning glory, was in reality its first decisive check – the cause and fore-runner of its downfall. . . .' After this, Christians as a body degenerated into intolerant persecutors of those who disagreed with them.[2]

It was much to be deplored, said O'Brien, that many religious truths had been overlaid and obscured by the absurd jargon of a professional priesthood. For example, there need be no mystery about the Trinity if, instead of trying to understand nonsense about 'Three Incomprehensibles in One Incomprehensible', people would regard the Deity 'from a three-fold point of view'. First, as the architect of material

---

[1] *National Reformer*, 8th and 22nd May 1847; *Political Register*, 27th January 1820. Gibbon wrote of Ambrose, Archbishop of Milan: 'Wealth was the object of his contempt; he had renounced his private patrimony; and he sold, without hesitation, the consecrated plate for the redemption of captives.' *Decline and Fall of the Roman Empire*, Ch. 27.

[2] O'Brien, *Human Slavery*, pp. 59–61, 69, 80–1; *Reynolds's*, 3rd August 1851.

creation and the fountain of all power, wisdom and knowledge; second, as the fountain of all love and all the pure affections; and third, as the fountain of all truth, conscience and conviction. Unless God be regarded in this way, it is impossible to make belief in the Deity the basis of any rational religion. To think of a God with infinite power, but without love and a strict regard for truth and justice, is to think of an infinitely powerful but capricious despot. 'Any man who takes the trouble to think, will find that unless we acknowledge God in his three-fold capacity, we might as well be Atheists as Theists.' It followed that God who creates human beings and endows them with consciousness of right and wrong, cannot be indifferent to their actions.[1] O'Brien, however, could not feel certain that eternal punishment was to be meted out to any soul; but he thought that, if it fell at all, it would fall upon 'those enormous sinners, whose crimes are, by their very nature, of an eternal character; such as the crimes of robbing the people of their land – of their free will – of their self-government – of all means of mental and moral culture, so as to perpetuate their degradation, corruption, and enslavement, to all future generations'.[2] Even for such crimes as these, however, God's mercy might temper the punishment, and, assuming the perfect justice of divine judgment, excessive punishment must be impossible.

To Bronterre O'Brien and those Chartists and others who shared his views, the indifference of the Christian churches to the manifold miseries and injustices suffered by the masses in agriculture and industry seemed utterly inconsistent with the spirit and teaching of Christianity. Joseph Arch, the famous farm labourers' champion and leader, reminds us that in the parish churches it was customary to allocate to the poor 'their lowly place . . . [where] they must sit meekly and never dare to mingle with their betters in the social scale . . . it was as if they were unclean'. And when a certain parson heard that nonconformist local preachers were holding services in a house in the village, he forbade the labourers to attend on pain of loss of their charities; 'no more soup and coals we should have. And it was no idle threat'. Alexander Somerville, touring the rural districts, was struck not only by the 'sulky servility of hopeless poverty', but by the hostility of the agricultural labourers and their wives to the parson. 'I boldly assert', he wrote, 'that the conditions of these people, their poverty, their hatred of the church, their external submission and inward bitterness against ecclesiastical dignitaries, is the rule among the country parishes of England, and its opposite is the exception'.

[1] O'Brien, *Dissertation and Elegy on Robespierre*, pp. 49–50n.
[2] O'Brien's Preface to *A Vision of Hell*.

213

Perhaps they had long memories and had not forgotten the tithe-wages riots of the early 1830s. There were, it is true, individual clergymen like Dr W. F. Hook, Vicar of Leeds from 1837 to 1859, who 'won the respect and even the affection of many of the working classes', and there were others who took the people's side, as did James Franks, Vicar of Huddersfield, Thomas Allbut, Vicar of Dewsbury, Richard Oglesby, Curate of Woodhouse, and others like Wyndham Madden and Josiah Bateman among the clergy of the industrial North, who put a new fervour into their parochial work. But these were exceptional. The majority of their colleagues came under O'Brien's lash because against 'almost every doctrine of holy writ', they persistently prostituted real religion to civil tyranny, and strove to preserve an evil social system. The so-called Christian churches, which should have been a tower of strength to the Radical reform movement, were riddled by the rot of reaction; hence their utter failure to give practical effect to the social teachings of their religion.[1]

It is now known that in the predominantly Protestant districts of England and Scotland in the mid-nineteenth century the working people's attitudes to religion ranged from the sort of smouldering hostility noted by Somerville, through apathy and inert indifference, to benevolent neutrality. Some of them – for example the handloom weavers and stocking knitters – had no Sunday clothes and were far too ashamed of their rags to appear in church or chapel, even if they had wished to go. Excluding the Roman Catholics, only about one working-class adult in four customarily attended church or chapel services, and these people were neither interested nor instructed in denominational or doctrinal differences. Indeed, they were usually broad-minded enough sometimes to attend church and at other times to 'give the chapel a turn', provided that the distance was not great and the building not too cold or otherwise uncomfortable; and this seems to have been equally true in both urban and rural districts. The degree of popularity of priest or preacher was, of course, another important factor. Many working-class parents even if they did not go to church or chapel themselves, sent their children to Sunday school (probably to secure a little peace and quiet in the house on Sundays!),

---

[1] *Bronterre's National Reformer*, 25th February 1837; McDouall's *Chartist and Republican Journal*, No. 19, August 1841; *People's Paper*, 7th and 31st July 1852; 19th February 1853; J. F. C. Harrison, *Learning and Living 1790–1960* (1961), pp. 158–62; J. F. C. Harrison, *Society and Politics in England, 1780–1960* (1965), pp. 174–6, 186–8; H. Pelling, *Popular Politics and Society* (1969), Ch. 2; E. Hobsbawn and G. Rudé, *Captain Swing* (1969), pp. 33–4, 105–18, 152–61.

but the majority of Protestant parents seem to have been very little concerned about the kind of religious instruction the children received. Bronterre O'Brien's approach and attitude to religion, especially his lack of dogmatism regarding the merits of any particular version of the Christian faith, doubtless made his Sunday discourses easily acceptable to his audiences at the Eclectic Institute.

Equally acceptable would have been O'Brien's opinions on church lands, which were, as one would expect, linked with his views on the land question in general. All church property, he argued, was public property; therefore the income from it should be put to beneficial public uses, such as 'home colonization' by the settlement of the unemployed on the land. Furthermore, as existing bishops and incumbents died, their revenues should be similarly applied, and the new bishops and other clergy should be supported by their congregations like the ministers of nonconformist churches. Thus complete disestablishment would gradually ensue. As for the poor curates, they might well be better off after disestablishment, for their congregations would almost certainly be more generous to them than the vicars and rectors who employed them under the existing Establishment.[1]

O'Brien, then, was implacably anti-clerical, but not anti-religious. He never embraced secularism, and we do not find him among the atheistic or agnostic members of the democratic movement, such as Hetherington, Watson, Carlile and Holyoake, but among the numerous body of Chartists, like Lovett, O'Neill and Collins, who remained loyal to the essence of Christianity, but were strongly anti-clerical. They had no love for the cloth and regarded almost all bishops and clergy as humbugs and 'pious pickpockets', concerned only to hold on to their livings and their easily-earned stipends.[2] It was O'Brien's considered opinion that 'when religion, degenerating into superstition and priestcraft, loses its divine character and becomes a mere cloak for hypocrisy and an instrument of oppression in the hands of tyrants, it . . . occasions a violent reaction against *all* religion . . . and the last stage of such reaction is Atheism'. A clear distinction must be drawn between 'a thing good in itself, and the perversion of that thing to wicked purposes'. True, genuine religion 'can never be other than an unmixed good to mankind'. From a similar partly critical, partly

---

[1] *Bronterre's National Reformer*, 15th January 1837; O'Brien, *Human Slavery*, p. 118; cf. Edward Miall's views in *Nonconformist's Sketch Book* (1842), Chs. 7–8 and Appendix. Almost all the Chartist leaders favoured complete separation of church and state.

[2] *Power of the Pence*, 2nd December 1848, p. 49; *Social Reformer*, 1st September 1849.

constructive attitude sprang the Chartist churches, through which Christian Chartists sought to re-create the essentials of primitive Christianity, to put an end to clerical domination, and to repudiate by deeds as well as words the 'ecclesiastical bellowing about Chartist infidelity'.[1] O'Brien's views harmonized with those of the Christian Chartists. It will be remembered that while he was in prison in 1841 he wrote of his pleasure at the news of 'the progress of Chartist Christianity (which is primitive Christianity) against the long-faced hypocritical pharisees of the day, whose religion consists in ... preaching slavery to the poor under the name of humility, and dutiful submission to the "powers that be", which powers they would fain make us believe, are "ordained by God"'.[2]

Evidently O'Brien's various activities made some impact in London Radical and Chartist circles, for about the middle of 1851 he was considered as a possible Chartist parliamentary candidate for Tower Hamlets, where George Thompson, the well-known, eloquent Anti-Slavery Radical, was the sitting member, having been elected by a very large majority in 1847. This east-end constituency included the Spitalfields silk weaving district where the hand-loom weavers, many of whom were descended from French Huguenot refugees, were suffering great depression and distress. The famous Spitalfields Acts, dating from 1773, which had prescribed legal minimum rates of pay for the London silk weavers, had been repealed in 1824, and the protection against imports of foreign silk fabrics had been much reduced between 1826 and 1851 as a result of the pressure of the free traders in Parliament, who were going from strength to strength. Meanwhile the unfortunate silk weavers were sinking ever deeper into poverty. Indeed in the late 1820s it was necessary for the Spitalfields Soup Society to give relief to many weavers on the verge of starvation.[3] It is significant that one London Board of Guardians, accustomed

---

[1] Pious middle-class people were, indeed, shocked at the tales of the Chartists' infidelity. 'We were pleased to hear,' wrote Caroline Fox in her Journal on 3rd April 1839, 'of the exile of the Chartists from Devizes by the public spirit of the inhabitants. Talked about their principles and the infidelity they have been preaching everywhere, our mines included. Sir Charles Lemon said they have been declaring that the difference between the rich and the poor abundantly proved the non-existence of a God. Someone remarked that it is the rich, not the poor, who become infidels; only those renounce Providence who do not feel the want of one.'

[2] *Northern Star*, 2nd January 1841.

[3] The London Weavers' Company subscribed £20 in response to the Spitalfields Soup Society's appeal in 1829, and £10 in 1832. Guildhall Library *MS*. 3655/20, ff. 76, 133b. On 'George Thompson, M.P.' see *Reynolds's Political Instructor* 17th November 1849.

though they were to dealing with extreme poverty and privation, resolved not to apprentice any more children to the silk weavers.[1] By the 1840s the weavers' well-known independence of spirit was quenched and the heart seemed to have gone out of them. There were, however, a number of Chartists in the district who, like Richard Cray, silk weaver and member of the L.W.M.A., had long been convinced that the only remedy 'is a fair Representation in the Commons house of Parliament' through universal suffrage. They felt that Bronterre O'Brien, so highly esteemed for his oratorical gifts and persistent advocacy of universal suffrage, might be able to revive the weavers' interest in politics. But this was easier to say than to do. Very few working weavers had the franchise; some, according to Richard Cray, were 'devoid of knowledge, wile others that is possest of knowledge cannot and will not make appearance among fellow men because they are . . . ashamed to mix in Society, having not sufficient Clothing'.[2] O'Brien did, in fact, address a few meetings, but his candidature seems to have lapsed after July 1851, probably because of progressive ill-health, for we know that in December 1851 he was suffering from what was described as 'a dangerous affection of the brain'. In the general election of 1852 the Chartist candidate in Tower Hamlets was not O'Brien, but William Newton, an engineer and leading trade unionist, who secured a favourable show of hands at the hustings, but polled only 1,095 votes in a five-cornered contest against two Whigs, who polled respectively 7,728 and 7,718, and two Liberal–Radicals who polled 4,568 and 2,792 votes.[3] Thus, Newton had received only 4½ per cent of the total votes cast; and it is a matter for conjecture whether O'Brien, even if fully restored to health, would have done any better.

Hyde Park in the summer of 1851 saw the opening of the Great Exhibition, which was housed in Paxton's astonishing transparent

[1] M. Sturt, *The Education of the People* (1967), p. 46.

[2] B.M. *MSS.* 34/245B. ff. 3–16; 37,773, fo. 9b. In August 1836 the newly-formed London Working Men's Association appointed a sub-committee, *viz.*, James Watson, the well-known book-seller; Charles Cole, secretary of the unofficial journeymen wavers' committee which collected and presented evidence to the Commissioner investigating the condition of the hand-loom weavers (1838–40); and Richard Cray, 'a weaver'. During the severe weather of January–February 1847, the Spitalfields Benevolent Society appealed urgently on behalf of the unemployed silk weavers and the 'many thousands of labouring men who herd together in the locality of Spitalfields'. *The Times*, 4th February 1847.

[3] *Glasgow Sentinel*, 26th July 1851; S. and B. Webb, *History of Trade Unionism* (1907 edn), pp. 188n–9; G. D. H. Cole, *British Working-Class Politics 1832–1914* (1941), pp. 21, 259. For William Newton's election address see *Star of Freedom*, 1st May 1852.

triumph, the 'Crystal Palace', – 900,000 square feet of glass held in place by 202 miles of standardized wooden sash bars – and aroused tremendous interest, attracting more than six million visitors of all classes in a little over five months. But the more thoughtful Chartists, Bronterre O'Brien among them, and some middle-class people as well, looked behind the dazzling display of thousands of articles of comfort and luxury to the men and women and children who made them. Was not the Exhibition, they asked, a glittering façade which masked shameful social conditions? 'Is the inanimate to gratify curiosity and afford wonder and pleasure, and the animate to be forgotten? The products to be esteemed and the producers unheeded?' [1] J. C. Fischer, a highly intelligent and prosperous Swiss industrialist who knew England and her expanding industries very well, made the following comment after visiting the Exhibition:

'I have just come back from England. In that country great things – I might say almost unbelievable things – have been achieved. . . . There is, however, another side of the picture. The situation of the actual producer of goods – the true worker . . . is not an enviable one, even though he may appear to be getting high wages. Not one of many thousands of English factory workers owns even a scrap of land. They cannot enjoy all the varied beauties of nature that we Swiss have. Even if they existed in England, they would be hidden by the great clouds of smoke which pour out of thousands upon thousands of chimneys.' [2]

And shortly afterwards *The Times* drew attention to yet another deficiency – the lack of provision of scientific and artistic instruction for the British people.

'Yet this country, as the centre of the commerce and industry of the world, would seem to require, more than any other, to have these wants supplied, and the Great Exhibition of 1851 has, in its results, convinced us that unless they be speedily satisfied this country will run serious risk of losing that position which is now its strength and pride.' [3]

In 1851, from June to December, Bronterre O'Brien was employed as London Correspondent of the *Glasgow Sentinel*, a Radical weekly

---

[1] *Glasgow Sentinel*, 3rd May 1851; G. M. Young (ed.), *Early Victorian England* (1934), I, pp. 212–23; C. R. Fay, *Palace of Industry* (1951); M. Argles, *South Kensington to Robbins* (1964), Chs. 1 and 2.

[2] Quoted by W. O. Henderson, *J. C. Fischer and His Diary of Industrial England* (1961), p. 44.

[3] *The Times*, 2nd December 1852, p. 3.

which was enlarged and reorganized in May of that year, when it made a declaration of policy, distinctly O'Brienite in flavour, declaring its aims to be 'the establishment of democracy' and persistent advocacy of the broad principle that 'the People is the source of all Political and Social Power', and promising that such all-important questions as parliamentary reform, national secular education, the rights of Labour, and home colonization compared with emigration, would be discussed. This appointment suited O'Brien admirably. He attended Chartist and Radical meetings in London and sent reports to the *Glasgow Sentinel*, in which, at the outset, he had a column and a half. Interspersed with these reports were his comments on current democratic and reactionary movements on the Continent, and on such burning questions of the day as Protection *versus* Free Trade. For instance, he declared himself in favour of free importation of all raw and manufactured produce not indigenous, or not producible in sufficient quantities in the United Kingdom; but he advocated effective protection for all commodities and productions which give employment to our artisans and labourers, and upon which the prosperity of native industry depends. Therefore, said Bronterre, he was opposed to

'. . . free trade merely to enrich idlers at home or speculators abroad, to the ruin and injury of the home producer . . . the cheap-labour, cheap-produce system benefits only a few leviathan manufacturers . . . a few millionaire-usurers, annuitants and tax eaters. . . . Why should this handful of worthless men be privileged to plunder and pauperize the rest of the country? At present this question is asked only in holes and corners – only by the intelligent few of the victimized classes. By and by, when the next commercial crisis occurs, you will hear it asked on the house tops and in the market places. It is doubtful to me if the middle classes will be able to adjourn the cry for universal suffrage beyond that day.'

It is hardly surprising that, in his reports to the *Glasgow Sentinel*, O'Brien often mentioned the meetings held in London under the auspices of the National Reform League; nor did he neglect to hold forth from time to time upon the ill-treatment and privations of the people of Ireland, pointing out to his readers that to produce wealth in great abundance, but to have no provisions for its just distribution is dangerous and might even be 'a source of impending revolution'.[1]

Also, in 1851, there had been a Chartist Convention[2] in which the

---

[1] *Glasgow Sentinel*, June–December 1851, *passim.*
[2] Held in the Parthenium Rooms, St Martin's Lane, London, from 31st March to 10th April 1851.

twenty-four delegates spent ten days discussing a draft programme which was distinctly characterized by O'Brienism. Although land nationalization was included only after a public protest by O'Brien himself, a number of other items show that his preaching and teaching on the essential interdependence of political and social reforms had not fallen upon deaf ears. The delegates, in fact, discussed a full social programme covering the land, church and state, education, the poor, public finance, the press, and the militia, and agreed upon the over-riding importance of unity and of using the wide appeal of Chartism to bring this about. Every section of the working class must rally and persistently attack class government in 'every one of its monopolies' and 'every one of its strongholds' – all leaves taken from O'Brien's book.[1] But this was the realm of theory; of policy for the future. The hard fact of the political present was that the chances of a Chartist revival were anything but bright.

Towards the end of 1851, O'Brien announced an ambitious new series of twopenny political tracts to be entitled *Bronterre O'Brien's European Letters and Tracts for the National Reform League*. These 'letters and tracts', he wrote in No. 1, published on 6th October 1851, '. . . will embrace the entire range of political, moral and social science . . . the fallacies and misrepresentations of historians, publicists, economists, politicans, and party, leaders; the solidarity of peoples; social rights home and foreign affairs, and the objects and prospects of the National Reform League in relation to agrarian, monetary and commercial reform'.[2] The second issue (13th December 1851) contained a bold reaffirmation of O'Brien's political faith and an explanation of his attitude to other Chartists and Chartist groups at this time. Addressing himself to the 'Chartists of England and Scotland' he wrote:

'In the National Reform League I am free from all the sinister influences which made me powerless for good among the Chartists so-called . . . I never refuse my services . . . on the contrary, I assist at all your meetings when I can, and give my Hall gratuitously to promote your cause when applied to for it by any Chartist society or locality. . . . Beyond this, I could be of no use at present. I have no faith in national organizations, nor in Executive Committees. I have seen too much of them. . . . [But] I am not the less attached to the sacred cause, which used, some thirteen or fourteen years ago, to draw us together in such

[1] E. E. Barry, *Nationalization in British Politics* (1965), pp. 38–9; J. Saville, *Ernest Jones, Chartist* (1952), pp. 257–63, Appendix III.
[2] Published by J. Watson, 3 Queen's Head Passage, Paternoster Row, and printed by Holyoake, Tyndale & Co. at the same address.

countless masses. . . . I am, though enfeebled in health and spirits, the same man in opinions, feelings and aspirations . . . in respect of the great essentials of our cause – in respect of those eternal rights, political and social, which I have ever advocated as the common inheritance, the common birthright of all mankind. . . . I still hold out for the right of every people to self-government by universal suffrage, exercised with the most absolute freedom of opinion. I still contend for a full, fair and free representation of the whole people in parliament and . . . in our municipalities, our vestries, our juries, our church, our religious and educational institutions, our army and navy, and every other department of the public service. . . .

But while true and steadfast to our ancient political creed . . . there is another creed . . . of infinitely greater consequence . . . the creed of social rights . . . i.e., those rights which every human being ought to have, as a *member of society* in exchange for the *natural* rights he gives up when he abandons the *savage* for the *social* state of existence . . . It is upon . . . these social rights that the real freedom and happiness of a people depends. Without liberty to produce and to distribute [wealth] freely amongst themselves, by equitable exchange, . . . they must ever remain paupers, or slaves to those who may control their labour. To a people so conditioned, political rights are illusory [for] . . . their destiny depends upon others – upon those who can give or withhold employment at pleasure and who, as at present in England, may force them, on pain of starvation, to accept what wages they choose to give. . . . To be of any use at all to them, the franchise must be available to restore to them their social rights.'

This testament of faith in universal suffrage and democratic government was followed in the same issue, by an announcement that 'Mr O'Brien is at present suffering from a dangerous affection of the brain . . . which may prevent his third European Letter from appearing next week . . . He writes with pain and difficulty'. In fact, this illness not only put an end to Bronterre's *European Letters*, but it resulted, also, in the termination of his appointment as London Correspondent of the *Glasgow Sentinel*.

When he had recovered from his illness, O'Brien, who was still on the right side of fifty, occupied himself mainly with the National Reform League and the development of his Eclectic Institute at Denmark Street. He had now transmuted violent political campaigning into peaceful adult education. The sorties and speeches, excitements and crises of militant agitation had given place to settled habits. The fire of his early days was not quenched, but its heat was tempered by hard knocks, hard times, poor health, and the moderation of approaching middle age. Occasionally he visited the provinces, but his main activities were in London, where he resided until his death. On several occasions during the summer of 1851, O'Brien and O'Connor, now reconciled (at least in public), spoke from the same platform. O'Brien also represented his N.R.L. at Harney's brave but abortive Democratic Conference; and at a public meeting later in the year O'Connor seconded, with O'Brien's support, a resolution 'hailing the arrival of the patriot Kossuth in England', followed by the presentation of an address of welcome to the Hungarian revolutionist and a public dinner at the Highbury Barn Tavern, at which Feargus O'Connor, Bronterre O'Brien and G. W. M. Reynolds were among the principal guests. On 3rd March 1852, Karl Marx told his friend, Engels, of 'a huge meeting' organized by the N.R.L. at which Ernest Jones seems to have been the chief speaker. Early in April 1852, a public tea party and musical soirée was held at the Eclectic Institute to celebrate Robespierre's birthday. Three members of 'the late French Assembly' and the 'late Editor of the *Populaire*' were present as guests of honour and 'the hall was crowded to excess'. O'Brien made a speech from the chair, and another speech was delivered by one of the French guests, Monsieur Etienne Cabet, a Radical historian and contributor to *Le Populaire*, who held Owenite-communist views. The speeches were 'interspersed with appropriate songs and music' and the audience left the Institute at 'a late hour, highly delighted with the combined instruction and amusement'. Just two months later, another grand soirée took place, this time at the John Street Institution, to raise funds for foreign democrats then living in England as refugees. A large group of Polish, German, Hungarian, Italian and French republican democrats attended, including Louis Blanc. Bronterre O'Brien, asked to speak to a proposition expressing the hope that Great Britain and the United States might arise to 'lead the way to the emancipation of Europe', astonished everybody by completely ignoring the proposition and asserting, with great vehemence, that nothing could be done for the refugees until the British people had obtained their social rights. This extraordinary outburst, which naturally provoked an angry reaction from the foreign democrats, points to a recurrence of O'Brien's mental illness, for it is diametrically opposed to his usual attitude of praise and support for men like Mazzini, Ledru–Rollin (who, he thought, ought to have been elected President of France instead of Louis Napoleon Bonaparte), and Cabet. As to Louis Kossuth, although at first O'Brien admired his services to the democratic cause in Europe, on closer acquaintance he waxed more

222

critical because the Hungarian, whose command of English was remarkable, willingly addressed public meetings organized by the predominantly middle-class Radicals of Birmingham and elsewhere (making long-winded, impassioned attacks upon the Austrian and Russian tyrannies), but seemed to ignore the working-class Chartist Movement. While O'Brien could appreciate some of Kossuth's difficulties as a visiting political figure, he could not forgive him for hobnobbing with the wrong people.[1]

With a general election in view in the spring of 1852, O'Brien had advised the working people in every borough to choose a candidate of their own and not to support candidates foisted upon them by middle-class politicians. Shortly afterwards, a Metropolitan Elections Committee, set up to find and help to support Radical candidates, proposed Bronterre O'Brien as candidate for the City of Westminster, and G. W. M. Reynolds for the Borough of Lambeth. But nothing further was done, and no Chartist candidates stood in either constituency in 1852.[2] O'Brien never thrust himself forward as a parliamentary candidate because, in his opinion, it was for the constituency to make the first approach. Moreover, neither his income nor the state of his health would permit him to become a candidate in 1852. With a wife and four children to support (the eldest still under fifteen), he was at this period always hard up and sometimes actually short of food.

Things were even more serious with Feargus O'Connor whose mental illness had evidently been growing upon him in 1847, if not before. Somerville speaks of a National Land Company shareholders' meeting, held in Manchester in October 1847, at which O'Connor

[1] *Reynolds's*, June–July 1851, *passim*, 14th September and 9th November 1851; *Star of Freedom*, 12th June 1852; *Star and National Trades Journal*, 10th April 1852; *People's Paper*, 3rd December 1853; Saville, *Ernest Jones, Chartist*, p. 236; *Bronterre O'Brien's European Letters*, No. 1, 6th December 1851; cf. *Hansard* (3rd Series), CVI, pp. 50, 386–7; The last issue of the famous *Northern Star* appeared on 13th March 1852. It was replaced a week later by the *Star and National Trades Journal*, which continued to agitate for the Charter, and especially Universal Suffrage, adding 'social and industrial effort', i.e. to link up with co-operative and trade societies, 'to help men, not only to political liberty but to industrial independence and social comfort'. A month later, on 17th April 1842, G. J. Harney resumed his editorship after a two-years' interval and announced that the *Star* was to become the *Star of Freedom* (incorporating the *Friend of the People*) and would be published weekly at 4½d. It would continue to advocate Chartism, Democracy, Trade Unionism and Co-operation; and this it did until 27th November 1852, when it was finally discontinued. Cobden had advised Kossuth 'from the first to be very chary of accepting invitations' (Morley, *Life of Cobden*, II, pp. 99–107).

[2] *Reynolds's*, 23rd May, 13th and 27th June, 4th and 18th July 1852; *People's Paper*, 3rd July 1852.

223

held forth, quite irrelevantly and with absurd exaggeration, on the number and nature of his duels. After the official enquiry in the following year, which led to the Company's liquidation, O'Connor's mental derangement worsened – although he had his lucid intervals – until, in June 1852, after a wild rampage around Westminster Hall, he had to be certified as insane and was committed to Dr Tuke's 'Retreat', an asylum [1] which was outstanding among the very few advanced, humane mental hospitals at that time.

At this period shortage of money was more acute than ever among the Chartists. Subscriptions were, indeed, so hard to raise that it took the National Charter Association four months to collect £33 to pay some of its debts. A laudable attempt to help O'Brien out of his acute money troubles was made by Robert Gammage and Ernest Jones towards the close of 1852, when they appealed for subscriptions to a 'permanent fund, to be kept up as long as needed'. Jones and Gammage agreed to serve upon the Testimonial Fund Committee; public meetings were organized to stimulate interest, and Jones undertook to receive subscriptions at the office of the *People's Paper*.

'Mr O'Brien still lectures [said the Appeal] to working-class audiences twice or thrice a week, as he has done for the last seven years, but the proceeds of these lectures are very small, after deducting payments for rent of lecture-rooms, and other charges. In short, unless timely relief be found, the Committee fear that his bodily, and even mental stamina, must be wrecked; but . . . could he be saved from the depressing influence of daily anxieties for mere subsistence, the literature of our country would not fail to be enriched by invaluable contributions from his pen.' [2]

When O'Brien himself addressed a meeting convened to arouse interest in the testimonial fund, he declared that, despite his poverty, he would never betray the working people in return for money from the middle classes. [3] The committee organized other meetings in and near London, while Gammage advertised the fund in the provinces. Eventually small donations began to trickle in, but the progress of the fund was painfully slow. [4] By 20th September 1853, only £21 18s 4d had been

[1] *Reynolds's* February–June 1852; *Star of Freedom*, 5th June, 9th October 1852; Read and Glasgow, *op. cit.*, p. 141; Somerville, *Autobiography*, p. 430n.

[2] *Reynolds's*, 5th December 1852; *People's Paper*, 27th August and 3rd September 1853.

[3] *Reynolds's*, 17th and 31st July 1853; cf. *National Reformer*, 24th April 1847, pp. 8–9.

[4] *Reynolds's*, August–November 1853, *passim*.

J—N B—T.   D—L—I.   L—D J—N R—S—L.   P—ST—N.

'The last Pantomime of the Season', by courtesy of *Punch*. The House
Commons rejected the Reform Bill introduced by Disraeli in 1859
a majority of 39.

8. The Eclectic Institute in Soho. The corner of Dudley Court (now Denmark Place) and Crown Street (now Charing Cross Road). The gable-end of O'Brien's Eclectic Institute can be seen to the left and, in the background, the top of the church spire of St Giles-in-the-Fields. From a water colour by 'Calvert'.

received. Of fifty subscription books issued, only fourteen had been returned,[1] and by the end of the year the net total did not exceed £30.[2]

Although O'Brien's health showed little lasting improvement in 1853, he was by no means completely *hors de combat*. At the National Hall, Holborn, on 13th April, he took the chair at a public celebration of the anniversary of Robespierre's birth. William Lovett, who owned the hall, had refused to exhibit the bills advertising this meeting, saying that had he known its object soon enough, the use of the hall would have been refused.[3] During the summer of 1853 O'Brien addressed several meetings, and as the autumn approached, the Eclectic Institute outlined the following weekly programme for the winter of 1853–4.

Mondays	Hall to be let for public meetings, concerts etc.
Tuesdays	Classes in grammar, composition, languages and literature.
Wednesdays	'Soirées musicales et dansantes'.
Thursdays	Lessons and lectures on scientific subjects.
Fridays	Social Science and Politics of the day.
Saturdays	Musical rehearsals.
Sundays	11 a.m. Theology and scriptural readings with commentary.
	Evening. History and biography, sacred and profane.[4]

An annual subscription of £1 gave admission to all the lectures, concerts, and amenities of the institute, including the coffee and reading rooms.

It was during the Christmas season of 1853 that a 'numerous company' gathered in the Hall of Science, City Road, to stimulate support for the *People's Paper*. O'Brien was present and apparently in good form at the time, for he made a trenchant speech praising the paper which, he said, 'had nobly stood its ground during the low ebb of public opinion'. He commended its articles, especially those on social rights, remarking that although 'the people surpassed their

[1] *Ibid.*, 2nd October 1853.

[2] *Ibid.*, 1st January 1854. The subscriptions to John Bright's testimonial fund at the end of the Anti-Corn Law agitation amounted to £5,048.

[3] In the following year the Robespierre commemoration meeting was held at the John Street Institution, and Bronterre O'Brien again presided. *Reynolds's*, 17th April 1853, 23rd April 1854.

[4] *Reynolds's*, 18th September 1853.

enemies in their powers of production . . . the manufacturers surpassed their workmen in keeping the fruits of their labour'. This speech was 'repeatedly applauded' and O'Brien sat down 'amid loud cheers'. Ernest Jones, too, made an eloquent speech which was received with equal appreciation and applause. On the surface no hint of trouble could be detected, all seemed 'calm and bright'; yet behind the scenes there was rising tension, and only three weeks later the *People's Paper* printed Ernest Jones's bitter allegation that a 'disgraceful plot' was afoot to wrest the paper from his control and 'to interfere in its management, for self-interested and sordid purposes', by forcing him to accept Bronterre O'Brien as joint-editor.[1] In point of fact a clause in the original prospectus of the *People's Paper* had stated, rather loosely, that 'the Chartist body shall annually elect a co-editor, with equal powers, and to receive a salary of £2 a week'. This clause, the root of the trouble, had remained in abeyance for two years, during which, Jones claimed, he alone had shouldered the burden and expenses, the labour and the losses, inseparable from the launching of the paper. Not only had he been the unpaid editor, but he had spent over £200 of his own money. O'Brien, on the contrary, had contributed nothing during this period.

'To the gentleman who is now proposed as editor,' said Jones, 'I offered when the paper was first started, three columns at his uncontrolled disposal – he refused with these words: "I will have nothing to do with it unless you give up your preposterous notion of sharing the profits with the people . . . let us share it together".'

Ernest Jones thought it quite intolerable that two years later, after the spadework had been done, the co-editor clause should be invoked in O'Brien's favour. On the other hand, there was evidently a good deal of outside support for the latter proposal (though pretty clearly it did not originate with O'Brien) from people who urged that O'Brien had studied the questions of social rights, currency and exchange 'to a greater extent than Mr Jones', who had, indeed, already used O'Brien's ideas extensively 'at second-hand' in the *People's Paper*. Moreover, it was urged that O'Brien's style of writing, so different from Ernest Jones's, would put more vigour and punch into the *People's Paper*.

[1] *People's Paper*, 31st December 1853, 21st and 28th January, 4th and 11th February 1854. Ernest Jones alleged that Robert Gammage 'was the first proposer of it in several places' in the North; but Gammage denied this and maintained that he had merely taken part in discussions of the proposal after it had been put forward by others.

226

At this point, Bronterre O'Brien could remain mute no longer. Excluded from the columns of the *People's Paper* because of the quarrel, he wrote and published, early in 1854, a four-page pamphlet entitled *Mr Ernest Jones*, in which he refers to a letter asking him whether he would be prepared to assist Ernest Jones 'gratuitously in the editing of his paper, till it reached a paying sale'. O'Brien flatly denied that he ever sought, directly or indirectly, the co-editorship or co-proprietorship of the *People's Paper*, nor did he try to interfere in any way with 'the rights or interests of the present management'. He further denied that members of the National Reform League moved or supported 'factious amendments' at Chartist meetings. 'What we do,' he declared, 'we do upon public grounds only, and always on the side of democracy and progress. Hence, though we are but a small body, the majority at public meetings is ever found on our side.' At one public meeting Ernest Jones had stated, *after O'Brien had left*, that he had offered the latter free use of his paper, but O'Brien had refused because he could not have 'the people's share of the profits'. This, said O'Brien was false nonsense:

'I expressed my willingness to write three columns of the *People's Paper* . . . gratuitously; provided Mr Jones himself wished it, and allowed me perfect freedom of opinion, the same as for himself . . . I had no wish to connect myself with his paper, unless of his own free will, and upon equal terms of mutual independence.'

In fact there were no profits; on the contrary, after a struggle lasting two years, 'the people's share of the profits amounted to exactly all the losses'. O'Brien then went on to make additional accusations against Jones, saying that

'Mr Jones burked an address of my testimonial committee at a time when my very existence might be said to hang upon its success with the public. . . . All we could learn after a fortnight's tramping backwards and forwards to the office [of the *People's Paper*] was that the "Copy was lost!".'

The same 'burking system', or – even worse – wilful perversions of facts, had been used against all meetings, soirées, etc., organized by the National Reform League, and all resolutions sent to the *People's Paper* by the League, or by 'the Chartist Locality, Soho'. Moreover, said O'Brien,

'I once asked him to receive an historical work from me at the rate of two columns a week. He declined on the alleged ground that his

227

columns were bespoke for a similar work on the same subject, which I have not yet seen there.'

O'Brien's pamphlet ends with a parting shot. 'If the tattered mantle of that once noted chief has fallen upon Mr E. Jones, I wish him joy of it – it may shelter him for a season, but he will find it a sad legacy in the end.' [1]

The threatening thunderclouds of war, which broke in March 1854, obscured for a time the Radical reform landscape, including the minor storm between the O'Brienite and Jonesite factions. The Crimean War – Britain, France and Turkey against Russia – was popular with the politicians and the urban crowds, who harboured many vague, delusive notions about the Russian menace.[2] Many of the foreign émigrés, too, welcomed the war, for they hoped that it would result in a crop of revolutionary uprisings on the Continent. Thinking wishfully, Kossuth declared that Russia must be crushed, and Karl Marx, who loathed Czarism and all its works, agreed because he saw in the vast, sprawling, despotic Russian Empire a formidable barrier to the march of revolutionary democracy. Comparatively few stood up boldly against the war. For instance, in Birmingham, apart from two Christian Chartist preachers, scarcely a parson or minister opposed it; but John Bright, Richard Cobden, and 'a small group of Manchester School Radicals, the apostles of peace and free trade', raised many a protest against 'this terrible crime',[3] 'I have hardly seen a madder business,' wrote Thomas Carlyle in his private journal. The eminent historian, E. A. Freeman, was angered by Britain's entry; while the Quakers actually sent a three-man deputation to the Czar of Russia – an extraordinary forlorn hope, led by the indomitable Joseph Sturge, who, in deep 'anguish and sorrow of soul' because of the threat of another war, set out from London in January 1854, with two fellow members of the Society of Friends, Robert Charleton and Henry Pease, to make a direct 'religious appeal' to the Czar. It is characteristic of Joseph Sturge that he was willing, at the age of sixty, to undertake a fortnight's journey by rail and sledge, in the middle of a Russian winter,

---

[1] J. Bronterre O'Brien, *Mr Ernest Jones* (1854). On the financial straits of the *People's Paper* in 1852, see letters from Marx to Engels, 19th August, 2nd and 23rd September 1852, printed in Saville, *Ernest Jones*, p. 237.

[2] Even after two years of war, Londoners hissed the heralds who proclaimed the peace treaty at Temple Bar on 30th March 1856. E. Longford, *Victoria R.I.* (1964), p. 255; *Illustrated London News*, 1856, p. 489.

[3] Hobhouse, *op. cit.*, p. 149; Morley, *Life of Richard Cobden* (1881), II, Ch. VI; Asa Briggs, *Victorian People* (1954), pp. 60–4; H. M. Hyndman, *Record of an Adventurous Life* (1911), p. 274.

in the slender hope of averting a war between the great powers.[1] From Riga the three Friends had to make a three-day journey in a six-horse sledge over the frozen snow to St Petersburg. 'They met with nothing but civility from the Russians, and had no serious mishaps, in spite of several adventures in the deep snowdrifts . . . on the banks of the great lake Piepus.' The Czar Nicholas received them with perfect courtesy. Affirming his abhorrence of war, he disclaimed any desire to conquer or ruin Turkey; but he went on to point out that 'he could not be indifferent to what concerned the honour of his country, and that the well-being of the Greek Church in Turkey . . . could not be sacrificed without dishonour'. The travellers, who now realized that it was already too late to prevent the war, returned empty-handed, to be greeted, most unfairly, by a violent storm of abuse from a press and people already in the first throes of war-fever.[2]

More than a decade after his association with Joseph Sturge and the Complete Suffrage Movement, Bronterre O'Brien found himself, once again, in agreement with Sturge, who had expressed the opinion that 'this sad war absorbs almost all that is good and promotes all that is evil'.[3] To the voices of the anti-war minority, O'Brien, equally clear-sighted, added his own protest, born of sincere conviction and independent judgment. Although he was not an out-and-out pacifist, he was against all dynastic wars; all territory-grabbing wars; all wars engineered in the interests of aristocratic rulers and capitalist adventurers. Many years before, when he was contributing, from prison, to the *Chartist Circular* and Peter McDouall's *Chartist and Republican Journal*, he wrote 'A Dialogue on War', between a 'Moral Force' Whig and 'Bronterre', a Chartist. Let those, says 'Bronterre', who have property abroad (e.g., in India) go there and fight as hard as they like. Let the owners of East India stock, or East India merchantmen; all the 'liver-coloured nabobs' and commercial speculators, go and fight for 'our Indian possessions', but 'let them not mock our degradation by asking us, working people, to fight along with them', for the workers have no 'possessions' *even in their own country*, having been robbed of everything by the upper and middle classes.[4] As for

[1] J. A. Froude, *Thomas Carlyle: A History of his Life in London, 1834–1881* (1884), II, p. 151. On the eve of his departure for Russia, Joseph Sturge wrote to his brother; 'Thou canst have hardly less hope than I have of good from our mission, and it seems more than probable that we shall have to return before getting to Petersburg.'
[2] Hobhouse, *op. cit.*, p. 143–9.
[3] *Ibid.*, p. 150.
[4] *Chartist Circular*, 29th May 1941; McDouall's *Chartist and Republican Journal* Nos 21 and 22 (August 1841).

the Crimean War, O'Brien loathed it as the negation of civilization and progress, and as certain to hold back parliamentary reform. It would, moreover, increase the national debts of the belligerents for the benefit of the monied classes. It was monstrous that although the British working people found all the money and nearly all the men for the war effort, they were not allowed to have even one man to represent them among the 658 members of the House of Commons.[1] The National Reform League brought out as a penny pamphlet *An Address to the Working Class on the war with Russia*, which reflects O'Brien's total opposition on the grounds that it decreased trade, increased prices, and would probably double the nation's debts and taxes. It would, moreover, reduce 'multitudes of our people to bankruptcy and pauperism in despite of their acknowledged thrift and industry'. The war, 'got up under false pretences', should be stopped, for it was a gigantic fraud upon the British public, and an outrage upon Europe. It was sheer hypocrisy to pretend that the war's aim was to protect the weak against the strong; to save Turkey from Russia and thereby to guarantee the interests of civilization and progress against the encroachments of Russian ambition, and the spread of Muscovite barbarism in the West.

'If Russia is ambitious, encroaching, self-aggrandizing, is not England more so? If Russia has pushed her frontiers in all directions by new annexations, had not England extended her empire all over the earth? . . . View it as we may . . . the present war is a monstrous iniquity . . . it is a war to rob, impoverish and decimate the industrious classes, for the gain of feudal tyrants, usurers and commercial vampires, speculating in the blood and calamities of their fellow creatures.'

Let the working people tell the hypocrites in plain terms that a parliament in which they, the producers, are not represented has no right to tax them, nor to claim military service from them, nor to involve them in costly and bloody wars designed to increase the slavery and poverty of their class.

Unfortunately, the warmongers easily prevailed, a frenzy of warfever swept the country, the war was started, and all too soon came news of the usual initial disasters, followed by a mounting toll of casualties, caused in this conflict more by the winter weather and incredibly bad supply services than by the resistance of the Russian forces. Then, in 1856, almost inevitably, the authorities decreed a 'Day of Fasting'; a pathetic gesture which drew from Bronterre a rhyming counterblast entitled 'Bronterre O'Brien's Sermon on the

[1] *Reynolds's*, 22nd July 1855.

Day of the Public Fast and Humiliation for England's Disasters in the Crimea.'

> 'Dearly Beloved, you have heard, of late
> How dire reverses have befall'n the State,
> And that our Sov'reign, mindful of her station,
> Has fixed this day for fast!—humiliation! [1]
> Our Bishops, too, to soothe her royal care,
> Have just prepar'd a godly form of pray'r,
> Wherewith to-day, exactly at eleven,
> They all beseig'd, for grace, the throne of heaven;
> Our Lords and Commons have confirmed the Act,
> And made the pious fiction a "great fact",
> Well, consid'ring how these great ones rule us,
> How oft they starve, and how they always fool us,
> 'Twere surely right that such transcendent sinners,
> Should go, at least one day, without their dinners;
> But will they? No! despite of church and steeple,
> They'll do it not – but they will *do* the people!
> Their sav'ry meals will reach them in due stages,
> While workmen they'll make fast for lack of wages;
> Or stint their children's bread to meagre slices,
> And even for that, exact confounded prices.
> Alas! we're fallen upon evil times,
> When poor folk must needs fast for rich men's crimes,
> For surely, friends, it is no fault of ours,
> That war had broken out amongst the Powers,
> *You* did not make our treaties, creeds, nor laws,
> Our wars – nor the calamities they cause;
>
> . . .
>
> You did not work our troops to death in trenches,
> Nor poison them with Balaclava stenches;
> You did not leave them without huts or clothes,
> To die of frost-bite, chills, and pelting snows;
>
> . . .
>
> These are your rulers' sins, as I have shown,
> But, now, let me inform you of your own,
> A wise, great man said, once upon a time,
> "They who permit oppression share the crime,"
>
> . . .

---

[1] In fact, Queen Victoria regarded public fasts as so much nonsense, but O'Brien did not know this. E. Longford, *op. cit.*, p. 190. For a vivid eye-witness account of the horrors of the Crimean War see Major-Gen. Sir George Bell, *Soldier's Glory* (ed. B. Stuart, 1956), Chs. 15–20; see also *Illustrated London News*, 1855–6, *passim*.

Passive obedience is the curse of slaves.
Now that's the people's sin! – your sin of sins!
Which makes you always lose whoever wins;

. . .

Grovel no longer in the mire like hogs,
Fling flunkeyism, like physic, to the dogs,

. . .

Then will that justice, which is everlasting,
Exchange the poor man's for the rich man's fasting,
God will, thenceforward, manifest his love,
And give you plenty *here*, and heav'n *above*.'

And at the end of all the Crimean carnage; after the fighting and fasting, the suffering and starvation, *The Times*, looking back in sorrow, admitted that the War had been the outcome of a mistaken policy, and that 'a gigantic effort and an infinite sacrifice had been made in vain'.[1]

Meanwhile, during the mid-1850s, O'Brien persevered in his educational and propagandist efforts at the Eclectic Institute under the auspices of the N.R.L. An advertisement issued in 1855 announced that

'Mr O'Brien lectures on the Principles of Political and Social Reform every Friday and Saturday evening at 8 o'clock at the Eclectic Institute. He also delivers discourses upon Theological Subjects every Sunday at 11 a.m. Admission free.'

Various N.R.L. tracts, addressed to 'all who desire a thorough Reform, by safe and legal means, of our Political and Social Institutions', were on sale at the Institute; there was a 'National Reform Library', and the coffee and reading rooms at 18 Denmark Street, adjoining the Institute, were open to both members and non-members, who were urged to 'frequent the Lecture Rooms of the society: above all, read the writings and attend the lectures of James Bronterre O'Brien'.

National Reform League Tract No. 5, issued in November 1855, during the penultimate stage of the Crimean War, is addressed to the 'Distressed Classes', and deals with 'the present famine prices of bread and other necessaries', the decline of employment and wages, and people anxiously asking – What is to become of the poor this winter? 'Dear bread and dear money is the cry from Land's End to

[1] Quoted by Hobhouse, *op. cit.*, p. 152.

Salway Firth'. Then follows Bronterre's bright vision of a welfare state:

'It is a sin and a shame that such a state of things should be. There is no necessity for it. . . . In a country like England . . . there should not be a single pauper . . . except the aged and infirm – and even these ought to be well-kept and happy. . . . There is land enough, labour enough, capital enough to sustain the whole population in the highest comfort.'

The great barrier is the fact that the landlords and profit mongers have made themselves the lords of society and masters of the government, 'holding every human being at their mercy'. Therefore, 'Manhood Suffrage must be the cry and watchword . . . [so as] to get honest laws passed upon Land, Credit, Currency and Exchange'.[1]

It was about this time that O'Brien wrote and published two more penny political 'poems', both prompted by the Crimean War and both in the form of 'odes', one to Lord Palmerston, who became Prime Minister early in 1855, and the other to the French Emperor, Louis Napoleon Bonaparte, who took the title, Napoleon III, in December 1852. Although Palmerston ('the Devil's son' to the Prussians) was regarded by many in England as 'the Whiskered Wonder', O'Brien disliked him intensely, deeming him an unscrupulous war-monger, closely leagued with capitalists who were every bit as ruthless. In O'Brien's ode Palmerston is accused of

> 'Changing with every scene, yet with one aim . . .
> Building on war and peace alike thy fame,
> Made great by acts that bring on others shame,
> Thriving at once on eulogy and blame. . . .'

The ode to Louis Napoleon, that 'contemptible fribble',

> 'Imperial puppet – idol of an hour!
> Drunk with the fumes of blood-begotten power.'

is equally outspoken and is fraught with much the same scathing invective as the ode to Palmerston.[2]

Prince Louis Napoleon, a nephew of Napoleon I, had been elected President of the new French Republic in 1848, 'the year of revolutions

---

[1] National Reform League *Tract No. 5* (November 1855).

[2] It is dated 31st March 1856 – the day after the proclamation of the Peace of Paris which ended the Crimean War – and was first published as a single sheet, priced at 1d. For Cobden's strictures on Palmerston see Morley, *Life of Cobden*, II, pp. 177–8, and for the story of Professor Victor Duruy's interview with Napoleon III, see Hyndman, *Record*, pp. 216–18.

in Europe' (but not in England), by an overwhelming popular verdict
of 5,434,220 votes, against an aggregate of only 1,835,000 votes cast
for his opponents, General Cavaignac, Ledru-Rollin, and Lamartine.
The newly-elected President took office as a strong supporter of
universal manhood suffrage, the introduction of social security services
(including assistance for sick and disabled workmen), better working-
class housing, and the proper care of orphans. But, in O'Brien's eyes,
he forfeited all honour and credit by forsaking his elective republican
presidency and allowing himself to be invested with hereditary imperial
status – taking the evocative title, Napoleon III. This fateful transformation seems to have sprung from a widespread popular demand
that an imperial crown should be bestowed upon him. 'Leaving
Strasbourg,' wrote Victor Duruy, 'to the cries of *Vive le President!*
he arrived at Bordeaux to the cries of *Vive l'Empereur!* – a cry which
Paris repeated in October [1852].' Bronterre O'Brien, unimpressed by
the shouts of the French populace, saw only the dangers of Louis
Napoleon's betrayal of his former liberal policies and promises, and a
revival of Napoleonic imperialism which would bring in its train a
series of wars paid for by the blood and toil and tears of the poor.
The Crimean War was the first stage on this road of death and disaster.
But, said Bronterre, with a flash of prophetic insight, evil would be
punished eventually and the arch-betrayer would be brought low.

> 'Yea! – the handwriting on the wall appears,
> To scathe thy guilty soul with conscious fears.
> Despite thy mouchards [1] and thy cuirassiers,
> In vain thy satellites would drown by cheers,
> The mother's curse, the widow's shrieks and tears.
>
> . . .
>
> Pretend not, tyrant, England takes thy part;
> Nor feels for those thy rod makes writhe and smart.
> England's base Government is not England's heart.
> England abhors thy every act and art,
>
> . . .
>
> For none knows better what a fiend thou art.
>
> . . .
>
> Talk not to us of "allies" and "free nations" –
> Names which but mask marauders in high stations –
> The lords of acres, gold, and Bourse "quotations",
> Proud squires and priests, and glutt'nous corporations,
>
> . . .

[1] Police spies.

Oh, Bonaparte, you once confessed these laws;
Yea, and wrote pamphlets, too, with some applause,
To prove yourself the friend of labour's cause!
How durst you now, without remorse or pause,
Treat all who preach such doctrines as outlaws,
Seal up their presses, and padlock their jaws? . . .'

The publication of such penny poems, evidently intended to sell
and circulate widely among the 'industrious classes' and the poor,
recalls to mind the singing and selling of the popular street ballads
of an earlier age. *Reynolds's* reviewer, of course, wrote enthusiastically
of O'Brien's verse as

'. . . a vehicle of withering exposures of exalted scoundrelism, the
promulgation of sound political principles, and the inculcation of all-
saving truths. . . . Mr O'Brien does not employ rhyme as a coral
rattle, with its silver bells for the amusement of grown-up babes and
sucklings'.[1]

A more impartial opinion was expressed by Alexander Somerville in a
book published in 1860:

'I have spoken with Bronterre O'Brien, though not knowing who he
was, and have read his politico-poetical maledictions. I know nothing
in literature like them . . . all the dictionaries have been ransacked and
exhausted for rhymes that follow in jangling succession . . . comically
for a time, until the clanging words become fiery bolts which strike
and make the heart quiver as shocks of electricity. They who have not
read Bronterre O'Brien have yet to become acquainted with literary
genius in one of its most weird and eccentric forms.' [2]

---

[1] Grant and Temperley, *Europe in the Nineteenth Century* (1931), pp. 215–23;
Reynolds's, 27th July 1856.
[2] A. Somerville, *Conservative Science of Nations* (1860), p. 217.

Chapter XI

THE WANE OF LIFE

As THE years slipped by, O'Brien's thoughts often returned to Robespierre, his hero of earlier days. The passage of time had in no way dimmed Robespierre's lustre in O'Brien's eyes, and in 1856 or 1857 he wrote an *Elegy on the Death of Robespierre, with a historical sketch of the three Assemblies which made the Revolution of 1789*, to which he added 'a brief notice of Robespierre's public life'. This work, first published in 1857 as a sixteen-page booklet, priced at twopence a copy,[1] was characterized by its author as an act of tardy justice and a tribute to 'the sacred frenzy' of a great reformer, who was murdered 'in order to effect a counter-revolution for the middle-classes'. O'Brien frankly admits that 'a few lines' of the *Elegy* 'are copied, literally' from *Lycidas*, Milton's poem of mourning for a dead friend; and 'also one or two exquisite passages . . . applicable to the "situation".' He regrets that he could not find even more 'inspirations of our sublimest poet . . . to render that homage to the Father of Social Democracy in France, which no other pen than Milton's could so worthily furnish'. The first of the poem's twenty stanzas begins with words spoken 'by a small group of brave, sorrowing workmen of the Faubourg St Antoine in Paris, a few days after the fatal 9th Thermidor, when they saw the last hopes of the Revolution extinguished in the blood of its most illustrious chief and his devoted friends'. The workmen are plucking laurel, myrtle and ivy berries, which they apostrophise in words freely adapted from Milton.

> 'Yet once more, O ye laurels, and once more
> Ye myrtles brown, with ivy never sere,
> We come with brimful eyes, and hearts full sore,
> To pluck your berries, rifle your sad store,
> To strew the hearse of him, to Frenchmen dear,
> A chief whose name will live for evermore,
> The man of men, whom myriads will deplore;

---

[1] Published by G. J. Holyoake & Co., Fleet Street, and E. Truelove, 240 Strand, London.

For Maximilian's dead! great Robespierre,
(Cropt in his flower – his five-and-thirtieth year),
And nowhere, on this earth, hath left his peer.

. . . He, whose inspiring voice . . .
Made millions rise, and crush with one same blow,
Th' internal traitor, and th' external foe;
Evok'd the force Democracies can wield,
Bade fourteen armies take the field;
And, through their might, triumphant all around,
Made every frontier, consecrated ground.

• • •

No! we'll not leave, to welter on his bier,
The great and good – our glorious Robespierre,
Without the meed of a melodious tear.

. . .

Begin, then, sisters of the sacred well,
That from beneath the seat of Jove doth spring!
Begin! and loudly, boldly, sweep the string,
For millions yearn to know what ye can sing;
Say why such cruel destiny befel,
The brilliant sage and chief ye lov'd so well.

. . .

Had we not seen in records of the past,
All god-like benefactors of our race,
End their careers in cruel deaths at last,
Else, wear out life in exile and disgrace?

. . .

Banish'd was Aristides, nam'd the just,
Poison'd was Socrates, the good and wise;
Flung from the Tarpeian rock, or roll'd in dust,
Was every chief the Romans learn'd to prize,
Some, whom th' Athenians would but ostracize.

As fared these patriots in Rome and Greece,
So fared our prophets in the Holy Land;
Likewise th' Apostles after Christ's decease,
And all preferring God's to Sin's command.

. . .

237

For when did knaves, who prey on others' labour,
E'er shrink from murd'ring their victims' friends?
When did that wretch fear God, or love his neighbour,
Who spurns the laws of both, for carnal ends?

. . .

A people wise, and master of just laws,
For land, for credit, and for fair exchange;
On rock of adamant hath bas'd its cause,
Beyond all revolutions' utmost range.

. . .

Yes, Robespierre! – our Revolution owes
All that enobled it to thee and thine;
Its crimes alone belong to thy fell foes,
Who spurn'd all justice, human and divine.

. . .

But, oh, the heavy change, now thou art gone;
Now thou art gone, and never must return;
Thee, chieftain, thee, the poor with looks so wan,
The bondsman and the labourer will mourn.

. . .

As killing as the canker to the rose,
Or taint worm to the weaning flocks unshorn,
Or east wind to young plants when fierce it blows,
Or desert-sands to verdure newly born.
Death-chilling as the frost to gay-rob'd flowers
(In summer's dawn, when first the hawthorn blows)
Whose life-warm fragrance, born of sun and showers,
Exhales, mid icy dews, their last perfumes.
Such, Robespierre, thy loss to freedom's cause,
So sweetly link'd by thee with Heav'n's own laws.

Men of the Faubourgs! think ye of the past!
Join your condolence with our sorrowing muse,
Beat up the vales and bid them hither cast
Their bells and flow'rets of a thousand hues:

Ye valleys deep, where Echo lonely sighs,
To plaintive winds and woods, and gushing brooks,
On whose fresh lap the swart star sparely looks;
Throw hither all your quaint enamel'd eyes,

That on the green turf suck the honied showers,
And purple all the ground with vernal flowers;
Bring the rathe primrose that forsaken dies,
The tufted crow–toe, and pale jessamine,
The white pink and the pansy freak'd with jet,
And spring's first-born, the fragrant violet;

The musk-rose, and the well-attired woodbine –
With cowslips wan that hang the pensive head,
And every flower that sad embroid'ry wears;
Bid Amaranthus all his beauties shed,
And daffodillies fill their cups with tears,
To strew the hearse where lies our sainted sage:
At once the pride and sorrow of our age.
Mayhap the bursting heart may find relief
In these poor outward offices of grief.

. . .

Weep no more, gallant Frenchmen, weep no more,
For Robespierre, your sorrow, is not dead;
Sunk though he be beneath a tide of gore,
So sinks the day-star in the ocean-bed,
But yet anon repairs his drooping head,
And tricks his beams, and with new spangl'd ore,
Flames in the fore-head of the morning sky;

. . .

As time and progress shall make facts more clear
And truths divine illume our hemisphere;
These will reveal that helmsman without peer,
Who taught what course republics ought to steer;
Whose virtues only Vice thought too austere;
Whose life was grand – whose death was sad and drear.'

. . .

In the following year, 1858, O'Brien produced what proved to be
the last outpouring of his 'vitriolic verse', under the title, *A Vision of
Hell, or Peep into the Realms below, alias Lord Overgrown's Dream*.
This was a personal attack on Jones Lloyd, Lord Overstone, who
helped to draft the famous Bank Charter Act, 1844; and a general tilt
against the ruling upper and middle classes and their unscrupulous

attempts 'to terrify poverty and ignorance into blind submission to arbitrary and wrongful rule'.

> 'And as for Rights – with all thy pompous prate,
> The useful classes are bereft of all!
> Thy system makes the rich alone *the State*,
> Down to the rank of brutes the workers fall;
>
> For not a man of them has vote nor voice,
> Where e'er thy felon politics prevail,
> The lords of land and gold alone rejoice
> Within thy boasted constitution's pale.'

A review of O'Brien's *Vision of Hell* appeared in the *National Union*,[1] which was the monthly organ of the National Political Union for the Obtainment of the People's Charter, a small group of London Chartists and O'Brienites, with Charles Murray, John Bedford Leno, and Thomas Martin Wheeler among its more active members.

'We are always glad,' wrote the reviewer, 'to receive and peruse anything from the pen of so able a scholar as the Political Schoolmaster of the age, Bronterre O'Brien, a man whose clear-sightedness every politician is more or less indebted to, and whose unwavering constancy in spite of every obstacle, warrants our warmest admiration . . .

We recommend all good haters of the profit-mongers . . . all who repudiate the use of the name of Christianity as a mask for the crimes of the Capitalist and the sins of the Statesman, to invest twopence in this outspoken scourger of their base iniquities.

In conclusion, we believe the author to be quite right in thus cataloguing hell's roasted and toasted occupants; and would applaud him, if there were no other reason, for his great discrimination in omitting ourselves from his list.'

From the *National Union* one learns that, at least as late as the end of 1858, Bronterre O'Brien was still running his Eclectic Institute, giving courses of lectures, selling his poems and the tracts of the National Reform League, and organizing social functions as occasion served. Like the Owenites, who were much given to dancing – 'cotillions, reels and waltzes' – O'Brien, too, held dances at the Eclectic Institute. In December 1858, for instance, the Institute announced

---

[1] *National Union*, No. 6, October 1858. Only nine numbers of this journal appeared; beginning in May 1858, it was discontinued after 11th December 1858.

'A Supper and Ball in commemoration of the 9th Anniversary
of the National Reform League at the Eclectic Institute on
Tuesday evening, 28th December 1858.

The President, Mr James Bronterre O'Brien, will preside.

Supper on Table at 7 o'clock. Ball to commence at 9.30.

Double tickets 4s 6d; Single 2s 6d; Admission to the Ball 1s 0d.'[1]

Such social gatherings put a little light and colour into many a drab
and dreary life.

Early in 1859 O'Brien's *Elegy on Robespierre* was re-issued as a
shilling booklet of ninty-four pages entitled

> '*A Dissertation and Elegy on the Life and Death of the immortal
> Maximilian Robespierre, revealing for the first time, the real
> causes and authors of his death; with true portraitures of the
> Three Assemblies that made the Revolution . . . and of their
> Historic Celebrities; showing how completely history has
> misrepresented the original:*
> *Also An Ode to Louis Napoleon Bonaparte.*'

O'Brien also included in this little volume (pp. 79–82), Robespierre's
'Declaration of the Rights of Man and the Citizen', describing it as
'the noblest, the sublimest, the most truly philosophic and christian
document of its kind the world has yet seen'. This booklet was the
subject of a letter to Joseph Cowen, the prominent and popular
Newcastle Radical and Member of Parliament, from H. E. Neal.

> '*5 New Burlington St,*
> *London.*
>
> *22 Feby 1859.*

My dear Sir,

Our unfortunate friend Bronterre O'Brien is desirous that you
should have a copy of the accompanying pamphlet in the hope that
you might possibly get it patronized a little in Newcastle; and I am
sorry to say that the sale of even a few copies would be of service to
him – such is his present condition! I have done what I could for him,
but that is little indeed, having (*entre nous*) met with a domestic
calamity lately which had nearly, if not quite ruined me.

O'Brien makes Robespierre a kind of idol – but I fancy the world
has got rather beyond him now. Yet the Eulogy on that celebrated

---

[1] *Ibid.*, No. 6, October 1858, p. 47; No. 8, December 1858, p. 59.

man is very interesting, and well worth a shilling. Perhaps you [can] get the Editor of the *Guardian* to notice it? . . .

Congratulating you on the successful efforts you are making in the North in futherance of Parliamentary Reform.'[1]

Bronterre, who was now nearing the end of the road, was often to be seen in the City at Cranston's Waverley Hotel in Lawrence Lane, and as we move into the 1860s we catch a glimpse of him through the eyes of William Edwin Adams, a young contemporary observer, then not quite thirty years of age, who, from beginnings as a journeyman printer had become a successful journalist. He came of a family of Chartists living in Cheltenham, and while still in his teens he was active in the Cause, which was then sliding into its decline. Later he was helped by Charles Bradlaugh who employed him for a time on his *National Reformer*. He worked, also, for Joseph Cowen in that ever-active Radical centre, Newcastle. Adams, who adopted the non de plume, 'Caractacus', eventually achieved marked success in the 1890s as editor of Cowen's *Newcastle Weekly Chronicle*. In his *Memoirs of a Social Atom*, published on 1903, he tells us that he remembered seeing Bronterre O'Brien in and around Fleet Street, 'towards the close of his career – shabby, snuffy, beery . . . a tribune of the people in the palmy period of Chartism . . . [and] . . . a good speaker even to the last, he was in demand at the Cogers and other debating halls of the metropolis', where his fee for opening a discussion was 'five shillings and his night's liquor'.

A popular discussion hall attached to a tavern meant good business for the tavern-keeper. In the Fleet Street neighbourhood there were three such halls: the Cogers Hall near St Bride's Church, the Temple Forum in Fleet Street, and the Discussion Hall in Shoe Lane. 'The Cogers' had been founded as far back as 1755 and its roll of members included such famous names as John Wilkes, Daniel O'Connell, Henry Hunt, and many other Radicals. Charles Dickens, too, was a member. The Temple Forum, despite its grand name, was held in a small ill-ventilated room at the back of the 'Green Dragon'. By contrast, the Shoe Lane Discussion Hall was a spacious, long, lofty room, comfortably furnished with seats and tables. It is easy to picture the scene. The president sat on a canopied chair and usually sipped brandy and water as he smoked a long churchwarden pipe. The rest of the company, including a number of distinguished men, Radical politicians, orators, agitators, editors, sub-editors and free-lance writers, were not slow to follow their president's example. From the walls portraits in oils of

---

[1] Cowen Collection No. C532, Newcastle-upon-Tyne City Library.

such celebrated Radicals as Thomas Hardy and William Carpenter looked down. The subjects for discussion at the next meeting and the name of the 'opener' were advertised beforehand in the tavern windows, and it was important to secure a good opener likely to attract a large attendance. After each speech the president called, 'The waiter's in the room, give your orders, Gentlemen'; and it is not surprising that, as the evening wore on, the exchange of views became more and more animated, though not always more logical and coherent, culminating in a general hubbub, every member holding forth to every other.

During the late 1850s and early 1860s many old Chartists joined hands with middle-class Radicals in an attempt to revive, on a nation-wide scale, the agitation for parliamentary reform. That Bronterre O'Brien did what lay in his power to further this movement we can infer from a letter written on 25th March 1860 by Robert Jones, a London Radical, to his friend, R. B. Reed, a Newcastle journalist and a friend of G. J. Holyoake, who once said of him that he had an 'instinct for incidents':

'Bronterre was arguing in the Discussion Hall, Shoe Lane, last night,' Jones wrote, 'that the last and newest recipients of the suffrage are always conservative against another importation as lessening the value of their privilege to them.' [1]

But, although O'Brien's spirit was still willing, the flesh was growing weak. From 1860–1 onwards he became, progressively, a prey to recurrent attacks of bronchitis, a disease doubtless much aggravated, especially in winter weather, by the polluted atmosphere in the close-built, coal-burning districts of inner London where he lived. He was also under ever-increasing pressure from poverty. His former tremendous capacity for sustained effort had gone for ever. A man of unusual intellectual power, he had given himself without stint, for more than thirty years, to a worthy, but apparently lost, cause. He continued to do what he could for the National Reform League, but as the shadows lengthened it became sadly obvious that his end was approaching. He could lecture no longer, he could write no more, his last trickle of income dried up. A few friends revived the Bronterre O'Brien testimonial fund, and young Charles Bradlaugh, who was already making a place for himself among the leaders of advanced

[1] W. E. Adams, *Memoirs of a Social Atom* (1903), I, p. 210; II, p. 316 (reprinted in 1968, with an introduction by John Saville); Cowen Collection No. C1326, Newcastle-upon-Tyne City Library. By the end of the nineteenth century the discussion halls were almost extinct; see G. R. Sims (ed.), *Living London* (1903), II, p. 290.

243

thought, lectured in aid of the fund, for 'real distress rarely appealed to him in vain'.[1] At the beginning of the year 1864 O'Brien's illness took a serious turn when his bronchitis developed into 'dropsy of the pulmonary circulation'.[2] Forced at last to take to his bed where, propped up by pillows – for towards the end he could not lie down – he lingered, in crushing penury and increasing pain, until Friday, 23rd December 1864, when he died at his home, No. 20 Hermes Street, Pentonville.

Charles Murray, his close friend and disciple, took charge of the funeral arrangements, and another friend, G. E. Harris, wrote to Victor Hugo, the famous French poet, novelist, republican-democrat, and implacable enemy of Napoleon III, inviting him to make a funeral oration. But time would not permit, for Hugo (then in his early sixties) was living in exile on the Channel Island of Guernsey. He sent, however, a courteous letter of apology and condolence.

> *'Hauteville House [St Peter Port],*
> *December 30th 1864.*
>
> *Sir,*
>
> Your excellent and touching letter reached me today, Friday, 30th December. The interment of your much regretted fellow-citizen takes place on Saturday, and our mail from Guernsey does not depart again for England until Monday, 2nd January. Judge of the impossibility in which I am of replying in person to your eloquent appeal. I reply to you immediately; but my letter – and it is for me a profound regret – is sure to reach you too late.
>
> I should have seized with earnestness this occasion of proving that national differences do not exist for the democrats, and of blending a French voice with English voices at the tomb of a man of courage and virtue. Progress, democracy, and liberty have lost much in losing the valiant and generous man whom you deplore. Let us not, however, mourn without hope. The dead, such as O'Brien, live, for they leave behind them their example.
>
> *Accept, Sir, my cordial salutations,*
> *Victor Hugo.'*

[1] H. Bradlaugh and J. M. Robertson, *Charles Bradlaugh* (1894), I, p. 219; *Working Man*, 1st January 1862. Thomas Cooper and many other Chartist leaders had fallen upon evil days. 'I can do no more than sympathize with you,' wrote Cooper to a friend, 'for I am at my wits' end to know how the week's bread is to be purchased.' Cooper to Edward Smith, 30th January 1855; London University *MSS*. and Autograph Letters.

[2] Certified Copy of an Entry of Death, dated 28th December 1864, in the registration district of Clerkenwell.

In the absence of such a literary giant as Victor Hugo, it is unlikely that the funeral at Abney Park Cemetery, Stoke Newington, at three o'clock in the afternoon of the last day of 1864 – when not only was the day waning, but the year – attracted very much public attention. We know that a number of faithful friends were there, and that six of them bore the coffin from the chapel to the grave, while five others served as pall bearers. Six 'chief mourners' are named, including James Francis Murray, but strangely enough the record does not mention the widow or any other member of O'Brien's family. Addresses at the graveside were delivered by three of his personal friends and disciples (C. Benzing, John Radford and John Rogers) who expressed deep sorrow at the loss of their 'revered teacher', mingled with admiration for the 'immutable doctrines' he taught, and above all for his 'unflinching and heroic struggle, extending over a period of thirty-five years, for the political and social rights of the masses'. At the conclusion of these addresses many of those present, with hands extended over the grave, 'pledged themselves in the most solemn manner to a life-long adherence to, and zealous propagation of, the doctrines of the deceased . . . as a beacon light to guide the people and an example to follow'.[1] This done, the mourners lingered a little, and then, in the fast-gathering December dusk, moved slowly and sadly away.

★   ★   ★

In the ensuing years some of them tried to honour their graveside pledge by keeping alive their master's ideas and proposals for a radical reformation of society, and by defending his memory and reputation against attack; for in their judgment Bronterre O'Brien would 'bear comparison with any man who has appeared in the public arena during the last forty years, for public virtue, unswerving fidelity, and enlightened views upon national reform'.[2]

The council of the National Reform League lost no time in calling a public meeting at the Eclectic Institute to launch a 'Bronterre O'Brien Memorial Fund' for the benefit of O'Brien's widow who was 'left

[1] Charles Bradlaugh's *National Reformer, Secular Advocate and Freethought Journal*, Vol. 6, 1865, pp. 15, 29 and 74; *Reynolds's*, 8th January 1865. The chief mourners named are James Francis Murray, George Messenger, James Lee, P. Brown, C. Benzing and (?)Turnbull. For the names of some of Bronterre O'Brien's disciples, with notes, see Appendix C.

[2] Letter addressed to the editor of the *Beehive*, after the death of Ernest Jones in 1869, signed by John Rogers, James Francis Murray, Charles Murray, John Radford, Edward Bedford, George Townsend, George Messenger, James Lea, Edward G. Smith, Thomas Boutwell, and James Flaxman (or Flexman?), perhaps related to the tenant of No. 18 Denmark Street who kept the coffee and reading rooms annexed to the Eclectic Institute); see pp. 205, 275.

wholly unprovided for'. A Memorial Committee issued an appeal for subscriptions in February 1865, and appointed George Messenger to act as London treasurer, and Robert Gammage, 'Surgeon, 18 Villiers Street, Sunderland', as 'provincial treasurer for the North of England'.[1] O'Brien's Scottish friend, Robert Cranston of Edinburgh, undertook a similar function for Scotland. Gradually a modest sum was collected, from which, no doubt with Mrs O'Brien's agreement, the cost of a memorial sarcophagus over O'Brien's grave was defrayed. This memorial can be seen today, impressive in its simple, grey dignity, undamaged by time or tempest, bearing but one brief inscription (still quite legible):

James Bronterre O'Brien
departed this life
December 23rd 1864
Aged 67

'His life was grand,
His death was sad and drear.'[2]

Here, in springtime,

'. . . robins flit among the greening trees,
One squats, a ruby, on a battered cross.
Here slant old stones commemorating loss,
Names known and unknown on their fading frieze.'[3]

And here, amidst a great multitude of fellow-citizens, Bronterre rests at last, his grave marked by a worthy memorial to

'A man whose heart was rent by every moan
That burst from every trodden, tortured slave . . .
He loved the people with a brother's love:
He hated tyrants with a tyrant's hate . . .
. . . misfortune's guest, . . . around thee gathered those
Who, poor and trampled patriots, were like thee.
Thou art not dead! Thy martyred spirit glows
In us, a band devoted of the free.'[4]

---

[1] Bradlaugh's *National Reformer*, Vol. 6, 1865, p. 119; see also p. 29 for some (very bad) 'Lines on James Bronterre O'Brien' by Hugh Fulton.

[2] Abney Park Cemetery, Stoke Newington; Grave No. 34497 in Section M.7. There is a curious error as to O'Brien's age on this inscription and on his Death Certificate, the age at death being given on both as sixty-seven, whereas his true age was sixty years ten months. The epitaph is taken from his *Elegy on Robespierre*.

[3] Lines from a poem by Edith Blake (1968).

[4] Adapted from William Maccall's verses on Bronterre O'Brien, published in the *Working Man*, 1st March 1867; reprinted in 1885.

Chapter XII
APPRAISAL

BRONTERRE O'BRIEN'S active political career, which spans the thirty years from his arrival in London from his native Ireland in 1830 to the final failure of his health after 1860, falls into two unequal parts, separated by his imprisonment from April 1840 to September 1841. In the first part, which covers slightly less than ten years, there were two peaks of intense activity: the struggle of the unstamped journals against the 'taxes on knowledge' from 1832 to 1834; and, some five years later, the feverish flurry of the Chartist agitation at its height.

For young O'Brien the fight, under Henry Hetherington's banner, to free the working men's papers from the iniquitous, crippling excise duties was probably the most exciting and satisfying of all the struggles in which he took part. At its height, for a period of some eighteen months during which Hetherington was often absent either in prison or in hiding to avoid arrest,[1] O'Brien, as editor of the *Poor Man's Guardian*, was Hetherington's right hand: the indispensable back-room boy, responsible, reliable, deputising for his chief and, at the same time, disseminating many remarkably advanced, penetrating and mature ideas of his own on Radicalism and the future of democracy.

The resounding victory won by the warriors of the Unstamped Press, to everybody's amazement, in the summer of 1834, did much to encourage the hope that the concession of universal suffrage could not be far away. But this hope proved delusive. Because the Chartists were in a great hurry – understandably so – they seriously under-estimated the time factor. Moreover, as everybody now knows, their Movement was torn asunder and sadly weakened by the moral force *versus* physical force issue, and when the physical force faction seemed to be getting the upper hand, the Government became alarmed and took firm repressive action. Bronterre O'Brien made the mistake of joining forces with the militants, whereas his talents, had he but known it, fitted him much better for a campaign of peaceful, though intense, forthright and, if need be, prolonged propaganda in the press and on the platform.

[1] G. Wallas, *Life of Francis Place* (rev. edn 1918), p. 348.

247

In the second part of his public career, from 1841 onwards, O'Brien adhered to his firm resolve, made during his imprisonment, never again to take part in activities likely to land him in prison. After 1841, although still completely loyal to the Chartist ideal, he recognized that henceforth less passion and more patience would be needed, for there could be no short cut to his objective; only steady plodding, year in, year out, along the propaganda road.

It was during the first phase referred to above – from 1832 to 1839 – that Bronterre O'Brien came to be known and accepted by working-class Radicals as 'the schoolmaster' of Chartism, or 'the political schoolmaster of the Age'. But was he a *good* 'schoolmaster'? Apparently, nobody ever asked this question. Of his natural intellectual endowment there can be no doubt. Born with a mind 'apt for learning', he had amply stored it by many years of assiduous study, wide reading and deep thinking, especially about existing social evils and the ideal society of the future. Of all the Chartist leaders, O'Brien was by far the most highly qualified and equipped by academic study and training. In addition to the classics and a good deal of history, he had read the works of many modern authors holding advanced opinions. For example, he wrote of his admiration for 'the immortal Jefferson'; of his respect for William Cobbett, whose *Legacy for Labourers* he wished to see in every cottage, for 'a more valuable legacy even Cobbett could not have left'; and of his debt to Tom Paine for a rich endowment of political knowledge. He had read with delight Paine's irreverent, iconoclastic, class-conscious writings, which aimed at clearing the cluttered ground in preparation for a new society incorporating social, or 'welfare', services,[1] all of which led O'Brien to formulate his own proposals to harness, in aid of the working class, the immense potential power of the State. O'Brien's grasp of his subject and his clear vision of the ultimate objective cannot be doubted. He certainly had a great deal to offer. Nor can his zeal and persistence be called in question. But he was prone to over-estimate the intellectual capacity of his working-class 'pupils', so that, from time to time, his 'lessons' were not suitably adapted to the end in view. This criticism applies especially to his heavily-annotated translation of *Babeuf's Conspiracy*, and his long, solid – and unfinished – biography of Robespierre. His series of articles on the American Constitution and his writings in several of his journals suffer from the same defect. Such large helpings of undiluted

---

[1] *Poor Man's Guardian*, 15th December 1832; *Bronterre's National Reformer*, 7th January 1837; T. Paine, *Rights of Man*, especially Part II; A. Plummer, 'Some Aspects of the History and Theory of Social Insurance', in *Economica*, June 1927.

Radical 'political instruction' could be digested only by a small, dedicated, almost fanatical, minority. On the other hand, it must be said, in fairness, that the majority of 'Schoolmaster' O'Brien's many 'lessons' were admirably adapted to the needs and interests of his 'classes'. His lectures and speeches were usually informative, stimulating and memorable, and much the same may be said of his editorials and leading articles in papers like the *Poor Man's Guardian*, the *Northern Star*, and the *British Statesman*. He was, for Chartism, an intellectual dynamo and a 'theorist of stature'; and although he never wrote a systematic treatise on social and political philosophy, his voluminous journalistic writings contain much of the raw material of later Socialist doctrine and a sheaf of sketch plans for a new democratic, egalitarian society, redeemed from the curse of Capitalism and the injustices of social privilege.

For more than thirty years O'Brien denounced Capitalism and advocated Chartism, pointing out that while the capitalists remained all-powerful, the masses of mankind would continue to be slaves; that the rich lived by exploiting the poor, who received but a small share of the wealth they produced; and that the control of the power of the State was the means by which this exploitation was achieved and perpetuated. He thus anticipated the fundamental ideas upon which Karl Marx based his famous book, *Das Kapital*, the first and principal volume of which was published in Hamburg in 1867.

When Karl Marx visited England in 1845, his friend, Friedrich Engels, drew his attention to the main stream of English radical and socialist literature, and it is known that he read with interest the works of Cobbett, Hodgskin, Thompson, and Bray. Although there appears to be no direct evidence that he read the periodicals containing Bronterre O'Brien's earlier articles, he can hardly have been ignorant of O'Brien's work, for he studied Chartism, he met Feargus O'Connor, and he had long, wide-ranging discussions with Engels, both before and after he settled in London in the summer of 1849, only four months before O'Brien's series of articles on 'The Rise, Progress and Phases of Human Slavery' began to appear in *Reynolds's Political Instructor*.[1] Marx certainly knew about O'Brien and his followers, for in January 1858, in one of his letters to Engels, he speaks of O'Brien as 'an irrepressible Chartist at any price'; and after O'Brien's death he refers to 'the sect of the late Bronterre O'Brien'. Hyndman once asked Marx 'how the conception of social surplus value and the social

[1] F. R. Salter, *Karl Marx and Modern Socialism* (1921), especially pp. 2, 41, 71–2; cf. H. M. Hyndman's recollections in his *Record of an Adventurous Life* (1911), pp. 275–6.

basis of exchange in social labour value occurred to him. He told me that . . . he believed the illuminating notion of the social economic forces of the time, working themselves out quite unconsciously and uncontrolled into monopoly and Socialism, beneath the anarchist competitions and antagonisms of the Capitalist system, first arose in a co-ordinated shape from his perusal of the works of the early English Economists, Socialists and Chartists'.[1] Bronterre O'Brien was certainly of this company.

Both O'Brien and Marx looked upon the orthodox political economists of their day as creatures of the ruling classes, and they challenged fiercely the assumptions and arguments currently used to justify Capitalism. O'Brien, as we know, wrote and spoke vehemently against the hypocritically disguised wage-slavery of modern industrial societies. So, too, did Marx, who maintained that

'In reality the worker belongs to capital before he sells himself to the capitalist. His economic bondage is at once caused and hidden by the periodical renewal of the sale of himself, by the change from one wage lord to another, and by the fluctuations in the market price of labour.'[2]

The articles in which O'Brien likens the capitalist to a sort of vampire, using his wealth as a means of sucking into himself the produce of others, are reflected in several passages in *Capital* in which Marx used the same simile. For example, on the lethal effects of excessive hours of day and night work he wrote:

'The prolongation of the working day beyond the limits of the natural day . . . into the night, acts only as a palliative. It can never more than slake the vampire thirst for the living blood of labour . . . In its blind, unbridled passion, its werewolf hunger for surplus labour, capital is not content to overstep the moral restrictions upon the length of the working day. It oversteps the purely physical limitations as well. It usurps the time needed for growth, development, and the healthy maintenance of the body.'[3]

Marx, like O'Brien, argued that great accumulations of wealth owned by the few meant a corresponding accumulation of wage-slavery, misery, and degradation for the working class. O'Brien's frequent

[1] Marx to Engels, 14th January 1858; Briggs and Saville (eds), *Essays in Labour History* (1960), p. 257; Hyndman, *Record*, p. 275.
[2] Karl Marx, *Capital* (Everyman edn, translated from the fourth German edition by E. & C. Paul, 1930), II, pp. 634–5.
[3] *Ibid.*, I, pp. 259, 269.

denunciations of the swarms of middlemen, crafty speculators, 'shopocrats', stock-exchange gamblers, usurers and bankers, and his contention that property-owners alone ought to be responsible for both the capital and interest of the national debt, and not the working class, 'seeing the debt was not borrowed by them nor for them, nor with their consent', find an echo in Marx's book, in which it is argued that the 'only part of the so-called national wealth that actually enters into the collective possession of modern peoples is – their national debt', and that 'a goodly share of every national loan accrues as capital fallen from heaven' to tax farmers, merchants, manufacturers, idle bond-holders, and financiers, and gives rise 'to gambling on the stock-exchange and to the modern bankocracy'.[1]

O'Brien taught that, in truth,

'... the upper and middle classes have no wealth but what consists of sub-tractions wrung from industry, through institutions of their own making. Those of them who have sprung from the "lower ranks" may boast as much as they like of their habits of industry as *workmen* and ascribe their wealth to that industry, but all who know anything know well enongh that it is not as workmen they acquired it, but as *hirers of workmen*. . . .

'That the producer does not, upon the average, receive a fourth of his produce is a certain fact. If the producers get back £125 millions out of a gross annual produce of £600 millions . . . it is the very extreme of their good fortune . . . the majority get less than a fourth . . . an Irish labourer or a London needle-woman does not, probably, receive a tithe of the value of their labour. . . .

'When a gentleman is said to have 10, 20, or 100 thousand pounds a year out of houses, trade, etc. . . . people do not reflect that [such incomes] are so many claims on the aggregate labour of the community to answer which the bones and sinews of the infant in the cradle are mortgaged by law. They do not consider that the effect of these claims upon future industry is to prevent the wealth-producer from enjoying a tenth of the fruits of his labours, in the shape of necessaries, till he has first wasted his health and strength in the production of luxuries for the aristocrat.'

We have already noted O'Brien's advanced views on the potential benefits of machinery used in the service of all, in a truly democratic society. But both he and Marx were fiercely critical of the capitalist's use of machinery to exploit the labour of women and children, as well as men. Such use of machinery, Marx declared, diminishes the part

[1] Marx, *op. cit.*, II, pp. 836–7.

251

of the working day in which the worker works for himself while increasing the part of the working day he gives to the capitalist for nothing; long spells of machine-tending heighten the intensity of labour, making slaves and paupers of the real producers.[1]

O'Brien's opinion that the blame for poverty and misery belongs to the economic and social system – the class-society – and not to individuals, for the latter are but the tools or instruments of their class, actuated 'by the silent operation of causes over which they have no control', appears to be accepted by Marx, who saw the evolution of the economic formation of society as a process of 'natural history', in which, in his own time, the natural laws of capitalist production were 'tendencies working with iron necessity towards inevitable results': the great concentrations of capital which would surely be the prelude to the downfall of Capitalism. This expropriation of the capitalists, said Marx, in the famous flourish at the end of chapter XXIV, will be ' . . . brought about by the operation of the immanent laws of capitalist production, by the centralization of capital. . . . The centralization of the means of production and the socialization of labour reach a point where they prove incompatible with their capitalist husk. This bursts asunder. The knell of capitalist private property sounds. The expropriators are expropriated'.[2] For many years Marx held this belief that the natural laws and trends of social evolution are inevitably on the side of the working class. O'Brien, on the contrary, held no such conviction. He maintained that the workers themselves must tackle the task of political organization; and that neither the progress of Capitalism nor anything else would do it for them. Social reconstruction would not begin until, through universal suffrage, the working class gained control of the law-making machinery of the State. Bearing in mind these earlier differences, it is interesting to see that the inaugural *Address to the Working Classes*, which Marx wrote in 1864 for the International Working Men's Association, was quite O'Brienite in tone, for it urged workmen everywhere to organize labour parties, to demand social reform, and to wage a relentless class war until they had captured political power and nationalized the means of production. 'The emancipation of the working classes must be achieved by the working classes themselves.'

The class struggle, then, was preached by O'Brien in the 1830s and 1840s, and it is clear that when Marx came upon the scene he found the theory of the class struggle already in existence. But, like the theory

---

[1] Marx, *op. cit.*, I, Ch. XIII.

[2] *Ibid.*, II, p. 846; cf. *The Communist Manifesto* (1848) which describes the fall of the bourgeoisie and the victory of the proletariat as 'equally inevitable'.

of surplus value, it received at his hands a far more academic, elaborate, and systematic treatment, and was woven into the pattern of his deterministic theory of social development.[1]

As we have seen (especially in Chapter II) O'Brien was strongly attracted to Owenism, because of its idealism, its essential humanity, its egalitarian elements, its enlightened attitude to the education and welfare of children, and its labour-for-labour scheme for the direct exchange of the products of the workman's skill. So we find many strands of Owenism running through the fabric of Bronterre O'Brien's social philosophy. But, O'Brien felt obliged to ask, could the Owenite community-making plan stand up to the severe tests and pressures of the real world? Reluctantly, he felt bound to answer, 'No; Owenism is not enough'. Since Owenite community-making must, inevitably, be extremely slow and limited in range, a far better and quicker way to build a new society, in O'Brien's opinion, would be to harness the immense latent power of the state, for this, wisely directed, could bring about not only the immediate or short-term relief of unemployment, under-employment, poverty and want, but the long-term continuous shaping of social change. And the golden key to this social regeneration was universal suffrage. 'Working-class political radicalism did not seek to replace Owenism, but to add another dimension to it.'[2]

Nobody saw more clearly than 'Schoolmaster' O'Brien that popular education and enlightenment would be essential to full success. He took it to be beyond dispute that free elementary and secondary education ought to be every citizen's right. There should be, also, in O'Brien's opinion, open access to adult education, developed from the 'political instruction' about their rights and the remedies for their wrongs which he always tried to give to all working men and women. Around this main centre of interest, in ever-widening circles, he hoped to inculcate a knowledge of the true principles upon which the new democracy should be founded, guided, and developed.

Bronterre O'Brien was second to none in his desire to secure beneficial reforms quickly, for as he observed and studied the onward march of industrial capitalism he saw and felt acutely

> '. . . How dear the penalty thus paid for wealth;
> Obtained through wasted life and broken health . . .
> The one his villa and a carriage keeps;
> His squalid brother in a garret sleeps.'[3]

---

[1] For an illuminating discussion of Marx's economic determinism, see A. D. Lindsay, *Karl Marx's Capital* (1925), Ch. 2.

[2] Cf. H. Silver, *The Concept of Popular Education* (1965), pp. 170–4, 235.

[3] William Osbourn, *A Poem* (1857).

Yet everything, he was convinced, might be so different. The crushing burden of poverty and suffering could be lifted and lightened without causing *real* harm to anybody. O'Brien thought he could discern the first faint outline of a future age of automation, short working weeks, and immense productivity:[1] a glimpse of an affluent and increasingly leisured society which was by no means absurdly utopian. Since O'Brien's time, science and technology, machines and materials, have undergone and are still undergoing a transformation so amazing in both range and rapidity that we now have actually within reach the material, if not the moral, basis for his well-regulated society in which men and women might live a good life as a right, giving in return a full contribution to production and government.

If the Chartist dream had turned into reality during the 1840s or 1850s, Bronterre O'Brien might well have won a seat in a new radically-reformed House of Commons, probably as a member for a politically-conscious, industrial constituency such as Newcastle-upon-Tyne.[2] This consummation, which, 'zealous politician' that he was,[3] he would have found entirely to his liking, went into the limbo of hopes deferred when the Chartist Movement failed to achieve unity and strength during the phase of partial recovery after 1841. Not until the last ten or twelve years of O'Brien's lifetime did encouraging signs begin to indicate that the efforts of the Radicals and Chartists in the 1830s and 1840s were at last about to bear fruit. First among the significant gains which certainly did not escape O'Brien's notice, and from which he may well have drawn a modicum of much-needed comfort and encouragement, were the successive repeals, between 1853 and 1861, of the obnoxious 'taxes on knowledge', against which such a good fight had been fought by the unstamped 'pauper press' over twenty years before. The advertisement duty, the remaining one-penny stamp, and the duty on paper were all abolished in O'Brien's lifetime.

As to parliamentary reform, O'Brien did not live quite long enough to witness the substantial instalment of franchise extension which resulted from the Reform Act of 1867; but this coming event was already throwing a shadow in the 1850s. It is on record that, in 1852, Macaulay had an earnest conversation with Joseph Hume 'about the necessity of a union of Liberals' in the course of which Hume 'said

---

[1] Bronterre O'Brien's speech at Second Co-operative Congress, 5th October 1831.

[2] At Newcastle in the 1906 General Election, Walter Hudson, standing for the newly-fledged Labour Party, was elected by the highest Labour poll in the country, 18,869 votes.

[3] Hetherington's *Twopenny Dispatch*, 'Bronterre's Letters', No. 4.

much about [the] Ballot and the Franchise'. Certainly every new straw in the wind was closely watched by Bronterre. For example, in November 1853, he told an audience that as soon as the serious industrial dispute in the cotton spinning district around Preston[1] was settled, 'they should direct their attention to the new Reform Bill, and take care it was not a hoax. If a hundred seats were disfranchised, they ought to be given to the unenfranchised in the manufacturing towns'.[2] Between 1852 and 1864 no fewer than four bills designed to alter and extend the franchise were introduced in Parliament, but for various reasons – chiefly fear of entrusting the vote to working-class citizens – all failed to reach the statute book. Nevertheless, when the property qualification for membership of Parliament was abolished in 1858, it must have been clear to O'Brien that time and pressure were at last eroding the obstacles and that a substantial step towards universal suffrage, that great prize for which he had fought for thirty years, could not be delayed for long. In fact, during his declining years, the parliamentary reform movement was rapidly gathering strength. John Bright stood forth and, shifting the weight of his appeal from interest to justice, sounded a clarion call with Chartism in every note:

'The class which has hitherto ruled in this country has failed miserably. It revels in power and wealth, whilst at its feet . . . lies the multitude it has neglected. If a class has failed, let us try the nation! That is our faith, that is our purpose, that is our cry: Let us try the nation!'[3]

At the same juncture, Gladstone, too, saw that franchise reform could not be held back much longer. Indeed, it so happened that only a few months after O'Brien died, Lord Palmerston's death (1865) opened the way, and Bright, Gladstone, Derby, Disraeli, all began to move in the same direction, towards 'freedom and an honest representation of the people'; but each moved at his own pace and with his own mental reservations. Derby and Disraeli it was who, as everybody knows, jumped in with the Reform Act of 1867 – that famous 'leap in the dark' – which, in the end, went further than they had originally intended, and drew from an alarmed and hostile Lord Dalhousie a despairing protest that 'the sluices of democracy' had been raised

---

[1] Charles Dickens, seeking inspiration and material for his book, *Hard Times*, visited Preston during this long, stubborn struggle.
[2] G. O. Trevelyan, *Life and Letters of Lord Macaulay* (1876: enlarged and complete edn 1908), p. 606; *People's Paper*, 3rd and 10th December 1853.
[3] John Bright, *Speeches* (ed. J. E. Thorold Rogers), Vol. II, p. 211; Asa Briggs, *Victorian People* (1954), pp. 233–4.

'not an inch but a foot'.[1] Bronterre O'Brien would have preferred a yard!

The reform Act of 1867, which conferred the parliamentary franchise upon 938,000 new voters,[2] thus increasing the electorate by 88 per cent, was passed less than three years after Bronterre O'Brien's death. It is, indeed, a matter for great regret that he was not spared to witness this major success for which he had done so much to pave the way. For he was an outstanding political pioneer, incessantly disseminating ideas which he hoped and believed would influence the destiny of society by extending the frontiers of political freedom and civilized life. Francis Place was right when he said that although such men may sometimes be ignorant of the best means of progressing and can seldom be persuaded that the immediate attainment of their objective is impossible, it is by their labours and sacrifices that the way is smoothed for others:

'Never without such persons . . . through their errors and misfortunes, would mankind have emerged from barbarism, and gone on as they have done, slow and painful as their progress has been.' [3]

Although many of O'Brien's ideas and suggestions have long since been absorbed into orthodox opinion and built into public policy, their formulation and dissemination in early-Victorian England required outstanding insight, originality, and courage, coupled with a passion for social and political progress. During a period in which the orthodox political economists and politicians were held fast in the grip of economic fatalism, Bronterre O'Brien was preaching the good news that man could yet be master of his fate. When authorities and rulers were afraid to tamper with the complex and delicate mechanism of the economic machine, O'Brien was boldly proposing to re-shape many of its parts and to scrap the remainder. When few men understood the true nature of the state, 'Schoolmaster' O'Brien was trying to teach the working men the alphabet of politics, using as his main incentive the argument that they could expect no improvement of their lot until they were able, by self-organization, to constitute themselves a social force strong enough to make *the* state, with its enormous potential power, *their* state. The spearhead of his attack was levelled against those supremely confident devotees of the cult of every man

---

[1] *Briggs, op. cit.*, Ch. 10. It is interesting to return to Justin McCarth's amusing Chapter LII on 'The Leap in the Dark' in his *History of Our Own Times*.

[2] C. Seymour, *Electoral Reform in England and Wales* (1918), p. 281. Voting by secret ballot was brought in by the Ballot Act, 1872.

[3] B.M. *Add.MSS.* 27,820(5), quoted by Wallas, *op. cit.*, p. 383.

for himself, the mighty middle class: iron masters, coal and cotton lords (the Railway King ascended the throne a little later), skilful manipulators of steam and steel and stocks and shares. To attack these forces in the world's workshop in the 1830s was to give battle to the Spirit of the Age; and this is exactly what Bronterre did.

One of the most striking characteristics of O'Brien's thought is the maturity of many of his ideas and judgments expressed in the early 1830s when he was still young and new to politics. Even those who cannot go along with him, can hardly deny the range and penetration of his mind; while his sincerity and constancy are beyond doubt. His optimism was, perhaps, as excessive as the pessimistic fatalism of many of his opponents, but, at least, his error was on the right side, namely, the side of Right. However, although he fully realized the importance of willing co-operation within the Chartist Movement, and unity in face of the enemy, his own personal contribution was not all that it might have been, for he was not always easy to work with. By nature he was impulsive and inclined to be hot-tempered, and could, on occasion, be seriously lacking in tact, discretion and for-bearance. Once he had taken offence, he became a formidable opponent in a war of words, and could not easily be reconciled. But, despite all his faults and failings, Bronterre O'Brien, with steadfast singleness of purpose, helped in no small measure to enlighten, encourage and lead 'the first genuinely democratic movement for social reform in modern history'.[1] Although he came from a petit-bourgeois family and, for more than eleven years, received a bourgeois-type education, he was one of the least conventional and most sensitive men of his class. No man, lacking direct industrial experience, ever felt more keenly, more personally, the misery and injustice suffered by the farm workers, the miners, foundrymen and metal-workers, the weavers, nailers, needle-women, and the rest; nobody had greater ability to stand in their shoes, or to win their hearts and minds. The political enterprise to which he devoted so much of his life was not, as we know, an immediate spectacular success; but when the Chartist Movement disintegrated, Chartism did not die. The organization withered away. but the essential spirit survived and passed into the democratic movements of the second half of the nineteenth century. And much the same may be said of O'Brienism. Bronterre O'Brien's ideas and influence penetrated into many sections of the British Labour and Socialist Movement where they were absorbed and blended with ideas and influences from other sources. For example, we have the impact of his unremitting advocacy of land nationalization and public ownership of mines, banking,

[1] Hovell, *op. cit.*, p. 312.

transport and other public utilities. It was O'Brien who supplied the arguments and original impetus which made land nationalization a live issue for many years after his death. Late in the 1860s a group of his disciples, including Martin Boon, Patrick Hennessey and Frederick Riddle, who had continued to meet and discuss his various theories and proposals, decided to agitate for land reform through O'Brien's National Reform League, which they re-named the Working Men's National Reform League. Other land nationalizers, notably Alfred Russel Wallace, President of the Land Nationalization Society, and Charles Wicksteed, following along lines almost identical with those sketched by O'Brien, fanned land nationalization into a burning question in the 1880s.[1] Wallace and Wicksteed worked out the details of a scheme of nationalization-with-compensation, on the assumption that land values would continue to rise, yielding a growing net surplus over all compensation and interest payments, which could be used to redeem land nationalization bonds and to relieve taxation. Wicksteed's mathematics led him to the conclusion that the whole take-over could be completed in from fifty-three to seventy-one years.[2] But these calculations were never tested in practice; the nettle of land nationalization has never been grasped in Britain. On the other hand, nearly all O'Brien's proposals for public ownership of mines, inland transport, gas, water, etc., were carried through during the first half of the twentieth century, either by direct state ownership or indirectly through the municipal corporations or public service boards. He was certainly one of the makers of the Britain we know today.

O'Brien's Eclectic Institute served a useful purpose in the early stages of the adult education movement for over twenty years, while his disciples continued to be active in the trade unions and in the English section of the International Working Men's Association. The National Reform League, founded by O'Brien in 1850, was still maintaining its steady, consistent propaganda in the late 1860s, and was the first English political society to affiliate to the I.W.M.A. It provided the English section with an ideology.[3] The local branches of

[1] A. J. Peacock, *Land Reform, 1881–1919: A Study of the Activities of the English Land Restoration Leagues and the Land Nationalization Society*. (An unpublished M.A. thesis, 1961; Southampton University), p. 12; E. E. Barry, *op. cit.*, pp. 49–65.

[2] A. R. Wallace, *Land Nationalization* (2nd edn 1882); A. J. Peacock, *op. cit.*, p. 85. The Georgeite Land Restoration League was against the compensation of land-owners, for they could not 'tolerate the idea that the people of England shall be compelled to buy back the land which is theirs by natural right'.

[3] H. Collins and C. Abramsky, *Karl Marx and the British Labour Movement* (1965), p. 301.

the I.W.M.A., of which there were more than twenty up and down the country, were propaganda bodies disseminating socialism according to Bronterre O'Brien 'whose followers formed the only coherent body of socialists in England at the time' (c. 1871–2). When Charles Murray took the chair at a meeting of the Mutual Land Emigration and Colonization Company – a society which sought to plant an O'Brienite colony in America – he spoke about 'just laws on land, credit, currency and exchange', and John Hales, secretary of the General Council of the I.W.M.A., later addressed the meeting on land nationalization. One of the earliest lectures given at the Manchester branch was on land, currency and credit, and when the West End branch of the I.W.M.A., in which Charles Murray and George Milner were leading lights, was addressed by Martin Boon of the National Reform League, he dealt with the land and currency laws and their vital importance to ordinary people. In the same period, too, Harrison Riley's *International Herald* was preaching O'Brienite state socialism. For many years Marx thought well of the O'Brienites because, in spite of what he called their 'currency quackery', they seemed to him more revolutionary than the majority of English trade unionists, 'firmer on the land question, less nationalistic, and not susceptible to bourgeois bribery in one form or another'.[1] In 1869 the Holborn branch of the N.R.L., still vigorous and progressive, resolved to convene the meetings which led to the formation of the Land and Labour League; a body whose programme clearly owed a great deal to O'Brienism – home colonization, suppression of private banks of issue, issue of paper money by the state alone, liquidation of the National Debt, and a national system of secular, free, compulsory education for children. Certainly the O'Brienites were leavening the lump to some purpose.

For all this, and much more which followed, credit in full measure must go to such men as Bronterre O'Brien who, possessed by their dreams and driven by a divine discontent, created for the masses a magnetic image of a Just Society, which was both a vision and a goal. Such men possess to a high degree the 'mysterious human quality' of self-sacrifice. Bronterre was seldom, if ever, influenced by considerations of personal advantage, because he belonged to that select, sensitive company

'. . . to whom the miseries of the world
Are misery, and will not let them rest.'

[1] *Ibid.*, p. 249, 252; *Manifesto* issued by the Social Democratic Associations, London, July 1883; M. Beer, *Fifty Years of International Socialism* (1937), pp. 133–4; R. Harrison, *Before the Socialists* (1965), pp. 215–23; *Working Man*, 1866–7, *passim*.

In his eyes 'the poor man's life' was of far more consequence than 'the middleman's gains'. O'Brien was a 'man of faith' as defined by the eminent historian, James Anthony Froude, in the third of three lectures delivered in Newcastle-upon-Tyne less than three years after O'Brien's death. 'By faith', said Froude, 'I do not mean belief in dogmas, but belief in goodness, belief in justice, in righteousness, above all belief in truth. . . . [Men of faith] are not contented with looking for what may be useful or pleasant to themselves; they look by quite other methods for what is honourable – for what is good – for what is just. They believe that if they can find out that, then at all hazards, and in spite of all present consequences to themselves, that is to be preferred. If individually and to themselves no visible good ever came from it . . . still they would say "Let us do that and nothing else. Life will be of no value to us if we are to use it only for our own gratification".' [1] For Bronterre O'Brien there was no careful balancing of debits and credits in terms of personal prosperity. He never counted the cost.

[1] J. A. Froude, *Short Studies in Great Subjects* (1894), I, pp. 114–5; cf. H. M. Hyndman's tribute to Bronterre O'Brien and other Chartist agitators 'who worked so hard and to all appearance so fruitlessly' to free the work people from the 'tyranny of capital and the misery of wage-slavery'. Hyndman, *Record*, p. 13. On J. A. Froude see A. L. Rouse, *The English Spirit* (rev. edn 1966), Ch. XXII.

Appendix A

Thomas A. Devyr on the Newport Rising and the Projected Rising in the Newcastle District

(From *The Odd Book of the Nineteenth Century*)

'THE first news that we at Newcastle-on-Tyne had of the [Newport] rising was through the London *Times*. It announced, by special correspondent, that Frost, at the head of 30,000 men, was in possession of South Wales.[1] A significant change on that instant appeared in Newcastle. For weeks previously not a group of three men would be suffered to stand together on the sidewalk. No political paper was suffered to appear on the walls. . . . As soon as the intelligence of Frost's movement reached us *all this was reversed*. The Reformers met in exultant groups, and several copies of a painted placard . . . were pasted up like this:

> "The hour of British Freedom has struck! John Frost is in possession of South Wales at the head of 30,000 men!"

Past these placards the policemen quietly walked. . . . Intelligence of the rising swept over the neighbourhood, and the following night delegates from 65 armed districts were assembled in Newcastle waiting for the expected Proclamation by Frost. The leaders were from the numerous districts lying close around. The two Shields, Sunderland, and the more distant districts of Durham and Northumberland were not present, but they were nearly or wholly as well appointed and prepared to rise at the expected signal. . . . While in the upper large room were assembled the earnest and gloomy chiefs of the insurrection, in the lower rooms were numbers of unthinking, good natured men, singing and playing music, even with their wives and daughters among them, waiting for the signal. . . . Here they were in midnight muster, waiting the signal to grasp the pike and level the musket – to give or receive death – driven to it by greedy and rapacious men, incredible in their selfishness. . . . But the more reflecting men are at the top of the house and I must go up to them. It was yet only midnight. We expected the gallop of a horse every instant. The proclamation was to radiate by horse express from the centre, Birmingham, all round. The night

[1] This is wrong. The report said, 'almost entire possession of the town' (Newport).

mail from London would be in by 2 o'clock, and *The Times* at least would throw some additional light upon the darkness.

'But there comes a rap to the door. An enquiry for me and a letter put into my hands. . . . The letter had been expressed up from Sunderland by Williams and Binns. They had just received it from a young friend named Batchelor, who resided in Newport and was a spectator of the conflict. It outlined the facts. . . .

> 'Three days' storm in the hills; only about 1,000 of the first division reach Newport, tired, drenched, at 8 a.m. instead of 2. [a.m.] The soldiers under cover, the rebels in the street. The slaughter all one one side. Frost prisoner.'

Next day, when the intelligence came out in the newspapers . . . an entire revulsion came over the public mind. Men seemed to be impressed with the thought that the Government was impregnable. All congratulated themselves that whatever course on our part had been taken, the Government knew nothing and could do nothing about it. A meeting was immediately held to found a penny subscription for the defence of Frost . . . there were about 500 pennies laid down, many present not having the penny with them.

'[In December 1839] a meeting was held at Dewsbury of delegates from most of the considerable towns in the North. It was there resolved that a simultaneous rising should take place in those towns on the night of the 12th of January (1840). . . . Men were now growing more desperate. . . . Respect for either life or property would no longer be permitted to stand in the way of success. . . . Every town took its own way to action. Ours [Newcastle] was this: Classes of twelve were formed, each with a leader chosen by themselves. . . . For the first time an oath was resorted to. Each member of the combination was, with a peculiarly impressive solemnity, sworn to impenetrable secrecy – to obey orders – to hold their lives of no account in the attainment of their object – and to execute death upon any one . . . found to betray information of our action to the governing authorities. . . . (It was decided not to injure the police or the municipal officials) . . . the several [police] station houses should be captured and used for the temporary imprisonment of the police, whilst the Mayor, municipality and other officials in power should be confined to their own houses or elsewhere. The work of accomplishing this we regarded as nothing. That of vanquishing the troops, consisting of some 800 infantry, two companies of dragoons, and two of artillery, we well knew to be the main difficulty. . . . On this there is but one opinion. The officers *hors de combat*, the troops would join us. Such was our firm belief, and I think it was well founded. The infantry, I remember, were principally young Irishmen – an inflammable race, that had given quite assuring indications of their good will. . . . Of powder used for blasting in the mines there was or could be no scarcity. . . .

'Thus time and act moved on toward the eventful Saturday night. Nothing practicable was left undone in Newcastle, and we relied undoubtingly on the Winlaton men that the explosives would be forthcoming. But they were not. Nor was this all. On the night of movement there assembled not quite seventy men, out of the secret enrolment of nearly ten times that number. Of course, those who did assemble were the most daring and desperate spirits in the movement; and finding that they were not in a condition for a stand up fight, it was strongly urged that the *torch* should be resorted to . . . [to] cause a waking up and excitement, under the influence of which every revolutionist would rush to arms. Others (the majority) resolved to wait events, and in case our friends made a successful rising in any one of the various towns . . . it was determined not to allow the troops on the Tyne or Wear to march against them. We would throw up barricades and give them work to do at home.

'. . . The most desperate were not at all reconciled to even a temporary inaction, and next morning I was informed that a party of them were assembled in a remote room . . . preparing to enter upon the horrible work that had been prevented the night before. Under guidance, I hastened to the spot through dark, intricate passages, and up tumble-down stairs. To my expostulations they replied that I was "too late". "Already" they said, "was the work commenced. . . . Before midnight . . . flames and combat would have full possession of New-castle; I might join in that combat, or I might not, but the fact I could not alter." I believed them, retired home, and spent such a night of anxiety and horror as stands alone in the record of my life. I threw myself on the bed, with my uniform blouse and arms on the table, and I now wonder at the mistaken sense of honour that made me prepare to join them on hearing the first shot.

'Day dawned in quietness, the most welcome I have even seen.'

Appendix B

Bronterre O'Brien's Address to the Electors and Non-electors of Newcastle-upon-Tyne

written in H.M. Prison, Lancaster Castle, in June 1841.

'GENTLEMEN, . . . I am a Conservative Radical Reformer in the just and obvious meaning of the words. . . . I am for peace founded upon liberty for all – for law founded upon justice for all – for order founded upon contentment for all. I am for unqualified obedience to the laws (even where they are bad and vicious) so long as any hope or chance remains of altering or amending them; but I am for giving to the people every facility of altering and improving them in conformity with the will of the majority. . . .

'I am for conserving all that is sound and valuable in our institutions, and for radically reforming all that is unsound. . . . I am . . . for unbounded liberty of opinion above and before all things else.

'I am for the perfect inviolability and security of all property, public and private . . . I consider . . . that only the voice of the entire public (constitutionally expressed by the vote of the majority) can justly or honestly appropriate or dispose of the property of the public. . . . As well, then, for the sake of conserving the property of the public to uses of the public and the public only – as for divers other just and imperative reasons, I shall deem it the first and most important of my parliamentary duties, to endeavour to get the national representation amended upon the plan and principles of the "People's Charter". . . .

'I consider the public has no more right to invade or appropriate the property of individuals (without their consent) than individuals or fractions of the people have to invade the property of the public . . . at the same time, I hold it to be perfectly just and competent for the legislature to interfere with any and every species of private property where such interference is required by the public interest, provided always that the parties interfered with be fully indemnified by compensation. . . .

'I am opposed to every species of monopoly, whether of wealth, power or knowledge. . . . I am for doing away with all laws and institutions which give one set of men facilities for acquiring wealth,

264

power or knowledge, denied to other men by the same laws and institutions. I am consequently opposed to the monopoly of the Bank of England. . . . The prerogative of making and issuing money I hold to be one which cannot be delegated or parcelled out to individuals without danger to the commonwealth. . . . I shall, therefore, deem it my duty to promote the abolition of all existing banks of issue, and to substitute for them a National Bank (with such branches as may be required for the public accommodation) which shall afford equal facilities to all classes alike . . . such banks should be under the surveillance and control of a legislature chosen by the people; otherwise its existence would be a curse, instead of a blessing.

'I am opposed to all restrictions on trade, commerce, and industry, for mere purposes of revenue, and doubly so, when imposed to create monopolies for particular interests. I am more particularly hostile to our corn and provision laws, which I consider most iniquitous. . . . I shall vote for their total and immediate repeal, but I shall also demand such repeal be accompanied with other measures for reducing the national debt and other public burdens and liabilities in proportion to the fall of prices consequent upon their repeal. Otherwise the repeal . . . would benefit only fundholders, mortgagees, userers, and men of fixed income (not immediately derived from the land) etc. . . . but to the millions of workpeople, who have only their daily labour to live by, to the numerous body of shop-keepers dependent upon their custom, and to the industrious classes generally, it would yield no benefit at all, while it would augment the burden of all . . . I am, therefore, for a Radical repeal of the corn and provision laws, but not for Whig repeal, which means robbing and no relief where relief is wanted.

'I am, of course, opposed to all restrictions on the liberty of the press, whether by bonds, stamp duties, or censorship.

'I am for abolishing all connection between Church and State. . . .

'I am opposed to placemen having seats in the House of Commons. . . .

'I am an advocate for free trade; but would first free the industry of the country from the enormous burdens and artificial shackles imposed upon it by our present cumbrous . . . and most expensive system of taxation. This, I believe, cannot be effectually done without, in the first place, greatly reducing the amount of the taxes, and, in the next, substituting for our system of excise and customs a system of direct taxation, to be raised from landed funds, and other property. Upon these and other points, however, I shall feel it my duty to consult you freely and often. . . . I shall feel it my duty, not only to visit you at the close of every Session, to give an account of my stewardship, but also to obey a summons from you, at any time, requiring my attendance at a public meeting of your body to be openly and fairly convened. . . .'

Appendix C

Some Notes on Twelve of Bronterre O'Brien's Friends and Disciples

MARTIN JAMES BOON, who had an ironmongery business at Clerkenwell Green, was a member of the National Reform League and the International Working Men's Association. He had, also, Owenite leanings, especially towards Owen's proposed 'labour exchanges'. Of all O'Brien's followers Boon was the most prolific propagandist and produced many pamphlets on the nationalization of land and public utilities, and on credit and emigration; e.g.,

> *Home Colonization . . . showing how all the Unemployed might have profitable work . . .* (1869).
>
> *A Protest against the present Emigrationists . . .* (1869).
>
> *Important to Ratepayers* (1870).
>
> *How to Nationalize the Commons and Waste Lands, Railways, Tramways, Waterworks, Gas Works, etc.* (1873).

Boon and Eccarius became the first joint secretaries of the Land and Labour League, founded in London in 1869; and it was at this time that Boon's pamphlet on Home Colonization was much discussed in Radical circles.

During the Franco-Prussian war Boon, 'a most pronounced republican', demanded active British intervention on the side of the new French Republic; but Marx, Engels and many others thought this policy too extreme. When the collapse of the Paris Commune was seen to be imminent in 1871, Boon, supported by G. E. Harris, called attention to the need to make preparations to receive French refugees, and wanted the I.W.M.A. to give a lead.

In the early 1870s Boon seems to have gone into publishing on a small scale, but 'his worldly affairs have fallen into confusion', he migrated, early in 1874, to South Africa where he lived for many years as a merchant in Bloemfontein, Orange Free State. After an interval of six or seven years he again felt the itch to write. Two pamphlets from his pen appeared in 1884: *Malthusian Quackery* and *How to Construct free State Railways*. As a staunch O'Brienite, Boon held that railways should be constructed and owned by the state, the capital cost to be met by the issue of paper currency secured on the railway's assets, and later redeemed by applying annually 5 per cent of the railway's net profits to cancel its notes, until the whole issue had passed from circulation, leaving the debt-free railway as a valuable property and source of income in the ownership of all the citizens.

Five other works followed swiftly:

National Paper Money,
How to Colonise South Africa
A History of the Orange Free State, and
Jottings by the Way, or Boon's Madness on the Road

In his writings on public affairs in the Orange Free State, Natal and Cape Colony, Boon advocated a scheme of peasant-ownership linked with an expansion of paper currency. He defended the 'poor Aborigines' and exposed their ill-treatment by the whites. He also attempted to expose corruption in official circles and 'semitic and Teutonic Rascality', all of which, he alleged, were rife in South Africa in the 1880s.

G. E. HARRIS traded as a bookseller at 60 Bell Street, Edgware Road; he was a member of the I.W.M.A. and was referred to in 1869 as 'the veteran G.E.H.'. He held that a national system of free education would not necessarily improve the existing state of things unless supplemented by adequate political instruction. He was a contributor to the *Working Man* and to Charles Bradlaugh's *National Reformer*. The letter to Victor Hugo, inviting him to deliver a funeral oration at O'Brien's burial, was written by Harris; and it is likely that he wrote the obituary notice and report of the funeral, published in Bradlaugh's *National Reformer* on 8th January 1865.

PATRICK HENNESSEY was a staunch advocate of land nationalization. In 1870 he became President of the Land and Labour League, and urged that all waste land should be bought, reclaimed and utilized by the state as a means of solving the problem of persistent unemployment. Ten years later he became one of the original members of the Land Nationalization Society, founded on the initiative of Alfred Russel Wallace to put forward a scheme – very similar to O'Brien's – for the gradual acquisition of the land by the state in four generations. Hyndman says that he was 'a well-known agitator' in the 1880s.

GEORGE MILNER, an Irishman; a member and, later, secretary of the National Reform League, *c.* 1868–72. He opposed shortening the

268

working day because he thought that total production would thereby be decreased; but he advocated demands for higher wages so that the workpeople would get a larger share of the wealth produced. He favoured co-operative production, sponsored by the trade unions, to give work to their unemployed members and, eventually, to emancipate all workers from the wages system. In the late sixties he was a member of the General Council of the I.W.M.A. and of the executive committee of the Land and Labour League. In 1872 he was elected Corresponding Secretary for England of the I.W.M.A.

CHARLES MURRAY and JAMES FRANCIS MURRAY were brothers. They had a Roman Catholic background and were intimate and loyal friends of Bronterre O'Brien, whose devotion to Chartism they shared. Charles Murray was a craftsman and a trade unionist. A prominent member of the small West-end of London Boot-closers' Society and one of its delegates to the I.W.M.A. (London), he was in due course elected to the General Council of the I.W.M.A. In the late 1850s he took a leading part in the proceedings of the short-lived Political Union for the Obtainment of the People's Charter. He stood for full freedom of the press, and attended the Exeter Hall meeting of the Association for Promoting the Repeal of the Taxes on Knowledge with O'Brien and John Rogers, on 1st December 1852. As an O'Brienite he was, of course, in favour of nationalization of the land, and was a member of the executive of the Land and Labour League, founded in 1869 to press for land nationalization. Later he served on the executive of the Land Nationalization Society (founded in 1881), of which Alfred Russel Wallace was President.

The other brother, James Francis Murray, was also an active Chartist and O'Brienite. He staunchly supported Boon's home colonization scheme and, in the 1880s, lectured on 'Labour Emancipation something more than Land Nationalization'. When Bronterre O'Brien died in December 1864, Charles Murray supervised the funeral arrangements, and, with James Murray, was among the chief mourners.

Both brothers, who outlived Bronterre O'Brien by twenty years or more, and became confirmed left-wing Socialists, were in at the inception of the Social-Democratic Federation. Hyndman records that early in 1881

' . . . several more or less important gatherings were held with a view to establishing a really democratic party. . . . Among those who took part in these preliminary meetings were Mr Joseph Cowen, then member for Newcastle . . . Professor Beesly, the well-known Positivist

269

who took the chair at the first public meeting of the "International" in 1864 . . . the two brothers James and Charles Murray, old Chartists . . . Morgan and Townsend and Oliver, also old Chartists . . . Justin McCarthy, the Irish M.P. and popular historian and writer . . . and many more'.

Hyndman tells of a visit made by the two Murrays and Bill Morgan, a slipper maker, who had been a boatswain in the Royal Navy, to Woolwich Arsenal – a story somewhat reminiscent of the visit made by 'the doctor', Peter Murray McDouall, to the same establishment over forty years before. As the new Democratic Federation began to gather strength

' . . . and it began to look as if one of those fine days we might have an active revolutionary party in London, an artillery officer, Major Edwards, who partially sympathized with our objects, invited several of our working men, including the two Murrays and Bill Morgan, down to Woolwich, where he treated them very well, and showed them one of the biggest guns from the Arsenal, "There," said the Major, "what is the use of you fellows talking about fighting and coming to close quarters with the upper classes? What could you do against a gun like that?" "Yes," replied Morgan, "and what should we be doing while you were getting that plaything into position?" '

(Hyndman, *Record of an Adventurous Life*, pp. 246, 254, 346;

The Murrays continued to serve the Social-Democratic cause in London well into the 1880s. James Murray died in 1889.

FREDERICK RIDDLE was one of the small band of London craftsmen who strove to keep alive the Chartist social programme which was originally worked out by O'Brien. Riddle was specially interested in the farm labourers, whose conditions he studied at first hand and later described to crowds of London working men assembled on Mile End Waste or Clerkenwell Green. He wanted all waste lands to be bought by the state, reclaimed by the labour of the unemployed, and subsequently let to working men 'in association or otherwise'. In the 1870s he co-operated closely with Patrick Hennessey, John Weston and other O'Brienites.

W. HARRISON RILEY was born in Manchester and worked in the clothing trade for some years before emigrating to America. Later, he returned to England and in 1871 he appeared in London where he came under

270

the influence of Marx and Engels. Early in the following year he began to edit and publish the *International Herald* as a fortnightly at first, but from 11th May 1872, as a weekly. Its statement of objects was markedly O'Brienite for it included universal suffrage, nationalization of land, railways, mines, canals, docks and harbours, currency reform and liquidation of the National Debt. Riley hoped to make his journal 'the special organ of such societies as are not specially represented by the *Beehive* or the *National Reformer*' and tried to combine the Chartists' principles and programme with producers' co-operation and O'Brien's state socialism. The I.W.M.A. received special notice and favourable comment from Riley at a time when the Association was widely misinterpreted and misunderstood. Early in May 1872 the *International Herald* declared itself the 'Official Organ of the British Section of the I.W.M.A.'; but it did not long remain so, for it collapsed after Riley had deviated into an attempt to found a 'Mutual Help' colony on Owenite lines. The *Herald's* last number appeared on 8th October 1873. Thereafter, Riley moved to Sheffield where, for a few months, he produced *The Socialist*.

Edward Carpenter in his *Sketches from Life in Town and Country* (1908) describes Riley (perhaps too favourably) as 'restless, inquisitive, sensitive; of rather searching mind, stimulating and paradoxical in his talk and writing . . .'; one of those who bridged 'the interval between the old Chartism of '48 and the Socialism of the early eighties'. Riley published two pamphlets: the first on *Strikes, their Cause and Remedy*, and the second (perhaps inspired by O'Brien's articles on slavery) entitled *British Slavery: A Tract dedicated to all Working Men*, (*c*. 1873).

JOHN ROGERS was one of the founder-members of the London Working Men's Association and became a member of its Committee on 24th July 1836, the day on which O'Brien was made an honorary member (*B.M.Add.MSS*. 37,773, ff. 2, 7b–8). The two men became friends and remained so for nearly thirty years. Rogers, with Charles Murray and O'Brien, spoke at the Essex Hall meeting on repeal of the newspaper duty in 1852. He was one of the pall bearers at O'Brien's funeral.

GEORGE TOWNSEND was a member of the General Council of the I.W.M.A. and was among those who signed the 'address on the Civil War in France' (1871). In the spring of 1895 Max Beer found Townsend in a room in Tottenham Court Road. Elderly and in reduced circumstances, he was 'sitting amidst a litter of papers and books, evidently from his library, of which . . . he desired to dispose'. He told Max Beer that in company with a few other O'Brienites he had sat with Marx on the General Council of the I.W.M.A. for several years. Marx, he said, looked like a lion but always behaved like a gentleman. Engels was very different: he was 'a domineering German, but he had the funds, and we needed his financial help'. Townsend wished that Bronterre O'Brien had lived a few years longer, for 'he would have been the man to argue currency matters out with Marx; none of us could' (Max Beer, *Fifty years of International Socialism*, 1935, pp. 133–4).

ALFRED A. WALTON of Brecon started his working life as a stonemason and was an active member of the Operative Masons' trade union before becoming, in later life, a builder and architect. In the 1840s he was connected with the National Association of United Trades. He was an Owenite but supported Chartism also. A member of the council of O'Brien's National Reform League, he became its President in 1867. He was a leading advocate of co-operative building and of state-sponsored self-supporting 'home colonies' to cure unemployment. It was, he thought, an ideal arrangement when a craftsman could also work a part-time small-holding. But complete 'emancipation of labour' would never be achieved 'while the entire social and legislatorial power of the State is in the hands of men whose order have ruled the world by force for ages'.

At the General Election in 1874, Walton stood as a 'Labour' candidate at Stoke-on-Trent, a two-member constituency, where he was opposed by two Liberals and a Tory. Although he polled 5,198 votes, he came bottom of the poll: Liberal (1) 6,777; Conservative 6,180; Liberal (2) 5,369; Walton 5,198. However, at a by-election at Stoke shortly afterwards Walton came second in a three-cornered contest: Liberal 6,110; Walton 4,168: Conservative 3,901 (Cole, *British Working Class Politics*, pp. 67, 69, 71, 262–3). Walton's published writings include *A History of the Landed Tenures of Gt Britain and Ireland* (1865); *Our Future Progress* (1867; second edn 1868); *Agricultural Depression and Distress* (1880), a pamphlet.

JOHN WESTON was an active member of O'Brien's National Reform League. In 1869 he was elected treasurer of the Land and Labour League which he represented, with Odger and Cremer, at the inaugural meeting, in 1871, of the short-lived (Liberal) Land Tenure Reform Association. He often addressed open-air meetings of working men, urging the necessity of land nationalization and state purchase, reclamation and home colonization of waste lands as a solution of the problem of unemployment.

He was known to Holyoake, who spoke well – almost affectionately – of him:

'John Weston – the thinnest, wiriest, gentlest, yet most ardent, prompt, and demonstrative of working-class politicians. There was nothing of him save his voice and his ceaseless energy. He was a workman who owed everything to himself. He was a cow-boy and a page-boy in his youth, and at last a hand-rail maker – a trade he learned himself. And no man knew it better, or so well, for he wrote a book upon it, which is an authority in the trade. He lived to be seventy-two, working ten to twelve hours a day at the bench, and making speeches when evening came. With the independence which only a good workman can afford to show, he carried his principles into every house, high or low, where he went, and gave his opinions upon public questions to the noblest employer who fell into conversation with him. He stood none of the Imperial Communism and State Socialism of Carl Marx, but confronted that master of agitation, and carried resolutions against him. Whatever good movement was on foot anywhere in the metropolis, Weston was soon in it, if, indeed, he were not there first; and yet there were more home difficulties in his way, of the Zantippe type, than any man save Socrates had to encounter. But no discomfort deterred him. Of all men of gentle spirit I have known, he was the fiercest worker. . . . He had the genuine passion of progress which brings good to others, but only gratitude and poverty to those who have it.'

(G. J. Holyoake, *Sixty Years of an Agitator's Life* (1902), II, pp. 263–4.)

Appendix D

The National Reform League, the Eclectic Institute and the 'Working Man'

EARLY in the 1860s the National Reform League acquired as its organ a small three-ha'penny monthly magazine entitled the *Working Man*, which was designed to be 'A Political and Social Advocate of the Rights of Labour and a Monthly Record of Co-operative Progress'. Although some of the initial capital was subscribed by members of the N.R.L., it seems likely that a good deal of money was advanced, both then and later, by the editor, Joseph Collett, who feared that the press was 'falling more and more into the hands of the capitalists, and threatens to become their monopoly'. There was a committee of shareholders and supporters of the *Working Man*, with A. C. Cudden as chairman and G. E. Harris as secretary. The publisher was Job Caudwell of 335 Strand, W.C.

Towards the end of 1861 the Council of the N.R.L. attempted to revive the Bronterre O'Brien Testimonial Fund, of which John Rogers was then the secretary. *The Working Man*, 1st January 1862, carried an address 'to the industrious classes – more especially the friends of political and social reform', stressing the urgent need to 'alleviate the privations' of Bronterre O'Brien and reminding readers of his great services to their cause through 'his teachings and struggles' over more than thirty years. 'His disciples are scattered all over the earth, from California . . . to Sydney and Melbourne; while the seeds of his teaching are sown . . . throughout the European Continent. For several years following the revolution of 1830–1 his house was at once a *rendezvous* and a school for the *Proscrits* of all nations. . . . We must, for our own sakes, as well as for his family's, endeavour to protect a life which we hope to render still more valuable to humanity than it has yet been'. This appeal was signed on behalf of the N.R.L., by G. Messenger, J. F. Murray, J. Flexman, and five other Council members. Apparently no complete accounts of the subscriptions received were ever published, but it was disclosed that at one lecture-meeting held in St George's Hall, Southwark, on 18th February 1862, upwards of £1 7s was collected for the Fund.

We get a last glimpse of the Bronterre O'Brien of former days in a report (*Working Man*, 1st May 1862, p. 125) of an address he gave at the Eclectic Institute on 9th April 1862 in celebration of the 102nd anniversary of Robespierre's birth; a full-length discourse described by a member of the audience as 'a masterpiece'.

The establishment, in August 1862, by the N.R.L. and the *Working Man*, of a Working Man's Central Circulating Library is not without interest as a pioneer effort. Individuals subscribed one penny a week, but working men's societies and institutes, co-operative societies, reading clubs, and the like could have a weekly parcel of books for a subscription of one guinea a year. According to the *Working Man* (1st August 1862) the scheme began with some 300 volumes.

By reason of personal and financial difficulties Joseph Collett had to discontinue the *Working Man* after November 1862; but he never lost interest and in January 1866, when another Reform Bill cauldron was beginning to boil, he revived the paper in a slightly larger format but with the same slogans as before: *Union is Strength* and *Knowledge is Power*. This 'new series' was published by F. Farrah at 282 Strand; price 1d.

During May 1866 we see the N.R.L. agitating for the widest possible extension of the franchise. 'Let working men aid those who are trying to shape this inadequate measure (i.e. Reform Bill) into a useful and profitable one.' At the same time Bronterre O'Brien was not forgotten and the propaganda pattern bequeathed by him was maintained. There were week-day and Sunday lectures at the Eclectic Institute on 'Political and Social Questions' such as the land, the currency, commerce, liberty, education, etc., many of them delivered by A. C. Cudden. From the *Working Man* (June and August 1867) one gathers that the O'Brienites had formed a Working Men's Educational Society which held weekly meetings at the Eclectic Institute.

About two years after O'Brien's death the *Working Man* announced that 'on 6th February next (1867) the members of the National Reform League intend to celebrate the anniversary of their late devoted President, James Bronterre O'Brien, by a Tea and Soiree to be held at the Eclectic Hall, Denmark Street, Soho'. On the day Robert G. Gammage, who had made a special journey from Sunderland, was in the chair, and 'full a hundred persons' sat down to the tea supplied from the adjacent tea and coffee rooms in Denmark Street by John Flexman, a loyal, useful member of the N.R.L. who was soon to become its treasurer. 'In the background of an improvised platform, richly hung with crimson drapery, *in relievo* was a cast of the late Mr O'Brien (taken after death), surmounted by a triangle on which was inscribed the motto of the League: *Liberty in right; Equality in law; Fraternity*

275

in interest. Encentred was a representation of the sun, emblematical of light, the whole being tastefully surrounded by *immortelles* and evergreens. Opposite the platform was seen a likeness of the late President Lincoln . . . [with] *immortelles,* evergreens and the American flag.' After tea letters were read from Mazzini, Louis Blanc, G. W. M. Reynolds, George White of Bradford, and many others who were unable to be present. Gammage delivered an eloquent address praising O'Brien's outstanding and unselfish services to the people's cause, 'which [services] would be duly appreciated at some future time', and pointing out that already there were fair prospects of an early reform of the franchise. Gammage was followed by John Rogers, 'one of the oldest disciples of our departed friend', who urged that just as Bronterre O'Brien had 'worked for future generations . . . so must we'. Other speakers offered their tributes, several songs were sung, and two poems specially written for the occasion by William Maccall and W. Dixon were recited. These were printed in the *Working Man,* 1st March 1867.

As to the revived *Working Man,* despite the devotion of its editor and a number of articles contributed by leading O'Brienites, such as G. E. Harris, it had to close down finally in the middle of August 1867.

Bibliography

MANUSCRIPTS

British Museum Additional Manuscripts, 27,789–27,792, 27,808, 27,809, 27,817–27,822, 27,835, 27,837, 29,820, 34,245 A & B, 35,143, 35,149, 35,154, 37,773, 37,949
Cowen Collection, Newcastle-upon-Tyne City Library
Dublin University Admission Register, 1769–1825
Granard R.C. Church, Register of Baptisms, 1804
Gray's Inn Admission Book, 1830
Holyoake Collection, Co-operative Union Library, Manchester
Home Office Papers, Public Record Office, 18 (various bundles), 19, 27(61), 40(43–51), 61(22), 64(4–6), 64(17–19)
Howell Collection of MSS., News Cuttings, Pamphlets, etc., Bishopsgate Institute, London
King's Inns, Dublin, Admission Book, 1826
London University MSS. and Autograph Letters
London Working Men's Association Minute Book, 1836, British Museum
National Complete Suffrage Union Minute Books, 1843–6, Birmingham Reference Library
Owen Collection, Co-operative Union Library, Manchester
Place Collection of Newspaper Cuttings, MSS., Letters, etc., British Museum
'Working Men's Association' Newspaper Cuttings, Letters, etc., 1836–43, Birmingham Reference Library

OFFICIAL PUBLICATIONS

Hansard's Parliamentary Debates
State Trials
Accounts and Papers, 1847–8, 1852–3
Board of Education in Ireland. *Eleventh Report:* Parish Schools, 1810; *Fourteenth Report:* 1812
Commissioners of Irish Education Enquiry: *Second Report:* 1826
Report on the Condition of the Hand-loom Weavers, 1840
Minutes of the Proceedings of the Court of Common Council (City of London), 1839

BIBLIOGRAPHY

PERIODICALS

Agitator 1833
Annual Register
Ayrshire Examiner 1839
Birmingham Journal 1839
British Statesman 1842
Bronterre's National Reformer 1837
Champion and Weekly Herald 1839
Charter 1839
Chartist 1839
Chartist Circular 1839–41
Chartist and Republican Journal (McDouall's) 1841
Cooper's Journal 1850
Cosmopolite 1832
Crisis 1834
Democratic Review 1849–50
Destructive and Poor Man's Conservative (afterwards *People's Conservative and Trade Union Gazette*) 1833–4
Dublin Monitor 1839
Eclectic Review 1846
Edinburgh Review 1820
Glasgow Liberator 1834
Glasgow Sentinel 1851
Hull Observer 1839
Hull Saturday Journal 1839
Labourer 1847–8
Leeds Times 1840–1
Lloyd's Weekly Newspaper 1845
London Democrat 1839
London Dispatch 1836–7
London Mercury 1836–7
Man 1833
Manchester Examiner 1846–7
Manchester Times 1839
Midland Representative and Birmingham Herald 1831
Morning Advertiser 1838
National Reformer and Manx Weekly Review (O'Brien's) 1846–7

National Reformer, Secular Advocate and Freethought Journal (Charles Bradlaugh's) 1865
Nonconformist 1842
Northern Liberator 1837–40
Northern Star 1838–40
Notes to the People 1852
Operative 1838–9
Penny Satirist 1837–46
People's Paper 1852–4
Pioneer 1834
Police Gazette (Cleave's) 1836
Political Letters (Carpenter's) 1830–1
Political Register (Cobbett's) 1827–1830
Poor Man's Guardian 1831–5
Power of the Pence (O'Brien's) 1848–9
Quarterly Review 1831–42
Republican 1834
Reynolds's Newspaper 1850–65
Reynolds's Political Instructor 1849–1850
Sheffield Iris 1839
Social Reformer 1849
Southern Star 1840
Standard 1833
Star of Freedom 1852
Statesman and Weekly True Sun 1840
The Times 1839–51
Tribune of the People (Benbow's) 1832
True Scotsman 1839
Twopenny Dispatch (Hetherington's) 1836
Tyne Mercury 1839
United Trades Co-operative Journal 1830
Weekly True Sun 1839
Working Man 1861–2 and 1866–7
Working Man's Friend 1832–3

AUTOBIOGRAPHIES, MEMOIRS AND TRAVELS

Adams, W. E. *Memoirs of a Social Atom* 1903 (Reprinted 1968, with an Introduction by John Saville)
Bamford, S. *Passages in the Life of a Radical* 1893
Burn, J. *James Burn, the Beggar Boy: An Autobiography* 1882
Cooper, T. *Life of Thomas Cooper* 1872
Croker, T. C. *Researches in the South of Ireland* 1834
Curwen, J. C. *Observations on the State of Ireland* 1818
Devyr, T. A. *Odd Book of the 19th Century* 1882
Edgeworth, R. L. *Memoirs* 1820
Edgeworth, F. A. *A Memoir of Maria Edgeworth* 1867
Frost, T. *Forty Years' Recollections* 1880
Holland (Lord) *Memoirs of the Whig Party* 1852–4
Holyoake, G. J. *Sixty Years of an Agitator's Life* 1900
Huish, R. *Life of Henry Hunt* 1835
Hunt, Henry *Memoirs* 1820–2
Hunt, L. *Autobiography* 1850
Hunt, L. *Correspondence* 1862
Hyndman, H. M. *Record of an Adventurous Life* 1911
Lovett, W. *Life and Struggles* 1876
Mill, J. S. *Autobiography* 1873
Richard, H. *Memoirs of Joseph Sturge* 1864
Solly, H. *These Eighty Years* 1893
Somerville, A. *Public and Personal Affairs* 1839; *Autobiography of a Working Man* 1848; *History of the British Legion and the War in Spain* 1839; *Conservative Science of Nations* 1860
Spencer, H. *Autobiography* 1904
Taylor, W. Cooke *Notes of a Tour in the Manufacturing Districts of Lancashire* 1842; *Factories and the Factory System* 1844
Wakefield, E. *An Account of Ireland* 1812
Young, A. *A Tour in Ireland* 1776–9 (ed. A. W. Hutton) 1892

OTHER BOOKS OF THE PERIOD

Andrews, A. *History of British Journalism* 1859
Bruce, W. N. *Life of General Sir Charles Napier* 1885
Cooper, T. *Life and Character of Henry Hetherington* 1849
Dove, P. E. *Science of Politics* 1850
Edgeworth, M. & R. L. *Practical Education* 1801
Edgeworth, R. L. *Essays on Professional Education* 1809
Gammage, R. G. *History of the Chartist Movement* 1854 (2nd edn 1894)
Gray, John *Efficient Remedy for the Distress of Nations* 1842

279

Gray, John   *The Social System* 1831
Hall, C.   *Effects of Civilization on the Peoples of European States* 1805
Hodgskin, W.   *Labour Defended against the Claims of Capital* 1825;
    Popular Political Economy 1827; *The Natural and Artificial Rights of
    Property Contrasted* 1832
Holyoake, G. J.   *Life and Character of Henry Hetherington* 1849
Kydd, Samuel ('Alfred')   *History of the Factory Movement* 1857
Lockhart, J. G.   *Narrative of the Life of Sir Walter Scott* 1848
Maceroni (or Macerone), F.   *Memoirs of the Life and Adventures of
    Colonel Maceroni* 1838
Mackay, C.   *Forty Years' Recollections* 1877
Mayhew, H.   *London Labour and London Poor* 1851
Morgan   *Revolt of the Bees* 1828
Napier, W. F. P.   *Life and Opinions of General Sir Charles J. Napier* 1857
O'Connor, F.   *A Practical Work on the Management of Small Farms* 1843
Owen, R.   *Observations on the Effect of the Manufacturing System* 1815;
    Book of the New Moral World 1836
Solly, H.   *What says Christianity to the Present Distress?* 1842
Somerville, A.   *Cobdenic Policy: the Internal Enemy of England* 1854
Taylor, John   *Catechisms of the Currency and Exchanges* 1836

PAMPHLETS, TRACTS, ARTICLES, ETC.
Anon.   *The Rise and Fall of Chartism in Monmouthshire* 1840; *The Black
    Book* 1820
Benbow, W.   *Grand National Holiday and Congress of the Productive
    Classes* 1832; *Censorship Exposed, or Letters to Lord Sidmouth* c. 1818
Bray, J. F.   *Labour's Wrongs and Labour's Remedy* 1839
Carpenter, W.   *Report of the Trial of Mr William Carpenter* 1831
Cleave, J.   *Brief Sketches of the Birmingham Conference* 1842
Cobbett, W.   *Lectures on the French Revolution and English Borough-
    mongering* 1830
Complete Suffrage Conference, *Report of the Proceedings* 1842
Co-operative Congresses, *Reports of the Proceedings,* 1831 and 1832
Lovett and Collins   *Chartism* 1840
Maceroni (or Macerone), F.   *Defensive Instructions for the People* 1832
Miall, E.   *The Politics of Christianity* (Reprinted from *The Non-
    Conformist* of 1847-8) 1863
National Reform League   *Tracts* 1855
O'Brien, J. B.   *Babeuf's Conspiracy for Equality* (A translation with
    notes and comments) 1836; *Life and Character of Maximilian Robespierre*
    (First published in instalments) 1838; *Vindication of his Conduct at*

the late Birmingham Conference 1842; *Rise, Progress and Phases of Human Slavery* (Newspaper articles originally published in 1849 and 1850: reprinted in book form in 1885); *State Socialism* 1850; *Bronterre O'Brien's European Letters* 1851; *Mr Ernest Jones* 1854; *Sermons on the Day of the Public Fast and Humiliation for England's Disasters in the Crimea* 1856; *Ode to Lord Palmerston* 1856; *Ode to Louis Napoleon Bonaparte* 1856; *A Vision of Hell, or Peep into the Realms below* 1859; *Dissertation and Elegy on Maximilian Robespierre* 1859

Roebuck, J. A.   *Pamphlets for the People* 1835

Somerville, A.   *Dissuasive Warnings to the People on Street Warfare* 1839

Sturge, J.   *Reconciliation between the Middle and Working Classes* 1841

WORKS OF REFERENCE

Burtchaell and Sadleir   *Alumni Dublinenses: 1593–1846*

Dublin University   *Calendars*

Dublin University   *Catalogues of Graduates: 1591–1868*

Lewis, S.   *A Topographical Dictionary of Ireland* 1837

Pigot & Co.   *City of Dublin and Hibernian Provincial Directory* 1824

The author gratefully acknowledges his indebtedness to the many writers, not mentioned above, whose works he has consulted. References to these are given in the footnotes

Index

Abney Park Cemetery, Stoke Newington, 245
Accrington, poverty in, 167
Adams, William Edwin, 242
Address to the Working Classes, Karl Marx's, 252
Affluent society, Bronterre O'Brien's vision of, 254
Agents provocateurs, see 'Spies'
Agrarian Justice, Thomas Paine's, 180
Ancient world, slavery in, 194–7
Anti-Corn Law Movement, 97, 135, 159–61, 169–70
Appeal for funds for Bronterre O'Brien, 162, 164, 167
Arch, Joseph, 213
Aristocracy, defined, 35–6
Arms and arming among Chartists, 91–3, 99–101, 105, 108–9, 111–112, 114, 117, 122, 131–8, 150–1, 192, 261–3
Ashton-under-Lyne, Chartists in, 134, 164
Association for Promoting the Repeal of the Taxes on Knowledge, 58, 131–8
Atcherley, Sergeant, 150
Attorney-General v. Hetherington, 54–5
Attwood, Thomas, 27, 41, 100, 170, 170n., 207, 208–9
Ayr, Richard, 149
Ayre, James, 145

Babeuf, Francis Noel, 55, 59–66, 71, 248
Ballot, secret, 52–3, 78, 110, 255
Barclay, Rev. John, 204n.
Barras, General, 63

Batty's Circus, Manchester, 105–6, 121–2, 150
Beaumont, Augustus Harding, 78, 91
Beaumont, George, 197n.
Beer, Max, 271
Bell, John, 73, 78, 80–2, 84
Benbow, William, 51, 53, 105, 124–128, 142, 198
Beniowski, Polish refugee and agitator, 143
Benzing, C., 245
Bereans, or Barclayites, 204
Bernard, J. B., 80–4
Birmingham, Chartists in, 112–13
Birmingham Political Union, 27, 89
Black, John Roberts, 78, 82
Blakey, Jon, 149
Blakey, Robert, 91
Blanc, Louis, 222, 276
Blanchard, Samuel Laman, 90
Bonnet Rouge, J. H. B. Lorymer's, 51, 53
Boon, Martin, 258, 267–9
Bradlaugh, Charles, 242–3
Bray, John Francis, 49
Bresson, William, 57
Bright, John, 228, 255
Brighton and district, Chartism in, 103–4, 139, 153–4, 174
Bristol, Chartists buying arms in, 136
British Statesman, 166–7, 249
Bronterre's National Reformer, 24, 73, 77–8, 80
Brougham, Henry, 29
Bull Ring, Birmingham, riot in, 120, 141, 143
Buonarroti, Philippe, on Babeuf's Conspiracy, 55, 59–66, 248

Burn, James, 47
Burnley, poverty in, 167
Bussey, Peter, 116, 135
Butterworth, William, 150

Cabet, Etienne, 222
Canada, rebellion in, 84
Capitalism, 38–9, 56, 249, 250–3
Cardo, William, 143
Carlile, Richard, 27, 28, 49, 121, 124, 215
Carlyle, Thomas, 228
Carpenter, Edward, 271
Carpenter, William, 33, 44, 50, 74, 78, 130, 137, 140, 143, 148, 243
Cartwright, John, 77
Catholic emancipation, 26
Cavaignac, General, 234
Central National Association, 80–4, 88
Chadwick, Edwin, 75–6
Charter, The, 148
Charter, The, see 'People's Charter'
Chartism, 15, 29, 87, 94, 201–2, 249, 257, 271–2
Chartist, The, 100
Chartist Churches, 119, 216, 228
Chartist Circular, 166, 229
Chartist National Conventions, see 'National Conventions'
Chartist Programme, 1851, 183
Chartist and Republican Journal, McDouall's, 142, 155, 229
Chartists' Petition, 79
Children, treatment of, 85
Cholera, 125
Christian Chartists, 170, 172
Christianity, see 'Religion'
Class struggle, theory of, 252–3
Cleave, John, 47, 49, 57, 89, 137
Cobbett, J. P., Barrister-at-law, 146
Cobbett, William, 25, 25n., 28, 29, 31, 65, 76, 120, 124–5, 206
Cobbett Club, 100

Cobden, Richard, 58, 170, 228
Cogers (Discussion) Hall, 242
Cole, Charles, 217n.
Coleridge, Mr Justice, 145, 147, 150–1
Collett, Joseph, 274
Collins, John, 113, 141, 148, 168–9, 174, 215
Colne, Lancs., poverty in, 167
Communism, 62–6, 194
Complete Suffrage Movement, 95, 166, 168–76, 229
Constitutional, The, 90
Conventions, Chartist, see 'National Conventions'
Cooper, Thomas, 162, 174–5, 198
Corn Laws, 37
Cowan, Joseph, 241–2, 269
Crabtree, Matthew, 97
Crawford, Sharman, 168
Cray, Richard, 86n., 217
Crimean War, 228–32
Cudden, A. C., 274–5
Currency laws, reform of, 177, 197, 206–10, 223, 259, 268, 272
Curwen, John Christian, 16–17

Dalhousie, Lord, 255–6
Daniel, Samuel, poet, 153
Deegan, John, 132
Democratic ideas, early, 77
Demonstrations, Chartist, on 12th August, 1839, 143
Derby, Lord, 255
Destructive and Poor Man's Conservative, Hetherington's, 53
Devonshire, Labourers arming in, 135
Devyr, Thomas Ainge, 90, 120, 136, 138, 145, 147–9, 261–3
Dewsbury, Chartists in, 262
Dickens, Charles, 29, 149
Disciples of Bronterre O'Brien, 202, 267–73
Discussion (or Debating) Halls, 242–3

Disraeli, Benjamin, 255
Dixon, W., 276
Doubleday, Thomas, 91
Douglas, P. H., 89
Dublin, King's Inns, 23–4
Dublin, University of, see 'Trinity College'
Dudley Court Chapel, 204–5
Duff, Isabella, Bronterre O'Brien's granddaughter, 120
Duff, Mrs Luisa St John, Bronterre O'Brien's daughter, 119
Durham Charter Association, 121

Eclectic Club, 198
Eclectic Institute, O'Brien's, 204, 220–2, 225, 240–1, 245, 258, 275–6
Edgeworth, Lovell, 18–22
Edgeworth, Maria, 17
Edgeworth, Richard Lovell, 18–20, 22
Edgeworthstown School, 18–22
Edinburgh and Midlothian Universal Suffrage Association, 117
Edinburgh Radicals, 89
Education, public, 40, 52, 199–200, 205–6, 220, 225, 253, 259
Election Address, Bronterre O'Brien's, June 1841, 157–8, 166, 264–6
Election Clubs proposed, 134
Election plan, O'Brien's, 83, 112–113, 115, 119, 157–9, 159n.
Elliott, Ebenezer, 89
Engels, Friedrich, 249, 267, 271–2
Erskine, Mr Justice, 145, 148
Europe, Continent of, political struggles, 27–8
European Letters, Bronterre O'Brien's, 220–1
Evans, Lt General Sir George De Lacy, 108
Examiner, The, 48
Exchange, equitable, of labour for labour, 125, 200, 208–10, 259

Faraday, Michael, 33
Fast Day Demonstration, 21st March 1832, 125–6
Fawkner, Henry, 136
Fielden, John, 75
Fieschi, would-be assassin, 66–7
Finch, John, 152
Fischer, J. C., 218
Fletcher, Matthew, 111
Flexman, John, 205, 274–5
Fonblanque, Anthony, 48–9
Fox, Charles James, 78
Fox, William Johnson, 176
France, revolution in, July 1830, 28
Franchise, extension of, 254–6, 276
Fraternal Democrats, Society of, 198, 200–3
Freeman, E. A., 228
French Revolution of 1789, certain aspects of, 59–72
French Revolution of 1848, 201
Friends, Society of, 228–9
Frost, John, 111, 131, 137, 261–2
Froude, John Anthony, 260
Fussell, Joseph, 113

Gammage, Robert G., 22, 95, 174, 188, 224, 246, 275–6
Gauntlet, Richard Carlile's, 49
General Convention of the Industrious Classes, see 'National Conventions'
General strike, 51, 102, 112, 122, 123–34, 151, 176
George, Henry, 72
George IV, death of, 27
Gladstone, William Ewart, 255
Glasgow Cotton Spinners, 119, 123
Glasgow Sentinel, 218–19, 221
Good, John, 154
Granard, Co. Longford, 15–17, 24
Granard Parochial School, 17–18, 90
Grand National Consolidated Trades Union, 52

Grand National Holiday, William Benbow's, 51, 53, 124, 128
Gray, Charles, 180
Great Exhibition of 1851, 217–18
Greenwich, Chartists in, 202
Greenwich, Woolwich and Deptford Patriot, 90
Greenwich Working Men's Association, 132, 204
Grey, Lord, 29

Hadley, Alderman Benjamin, 96
Hales, John, 259
Halifax, Chartists in, 138
Hall, Charles, 180, 180n.
Hall of Science, City Road, 225
Harmer, Alderman James, 74n.
Harney, George Julian, 46, 66, 98, 113, 130, 147, 149, 172, 184, 191–2, 198, 201–3, 222
Harris, G. E., 244, 268, 274, 276
Hart, Richard, 200
Hartshead Moor, see 'Peep Green'
Hartwell, Richard, 81, 89, 132
Heckmondwike Chartists and the Newport rising, 135
Henderson, Report for *Tyne Mercury*, 146–8
Hennessey, Patrick, 258, 268, 270
Hetherington, Henry, 27, 29, 31, 43, 46, 49, 50, 51, 53–7, 59, 81–2, 89, 125, 131, 137, 190, 215, 247
Heywood, Abel, 48
Heywood, Chartists in, 132
Heyworth, Lawrence, 176
Hibernian Society, 90
Higgins, Timothy, 134
Hill, William, 170, 171n.
Hobson, Joshua, 49
Hodgskin, Thomas, 180
Holyoake, George Jacob, 178, 190, 203, 215, 243, 273
Home colonization, 36, 184, 188, 199, 259, 267–9, 270, 272
Hope Coffee House, James Cleave's, 49

Hugo, Victor, 244–5, 268
Human Slavery, The Rise, Progress and Phases of, by Bronterre O'Brien, 194–7, 202, 249
Hume, Joseph, 254–5
Hunt, Henry, 27, 29, 31, 35, 43, 120, 124
Hustings candidates, see 'Election plan'
Hyndman, H. M., 249–50, 268–70

Insurrection, attempted at Newport, Mon., 135–8
Insurrection, preparations for, 92–93, 101, 105, 108–9, 115, 122, 134–5, 138, 192
International Herald, W. Harrison Riley's, 259, 271
International Working Men's Association, 252, 258–9, 267–72
Ireland, rebellion in, 15–16
Ireland, union of, with Great Britain, 33–4
Irish poor, plight of, 24–5, 34–5, 85, 189–90, 196, 198

Jackson, Rev. William Vickers, 150–1
Jacobins, 32, 62
Jerrold, Douglas, 58, 178
John Street Literary and Scientific Institution, 190, 194, 202, 205, 222
Jones, Ernest, 188, 190, 198, 202–4, 224, 226–8
Jones, Robert, 243
Jones, Thomas, 136
Jones, William, 137
Jude, Martin, 189n.

Kennington Common, Meetings and demonstrations on, 143, 192
Kerr, Police Sergeant, arrested Bronterre O'Brien, 144–5
Kersal Moor, Meeting and demonstration on, 92, 115–16

Kildare Place Society, 17, 90
King's Inns, Dublin, 23–4
Kingsley, Charles, 188
Kossuth, Louis, 203, 222–3, 228

Land and Labour League, 259, 267–9, 272
Land Nationalization Society, 268–269
Land ownership and nationalization, 177, 179–84, 199
Land Tenure Reform Association, 272
Laski, Harold, 66
Lawrie, Sir Peter, magistrate, 46
Ledru-Rollin, 203, 222, 234
Lee, R. E., 45, 49
Legacy for Labourers, William Cobbett's, 248
Leicester, Chartists in, 162, 174–5
Leigh, Lancs., Chartists in, 162
Lemon, Mark, 43
Leno, John Bedford, 240
Lewis, Thomas Frankland, 75
Lincoln, President Abraham, 276
Literary Institution, Leicester Square, 200
Lloyd's Weekly News, 58
London, Chartists in, 78–9, 88–90, 96, 100, 102, 106–8, 137, 190–2
London, City of, 29, 101–2
London Democratic Association, 46
London Dispatch and People's Political and Social Reformer, Hetherington's, 57, 81–2, 139
London Mercury, John Bell's, 73, 80–2, 84, 88
London Radical Reform Association, 27, 29, 31–2
London Working Men's Association, 77–82, 88, 100, 119, 217, 271
Lorymer, J. H. B., 49
Louis-Philippe I, King of France, 28, 66–7, 190
Lovett, William, 31, 43, 49, 50, 53,

59, 77, 79, 88–9, 96–7, 99, 113, 119, 125–6, 129, 135, 141, 148, 168–9, 174–6, 188, 198, 215, 225
Lowery, Robert, 89, 111, 116, 147–148
Lyndhurst, Lord, 54–5

Maccall, William, 276
M'Crae, John, 119, 156–7
McDouall, Peter Murray, 98, 105, 108, 120, 130, 142, 154, 172–3, 176, 192, 270
Maceroni (Macerone), Colonel Francis, 108–9, 134
Machinery, abuses and advantages of, 36–7, 87, 251–2
Malthus, Rev. T. R., 75, 267
Man, R. E. Lee's, 53
Manchester Cathedral, Chartists in, 133
Manchester Guardian, 151
Manchester Times, 105
Manifeste des Egaux, 63
Manifesto (Chartist) on Ulterior Measures, 97, 112–13, 130
Maréchal, Silvain, 63
Marsden, Richard, 130
Marx, Karl, 72, 209, 222, 228, 249–253, 267, 271–3
Mason, John, 145, 160
Mayhew, Henry, 43, 47n.
Mayhew, Thomas, 43
Mazzini, Giuseppe, 203, 276
Mechanics' Institute, 198
Melbourne, Lord, 48, 157
Messenger, George, 246, 274
Metropolitan Charter Association, 153
Metropolitan Elections Committee, 223
Metropolitan Police, see 'Police'
Metropolitan Union of Radical Reform, 27
Miall, Edward, 168
Mill, John Stuart, 28
Milner, George, 259, 268–9

287

Milton's *Lycidas*, 236
Mines, Nationalization of, 183, 193, 199, 257–8, 271
Missionaries, Chartist, 102–4
Mitchell, Joseph, 124
Monkton Moor, Meeting on, 117
Moral Force, 92, 99, 117, 247
Morning Advertiser, 115
Morning Chronicle, 155, 196
Morrison, James, 49
Mortier, Marshal Eduard, 67
Murray, Charles, 58, 240, 244, 259, 269–70
Murray, James Francis, 245, 269–270, 274
Mutual Land Emigration and Colonization Company, 259

Napier, Maj. Gen. Sir Charles, 109–10, 116
Napoleon III (Louis Napoleon Bonaparte), 222, 233–5, 244
National Charter Association, 158, 200, 202, 224
National Conventions, 56, 87, 89, 92, 94, 99–103, 106–7, 116, 119, 123, 129–32, 134–5, 219–20
National Debt, 161, 259, 271
National Petition (Chartist), 89, 92, 94, 96, 98, 102–5, 130, 150
National Reform League, Bronterre O'Brien's, 198–201, 204–6, 209, 219–20, 230–2, 240–1, 245, 258–9, 268, 272, 274–6
National Reformer, Chas. Bradlaugh's, 242, 268
National Reformer and Manx Weekly Review, Bronterre O'Brien's, 177–9
National Rent, 89, 92, 96–8, 103
National Union, 240
National Union of the Working Classes, 89, 125, 127
Nationalization of banking, currency and credit, 40, 42, 183, 193, 200, 210, 257–8

Nationalization of industries, 40, 183
Nationalization of land, 42, 179–184, 193, 197, 199, 220, 223, 257–8, 268–9, 271–2
Neal, H. E., 241
Newcastle Assizes, Bronterre OBrien's trial at, 121
Newcastle-upon-Tyne, Chartists in, 90–3, 120, 136, 138, 145–6, 157–9, 261–3
Newcastle Weekly Chronicle, Joseph Cowan's, 242
Newport, I.W., Chartists in, 103, 174, 261–2
Newport, Mon., Chartism and the rising in, 92, 135–8
Newton, William, 217
Nicholas, Czar of Russia, 229
Nicholls, George, 75
Nonconformist, The, 169
Northern Liberator, 90–3, 120, 141, 146–9
Northern Political Union, 91
Northern Star, Feargus O'Connor's, 84–7, 115, 116n., 133, 139, 149, 152–4, 163–5, 170, 172, 178, 190, 223n., 249
Norwich, Chartists arming in, 135

Oastler, Richard, 75, 85, 110, 120
O'Brien, Daniel and Mary, parents of James Bronterre O'Brien, 17–18
O'Brien, James Bronterre, birth, 15; education, 17–24; joins the Radicals, 24–5, chap. II; speech at London Tavern, Jan. 1831, 31; opposes 'Whig Reform', 31–32; early articles in Radical papers, 33–7; edits the *Midland Representative and Birmingham Herald*, 37; speech at 2nd Co-operative Congress, 38–9; attitude to Robert Owen and Owenism, 40–2; edits the *Poor*

Man's Guardian, 43–58; edits other papers for Hetherington 53, 55–7; translates Buonarroti's history of Babeuf's Conspiracy, 59–66; his visits to Paris, 66–8; publishes a *Life of Robespierre* (vol. I), 69; his belongings seized for debt, 71; launches *Bronterre's National Reformer*, 73; opposes new Poor Law, 74–76; elected hon. member of L.W.M.A., 78; member of Central National Association, 80–3; stands as hustings candidate at Manchester, 84; writes for the *Northern Star*, 84–7; edits the *Operative*, 87–8; his oratory, 95–96; becomes member of Chartist National Convention, 96; tours the South-east, 102–4; and the North, 105–6; meets Mme Flora Tristan, 106–7; in Birmingham, 112–13; tours Scotland, 116–18; and Yorkshire, 121; opposes the general strike, 130–1; drafts final address for the 1839 Convention, 134; helps the Frost defence fund, 137; proposes tour in North, 139; launches the *Southern Star*, 139–40; his trials at Newcastle and Lancaster Assizes, 142–52; his imprisonment, 152–63; speeches at Carlisle and Dalston, 149; abandons physical force, 153; letters from Lancaster Gaol, 154–7; election address written in prison, 157–8, 264–6; his release from prison, 162–3; edits the *British Statesman*, 165–77; his tours in England and Scotland, 167; supports the Complete Suffrage Movement, 168–76; his quarrel with O'Connor, 171–6; moves to Isle of Man, 177–9; his *National Reformer and Manx Weekly*

Review, 177–8; loses money, 178–9; he denounces landlordism, 180–1; advocates land nationalization, 179–84; attacks O'Connor's land scheme, 186–8; resigns from Chartist Convention of 1848, 191–2; brings out *The Power of the Pence*, 193; his essays on *Human Slavery*, 194–7; founds the National Reform League, 197–201; his pamphlet *State Socialism*, 201; lectures at John St Institution, 202; other activities in the 1850s, 203–4, 222; opens the Eclectic Institute, 204–5; lectures and classes there, 205–16; a possible parliamentary candidate for Tower Hamlets, 216–17; ill-health, 217; London correspondent of *Glasgow Sentinel*, 218–19; proposed parliamentary candidate for Westminster, 223; his money troubles, 224–5; quarrels with Ernest Jones, 226–8; views on war, 229–32; his political poems, 233–5, 239–44; his *Elegy* on Robespierre, 236–9; a speaker in Discussion Halls, 242–3; his last illness and death, 243–4; his funeral, 244–5; his tomb, 246; appraisal of his life's work, 247–260

O'Brien, Mrs, 68, 144, 152–4, 156, 245–6

O'Brien, William Smith, 203

O'Connell, Daniel, 26, 27, 31, 33, 74

O'Connor, Feargus, 78, 80–1, 83–7, 89, 96, 98, 105, 107, 110–12, 114–15, 119, 120, 129–31, 135, 137, 139–40, 142–4, 150, 155, 159–63, 170–6, 184–9, 190–1, 198, 222–4, 249

Ogilvy, William, 180, 182

O'Neill, Arthur, 164n., 168, 172, 215

Operative, The, 87–8, 94, 99, 139

Overstone, Lord, 239–40

Owen, Robert, and Owenism, 35, 38, 40–2, 52, 78, 152, 194, 199, 201, 208–9, 253, 271–2

Paine, Thomas, 180, 182

Palmerston, Lord, 233, 255

Paris, condition of poor in, 76–8

Pauper Press, see 'Unstamped journals'

Peel, Frank, 95

Peep Green, Meetings on, 115

Penny Magazine, Knight's, 54

Penny Satirist, 109, 120

People's Charter, 15, 77–9, 87–9, 117, 120, 129, 166, 169, 175–7, 202

People's Charter Union, 198

People's Conservative and Trade Union Gazette, 53

People's League, 198

People's Paper, 224–7

Physical force, 91–2, 99–101, 105, 107–8, 117, 119, 247

Pioneer, James Morrison's, 53

Place, Francis, 28, 33, 78, 85, 88–9, 123, 168, 256

Plug drawing in Lancashire and Yorkshire, 176

Police, Metropolitan, 30, 126, 141

Police Gazette, John Cleave's, 47

Political Instructor, Reynolds's, 194, 199, 202–4

Political Letters, Wm. Carpenter's, 33–4, 44, 50

Political Register, Cobbett's, 125

Poor Law, new, 56, 74–7, 85, 126, 199

Poor Man's Guardian, 43, 44–58, 59, 60, 85, 89, 108, 113, 140, 166, 247–9

Populaire, Le, 222

Population, 75–6

Power of the Pence, O'Brien's, 193

Press, The Radical, and the taxes on, 33–4, 58

Press Fund, Bronterre O'Brien's, see 'Appeal for funds'

Proletarians, defined, 195–6

Property qualification for membership of Parliament, 171, 255

Prosecution of Chartists by Government, 140–57

Public utilities, 183, 200, 257–8, 271

Quaker mission to Russia in 1854, 228–9

Queen v. Frost (1839–40), 138n.

Queen v. Hetherington (1840), 55

Radford, John, 245

Radical reform, 29, 31–2, 73, 85, 108

Railways, nationalization of, 183, 267

Rates, local, 76–7, 199

Rational religion, Robert Owen's views, 201

Reasoner, Holyoake's, 178

Reed, R. B., 243

Reform Act, 1832, 29, 31–2, 41, 43, 91, 108, 127, 145

Reform Act, 1867, 254–6

Religion, Bronterre O'Brien's views on, 56, 210–15, 240

Reynolds, G. W. M., 198, 200, 202, 204, 222–3, 276

Reynolds's Political Instructor, see 'Political Instructor'

Reynolds's Weekly Newspaper, 203–4

Richardson, Reginald John, 97, 105–6, 131, 150–1, 172

Richmond, Duke of, 77

Riddle, Frederick, 258, 270

Riley, W. Harrison, 259, 270–1

Riots, 'Swing', in rural districts, 30

Riots in London, 30

Roberts, William Prowting, 98

Robespierre, Maximilien, 62, 66–71, 202–3, 236–9, 241–2, 248, 275
Rochdale, Chartists in, 132, 164
Roebuck, John Arthur, 88–9
Rogers, John, 58, 81, 137, 199, 245, 269, 271, 276
Ross, Sir Hew, 109–10
Rotunda, The (Blackfriars), 28
Rucastle, John, 148
Russell, Lord John, 143

Sacred Month, see 'General strike'
St Paul's Cathedral, Chartists in, 133
Salt, T. C., 96
Scales, Alderman, 140
Scottish Chartists, 100, 116, 118–119, 164, 172
Scottish friends, Bronterre O'Brien's, 118–20
Scottish Patriot, 164
Secret Committee of War, 107–8, 135
Shaw-Lefevre, J. G., 75
Sheffield, arms found in, 138
Shoe Lane Discussion Hall, 242–3
Silk weavers in Spitalfields, 49, 57, 77, 86, 216–17
Slavery, see 'Wage-slavery'
Small holdings, Feargus O'Connor's land scheme, 184–9, 223–4
Smedley, Francis, 89
Smiles, Samuel, 89
Smith, James (Shepherd), 120
Smith, Rev. Sydney, 27
Social Democratic Federation, 269
Social Reformer, Bronterre O'Brien's, 166, 198
Socialism, 85, 201, 269, 271, 273; see also 'State Socialism'
Socialist, early use of word, 47
Socialist, W. Harrison Riley's, 271
Society for the Education of the Poor in Ireland, see 'Kildare Place Society'

Solly, Rev. Henry, 95, 168, 175
Somerville, Alexander, 107–9, 137, 235
Southampton Working Men's Association, 104
Southern Star and Brighton Patriot, Bronterre O'Brien's, 139–40, 148, 152–4
Spence, Thomas, 180
Spencer, Herbert, 169
Spencer, Rev. Thomas, 168–9
Spies, 50–1, 53–4, 63, 105, 116n., 164, 234n.
Standard, The, 50
State Socialism, Bronterre O'Brien's pamphlet, 201
Statesman and Weekly True Sun, 88, 138
Stephens, Rev. Joseph Rayner, 75, 81, 85, 113, 120, 134n., 141
Stockport, Chartists in, 121–2, 164
Sturge, Joseph, 168–76, 228–9
Sue, Eugene, 203
Sunderland Chartists, 91–2, 120–1, 261–2
Surrey Political Union, 137–8
Sutton-in-Ashfield, plight of framework knitters, 110

Taxation, Tree of, cartoon in Northern Liberator, 118
Taylor, Dr John, 107, 113, 116, 118–19, 120, 134, 142–3
Taylor, Dr W. Cooke, 167
Taylor, Rev. James, 130
Temperance hotels, Robert Cranston's, 119, 242
Temple Forum Discussion Hall, 242
Thomason, William, 145–6
Thompson, George, 216
Thomson, William, 166
Times, The, 112, 144, 183, 218, 261–2
Tolpuddle labourers, 52, 126–7
Tower Hamlets, parliamentary election in 1852, 217

Townsend, George, 271–2

Trade depressions and crises, 190

Trades Free Press, Wm. Carpenter's, 74

Trials of Bronterre O'Brien and other Chartists, see 'Prosecutions'

Tribune of the People, Wm. Benbow's, 45

Trinity College, Dublin University, 22–3

Tristan, Mme Flora, 106–7

True Scotsman, 116–17

True Sun, 43, 80, 90

Twopenny Dispatch, Hetherington's, 55–7, 60, 79

Tyne Mercury, 146

Ulterior measures, 97, 102, 112–13, 129–30, 134, 150

Unemployment, 184, 199, 269–70, 272

United Irishmen and the Rebellion of 1798, 15–16

Universal Suffrage, 27, 29, 31, 41, 52–3, 56, 78–81, 83, 85, 87–8, 91, 94, 110, 115, 117, 166, 169–170, 177, 187, 193, 198, 206, 221, 255, 271

Unstamped journals, struggle against taxes on newspapers, 44–58, 247, 254

Value, theory of, 209

Victims' Fund, 45, 49

Victoria, Queen, petitions to, 138, 191

Vincent, Henry, 81, 113, 131, 141, 148, 168–9, 172, 174

Voice of the West Riding, Joshua Hobson's, 49

Wade, Rev. A. S., Vicar of Warwick, 43, 110n., 131, 138, 168

Wage-slavery, 39, 194–7, 200

Wakley, Thomas, 31, 76

Wallace, Alfred Russel, 258, 268

Walter, John, 76

Walton, Alfred A., 272

Watson, James, 49, 69, 125–6, 178, 215

Weavers of London, their case stated in 1649–50, 77

Weekly Dispatch, James Harmer's, 74, 98

Weekly Police Gazette, John Cleave's, 49, 57

Welfare State, Bronterre O'Brien's vision of, 232

Wellington, Duke of, 26, 48

Wemyss, Colonel, 109, 110n.

West of Scotland Radical Association, 119

Weston, John, 270, 272–3

Wheeler, Thomas Martin, 186n., 240

Whigs, alleged insincerity of, 31, 35, 42–3, 73, 159–62

White, George, 276

Whitsuntide meetings, 1839, 129

Wicksteed, Philip H., 258

William IV, 29

Williams, Zephaniah, 137

Wilson, Samuel, Lord Mayor of London, 101–2

Winlaton, Chartists in, 263

Woolwich Arsenal, Chartists' visits to, 108, 270

Working Man, 268, 274–6

Working Man's Central Circulating Library, 275

Working Men's Educational Society, 275

Working Men's National Reform League, 258